Formal Approaches in Categorization

The process of constructing concepts underpins our capacity to encode information in an efficient and competent manner and also, ultimately, our ability to think in terms of abstract ideas such as justice, love, and happiness. But what are the mechanisms which correspond to psychological categorization processes? This book unites many prominent approaches in modelling categorization. Each chapter focuses on a particular formal approach to categorization, presented by the proponent(s) or advocate(s) of that approach, and the authors consider the relation of this approach to other models and the ultimate objectives in their research programmes. The volume evaluates progress that has been made in the field and where it goes from here. This is an essential companion to any scientist interested in the formal description of categorization and, more generally, in formal approaches to cognition. It will be the definitive guide to formal approaches in categorization research for years to come.

Emmanuel M. Pothos is a reader in the Department of Psychology at Swansea University.

Andy J. Wills is an associate professor in the School of Psychology at the University of Exeter.

Formal Approaches in Categorization

Emmanuel M. Pothos and Andy J. Wills

Editors

CAMBRIDGE
UNIVERSITY PRESS

CAMBRIDGE UNIVERSITY PRESS
Cambridge, New York, Melbourne, Madrid, Cape Town, Singapore,
São Paulo, Delhi, Dubai, Tokyo, Mexico City

Cambridge University Press
The Edinburgh Building, Cambridge CB2 8RU, UK

Published in the United States of America by Cambridge University Press, New York

www.cambridge.org
Information on this title: www.cambridge.org/9780521140720

© Cambridge University Press 2011

First published 2011

Printed in the United Kingdom at the University Press, Cambridge

A catalogue record for this publication is available from the British Library.

Library of Congress Cataloguing in Publication data
Formal Approaches in Categorization / Emmanuel M. Pothos,
    Andy J. Wills, Editors.
        p.   cm
    Includes bibliographical references and index.
    ISBN 978-0-521-19048-0 (hardback) – ISBN 978-0-521-14072-0 (paperback)
    1. Categorization (Psychology)   I. Pothos, Emmanuel M., 1973–
    II. Wills, Andy J., 1972–
    BF445.F66   2011
    153.2–dc22
    2010045712

ISBN 978-0-521-19048-0 Hardback
ISBN 978-0-521-14072-0 Paperback

Contents

List of figures   *page* vii
List of tables   x
List of contributors   xi

1 Introduction   1
   EMMANUEL M. POTHOS AND ANDY J. WILLS

2 The generalized context model: an exemplar model
   of classification   18
   ROBERT M. NOSOFSKY

3 Prototype models of categorization: basic formulation,
   predictions, and limitations   40
   JOHN PAUL MINDA AND J. DAVID SMITH

4 COVIS   65
   F. GREGORY ASHBY, ERICK J. PAUL AND
   W. TODD MADDOX

5 Semantics without categorization   88
   TIMOTHY T. ROGERS AND JAMES L. MCCLELLAND

6 Models of attentional learning   120
   JOHN K. KRUSCHKE

7 An elemental model of associative learning and memory   153
   EVAN LIVESEY AND IAN MCLAREN

8 Nonparametric Bayesian models of categorization   173
   THOMAS L. GRIFFITHS, ADAM N. SANBORN,
   KEVIN R. CANINI, DANIEL J. NAVARRO AND
   JOSHUA B. TENENBAUM

9 The simplicity model of unsupervised categorization   199
   EMMANUEL M. POTHOS, NICK CHATER AND
   PETER HINES

10 Adaptive clustering models of categorization   220
    JOHN V. MCDONNELL AND TODD M. GURECKIS

11 COBWEB models of categorization and probabilistic
    concept formation   253
    WAYNE IBA AND PAT LANGLEY

12 The knowledge and resonance (KRES) model of
    category learning   274
    HARLAN D. HARRIS AND BOB REHDER

13 The contribution (and drawbacks) of models to the
    study of concepts   299
    GREGORY L. MURPHY

14 Formal models of categorization: insights from
    cognitive neuroscience   313
    LUKAS STRNAD, STEFANO ANZELLOTTI AND
    ALFONSO CARAMAZZA

15 Comments on models and categorization theories:
    the razor's edge   325
    DOUGLAS MEDIN

Index   332

Figures

2.1 Schematic illustration of a category structure to explain
the workings of the GCM. *page* 20
2.2 Confusion matrices for an identification and classification
experiment. 25
2.3 Schematic illustration of four category structures which
have been used to test the GCM. 31
2.4 GCM predictions versus observed data. 33
3.1 Examples of the dot-pattern stimuli which have been
used in tests of the prototype model. 44
3.2 Categorization performance with the dot-pattern stimuli. 45
3.3 Simulated predictions of the prototype model,
assuming a categorization mode based on prototypes. 51
3.4 Further simulations with the prototype model. 52
3.5 Fitting the prototype model to hypothetical classification
data, which reflect either linearly separable or non-linearly
separable classifications. 55
3.6 Fitting the prototype model to two hypothetical sets of
classification data. 57
4.1 Schematic illustration of the architecture of the COVIS
procedural system. 72
4.2 COVIS simulations and corresponding empirical data. 79
5.1 An example of the neural network considered in this
chapter. 96
5.2 An example of the graphical interface of the PDPTool
Matlab application. 101
5.3 Progressive differentiation of concepts and preservation
of superordinate information in the PDP model. 104
5.4 Naming data using more or less general category terms
and corresponding semantic dementia patient data. 106
5.5 The similarity structure of the same objects in different
contexts. 109

5.6	Activation of an object property for different objects, depending on context.	111
6.1	Category structures that illustrate the benefits of selective attention.	121
6.2	General framework for models of attentional learning.	128
6.3	The RASHNL model.	130
6.4	The EXIT model.	133
6.5	The ATRIUM and POLE models.	137
6.6	Locally Bayesian learning.	141
7.1	A simple connectionist system.	154
7.2	Representation of a stimulus dimension in a connectionist system.	157
7.3	A model architecture based on McLaren and Mackintosh (2000, 2002).	158
7.4	Examples of 'icon' stimuli.	161
7.5	Data from Oakeshott (2002) and simulation.	163
7.6	Data and simulation.	165
8.1	Example stimuli.	178
8.2	Hierarchical Dirichlet process.	181
8.3	Local MAP, particle filtering, and Gibbs sampling approximation algorithms.	186
8.4	Results of the approximation algorithms compared to the exact posterior.	187
8.5	Data and simulation for Smith and Minda (1998, Experiment 2).	192
9.1	Illustrating the kind of similarity employed by the simplicity model.	206
9.2	Examining the predictions of the simplicity model.	207
10.1	Schematic illustration of SUSTAIN.	224
10.2	The stimulus encoding process and cluster representation.	228
10.3	Simulation of Younger and Cohen (1986, Experiment 2).	237
10.4	Gureckis and Goldstone's (2008) experimental design and results.	240
11.1	A concept hierarchy.	264
11.2	Multiple alternative updates to a concept hierarchy.	265
12.1	A KRES network.	277
12.2	Fitting a KRES model to data from Hoffman *et al.* (2008).	284
12.3	Further fits of a KRES model to data from Hoffman *et al.* (2008).	285
12.4	An alternative KRES network.	289

12.5 Fitting the alternative KRES network to data from
Wattenmaker *et al.* (1986). 291
12.6 Effect of knowledge parameter variation on KOVE models
simulating the experiments of Wattenmaker *et al.* (1986). 292

Tables

2.1 Maximum-likelihood parameters and summary fits
for full and restricted versions of the exemplar-similarity
categorization model (reprinted from Nosofsky, 1989)   *page* 30
3.1 Category set from Medin and Schaffer (1978)   49
3.2 Non-linearly separable category set   56
4.1 COVIS parameter values used in the simulations of
Figure 4.2   80
6.1 Training designs for blocking and highlighting   123
7.1 Stimulus dimension used by Oakeshott (2002)   162
8.1 Categories A and B from Smith and Minda (1998)   191
9.1 Three datasets exploring variations of a simple
two-cluster category structure   210
10.1 Best fit parameters from Love *et al.* (2004)   234
11.1 Generic algorithm for the family of COBWEB models   261
12.1 KRES/D and KOVE/D fits to Hoffman *et al.*'s (2008)
accuracy data   283
12.2 Category structure from Wattenmaker *et al.* (1986)   288

Contributors

STEFANO ANZELLOTTI Cognitive Neuropsychology Laboratory, Psychology Department, Harvard University

F. GREGORY ASHBY Department of Psychology, University of California, Santa Barbara

KEVIN R. CANINI Computer Science Division, University of California, Berkeley

ALFONSO CARAMAZZA Cognitive Neuropsychology Laboratory, Psychology Department, Harvard University and Center for Mind/ Brain Sciences, University of Trento

NICK CHATER Department of Psychology, University College London

THOMAS L. GRIFFITHS Department of Psychology, University of California, Berkeley

TODD M. GURECKIS Department of Psychology, New York University

HARLAN D. HARRIS Department of Psychology, New York University

PETER HINES Department of Computer Science, University of York

WAYNE IBA Computer Science Department, Westmont College

JOHN K. KRUSCHKE Department of Psychological and Brain Sciences, Indiana University

PAT LANGLEY Computational Learning Laboratory, Center for the Study of Language and Information, Stanford University

EVAN LIVESEY School of Psychology, University of Sydney

W. TODD MADDOX Department of Psychology, The University of Texas, Austin

JAMES L. MCCLELLAND Department of Psychology, Stanford University

JOHN V. MCDONNELL Department of Psychology, New York University

IAN MCLAREN School of Psychology, University of Exeter

DOUGLAS MEDIN Department of Psychology, Northwestern University

JOHN PAUL MINDA Department of Psychology, The University of Western Ontario

GREGORY L. MURPHY Department of Psychology, New York University

DANIEL J. NAVARRO School of Psychology, University of Adelaide

ROBERT M. NOSOFSKY Department of Psychological and Brain Sciences, Indiana University

ERICK J. PAUL Department of Psychology, University of California, Santa Barbara

EMMANUEL M. POTHOS Department of Psychology, Swansea University

BOB REHDER Department of Psychology, New York University

TIMOTHY T. ROGERS Department of Psychology, University of Wisconsin-Madison

ADAM N. SANBORN Gatsby Computational Neuroscience Unit, University College London

J. DAVID SMITH Department of Psychology and Center for Cognitive Science, University at Buffalo, The State University of New York

LUKAS STRNAD Cognitive Neuropsychology Laboratory, Psychology Department, Harvard University

JOSHUA B. TENENBAUM Department of Brain and Cognitive Sciences, Massachusetts Institute of Technology

ANDY J. WILLS School of Psychology, Exeter University

1 Introduction

Emmanuel M. Pothos and Andy J. Wills

Categorization is one of the most fascinating aspects of human cognition. It refers to the process of organizing sensory experience into groups. This is an ability we share to some extent with other animals (e.g. Herrnstein & Loveland, 1964), and is key to our understanding of the world. Humans seem particularly adept at the systematic and productive combination of elementary concepts to develop complex thought. All in all, it is hard to envisage much of cognition without concepts.

The study of categorization has a long history (e.g. Hull, 1920). It is usually considered a particular research theme of cognitive psychology, cognitive science, and cognitive neuroscience. Categorization relates intimately to many other cognitive processes, such as learning, language acquisition and production, decision making, and inductive reasoning. What all these processes have in common is that they are inductive. That is, the cognitive system is asked to process some experience and subsequently extrapolate to novel experience.

A *formal* model of categorization is taken to correspond to any description of categorization processes in a principled, lawful way. Formal models of categorization are theories that allow quantitative predictions regarding the categorization behaviour of participants. Some formal models also make predictions about the underlying neuroscience.

Selecting the models to be discussed in this volume was difficult. Our goal was to create an accessible volume with a reasonably small number of models. As a result, there are many excellent models which we were not able to include. Notable omissions include Heit's (1997) proposal for how to modify exemplar theory to take into account the influences of general knowledge, Kurtz's (2007) auto-associative approach to categorization, Lamberts's (2000) model of the time course of categorization decisions, Rehder's (2003) view of categorization as causal reasoning, Schyns's (1991) model of concept discovery based on Kohonen nets, Vanpaemel and Storms's (2008) attempt to integrate prototype and exemplar theory, several models of statistical clustering (e.g. Fisher, 1996; Fraboni & Cooper, 1989), and interesting developments based on the mathematics of quantum mechanics (e.g. van Rijsbergen, 2004).

We hope that the models we have selected will help to illustrate some of the key ideas in the formal modelling of categorization. In the next sections, we summarize some of these ideas. We then go on to summarize briefly each of the models presented in this volume, and finish with some thoughts about how these models might be compared.

Supervised and unsupervised categorization

Categorization processes can be distinguished into supervised and unsupervised – in other words, processes that require external feedback versus those that do not. This is an important distinction, and one that has had a substantial influence on the development of categorization research. For example, most categorization models are proposed as either specifically supervised categorization models or as unsupervised ones. The majority of categorization research concerns supervised categorization and, in this volume, we have included the most prominent corresponding models. Equally, we have attempted to include contributions which cover some of the successful unsupervised categorization models.

In brief, supervised categorization concerns the processing of novel experience in relation to a pre-defined set of categories. Simply put, a child might see a round object which looks like it is edible, and wonder how it fits to its existing categories of oranges, lemons, or apples. She might attempt a guess and an adult might point out whether the guess is correct or not; this process of corrective feedback is one of the possible ways in which categories can develop in a supervised way (although it is unclear as to how central this process is in human conceptual development). In the laboratory, supervised categorization often involves creating a set of artificial stimuli, determining how they should be classified (this is done by the experimenter prior to the experiment), asking a participant to guess the classification of each stimulus one by one, and providing corrective feedback.

It seems uncontroversial to say that supervised categorization plays a part in the acquisition of many real-world concepts. However, one can reasonably ask where concepts come from in the first place. A related intuition with respect to real life concepts is that certain concepts are less ambiguous than others (for example, compare 'chair' with 'literature'; with respect to the latter, many naive observers would disagree as to which instances should be considered 'literature'). Both these problems are problems of unsupervised categorization.

Unsupervised categorization concerns the spontaneous creation of concepts. For example, in the laboratory, participants might be presented with a set of artificial stimuli with instructions to classify them in any way they like. A key goal of unsupervised categorization research is to determine why certain classifications are preferred, compared to others. With respect to real concepts, one can ask what determines the particular division of experience into concepts. Why, for example, do we have separate concepts for 'chairs' and 'armchairs', rather than a single one to encompass all relevant instances? The particular divisions we acquire seem to be affected by the category labels our culture provides (e.g. Roberson *et al.*, 2005; this would correspond to a supervised categorization process), but they must also be influenced by prior intuitions of which groupings are more intuitive. Other things being equal, more intuitive classifications should be easier to learn, and so unsupervised categorization models can also be applied to the problem of predicting which classifications are easier to learn compared to others (of course, some classes of supervised categorization models are suitable for addressing this problem as well).

How fundamental is the distinction between supervised and unsupervised categorization? Consideration of the models of supervised and unsupervised categorization included in this volume reveals several important common features. For example, nearly all the models considered are driven by some function of psychological similarity. Also, some researchers have argued that supervised categorization models are logically equivalent to unsupervised ones (cf. Pothos & Bailey, 2009; Zwickel & Wills, 2005); such an argument for the equivalence of supervised and unsupervised categorization is based on the general computational properties of categorization models. However, even if it is computationally feasible to create a model which can account for both supervised and unsupervised categorization results within the same formalism, psychologically it might be the case that these are separate cognitive processes.

The SUSTAIN model (Love, Medin, & Gureckis, 2004; Chapter 10) was one of the first attempts to account for both supervised and unsupervised categorization within the same model. The model's architecture is specified around a parametric combination of two components. The first component develops category representations as a result of an external supervisory signal and the second component spontaneously generates clusters based on a principle of similarity (that is, more similar items end up in the same cluster). This model is interesting since it embodies a particular assumption about the relation between supervised and unsupervised categorization processes, namely that they are distinct but related.

Exemplars and prototypes

The contrast between exemplar and prototype theory has been at the heart of the development of (supervised) categorization research. Equally, these are the two theories that psychologists without any particular categorization expertise are most likely to recognize. Accordingly, the first two chapters cover a prominent version of exemplar theory, the generalized context model (Nosofsky, 1988; see also Medin & Schaffer, 1978) and prototype theory (Hampton, 2000; Minda & Smith, 2000), respectively. Contrasting these two formalisms is a complicated issue. In principle, it is possible to identify stimulus sets that allow differential predictions (e.g. Medin & Schaffer, 1978; Medin & Schwanenflugel, 1981). In practice, sometimes the comparisons hinge on the role of particular parameters, whose psychological relevance has to be carefully justified. The effort to compare prototype and exemplar theory has led some researchers to examine formal comparisons (e.g., Nosofsky, 1990; see also Ashby & Alfonso-Reese, 1995). Such comparisons and related analyses (e.g., Navarro, 2007; Smith, 2007; Vanpaemel & Storms, 2008) have led to a profound understanding of the formal properties of exemplar and prototype models, to an extent that is rare in psychology.

Unitary and multi-process models

Should categorization be understood as a unitary process (e.g. Nosofsky & Kruschke, 2002) or a combination of independent processes? Chapter 4 covers the COVIS model (COmpetition between Verbal and Implicit Systems; Ashby *et al.*, 1998), which has been built on the assumption that human (supervised) categorization is supported by at least two separate, competing systems. COVIS is also notable as it is currently the only model which has been developed to provide categorization predictions at both the behavioural and neuroscience level. Indeed, COVIS motivated many of the early investigations which have allowed categorization researchers to consider ways in which the impressive recent advances in neuroscience could help the development of categorization theory (e.g. Nomura *et al.*, 2007; Zeithamova & Maddox, 2006).

Parallel distributed processing

Parallel distributed processing (PDP) models are generally considered to have a certain degree of biological plausibility – in other words, the architecture of the models is said to mimic some aspects of brain architecture. PDP models are often built to describe particular aspects of cognitive development (e.g. Plunkett *et al.*, 1997) or psychopathology (Plaut & Shallice, 1993). McClelland and Rumelhart (1986) have led an extensive connectionist research programme; Chapter 5 covers the extension of this work in categorization behaviour. Unlike most categorization models, which are tested with respect to either the classification of novel instances or the spontaneous generation of categories, the PDP model of Chapter 5 is supported through known developmental aspects of the categorization process and how categorization competence breaks down in specific cases of brain pathologies (such as semantic dementia). Chapter 7 considers the feature-based approach to stimulus representation assumed by PDP models.

Attentional processes

The acquisition of categories seems to result in the direction of attention towards those aspects of the stimuli that are most useful in determining category membership. Most formal models of categorization posit some form of attentional process; the focus of Chapter 6 is these processes. It also extends these ideas to both mixture of experts models (see also Chapter 4) and considers how they might be formulated within a Bayesian framework (see also Chapter 8).

Optimal inference models

Categorization is an example of an inductive problem, which requires the determination of category membership from the limited information provided by the features of a stimulus. The mathematics of Bayes's theorem can be employed to develop accounts of optimal performance on inductive problems. Often, this kind of approach takes a step back from psychological processes to consider how ideal solutions to the inductive problem of categorization might shed light on the behaviour of humans and other animals. Such an approach is embedded in the general effort to understand cognition in terms of Bayesian probabilistic principles (e.g., Griffiths, Steyvers, & Tenenbaum, 2007; Tenenbaum & Griffiths, 2001). Bayesian principles can also be extended to more powerful frameworks (e.g., based on quantum probability; Busemeyer, Wang, & Townsend, 2006). Chapter 8 illustrates the application of Bayesian principles in categorization, in terms of an extension to Anderson's Bayesian model of unsupervised categorization (Anderson, 1991).

Minimum description length

An approach similar to the above is possible if one considers categorization as a process of data reduction. In other words, perhaps one of the reasons we have categories is that they allow a more efficient (less memory intensive) representation of the world. A minimum description length (a.k.a. *simplicity*) framework is basically an algorithmic coding scheme. It allows a researcher to define the codelength for data and hypotheses for the data. Then, the problem of choosing an appropriate hypothesis is translated to a problem of finding the hypothesis which leads to the greatest overall reduction in codelengths. Pothos and Chater (2002) suggested that categories can be considered as hypotheses regarding structure in the similarity relations between a set of stimuli. A particular classification will be preferred if it can simplify the description of similarity information to a greater extent. Thus, simplicity principles naturally lead to a model of unsupervised categorization, which is described in Chapter 9.

It is interesting that the normative computational frameworks of Bayesian probability and MDL can both lead to unsupervised categorization models – perhaps this is because the lack of an external teaching signal in unsupervised categorization is replaced by the assumptions each model makes regarding structure (cf. Chater, 1996).

Machine learning

Categorization research in psychology concerns the organization of objects into categories. Clearly, this process is relevant in many areas of machine learning and statistical clustering. A common problem in such areas is to infer whether it is meaningful to organize some instances into clusters – this is a problem of unsupervised categorization. Chapter 11 covers some related modelling work, in relation to a class of models based on category utility, that is the probability that an instance has certain features given membership to a particular category (i.e., how 'useful' the category is, for the purpose of predicting the features of its members, e.g., Corter & Gluck, 1992). Clearly, category utility is closely related to the Bayesian approach described in Chapter 8.

Considering a machine learning approach to categorization raises several interesting questions. How much convergence should we expect between human and machine learning categorization? Are there categorization methods more efficient or useful than the one employed by the human cognitive system? How domain-dependent is the selection of the optimal categorization strategy?

General knowledge

Murphy and Medin (1985) pointed out that conceptual coherence, the 'glue' that binds the instances of a concept together in a meaningful and intuitive way, has to be more than just, for example, similarity relations. Each concept is an inseparable part of our overall knowledge of the world and, conversely, without this knowledge it is impossible to appreciate the significance of a concept. Compelling as these intuitions about categorization have been, it has proved remarkably difficult to formalize a putative role of general knowledge in categorization (cf. Fodor, 1983). Chapter 12 covers a proposal for a model about how categories develop based in part by some aspects of general knowledge.

Outline of this book

In this section we highlight some of the key aspects of the models covered in this volume. The models are described in detail in their respective chapters. Our purpose is not to repeat this material, rather to draw the attention of the reader to such model features that might enable a better understanding of model differences and commonalities.

Chapter 2 – The generalized context model

The generalized context model (GCM) is an exemplar model of supervised categorization. A novel stimulus is classified into a pre-existing category based on its similarity to known members of that category (and to members of other known categories). Similarity in the GCM is specified in terms of distances in a psychological space, as proposed by, for example, Shepard (1987). So, at the heart of the GCM is a principle of psychological similarity. A fundamental aspect of the GCM is that it computes similarity relations not just on the basis of the original psychological space, but also any transformations of this space that are possible through (graded) attentional selection or compression/stretching of the psychological space as a whole. In this way, the GCM is a very powerful model: it is most often the case that its parameters can be set in a way that human data in a supervised categorization can be closely reproduced.

The GCM makes relatively few prior assumptions about the categorization process. For example, parameters governing attentional weighting, the form of the similarity function, the metric space, the nature of responding (probabilistic versus deterministic) can all be set in response to fitting particular human data. The price for this flexibility is, of course, the relatively large number of free parameters. Some key psychological assumptions embodied in the GCM (apart from the obvious one, that category representation is based on individual exemplars) are that graded attentional weighting of stimulus dimensions and stretching/compression of psychological space are possible as a result of learning.

Chapter 3 – Prototype models of categorization

The extensive research on the relation between exemplar and prototype theory has led to computational implementations of these ideas in a way that their form is as similar as possible, and differs only with regards to the key psychological assumptions which are unique in each approach. This is a highly desirable situation, as it enables precise comparisons between the two formalisms. According to prototype theory, a novel instance is more likely to be classified into a category if the similarity between the instance and the category prototype is high; prototypes are typically operationalized as averages of category members. As with exemplar theory, more recent versions of prototype theory allow the same transformations of psychological space as the GCM. Another common feature of the two approaches is that they both postulate a single system of categorization.

Prototype theory is very similar to exemplar theory, but for a critical difference. The former is consistent only with linearly separable, convex-shaped categories, but the latter allows any kind of category shape. To see intuitively why this has to be the case, consider that for a category to have a meaningful prototype representation, the prototype (which is the average of the instances) must be included in the area (or volume) of psychological space which is occupied by the category.

Chapter 4 – COVIS

The COVIS model postulates that category learning is mediated by two, competing systems. The first system attempts to develop explicit, verbalizable rules that describe the required categorization. The rule-based system will be favoured to the extent that such rules exist, are simple, and allow accurate classification performance. It is assumed to be supported by the prefrontal cortex, anterior cingulate, the anterior striatum, and the hippocampus. The second system is a procedural learning system, which allows the learning of classifications such that information from all available dimensions is taken into account. Accordingly, the procedural system involves a mechanism of information integration. The brain areas associated with this system are principally the posterior striatum and the inferotemporal cortex. The two systems compete with each other; for any particular stimulus, preference for one of the two competing systems is determined by confidence in the predicted response and the overall track record of the system.

The unique element of COVIS is that its computational implementation is specified with respect to the known neurophysiology of the brain. For example, the equation determining perseveration for a rule involves a free parameter which is linked to dopamine levels in the striatum. In this way, COVIS can be tested both with behavioural data (e.g., participant performance in a categorization experiment) and neuroscience data (e.g., fMRI studies of how brain activity varies with different categorization tasks).

Chapter 5 – Semantics without categorization

This chapter summarizes the progress in an extensive research programme to model human categorization behaviour with a multi-layer, feedforward, backpropagation network. An underlying hypothesis in this programme is that categories do not exist as distinct representational entities, rather categorization behaviour (of any kind, for example, classification of new instances or inference about the unseen properties of a shown stimulus) arises from the way environmental input affects the connections in a network. A particular feature of the postulated network architecture is the existence of a set of context units, which take into account the particular situation in which the categorization of a new instance takes place (cf. Chapter 12). Different contexts can result in different categorizations for the same instance.

Chapter 6 – Models of attentional learning

This chapter summarizes some of the evidence in support of the idea that categorization involves selective attention, and then discusses the development of models to account for this phenomenon. Starting with approaches related to the global stretching and compression of psychological dimensions implemented in the GCM, a proposal is presented for how attentional allocation may be exemplar specific, and how attentional allocation may be allocated between competing cognitive systems (cf. COVIS). There is also consideration of how attentional allocation might occur within a Bayesian framework (cf. Chapter 8), where multiple hypotheses about category structures are maintained simultaneously.

Chapter 7 – An elemental model of associative learning and memory

This chapter considers a feature-based (a.k.a. *elemental*) approach to modelling categorization (see also Chapter 5). Specifically, the phenomenon of peak shift is discussed, for which (in both humans and pigeons) an elemental account may be more appropriate than an exemplar-based account (cf. Chapter 2). Peak shift is the phenomenon that, under certain circumstances, classification accuracy may increase with *decreasing* similarity to the members of category into which the item is classified. A formal elemental model of categorization is presented that provides an account of some of the situations where peak shift does, and does not, occur.

Chapter 8 – Nonparametric Bayesian models of categorization

According to this approach to unsupervised categorization, a model of category learning can be developed by considering how one can compute the category membership of a novel stimulus, given the appearance of the stimulus. In other words, the problem of categorization can be reframed as a problem of estimating the probability distribution of different objects with the same category label. Employing a Bayesian probabilistic framework to make this idea more concrete can lead to a number of implementation options, a key difference of which is whether the estimation of the required probability distribution is parametric (some assumptions are made regarding the general form of the distribution) or nonparametric (no assumptions made). This chapter describes a particular categorization model based on the latter approach, so that the prior assumptions about structure in the world are minimal; the model can be seen as an extension of Anderson's (1991) rational model of categorization.

A strength of this Bayesian approach to categorization is that it provides a framework for specifying a family of categorization models, including ones which are analogous to standard exemplar or prototype models (two parameters can determine whether a particular instantiation behaves more like an exemplar or a prototype model).

Chapter 9 – The simplicity model of unsupervised categorization

Chapter 9 describes the second model of (just) unsupervised categorization that is considered in this volume. The simplicity model is based on principles similar to those underlying the Bayesian probabilistic framework explored in Chapter 8. According to the simplicity model, categorization has a functional role, namely that of providing a more efficient description of any encountered stimuli. This 'simplicity' prerogative (informally equivalent to Ockham's razor) is formally implemented in a MDL framework, which is just a set of rules for deciding when a particular description for some data should be preferred. In the case of categorization, the data correspond to the perceived stimuli and descriptions to possible classifications.

A minimum description length framework is equivalent to a Bayesian one when the priors employed in the latter correspond to the so-called universal priors (Chater, 1996). Therefore, the simplicity model of Chapter 9 can be seen as a special case of the (parametric versions of) Bayesian classifiers presented in Chapter 8. Two noteworthy aspects of this approach are, first, that it involves no parameters at all and, second, that its input can be relational (for example, whether two stimuli are more similar than two other stimuli, as opposed to particular information about the features of the stimuli). Finally, the simplicity model assumes that all stimuli are presented concurrently.

Chapter 10 – Adaptive clustering models of categorization

This chapter outlines the SUSTAIN model, which embodies a proposal for understanding the relation between supervised and unsupervised categorization. The model's implementation is based on combining two components. The first component allows categories to develop on the basis of a supervisory signal, as is the case in exemplar or prototype theory. The second component supports the spontaneous creation of categories. In the absence of feedback, items will be assigned to the pre-existing category representation to which they are most similar. If an item does not fit any of the existing category representations very well, then a new category representation is created. SUSTAIN assumes trial-by-trial stimulus presentation, so this modelling approach predicts order effects in the creation of categories. In this respect, SUSTAIN is analogous to the early Bayesian categorization work presented in Chapter 8 (Anderson, 1991).

According to this approach, categorization is assumed to be driven by similarity. However, it is possible to modify the attentional weighting of stimulus dimensions. This ability is, of course, essential for supervised categorization, but an analogous mechanism exists for unsupervised categorization as well.

Chapter 11 – Constructing concept hierarchies using category utility

Chapters 2–10 describe attempts to understand human categorization which are primarily motivated from particular empirical findings. Another approach is possible through the consideration of artificial systems for the creation of 'useful' categories. This chapter describes an unsupervised system that develops conceptual hierarchies using the psychological principle of *category utility*. According to category utility (Corter & Gluck, 1992), categories are useful to the extent that they allow accurate prediction of the features of their instances.

Chapter 12 – Knowledge resonance in models of category learning and categorization

Cognitive scientists have mostly avoided attempts to incorporate putative general knowledge influences (such as semantics) in formal models (cf. Fodor, 1983). In categorization, such an approach leads to mixed reactions. On the one hand, there is no doubt that formal models driven entirely by similarity, or other low-level properties of the categorized stimuli, can be incredibly successful. On the other hand, most cognitive scientists would agree that a complete account of categorization has to take into account semantics as well. The relevant challenge is taken up in the model described in this chapter, KRES, which provides a formal approach for how semantic information can affect the formation of categories. Other features of the model include the assumptions that categories are represented with prototypes and that a category representation interacts with the representation of the currently processed stimulus.

Prior knowledge in KRES is encoded in two ways. First, additional relations are specified between stimulus features, which would correspond, for example, to knowledge that if a particular feature is present then another feature should be present as well. Second, the model embodies representations of 'prior concepts', which can affect the learning of a new category, when it is assumed that the new category is similar to a prior concept.

Chapters 13, 14, 15 – Commentaries

The final three chapters comprise three invited commentaries on the models presented in Chapters 2–12. In Chapter 13, Murphy takes a step back from the details of specific models, and asks what the advantages (and drawbacks) of formal modelling might be. In Chapter 14, Strnad, Anzellotti, and Caramazza put the case from neuropsychology and imaging that category representation is domain specific, and suggests this may pose a serious challenge to the domain-general models presented in this volume (see also Plunkett & Bandelow, 2006; Tyler *et al.*, 2003). In Chapter 15, Medin concludes the volume by considering what progress has been made in the study of categorization in the last 30 years.

Comparing models

The above summary of the models presented in this volume suggests many dimensions along which different models could potentially be compared. For example, an important dimension is between supervised and unsupervised categorization, which we have already considered extensively. From a theoretical point of view, it is clearly essential to appreciate which model characteristics relate to some fundamental assumption about psychological processes and which are incidental to a particular implementational philosophy. For example, in the cases of many models the distinction between supervised and unsupervised categorization is not fundamental: a model is presented as, for example, a model of supervised categorization not specifically because there is an underlying assumption that the psychology of unsupervised categorization is separate from that of unsupervised categorization, but rather because the modeller just happened to be interested primarily in supervised categorization. Of the models reviewed above, only SUSTAIN makes an explicit claim regarding the psychological relation between supervised and unsupervised categorization.

A model characteristic which does appear fundamental is whether the model proposes a unitary categorization system or a categorization faculty which is supported through the combination (and possibly competition) of independent components. COVIS is the only model in this volume in which there is a strong claim of multiple systems, with regards to its two systems of rule-based category learning versus information integration learning. SUSTAIN arguably involves two separate systems for supervised and unsupervised categorization, although it is not clear whether the theory assumes these to be separate, independent systems (and no corresponding tests have been provided).

The role of similarity in categorization is arguably one of the most important considerations in categorization research. Of course, all models assume there is 'similarity structure' in the world, that is, certain instances are more similar than others (if that were not the case, arguably a meaningful process of categorization would not be possible in the first place). However, models differ in the extent to which similarity is employed beyond the level of an input representation. For example, the GCM predicts (subject to the effects of, for example, attention and response bias) that a novel item is most likely to be classified into the category to which it is most similar. In contrast, certain Bayesian approaches (e.g. Anderson, 1991; Chapter 8) predict that a novel item will be placed into the category which best predicts the novel item's features.

Models also differ in the attentional mechanisms they assume. Some models allow coarse attentional selection (e.g., the simplicity model, which has the option of completely ignoring certain dimensions), other models allow graded, fine attentional modulation of stimulus dimensions, and in some models it is possible to stretch or compress psychological space (e.g., prototype and exemplar theory). Thus, it appears possible to compare formal categorization models in terms of the transformations of psychological space that they allow.

Most (but not all) models of categorization assume that stimuli are processed one by one. Should we consider the distinction between concurrent presentation of the available stimuli versus one by one presentation to be fundamental for our understanding of the psychology of categorization? This seems unlikely. Ultimately, it seems clear that the development of categorical knowledge is incremental, in the simple sense that we rarely, if ever, have all relevant category instances available at the same time. Equally, there are situations when we have strong intuitions about how a set of concurrently available stimuli should be spontaneously categorized. It would seem extremely unlikely that the principles that guide categorization in a trial-by-trial case are entirely different from those in the case of concurrent presentation. It then becomes an implementational challenge to develop models that naturally allow categorization in both modes.

The nature of category representation has been the focus of controversy for many categorization studies. Categories can be represented as prototypes, individual exemplars, decision boundaries, have flexible representations which can oscillate between more specific (exemplar) or more abstract (prototype) versions, or verbal rules. The issue of category representation is clearly a very fascinating one. A potential problem with progress on this issue is that sometimes the representational assumptions embodied in a model are confounded with other implementation details – so that it is not clear which aspect of the model is responsible for its behaviour. This problem has been addressed most compellingly in the comparison between exemplar and prototype theory, as, in the case of this particular controversy, versions of prototype and exemplar models have been built which are equivalent in all respects apart from the way categories are represented.

In this section our aim has been to highlight some dimensions along which the models covered in this chapter could be compared. This naturally leads to the question of how to compare categorization models. Ideally, in comparing two models we would like to be able to determine the circumstances when the performance (e.g., in predicting human data) of one model is superior to another model. Moreover, it would be important to determine when two models should be considered sufficiently similar so that they embody effectively equivalent claims about the nature of human categorization. Unfortunately, arguably, this is the single most important current obstacle in the further development of categorization research: the lack of comparative studies between different modelling approaches, which is a somewhat inevitable result of the increasing complexity of the available models. In the few instances when detailed computational and mathematical comparisons have been carried out, such as in the instance of the debate between exemplar and prototype theory, psychologists have been able to develop a profound understanding of the underlying differences in assumptions about the psychological process of categorization. We think that careful comparative work between formal approaches in categorization is an essential prerequisite for the further development of categorization theory. It is hoped that this volume can help.

REFERENCES

Anderson, J.R. (1991). The adaptive nature of human categorization. *Psychological Review*, **98**, 409–429.

Ashby, G.F., & Alfonso-Reese, A. L. (1995). Categorization as probability density estimation. *Journal of Mathematical Psychology*, **39**, 216–233.

Ashby, G. F., Alfonso-Reese, L. A., Turken, A. U., & Waldron, E. M. (1998). A neuropsychological theory of multiple systems in category learning. *Psychological Review*, **105**, 442–481.

Busemeyer, J. R., Wang, Z., & Townsend, J. T. (2006). Quantum dynamics of human decision making. *Journal of Mathematical Psychology*, **50**, 220–241.

Chater, N. (1996). Reconciling simplicity and likelihood principles in perceptual organization. *Psychological Review*, **103**, 566–591.

Corter, J. E., & Gluck, M. A. (1992). Explaining basic categories: feature predictability and information. *Psychological Bulletin*, **2**, 291–303.

Fisher, D. (1996). Iterative optimization and simplification of hierarchical clusterings. *Journal of Artificial Intelligence*, **4**, 147–179.

Fodor, J. A. (1983). *The Modularity of Mind*. Cambridge, MA: MIT Press.

Fraboni, M., & Cooper, D. (1989). Six clustering algorithms applied to the WAIS-R: the problem of dissimilar cluster analysis. *Journal of Clinical Psychology*, **45**, 932–935.

Griffiths, T. L., Steyvers, M., & Tenenbaum, J. B. (2007). Topics in semantic representation. *Psychological Review*, **114**, 211–244.

Hampton, J. A. (2000). Concepts and prototypes. *Mind and Language*, **15**, 299–307.

Heit, E. (1997). Knowledge and concept learning. In K. Lamberts & D. Shanks (eds.), *Knowledge, Concepts, and Categories* (pp. 7–41). London: Psychology Press.

Herrnstein, R. J., & Loveland, D. H. (1964). Complex visual concept in the pigeon. *Science*, **146**, 549–551.

Hull, C.L. (1920). Quantitative aspects of the evolution of concepts: an experimental study. *Psychological Monographs*, **28** (1), Whole No. 123.

Kurtz, K.J. (2007). The divergent autoencoder (DIVA) model of category learning. *Psychonomic Bulletin & Review*, **14**, 560–576.

Lamberts, K. (2000). Information-accumulation theory of speeded categorization. *Psychological Review*, **107**, 227–260.

Love, B.C., Medin, D.L., & Gureckis, T.M. (2004). SUSTAIN: a network model of category learning. *Psychological Review*, **111**, 309–332.

McClelland, J.L., & Rumelhart, D.E. (eds.) (1986). *Parallel Distributed Processing: Explorations in the Microstructure of Cognition*. Cambridge, MA: MIT Press.

Medin, D.L., & Schaffer, M.M. (1978). Context theory of classification learning. *Psychological Review*, **85**, 207–238.

Medin, D.L., & Schwanenflugel, P.J. (1981). Linear separability in classification learning. *Journal of Experimental Psychology: Human Learning and Memory*, **75**, 355–368.

Minda, J.P., & Smith, J.D. (2000). Prototypes in category learning: the effects of category size, category structure, and stimulus complexity. *Journal of Experimental Psychology: Learning, Memory, and Cognition*, **27**, 775–799.

Murphy, G.L., & Medin, D.L. (1985). The role of theories in conceptual coherence. *Psychological Review*, **92**, 289–316.

Navarro, D.J. (2007). Similarity, distance, and categorization: a discussion of Smith's (2006) warning about 'colliding parameters'. *Psychonomic Bulletin & Review*, **14**, 823–833.

Nomura, E.M., Maddox, W.T., Filoteo, J.V., Ing, A.D., Gitelman, D.R., Parrish, T.B., Mesulam, M.M., & Reber, P.J. (2007). Neural correlates of rule-based and information-integration visual category learning. *Cerebral Cortex*, **17**, 37–43.

Nosofsky, R.M. (1988). Similarity, frequency, and category representation. *Journal of Experimental Psychology: Learning, Memory, and Cognition*, **14**, 54–65.

(1990). Relations between exemplar-similarity and likelihood models of classification. *Journal of Mathematical Psychology*, **34**, 393–418.

Nosofsky, R.M., & Kruschke, J.K. (2002). Single-system models and interference in category learning: commentary on Waldron and Ashby (2001). *Psychonomic Bulletin & Review*, **9**, 169–174.

Plaut, D.C., & Shallice, T. (1993). Deep dyslexia: a case study of connectionist neuropsychology. *Cognitive Neuropsychology*, **10**, 377–500.

Plunkett, K., & Bandelow, S. (2006). Stochastic approaches to understanding dissociations in inflectional morphology. *Brain and Language*, **98**, 194–209.

Plunkett, K., Karmiloff-Smith, A., Bates, E., & Elman, J.L. (1997). Connectionism and developmental psychology. *Journal of Child Psychology & Psychiatry & Allied Disciplines*, **38**, 53–80.

Pothos, E.M., & Bailey, T.M. (2009). Predicting category intuitiveness with the rational model, the simplicity model, and the Generalized Context Model. *Journal of Experimental Psychology: Learning, Memory, and Cognition*, **35**, 1062–1080.

Pothos, E. M., & Chater, N. (2002). A simplicity principle in unsupervised human categorization. *Cognitive Science*, **26**, 303–343.

Rehder, B. (2003). Categorization as causal reasoning. *Cognitive Science*, **27**, 709–748.

Roberson, D., Davidoff, J., Davies, I. R. L., & Shapiro, L. R. (2005). Color categories: evidence for the cultural relativity hypothesis. *Cognitive Psychology*, **50**, 378–411.

Schyns, P. G. (1991). A modular neural network model of concept acquisition. *Cognitive Science*, **15**, 461–508.

Shepard, R. N. (1987). Toward a universal law of generalization for psychological science. *Science*, **237**, 1317–1323.

Smith, J. D. (2007). When parameters collide: a warning about categorization models. *Psychonomic Bulletin & Review*, **13**, 743–751.

Tenenbaum, J., & Griffiths, T. L. (2001). Generalization, similarity, and Bayesian inference. *Behavioral and Brain Sciences*, **24**, 629–641.

Tyler, L. K., Bright, P., Dick, E., Tavares, P., Pilgrim, L., Fletcher, P., Greer, M., & Moss, H. (2003). Do semantic categories activate distinct cortical regions? Evidence for a distributed neural semantic system. *Cognitive Neuropsychology*, **20**, 541–559.

Vanpaemel, W., & Storms, G. (2008). In search of abstraction: the varying abstraction model of categorization. *Psychonomic Bulletin & Review*, **15**, 732–749.

van Rijsbergen, K. (2004). *The Geometry of Information Retrieval*. Cambridge: Cambridge University Press.

Zeithamova, D., & Maddox, W. T. (2006). Dual-task interference in perceptual category learning. *Memory & Cognition*, **34**, 387–398.

Zwickel, J., & Wills, A. J. (2005). Integrating associative models of supervised and unsupervised categorization. In A. J. Wills (ed.), *New Directions in Human Associative Learning*. London: LEA.

2   The generalized context model: an exemplar model of classification

Robert M. Nosofsky

Model description

Conceptual overview

According to the *generalized context model* (GCM) (Nosofsky, 1986), people represent categories by storing individual exemplars (or examples) in memory, and classify objects based on their similarity to these stored exemplars. For example, the model assumes that people represent the category of 'birds' by storing in memory the vast collection of different sparrows, robins, eagles, ostriches (and so forth) that they have experienced. If an object is sufficiently similar to some of these bird exemplars, then the person would tend to classify the object as a 'bird'. This exemplar view of categorization contrasts dramatically with major alternative approaches that assume that people form abstract summary representations of categories, such as rules or idealized prototypes.

The standard version of the GCM adopts a *multidimensional scaling* (MDS) approach to modelling similarity relations among exemplars (Shepard, 1958, 1987). In this approach, exemplars are represented as points in a multidimensional psychological space. Similarity between exemplars is a decreasing function of their distance in the space. In many applications, a first step in the modelling is to conduct similarity-scaling studies to derive MDS solutions for the exemplars and to discover their locations in the multidimensional similarity space (Nosofsky, 1992b).

A crucial assumption in the modelling, however, is that similarity is not an invariant relation, but a highly context-dependent one. To take an example from Medin and Schaffer (1978), humans and mannequins may be judged as highly similar in a context that emphasizes structural appearance, but would be judged as highly dissimilar in a context that emphasizes vitality. In the GCM, the context-dependent nature of

The writing of this chapter was supported by grants FA9550-08-1-0486 from the Air Force Office of Scientific Research and MH48494 from the National Institute of Mental Health.

similarity is modelled in terms of a set of selective-attention weights that systematically modify the structure of the psychological space in which the exemplars are embedded (Carroll & Wish, 1974). As will be illustrated below, the weights serve to 'stretch' the psychological space along highly attended, relevant dimensions, and to 'shrink' the space along unattended irrelevant dimensions. This stretching and shrinking can have profound influences on similarity relations among exemplars and on the resulting classification predictions from the model.

Finally, the model assumes that the individual exemplars may be stored in memory with differing memory strengths. The memory strength of an exemplar may be influenced by factors such as frequency of presentation, recency of presentation, different forms of feedback provided during learning, and so forth. When a test item is presented so as to be classified, the exemplars that are most likely to be retrieved (and therefore to influence most strongly the classification decision) are those that are highly similar to the test item and that have high memory strengths. However, because exemplar retrieval is a probabilistic process, all exemplars stored in memory may influence classification decision making.

The conceptual ideas summarized above are illustrated schematically in Figure 2.1. Consider first the top panel. We suppose that there are two categories, A and B, with five exemplars in each category. The exemplars are composed of two dimensions. Exemplars A2 and B4 are close together in the space, so are highly similar to one another; whereas exemplars A5 and B2 are far apart, so are highly dissimilar. (The symbols used to illustrate the exemplars vary in their size in order to illustrate that the exemplars may be stored in memory with differing strengths.) Imagine that the observer is asked to classify test stimulus i into one of the two categories. According to the model, the observer sums the similarity of test item i to all of the exemplars of Category A and to all of the exemplars of Category B (weighted by the memory strengths of the examplars), and the classification decision is based on the relative magnitude of these summed similarities. In the top panel of Figure 2.1, test item i is roughly equally similar to the exemplars of the two categories, so the observer would classify the test item into the two categories with roughly equal probability.

Notice, however, that the horizontal dimension is far more relevant than is the vertical dimension for discriminating between the members of the two categories. (That is, all exemplars of Category B tend to have large values along the horizontal dimension, whereas all exemplars of Category A tend to have small values along the horizontal dimension.) Presumably, an experienced observer would learn this aspect of the

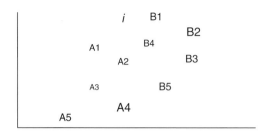

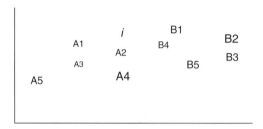

Figure 2.1 Schematic illustration of a category structure to explain the workings of the GCM. The top panel illustrates the category structure with equal attention to both dimensions. The bottom panel illustrates the structure following selective attention to the horizontal dimension.

category structure, so would learn to give greater attention to the more relevant horizontal dimension than to the less relevant vertical dimension. The bottom panel of Figure 2.1 illustrates the same category structure, but now assuming the above-described selective-attention strategy. The space is 'stretched' along the more-attended horizontal dimension and is 'shrunk' along the less-attended vertical dimension. In effect, by implementing this selective-attention strategy, the observer is attempting to optimize similarity relations for the given classification task (Nosofsky, 1984, 1986). There is now greater separation between the exemplars of contrasting categories (lowered between-category similarity), yet less separation among the exemplars within each category (heightened within-category similarity). Furthermore, note that this selective-attention strategy has a profound influence on the classification predictions from the model. In the top panel, item i was roughly equally similar to the exemplars of the two categories; however, following selective attention to the relevant dimension (bottom panel), the test item is now far more similar to the exemplars of Category A. Thus, in the latter situation, the exemplar model predicts that the test item would be classified into Category A with high probability.

Computational assumptions

In this section I present a brief description of how the GCM is formalized. The description assumes that there is an initial training phase in
which observers are presented with n unique training exemplars. The
training phase is followed by a test phase in which both training items
and new transfer items might be presented. On each trial during the
test phase, the observer classifies the test item into one of K_N categories.
According to the model, the probability with which item i is classified
into Category J during the test phase is given by:

$$P(J \mid i) = \frac{b_J \left[\sum_{j=1}^{n} V_{jJ} s_{ij} \right]^{\gamma}}{\sum_{K=1}^{K_N} b_K \left[\sum_{k=1}^{n} V_{kK} s_{ik} \right]^{\gamma}}, \tag{1}$$

where s_{ij} denotes the similarity between item i and exemplar j; V_{jJ} denotes
the memory strength of exemplar j with respect to Category J; γ is a
freely estimated response-scaling parameter $(0 < \gamma)$; and b_J $(0 < b_J)$
denotes the response-bias for Category J. Thus, according to the model,
the observer sums the similarity of item i to all exemplars j belonging
to Category J, weighted by their Category J memory strengths (and by
any differential response bias). This summed similarity constitutes the
'evidence' in favour of Category J. This evidence is then divided by the
summed evidence for all of the categories to predict the Category-J classification probability.

The parameter γ in Equation 1 is a response-scaling parameter
that influences the degree of determinism in classification responding
(Ashby & Maddox, 1993; Nosofsky & Zaki, 2002). When $\gamma = 1$, the
observer responds probabilistically by 'probability matching' to the relative summed similarities of each category; whereas when γ grows greater
than 1, observers respond more deterministically with the category that
yields the largest summed similarity. The memory-strength values (V_{jJ})
in Equation 1 are typically not free parameters but rather are given by
the nature of the experimental design. Usually, they are set equal to the
relative frequency with which each exemplar j is provided with Category
J feedback during the classification training phase. (In the most usual
classification learning paradigms, the exemplars are presented with equal
frequency and each exemplar is assigned to only a single category. In
that simple case, all exemplars j that are assigned to Category J receive

memory strengths equal to 1; whereas the memory strength of an exemplar with respect to all its unassigned categories is equal to 0.)

To apply Equation 1, one needs to compute the similarity between item i and each exemplar j, s_{ij}. In the standard version of the GCM, each exemplar j is represented as a single point in an M-dimensional psychological space. Let x_{jm} denote the value of exemplar j on Dimension m. The distance between item i and exemplar j is given by the weighted Minkowski power model,

$$d_{ij} = \left[\sum_{m=1}^{M} w_m \mid x_{im} - x_{jm} \mid^r \right]^{1/r} ,$$

(2)

where the value r determines the form of the distance metric. In situations involving highly separable-dimension stimuli (Garner, 1974; Shepard, 1964), the value r is typically set equal to 1, which yields a city-block distance metric. By contrast, in situations involving integral-dimension stimuli, the value r is set equal to 2, which yields a Euclidean distance metric. The w_m values in Equation 2 are freely estimated attention-weight parameters (with $0 \leq w_m \leq 1$, and $\Sigma w_m = 1$), reflecting the degree of attention that observers give to each dimension m in making their classification judgments.[1] A geometric interpretation for the operation of the attention weights is that of stretching and shrinking the psychological space along its component dimensions (see Figure 2.1).

Finally, the similarity between item i and exemplar j is given by

$$s_{ij} = e^{-cd_{ij}^p},$$

(3)

where c is a freely estimated sensitivity parameter that reflects the rate at which similarity declines with distance. When c is large, the similarity gradient is steep; that is, similarity falls off rapidly with increasing distance in the space. In this situation, the GCM acts very much like a nearest-neighbour classifier (i.e., one in which classification decisions are based primarily on the category membership of a test item's nearest neighbour). When c is small, the similarity gradient is shallow, and

---

[1] More precisely, the weights measure the span of each dimension *relative* to some prior, 'neutral' scaling or physical specification of the stimuli. To the extent that a prior scaling was obtained under conditions in which each dimension was equally relevant, then the weights estimated in a classification task can be interpreted in terms of the amount of 'attention' devoted to each dimension for purposes of the classification.

numerous exemplars may make major contributions to the classification decision. The value p in Equation 3 determines the shape of the function relating similarity to distance. In most cases, p is set equal to one, which yields an exponential relation between similarity and psychological distance (Shepard, 1987). In situations involving highly confusable stimuli, however, p is sometimes set equal to 2, yielding a Gaussian relation between similarity and distance (Nosofsky, 1985; for a theoretical interpretation, see Ennis, 1988).

In sum, the free parameters used for fitting the GCM to classification data are the sensitivity parameter c in Equation 3, the set of attention weights w_m in Equation 2, and the response-bias parameters and response-scaling parameter γ in Equation 1. (Because they can be constrained to sum to one, there are only $M - 1$ freely varying attention weights and $K_N - 1$ freely varying response-bias parameters.) All other quantities, including the x_{im} coordinate values (Equation 2), the V_{kK} memory strengths (Equation 1), the distance metric (value of r in Equation 2), and the similarity gradient (value of p in Equation 3) are fixed by the nature of the experimental design or are derived from independent sources.

Motivation

The GCM is a generalization of the original context model proposed by Medin and Schaffer (1978). Nosofsky (1984, 1986) integrated the Medin–Schaffer context model with classic theories developed in the areas of choice and similarity. This integration provided a firm theoretical foundation for the context model and allowed the original version to be extended to more widely varying classification paradigms. For example, the original context model was applied in highly simplified domains involving stimuli that varied along only binary-valued, separable dimensions. By comparison, most applications of the GCM are in continuous-dimension domains. In addition, the GCM is readily applied to predict classification performance involving integral-dimension stimuli as well as separable-dimension stimuli (Nosofsky, 1987). Moreover, when the GCM is used in combination with MDS approaches (in order to locate exemplars in psychological similarity spaces), it can be applied to predict classification performance in rich and complex domains in which the underlying stimulus dimensions may not be known (e.g., Shin & Nosofsky, 1992).

In the original version of the context model, Medin and Schaffer proposed what is essentially Equation 1 as a choice rule for classification. (Their equation did not include the memory-strength terms, bias parameters, or the γ response-scaling parameter.) However, they did not provide a strong justification for the use of the choice rule beyond the fact that it seemed to work. Nosofsky (1984, 1986) provided a deeper foundation for the context-model response rule by noting a strong relation between it and the classic *similarity-choice model* (SCM) for predicting confusions in identification paradigms (Luce, 1963; Shepard, 1957). I briefly review this motivating relation here.

In an identification paradigm, there are n distinct stimuli, and each stimulus is assigned a unique response. The data are summarized in an $n \times n$ identification confusion matrix (see left panel of Figure 2.2), where each cell (i, j) of the matrix gives the conditional probability with which stimulus i is identified as stimulus j. The SCM is one of the leading descriptive models for predicting confusion probabilities in identification paradigms. According to the SCM, the probability with which stimulus i is identified as stimulus j is given by

$$P(j \mid i) = \frac{b_j s_{ij}}{\sum\limits_{k=1}^{n} b_k s_{ik}}, \tag{4}$$

where b_j $(0 < b_j)$ is the bias for response j, and where s_{ij} $(0 < s_{ij}, s_{ij} = s_{ji})$ is the similarity between stimuli i and j.

In a classification paradigm, the n stimuli are assigned to one of K_N categories $(K_N < n)$. The data are summarized in an $n \times K_N$ confusion matrix, where cell $(i, \mathcal{J})$ of the matrix gives the conditional probability with which stimulus i is classified in Category $\mathcal{J}$. An illustration with $K_N = 2$ is provided in the right panel of Figure 2.2.

An intuitively compelling idea for predicting classification confusions from identification confusions was first proposed by Shepard, Hovland, and Jenkins (1961). The idea was that, in a classification paradigm, any time a stimulus is confused with another member of its own category, it would result in a correct classification response. Only between-class stimulus confusions would result in classification errors. Coined the *mapping* hypothesis[2] by Nosofsky (1986), the idea is illustrated schematically in Figure 2.2. In the figure, we imagine that stimuli 1–4 belong to Category A, whereas stimuli 5–8 belong to Category B. As illustrated in Figure 2.2, according to the mapping hypothesis, stimulus 3 would

---

[2] Identification paradigms involve a one-to-one mapping of stimuli onto responses. Classification paradigms involve a many-to-one mapping of stimuli onto responses. The mapping hypothesis allows one to use data from one-to-one mapping paradigms to predict performance in many-to-one mapping paradigms.

MAPPING   HYPOTHESIS

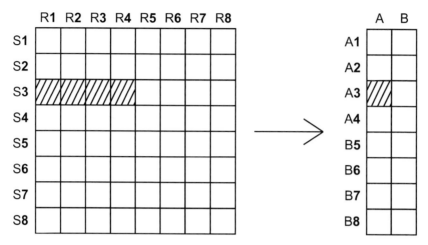

Figure 2.2 Left panel: an 8 × 8 stimulus-response (S-R) confusion matrix for an identification experiment. Right panel: an 8 × 2 S-R confusion matrix for a classification experiment (the same stimuli are used as in the identification task). Stimuli 1–4 are assigned to Category A, and stimuli 5–8 are assigned to Category B. According to the mapping hypothesis, one predicts the probability that stimulus 3 is classified in Category A by summing over the probabilities that stimulus 3 is identified as either stimulus 1, 2, 3, or 4 in the identification task. (From Nosofsky (1986), published by APA. Reprinted with permission.)

receive the correct response in the classification paradigm whenever it is confused with stimuli 1–4 in the identification paradigm.

More generally, if the mapping hypothesis is correct, then the probability that stimulus i is classified into Category J would be found by summing over the probabilities that it is confused with any member of Category J in the identification paradigm. It is straightforward to show that, if the SCM (Equation 4) describes these identification confusion probabilities, then the predicted classification probabilities are given by what is essentially Equation 1, i.e., the context-model response rule. The main difference is that because the response set has changed, the individual-item response bias parameters are replaced with category-level response bias parameters.[3]

---

[3] A further requirement for the mapping hypothesis to hold is that the γ response-scaling parameter be equal to one, which was true in the original formulation of the context model.

Although intuitively compelling, Shepard *et al.* (1961) observed systematic failures in using the mapping hypothesis to predict classification confusions on the basis of identification confusions. Although a full discussion goes beyond the scope of this chapter, Nosofsky (1984, 1986) proposed that the mapping hypothesis not be abandoned completely. The key idea was that the similarity parameters that operate in Equations 1 and 4 may change systematically across the identification and classification paradigms, because of the operation of the selective-attention processes depicted in Figure 2.1. Thus, Nosofsky (1986) proposed that rather than there being a *direct* mapping relation, a more abstract *indirect* mapping relation may connect identification and classification performance. According to this proposal, performance in both paradigms is governed by similarity relations among distinct exemplars, as formalized in Equations 1 and 4. However, these inter-exemplar similarity relations change systematically across the paradigms because of the operation of selective attention. Nosofsky (1984, 1986, 1987) provided strong support for this idea in theoretical and empirical work that investigated relations between identification and classification performance.

The motivation for the similarity equations used in the GCM (Equations 2 and 3) grows directly from decades of research and theoretical development in the area of similarity. MDS approaches to modelling similarity have long been among the most general and successful approaches in the field. Indeed, so successful have been those approaches that some of the discovered regularities have been proposed as candidates for universal laws of psychological generalization (Shepard, 1987). In particular, there is a great deal of support for the idea that psychological distance relations among integral-dimension stimuli are well described by embedding the stimuli in multidimensional Euclidean spaces, whereas psychological distance relations among separable-dimension stimuli are better approximated by a city-block distance metric. Furthermore, Shepard (1987) reviewed decades of research that point to an approximately exponential relation (Equation 3 with $p = 1$) between similarity, measured in terms of probability of stimulus generalization, and distance in these psychological spaces.

In their original formulation of the context model, Medin and Schaffer (1978) proposed an inter-dimensional multiplicative rule for computing stimulus similarity. The similarity between stimuli i and j was given by

$$s_{ij} = \prod_{m=1}^{M} s_m^{\delta_m(i,j)}, \qquad (5)$$

where s_m ($0 \leq s_m \leq 1$) is a freely estimated dimension-m similarity parameter; δ is an indicator variable set equal to 1 if stimuli i and j mismatch on dimension m, and set equal to zero if they match on dimension m. Thus, the overall similarity between stimuli i and j is simply the product of their similarities along each of their mismatching dimensions. This inter-dimensional multiplicative rule is a special case of the MDS approach to modelling similarity that is embodied in Equations 2 and 3 of the GCM. In particular, an inter-dimensional multiplicative rule arises whenever $p = r$ in Equations 2 and 3 (see Nosofsky, 1986, p. 42, for further discussion). The particular highly constrained rule used by Medin and Schaffer (Equation 5) arises when, in addition, the stimuli vary along a set of independent, binary-valued dimensions. However, as explained above, use of the MDS approach in the GCM allows for a far more general application of the model to diverse classification domains.

Because of its combination of assumptions involving an exemplar-based category representation and a non-linear similarity rule, the GCM is highly sensitive to effects of specific exemplars and to within-class correlational structure in categories (for extensive discussion, see, for example, Medin & Schaffer, 1978; Nosofsky, 1992a). A variety of experiments have been reported for illustrating the importance of such sensitivity. For example, in some studies, category structures have been designed in which an individual stimulus i is more similar than is stimulus j to the prototype (central tendency) of their category; yet, stimulus j has high similarity to specific exemplars of the category, whereas stimulus i does not. In such studies, it is often found that subjects classify more accurately the stimulus with high exemplar-specific similarity than the stimulus with high similarity to the prototype (for reviews and examples, see Nosofsky, 1992a, 2000; Nosofsky & Zaki, 2002). Exemplar models with non-linear similarity rules (such as the GCM) account naturally for such effects, whereas major alternative models, such as prototype models, do not.

Implementation recommendations

In the present section I present some practical advice on implementing the GCM. The key free parameters that are almost always estimated are the sensitivity parameter (c) in Equation 3 and the attention-weight parameters (the w_m) in Equation 2. An interesting working hypothesis is that, with learning, the participant may adopt a set of ideal-observer weights, for example, a set of weights that would allow the participant to maximize his or her percentage of correct classifications. Thus, it is interesting to compare the best-fitting attention-weight parameters to the ideal-observer weights. In many situations, the best-fitting weights turn out to approximate the ideal-observer weights (e.g., Nosofsky, 1984, 1986, 1991b).

Unless there are strong experimental manipulations involving differential category payoffs or frequencies, the response-bias parameters tend not to contribute substantially to the model fits, and can generally be set equal to one. The γ response-scaling parameter (Equation 1) is important when modelling performance at the individual-observer level, to allow the model to capture the deterministic response strategies that individual observers sometimes use (e.g., McKinley & Nosofsky, 1995; Nosofsky & Zaki, 2002). Practical experience suggests, however, that in fitting averaged data, γ can be held fixed at one without much loss in predictive accuracy.

As discussed in the introduction, in situations involving fairly discriminable stimuli, an exponential decay function for relating similarity to distance ($p = 1$ in Equation 3) is always assumed. For integral-dimension stimuli, a Euclidean metric ($r = 2$) is assumed in Equation 2; whereas for highly separable-dimension stimuli, a city-block metric ($r = 1$) is assumed. By contrast, in situations involving highly confusable perceptual stimuli, the values $p = 2$ and $r = 2$ tend to provide much better fits. (These parameter settings are probably reflecting extensive perceptual noise in the stimulus representations that exists in high-confusability situations – see Ennis (1988) for further discussion.)

The memory-strength values (Equation 1) are generally not treated as free parameters. Instead, they are usually set proportional to the relative frequency with which each stimulus is presented in combination with associated category feedback during the training phase of the experiment. In cases in which one models trial-by-trial performance data, a memory-strength value is often attached to each individual exemplar presented on each trial; in this case, the memory strengths are assumed to decay exponentially with lag of presentation of the exemplars (e.g., McKinley & Nosofsky, 1995).

In general, the GCM is fitted to classification choice-probability data by using a maximum-likelihood criterion, under the assumption that the distribution of responses into categories is multinomial in form (see Nosofsky, 1989, for examples). Hierarchically nested versions of the model, in which some parameters are held fixed at default values, can be tested against the full version of the model by using standard likelihood-ratio techniques (see Nosofsky, 1989, for examples) or alternative methods such as AIC or BIC that penalize models for their number of free parameters. Because analytic solutions for the maximum-likelihood parameters are generally not available except in exceedingly simple cases, a computer search is used for locating the best-fitting parameters. As is the case for fitting any highly non-linear model to data, multiple starting configurations should be used in the parameter searches to guard against local minima.

The GCM has been a highly successful and widely applied model. In addition, its free parameters are easily interpretable and provide measurements of psychological processes of fundamental interest. For example, researchers may be interested in the extent to which different populations of subjects adopt alternative patterns of selective attention to the dimensions that compose a set of stimuli (e.g., Viken *et al.*, 2002). The derived attention-weight parameters from the model provide such information. For these reasons, an important recent development is the availability of a general-purpose computer package for conducting Bayesian analyses of the GCM (Vanpaemel, 2009; see also Lee, 2008). The package provides estimates of the posterior distributions of the model's parameters to allow for easy inference and interpretation of the effects of different experimental manipulations on psychological processing.

Application to an example

An example application of the GCM to a previously published data set (Nosofsky, 1989) is briefly reviewed in Table 2.1 and Figure 2.3. Because the fits are to averaged data, they should be considered as merely illustrative. The stimuli were a set of semicircles with an embedded radial line. The semicircles varied orthogonally in their size (four levels) and in the angle of orientation of the radial line (four levels) to create a 16-member stimulus set. Subjects were tested in four different categorization conditions, which are illustrated schematically in Figure 2.3. In the figure, the columns of each 4×4 grid correspond to the different levels of angle, and the rows correspond to the different levels of size. Cells that are marked in their centre with a boldface 1 represent training exemplars of Category 1, whereas cells marked with a 2 were training exemplars of Category 2. Unmarked cells were unassigned transfer stimuli. During an initial training phase, subjects were presented with only the training exemplars and were provided with trial-by-trial corrective feedback. During a subsequent test phase, subjects were presented with both training and transfer stimuli. Feedback continued to be provided on trials in which training exemplars were presented, but was withheld on trials in which unassigned transfer stimuli were presented.

As can be seen in the figure, to provide evidence of generality, a variety of different category structures were tested. The Size and Angle categorizations provide examples of 'unidimensional' category structures, in

Table 2.1 *Maximum-likelihood parameters and summary fits for full and restricted versions of the exemplar-similarity categorization model (reprinted from Nosofsky, 1989)*

Condition	Model	Parameters			Fits		
		c	w_1	b_1	SSE	%Var	$-\ln L$
Size	Unconstrained	1.60	0.10	0.50	0.015	99.4	40.8
	Equal attention	2.38	(0.50)	0.49	0.077	97.0	72.0
	Equal bias	160	0.10	(0.50)	0.015	99.4	40.8
Angle	Unconstrained	3.20	0.98	0.43	0.010	99.6	44.3
	Equal attention	3.57	(0.50)	0.45	0.305	86.4	164.3
	Equal bias	3.09	1.00	(0.50)	0.029	98.7	56.8
Criss-cross	Unconstrained	1.62	0.80	0.45	0.025	95.2	47.7
	Equal attention	1.23	(0.50)	0.45	0.087	83.1	64.6
	Equal bias	3.00	0.93	(0.50)	0.046	91.1	56.7
Diagonal	Unconstrained	2.42	0.81	0.49	0.023	98.4	483
	Equal attention	1.81	(0.50)	0.48	0.217	85.0	109.4
	Equal bias	2.42	81	(0.50)	0.021	98.6	49.1

Values in parentheses were constrained a priori. The parameter w_1 gives the attention weight for Angle, and $1 - w_1$ the attention weight for Size. SSE is the sum of squared deviations between predicted and observed Category 1 probabilities; %Var is the percentage of variance accounted for; $\ln L$ is the log likelihood.

which one dimension is far more relevant than is the other for purposes of classification. These structures were tested to provide clear evidence of the role of selective attention in classification. Consider, for example, the Angle categorization. Note that stimulus 14 is an unassigned transfer stimulus. In terms of 'overall similarity', stimulus 14 is more similar to the exemplars of Category 2 than to the exemplars of Category 1 (it lies extremely close to exemplar 15 of Category 2). However, if subjects attend selectively to the relevant angle dimension, then the space will be stretched along the horizontal angle dimension, and shrunk along the vertical size dimension, rendering stimulus 14 more similar to the exemplars of Category 1. An analogous situation holds for stimulus 9 of the Size categorization. The Criss-cross categorization provides an example of a continuous-dimension biconditional structure. Note that the structure is non-linearly separable, i.e., the members of the contrasting categories cannot be separated by drawing a straight line through the space. Whereas various categorization models are applicable only in cases involving linearly separable categories, the GCM applies generally regardless of the form of the category structure. Finally, the Diagonal

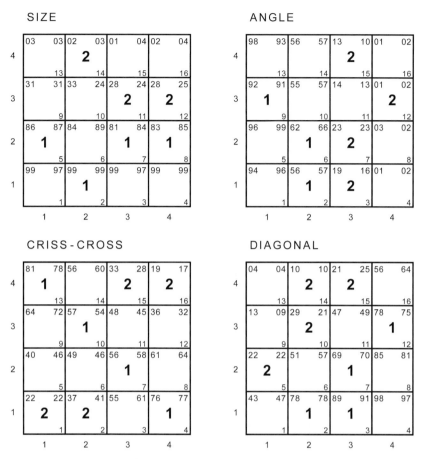

Figure 2.3 Schematic illustration of the four category structures tested by Nosofsky (1989). Cells marked with a 1 (2) depict training exemplars of Category 1 (2). Unmarked cells depict unassigned transfer stimuli. Top-left value in each cell is the predicted Category-1 response probability from the GCM. Top-right value in each cell is the observed Category-1 response probability. (Reprinted from Nosofsky, 1989.)

categorization provides an example of a fairly 'natural' two-dimensional category structure in which the exemplars of contrasting categories can be separated by drawing a diagonal line through the space.

In a preliminary similarity-scaling study involving the collection of identification confusion data (see Nosofsky, 1989, for details), a two-dimensional scaling solution was derived for the set of 16 stimuli. Not surprisingly, the derived two-dimensional solution closely reflected the 4 × 4 grid structure of the stimulus set (see Nosofsky, 1989; Figure 2.3). This two-dimensional scaling solution was then used in combination with the GCM to predict the classification data obtained in each of the four categorization conditions. The free parameters in the 'full' version of the model were the sensitivity parameter c, the dimension-1 attention weight w_1 (with $w_2 = 1 - w_1$), and the Category-1 response-bias parameter b_1 (with $b_2 = 1 - b_1$). All other parameters were set at the default values described previously in this chapter. (Because the stimuli were highly confusable, the Gaussian-Euclidean version of the model was used, with $p = 2$ and $r = 2$.) Parameters were estimated for each individual categorization condition that provided a maximum-likelihood fit to the data. In addition, special cases of the model were also fit to the data. In one special case, the attention weights were held fixed at $w_1 = w_2 = 0.5$; and in a second special case, the bias parameters were held fixed at $b_1 = b_2 = 0.5$. By comparing the fits of the special-case versions to the full version of the GCM, one gains evidence regarding the importance of the various free parameters.

The results of the model fitting are reported in Figures 2.3 and 2.4 and in Table 2.1. In Figure 2.3, the top-right value in each cell gives the observed probability with which subjects classified the stimulus into Category 1, whereas the top-left value gives the predicted probability from the GCM. A summary of all of these observed-against-predicted probabilities for all four categorization conditions is provided in the scatterplot in Figure 2.4. It can be seen from inspection that the model provides extremely accurate predictions of the data in all four conditions. The quantitative summary fits from the model are also reported in Table 2.1. Although the criterion of fit was to maximize likelihood (or, equivalently, to minimize the negative log-likelihood), the table also reports the sum-of-squared deviations between the predicted and observed classification probabilities, as well as the percentage of variance accounted for in each condition.

Finally, the table reports the fit results for the special-case models described above. Of greatest interest are the results for the special-case version that assumes equal attention to the two stimulus dimensions. In all conditions, this special-case model fits significantly worse than does the full version (see Nosofsky, 1989, for detailed reports of likelihood-ratio tests that compare the full version to the special cases). These results provide clear evidence of the need to incorporate assumptions about selective attention into the modelling. They can be understood most easily by considering the results for the critical transfer stimuli

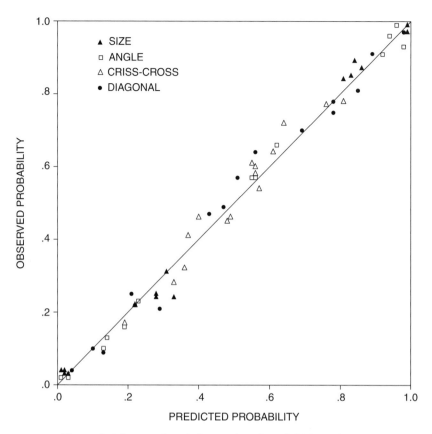

Figure 2.4 Scatterplot of observed against GCM-predicted Category-1 response probabilities for each stimulus in all four categorization conditions. (Reprinted from Nosofsky, 1989.)

described above. For example, in the Angle categorization, the equal-attention model predicted that transfer stimulus 14 would be classified into Category 2 with high probability, because it has greater overall similarity to the exemplars of Category 2 than to Category 1. However, the full version of the model, which allows for selective attention to the relevant angle dimension, predicts correctly that transfer stimulus 14 is classified with somewhat higher probability into Category 1. Indeed, the maximum-likelihood estimate for the attention-weight parameter in the Angle categorization is $w_1 = 0.98$ (see Table 2.1), providing clear evidence for the operation of selective attention in this condition.

Whereas the role of the selective-attention parameters in the GCM has been emphasized and studied systematically in past research, much less emphasis has been placed on the role of the response-bias parameters. However, in the same way that certain patterns of selective attention may yield better classification performance than others (depending on the category structure), so may certain patterns of response bias yield better performance than others (for examples in situations involving categories with differing variabilities, see Cohen, Nosofsky, & Zaki, 2001). Thus, to the extent that human observers are adaptive and adjust parameter settings to achieve task goals, it would not be surprising to find evidence of systematic shifts in patterns of category response bias as a function of experimental conditions.

Relations and extensions

Although a detailed discussion goes beyond the scope of this chapter, it is important to remark that the GCM is closely related to a variety of rational, Bayesian, and powerful statistical/machine-learning models of categorization (e.g., Anderson, 1990; Ashby & Alfonso-Reese, 1995; Jakel, Scholkopf, & Wichman, 2008; Nosofsky, 1990, 1991a; Shepard, 1987). Thus, it is interesting to speculate that exemplar-based classification schemes evolved because they provide highly adaptive and flexible solutions to the goals of classification given the structure of natural categories and limits on the computational complexity of the mind (Anderson, 1990). Furthermore, perhaps because the GCM builds upon classic past models in the fields of similarity and classification, and it has itself been a highly successful and widely applied model, there have also been numerous extensions of the GCM. In this final section I briefly review some of these extensions.

One extension is Kruschke's (1992) highly influential ALCOVE (attention-learning covering-map) model. In essence, ALCOVE adopts the GCM's exemplar-based representational assumptions, its MDS-based similarity assumptions, and its assumptions about selective attention, and embeds them within the framework of a connectionist learning network. A key potential advantage is that, whereas the selective-attention weights are free parameters in the GCM, ALCOVE provides a mechanism that *learns* the attention weights on a trial-by-trial basis. In addition, in standard applications of the GCM, the memory strengths associated with individual exemplars are assumed simply to be proportional to the frequency with which each exemplar is presented in combination with given category feedback. By contrast, in ALCOVE, learning is error driven, and association weights develop between exemplars and categories that are more intricate and potentially more adaptive than those allowed by the GCM.

Whereas the GCM is limited to predicting choice-probability data in classification, other major extensions of the model enable it also to predict classification response times (RTs). Nosofsky and Palmeri's (1997) *exemplar-based random-walk* (EBRW) model adopts the same representational assumptions as does the GCM. However, classification decision-making is governed by a random-walk process. The random walk is driven by exemplars that are retrieved from memory. Importantly, in a two-category experiment, the GCM response-rule (Equation 1) emerges as a special case of the EBRW model, so the EBRW provides a process-level interpretation for the GCM. It also predicts successfully a wide variety of fundamental effects involving classification RT data, including effects of distance-from-boundary, familiarity, practice, and probabilistic feedback (Nosofsky & Palmeri, 1997; Nosofsky & Stanton, 2005). Another major extension is Lamberts's (2000) *extended generalized context model for response times* (EGCM-RT). This extension also adopts the GCM's exemplar-based representational and similarity assumptions. However, it assumes that categorization involves the gradual construction of a perceptual representation through a process of information accumulation. In particular, the perceptual representation of a stimulus is gradually built through a process of stochastic, parallel sampling of the stimulus's individual dimensions. Classification RTs are determined by the length of time with which the sampling process operates, which in turn is closely related to outputs from the GCM response rule.

A long-standing debate in the classification literature has involved a contrast between exemplar and prototype models. Whereas exemplar models assume that categories are represented in terms of individually stored exemplars, prototype models assume instead a single summary representation that is the central tendency of the individual exemplars. In Chapter 3 of this volume, Minda and Smith consider prototype models. They argue that prototype models provide better accounts of data than do exemplar models in a variety of experiments involving visual categories. However, this conclusion has been disputed in numerous studies (see e.g., Busemeyer, Dewey, & Medin, 1984; Nosofsky, 2000; Nosofsky & Zaki, 2002; Palmeri & Flanery, 2002; Rehder & Hoffman, 2005; Stanton, Nosofsky, & Zaki, 2002; Zaki & Nosofsky, 2004, 2007; Zaki *et al.*, 2003). An intermediate view is that multiple prototypes may be formed to represent a category, where a varying number of exemplars may be averaged together to form each individual prototype. In the *varying abstraction model* (VAM) of Vanpaemel and Storms (2008), all possible multiple-prototype representations are considered, and the version that fits best is taken as the underlying category representation. Although the VAM is far more complex than the GCM, results from

Vanpaemel and Storms suggest that the added complexity is justified in terms of one's ability to accurately predict human classification performance. A closely related alternative idea is the Rex Leopold I model of De Schryver, Vandist, and Rosseel (2009). This model posits that categories are not represented in terms of the complete set of experienced exemplars, but in terms of reduced subsets of the exemplars. Analogous to the VAM, all possible reduced subsets are considered, and the best-fitting subset is taken as the category representation.

Another important extension of the GCM is Stewart and Brown's (2005) *similarity-dissimilarity exemplar model*. This model posits that the evidence in favour of a category is not based solely on the similarity of a test item to the exemplars of that category, but on its *dissimilarity* to the exemplars of contrast categories. This extended model accounts successfully for the use of difference information and category-contrast effects in classification. A final example is Pothos and Bailey's (2009) extension of the GCM to judgments of category intuitiveness and unsupervised categorization. This unsupervised GCM operates by computing, for any given partitioning of exemplars into categories, the overall prediction error associated with that partitioning. The category assignment that results in the smallest prediction error is considered to be the most intuitive.

Finally, although I have focused on the issue of categorization in this chapter, perhaps the most important achievement of the GCM is that essentially the same model has been used to account for varieties of other fundamental cognitive processes, including individual-item identification, the development of automaticity, and old-new recognition performance (e.g., Nosofsky, 1986, 1987, 1988, 1991b; Nosofsky & Stanton, 2006; Nosofsky & Zaki, 1998; Palmeri, 1997). The successful applications of the GCM in these domains, and the use of the model to explain relations between categorization and performance in other fundamental tasks, suggests the possibility of developing unified, exemplar-based theories of cognitive representation and processing.

REFERENCES

Anderson, J. R. (1990). *The Adaptive Character of Thought*. Hillsdale, NJ: LEA.

Ashby, F. G., & Alfonso-Reese, L. (1995). Categorization as probability density estimation. *Journal of Mathematical Psychology*, **39**, 216–233.

Ashby, F. G., & Maddox, W. T. (1993). Relations between exemplar, prototype, and decision bound models of categorization. *Journal of Mathematical Psychology*, 37, 372–400.

Busemeyer, J. R., Dewey, G. I., & Medin, D. L. (1984). Evaluation of exemplar-based generalization and the abstraction of categorical information.

Journal of Experimental Psychology: Learning, Memory, and Cognition, **10**, 638–648.

Carroll, J.D., & Wish, M. (1974). Models and methods for three-way multi-dimensional scaling. In D.H. Krantz, R.C. Atkinson, R.D. Luce, & P. Suppes (eds.), *Contemporary Developments in Mathematical Psychology* (Vol. 2). San Francisco, CA: W.H. Freeman.

Cohen, A.L., Nosofsky, R.M., & Zaki, S.R. (2001). Category variability, exemplar similarity, and perceptual classification. *Memory & Cognition*, **29**, 1165–1175.

De Schryver, M., Vandist, K., & Rosseel, Y. (2009). How many exemplars are used? Explorations with the Rex Leopold I model. *Psychonomic Bulletin & Review*, **16**, 337–343.

Ennis, D.M. (1988). Confusable and discriminable stimuli: comment on Nosofsky (1986) and Shepard (1986). *Journal of Experimental Psychology: General*, **117**, 408–411.

Garner, W.R. (1974). *The Processing of Information and Structure*. New York: Wiley.

Jakel, F., Scholkopf, B., & Wichman, F.A. (2008). Generalization and similarity in exemplar models of categorization: insights from machine learning. *Psychonomic Bulletin & Review*, **15**, 256–271.

Kruschke, J.K. (1992). ALCOVE: an exemplar-based connectionist model of category learning. *Psychological Review*, **99**, 22–44.

Lamberts, K. (2000). Information accumulation theory of categorization response times. *Psychological Review*, **107**, 227–260.

Lee, M.D. (2008). Three case studies in the Bayesian analysis of cognitive models. *Psychonomic Bulletin & Review*, **15**, 1–15.

Luce, R.D. (1963). Detection and recognition. In R.D. Luce, R.R. Bush, & E. Galanter (eds.), *Handbook of Mathematical Psychology* (pp. 103–189). New York: Wiley.

McKinley, S.C., & Nosofsky, R.M. (1995). Investigations of exemplar and decision bound models in large, ill-defined category structures. *Journal of Experimental Psychology: Human Perception and Performance*, **21**, 128–148.

Medin, D.L., & Schaffer, M.M. (1978). Context theory of classification learning. *Psychological Review*, **85**, 207–238.

Nosofsky, R.M. (1984). Choice, similarity, and the context theory of classification. *Journal of Experimental Psychology: Learning, Memory, and Cognition*, **10**, 104–114.

(1985). Overall similarity and the identification of separable-dimension stimuli: a choice model analysis. *Perception & Psychophysics*, **38**, 415–432.

(1986). Attention, similarity, and the identification-categorization relationship. *Journal of Experimental Psychology: General*, **115**, 39–57.

(1987). Attention and learning processes in the identification and categorization of integral stimuli. *Journal of Experimental Psychology: Learning, Memory, and Cognition*, **13**, 87–109.

(1988). Exemplar-based accounts of relations between classification, recognition, and typicality. *Journal of Experimental Psychology: Learning, Memory, and Cognition*, **14**, 700–708.

(1989). Further tests of an exemplar-similarity approach to relating identification and categorization. *Perception & Psychophysics*, **45**, 279–290.

(1990). Relations between exemplar-similarity and likelihood models of classification. *Journal of Mathematical Psychology*, **34**, 393–418.

(1991a). Relation between the rational model and the context model of categorization. *Psychological Science*, **2**, 416–421.

(1991b). Tests of an exemplar model for relating perceptual classification and recognition memory. *Journal of Experimental Psychology: Human Perception and Performance*, **17**, 3–27.

(1992a). Exemplars, prototypes, and similarity rules. In A. F. Healy & S. M. Kossyln (eds.), *Essays in Honor of William K. Estes, Vol. 1: From Learning Theory to Connectionist Theory* (pp. 149–167). Hillsdale, NJ: LEA.

(1992b). Similarity scaling and cognitive process models. *Annual Review of Psychology*, **43**, 22–53.

(2000). Exemplar representation without generalization: comment on Smith and Minda's (2000) 'Thirty categorization results in search of a model'. *Journal of Experimental Psychology: Learning, Memory, and Cognition*, **26**, 1735–1743.

Nosofsky, R. M., & Palmeri, T. J. (1997). An exemplar-based random-walk model of speeded classification. *Psychological Review*, **104**, 266–300.

Nosofsky, R. M., & Stanton, R. D. (2005). Speeded classification in a probabilistic category structure: contrasting exemplar-retrieval, decision-boundary, and prototype models. *Journal of Experimental Psychology: Human Perception and Performance*, **31**, 608–629.

(2006). Speeded old-new recognition of multidimensional perceptual stimuli: modeling performance at the individual-participant and individual-item levels. *Journal of Experimental Psychology: Human Perception and Performance*, **32**, 314–334.

Nosofsky, R. M., & Zaki, S. R. (1998). Dissociations between categorization and recognition in amnesic and normal individuals: an exemplar-based interpretation. *Psychological Science*, **9**, 247–255.

(2002). Exemplar and prototype models revisited: response strategies, selective attention, and stimulus generalization. *Journal of Experimental Psychology: Learning, Memory, and Cognition*, **28**, 924–940.

Palmeri, T. J. (1997). Exemplar similarity and the development of automaticity. *Journal of Experimental Psychology: Learning, Memory, and Cognition*, **23**, 324–354.

Palmeri, T. J., & Flanery, M. A. (2002). Memory systems and perceptual categorization. In B. H. Ross (ed.), *The Psychology of Learning and Motivation: Advances in Research and Theory* (pp. 141–189). San Diego, CA: Academic Press.

Pothos, E. M., & Bailey, T. M. (2009). Predicting category intuitiveness with the rational model, the simplicity model, and the Generalized Context Model. *Journal of Experimental Psychology: Learning, Memory, and Cognition*, **35**, 1062–1080.

Rehder, B., & Hoffman, A. B. (2005). Thirty-something categorization results explained: selective attention, eyetracking, and models of category learning.

Journal of Experimental Psychology: Learning, Memory, and Cognition, **31**, 811–829.

Shepard, R. N. (1957). Stimulus and response generalization: a stochastic model relating generalization to distance in psychological space. *Psychometrika*, **22**, 325–345.

(1958). Stimulus and response generalization: tests of a model relating generalization to distance in psychological space. *Journal of Experimental Psychology*, **55**, 509–523.

(1964). Attention and the metric structure of the stimulus space. *Journal of Mathematical Psychology*, **1**, 54–87.

(1987). Toward a universal law of generalization for psychological science. *Science*, **237**, 1317–1323.

Shepard, R. N., Hovland, C. I., & Jenkins, H. M. (1961). Learning and memorization of classifications. *Psychological Monographs*, **75** (13), Whole No. 517.

Shin, H. J., & Nosofsky, R. M. (1992). Similarity-scaling studies of dot-pattern classification and recognition. *Journal of Experimental Psychology: General*, **121**, 278–304.

Stanton, R. D., Nosofsky, R. M., & Zaki, S. R. (2002). Comparisons between exemplar similarity and mixed prototype models using a linearly separable category structure. *Memory & Cognition*, **30**, 934–944.

Stewart, N., & Brown, G. D. A. (2005). Similarity and dissimilarity as evidence in perceptual categorization. *Journal of Mathematical Psychology*, **49**, 403–409.

Vanpaemel, W. (2009). BayesGCM: software for Bayesian inference with the Generalized Context Model. *Behavior Research Methods*, **41**, 1111–1120.

Vanpaemel, W., & Storms, G. (2008). In search of abstraction: the varying abstraction model of categorization. *Psychonomic Bulletin & Review*, **15**, 732–749.

Viken, R. J., Treat, T. A., Nosofsky, R. M., McFall, R. M., & Palmeri, T. J. (2002). Modeling individual differences in perceptual and attentional processes related to bulimic symptoms. *Journal of Abnormal Psychology*, **111**, 598–609.

Zaki, S. R., & Nosofsky, R. M. (2004). False prototype enhancement effects in dot pattern categorization. *Memory & Cognition*, **32**, 390–398.

(2007). A high-distortion enhancement effect in the prototype learning paradigm: dramatic effects of category learning during test. *Memory & Cognition*, **35**, 2088–2096.

Zaki, S. R., Nosofsky, R. M., Stanton, R. D., & Cohen, A. L. (2003). Prototype and exemplar accounts of category learning and attentional allocation: a reassessment. *Journal of Experimental Psychology: Learning, Memory, and Cognition*, **29**, 1160–1173.

3   Prototype models of categorization: basic formulation, predictions, and limitations

John Paul Minda and J. David Smith

Summary

The prototype model has had a long history in cognitive psychology, and prototype theory posed an early challenge to the classical view of concepts. Prototype models assume that categories are represented by a summary representation of a category (i.e., a prototype) that might represent information about the most common features, the average feature values, or even the ideal features of a category. Prototype models assume that classification decisions are made on the basis of how similar an object is to a category prototype. This chapter presents a formal description of the model, the motivation and theoretical history of the model, as well as several simulations that illustrate the model's properties. In general, the prototype model is well suited to explain the learning of many visual categories (e.g. dot patterns) and categories with a strong family-resemblance structure.

Prototype models of categorization: basic formulation, predictions, and limitations

Categories are fundamental to cognition, and the ability to learn and use categories is present in all humans and animals. An important theoretical account of categorization is the prototype view (Homa & Cultice, 1984; Homa *et al.*, 1973; Minda & Smith, 2001, 2002; Posner & Keele, 1968; J. D. Smith & Minda, 1998, 2000, 2001; J. D. Smith, Redford, & Haas, 2008). The prototype view assumes that a category of things in the world (objects, animals, shapes, etc.) can be represented in the mind by a prototype. A prototype is a cognitive representation that captures the regularities and commonalities among category members and can help a perceiver distinguish category members from non-members. The

This work was completed with the assistance of a grant from the National Science and Engineering Research Council of Canada (Minda) and grant HD-38051 from the National Institute of Child Health and Human Development (Smith).

prototype of a category is often described as the central tendency of the category, as a list of frequently occurring features, or even as an ideal category member. Furthermore, the prototype is similar to category members within the category and less similar (or very dissimilar) to members of other categories. According to the prototype view, objects are classified by first comparing them to the prototypes that are stored in memory, evaluating the similarity evidence from those comparisons, and then classifying the item in accord with the most similar prototype.

The prototype view can be realized as a computational model (i.e. the prototype model) that enables a researcher to make specific predictions about the category membership of novel exemplars within a prototype-based framework. The prototype model has been influential in categorization research for several decades as a complementary and balancing perspective to exemplar theory. In this chapter, we present a detailed description of the prototype model (Minda & Smith, 2001; J. D. Smith & Minda, 1998, 2000), we review the historical development of the prototype model, and we present several key predictions of the prototype model.

Description of the model

In this section, we provide a basic formulation of how the prototype model calculates similarity and makes a classification decision (Minda & Smith, 2001; Nosofsky, 1992). The formulation of the basic prototype model is closely related to the generalized context model of Nosofsky (Nosofsky, 1986, 1987), which is covered in Chapter 2 of this volume. Of course, the key difference is that to-be-categorized items are compared to prototypes, rather than multiple, specific exemplar traces as in the context model. The prototype model makes a classification decision in two steps: comparison and decision. In the comparison phase, a to-be-classified item is compared to the stored prototypes (usually calculated as the modal or average feature values) and the psychological distance between them is converted to a measure of similarity. In the decision phase, the model calculates the probability of the item's category membership based on the similarity of the item to one prototype divided by the similarity of the item to all the prototypes.

The model can be formulated with three equations. First, the distance between the item i and the prototype P is calculated by comparing the two stimuli along each weighted dimension k (see Equation 1):

$$d_{iP} = \left[\sum_{k=1}^{N} w_k \left| x_{ik} - P_k \right|^r \right]^{1/r} . \tag{1}$$

In this case, a dimension usually corresponds to some variable feature (for example, if a set of stimuli appear as either green or blue, colour would be a dimension).[1] The value of r is used to reflect two common ways to calculate distance. When $r = 1$ the model uses a city-block distance metric which is appropriate for separable-dimension stimuli. When $r = 2$ the model uses a Euclidean distance metric which is appropriate for integral-dimension stimuli. All of the simulations in this chapter use stimuli with separable dimensions and so r can be set to 1. Each dimension can be weighted to reflect how much attention or importance it is given by the model. In the present case, each attentional weight (w) varies between 0.0 (no attention) and 1.0 (exclusive attention). Attentional weights are normally constrained to sum to 1.0 across all the dimensions. The results of these weighted comparisons are summed across the dimensions to get the distance between the item and the prototype.

This distance (d_{iP}) between the item and the prototype is then converted into a measure of similarity (η_{iP}), following Shepard (1987), by taking:

$$\eta_{iP} = e^{-cd_{iP}} \tag{2}$$

which gives a measure of similarity of an item i to a prototype P. It is the exponent in Equation 2 that allows for the exponential-decay of similarity (meaning that trait dissimilarities tend to decrease psychological similarity very steeply at first, and then more gradually later on) and allows for the close correspondence between the prototype model and the generalized context model of Nosofsky (1992). The exponent is distance (d_{iP}) multiplied by the scaling or sensitivity parameter c. This parameter is a freely estimated parameter that can take on values from 1 to ∞ and reflects the steepness of the decay of similarity around the prototype. Low values of c indicate a gradual, more linear decay. High values of c indicate a steep, exponential decay. Generally, higher values of the sensitivity parameter will result in stronger category endorsements for typical items, and lower values of c will result in classification probabilities that are closer to chance.

The process of item-to-prototype comparison is repeated for all the prototypes (in this case P_A and P_B, but typically one to four in experimental settings). Once the item has been compared to the prototypes

---

[1] Most of the work with this model or related models like the GCM assumes that the dimensions exist in a psychological space that is representative of physical space. The dimensions of this psychological space can be derived from similarity scaling studies, or by making a simplifying assumption that each perceptual component will be interpreted as a dimension.

the probability of a Category A response is calculated for each stimulus. Prototype A similarity (d_{iP_A}) is divided by the sum of Prototype A and Prototype B similarity to generate the model's predicted probability of a Category A response $(P(R_A))$ for stimulus (S_i) as shown in the probabilistic choice rule in Equation 3:

$$P(R_A \mid S_i) = \frac{\eta_{iP_A}}{\eta_{iP_A} + \eta_{iP_B}}. \tag{3}$$

This is the standard version of the model, and the one that was used by Nosofsky and colleagues to argue in favour of exemplar theory and that was used by Smith and Minda to argue against exemplar theory and in favour of prototype theory (Nosofsky, 1992; J. D. Smith & Minda, 1998, 2000; J. D. Smith et al., 1997). The basic prototype model makes precise, prototype-based predictions about stimuli, and can be used to estimate the effectiveness of the prototype view in comparison to other computational accounts. Fitting the model involves parameter estimation and is described in the 'Implementation' section. In later work, Smith and Minda considered an alternative model that was prototype based, but included an exemplar-memorization process as well (Minda & Smith, 2001, 2002; J. D. Smith & Minda, 1998, 2000). This chapter is primarily concerned with prototype-based processing and readers may wish to consult these other papers for work on the mixture model.

Motivation

The modern version of the prototype model can trace its history back to several key developments in cognitive psychology. The first of these was the influential dot-pattern research of Posner and Keele, and Homa and colleagues (Homa & Cultice, 1984; Homa et al., 1973; Posner & Keele, 1968). In a series of elegant experiments, subjects were shown distortions of a dot pattern or polygon (i.e., the prototype). The details for the creation of the stimuli can be found in any of the papers, and an example can be seen in Figure 3.1. In the figure, the prototype is shown at the top. The distortions were similar to, but not exactly like, the originating prototype. To create the distortions, each dot was subjected to a probabilistic function to determine whether it would keep the same position it had in the prototype and, if not, how far its position would change. Small adjustments of the location of some dots resulted in items that were 'low distortions' of the originating prototype, and larger adjustments resulted in 'high distortions'.

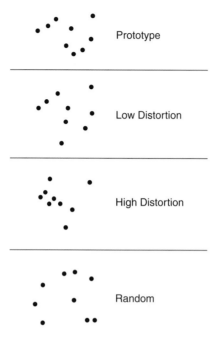

Figure 3.1 This figure shows an example of four kinds of dot-pattern items. The prototype is the original configuration of dots. Low-distortion items result from a smaller probabilistic move for each dot and the high-distortion items result from a larger probabilistic move for each dot. The random items are not related to the prototype and are a new arrangement of the nine dots.

Subjects were generally trained on high-distortion items. Crucially, subjects were never shown the prototype during the training session. Later, during a test phase, subjects were usually shown the old patterns, some new distortions of varying levels of typicality, and the originating prototype. Studies using these dot patterns have generally found consistent results. First, subjects often performed as well on the prototype as they did on the old patterns, even though the prototype was originally unseen. Second, if the test was delayed by several hours or days, performance on the training items declined whereas performance on the prototype remained strong (or declined less). Finally, the endorsement of new items showed a predictable typicality effect (like that shown in Figure 3.2), such that items that are physically closer to the prototype are endorsed more strongly as category members than items that are physically more distant (Homa & Cultice, 1984; Homa *et al.*, 1973; Knowlton & Squire, 1993; Posner & Keele, 1968; Reber, Stark, & Squire, 1998a,

Performance on Dot Pattern Tasks

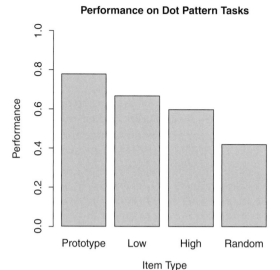

Figure 3.2 This figure shows the average dot pattern performance by control subjects from Knowlton and Squire (1993) along with the subjects in two papers by Reber and colleagues (Reber *et al.*, 1998a, 1998b). The performance on the prototype pattern is best, followed by performance on the low distortions (which are most like the prototype), the high distortions and the random items.

1998b; J. D. Smith & Minda, 2001; J. D. Smith *et al.*, 2008). In addition, some of this work suggested that prototypes were especially important for larger categories (Homa & Cultice, 1984).

One of the most important contributions of this research programme was the notion that the prototype is abstracted from experience with individual exemplars. By this account, there is no need to store every training exemplar, but the average of the exemplar experience is stored and used for subsequent classification decisions. Not surprisingly, the theoretical work with dot-pattern stimuli has generally favoured prototype theory (Ashby & Maddox, 2005; J. D. Smith & Minda, 2001; J. D. Smith *et al.*, 2008). A second key development in cognition was the influential work in the 1970s of Eleanor Rosch (Rosch & Mervis, 1975; Rosch *et al.*, 1976). Rosch followed Wittgenstein (1958/2001) by introducing to cognitive psychology the idea of 'family resemblance' as an alternative to the classical rule-based models that were dominant at the time. Rosch argued that for many categories, the prototype was an abstract representation with the highest family resemblance to the other category members. In some cases this prototype might correspond to an actual category member, but in other cases it is simply a person's best idea about a category. Rosch's use of prototype-cantered categories seemed uniquely able to explain the strong typicality gradients that character-ized many natural-kind categories. Rosch's work, in conjunction with Posner's and Homa's research, provided the groundwork for the domin-ance of prototype theory in the 1970s and 1980s.

An early mathematical formulation of the prototype model was pro-vided by Edward Smith and Doug Medin in their book *Categories and Concepts* (1981). In this text, the authors presented the prototype model as a plausible alternative to the classical view. The classical view assumed that concepts were essentially defined by necessary and sufficient con-ditions. Unlike the classical view, the prototype model accounted for the typicality effects observed by Rosch and others. The dominance of the prototype model waned, however, as research by Medin, Nosofsky, and others (Medin & Schaffer, 1978; Medin & Schwanenflugel, 1981; Nosofsky, 1986, 1987, 1988) suggested that exemplar models such as the generalized context model sometimes provided a better account of categorization behaviour than did the prototype model. The prototype model was generally regarded as inferior to the exemplar model during this period.

It is critical to point out three aspects of that later research that should have tempered the theoretical climate of that era. First, researchers were often relying on small categories with only a few exemplars in their stud-ies. These categories were easily memorizable as specific exemplars, and moreover they were repeated dozens of times during category learning, so participants had little impetus to abstract prototypes. Second, the categories in use at the time were poorly structured with weak family-resemblance relationships, so that once again participants had little to gain from prototype abstraction. Indeed, research by Blair and Homa (2004) showed that in one of the most commonly used category sets, participants appeared not even to categorize, but simply to memorize the frequently recurring specific items.[2] Third, it was the practice of the time to model the performance of whole subject groups. But it is now known that this homogenizes performance profiles in a way that disfa-vours the prototype model for non-psychological reasons. For example, Smith *et al.* (1997) used simulations to demonstrate that the common practice of averaging data together nearly always produced performance that was a better match to the predictions of the exemplar model, even when the average was created from known individual prototype-based

---

[2] Blair and Homa demonstrated that there was no advantage for category learning versus individual-stimulus identification learning for the Medin and Schaffer 5/4 stimuli.

performances. Accordingly, the prototype model has enjoyed renewed interest since the late 1990s. In a series of papers, Smith and Minda showed that the prototype model often provided a better account of categorization behaviour than the exemplar model (or rule-based models). For example, Smith *et al.* (1997) found that prototype models often had the advantage over an exemplar model in fitting the data from individual subjects (not whole groups). They found that averaging the individual data together can smooth away the steeper typicality gradients associated with prototype-based performance and present the models with shallower typicality gradients of the kind usually produced by exemplar-based performance. This was true even when the average samples contained known prototype-based performances. Of course the fit of a model to an individual's data is the appropriate level of analysis in the psychological study of category learning. Other research demonstrated that when fitting data at earlier stages of learning, the prototype often performed better than the exemplar model (J. D. Smith & Minda, 1998). Smith and Minda found that early in the learning of certain kinds of categories known as 'non-linearly separable' categories, subjects often miscategorized exception items, even while they performed very well on more prototypical items. The prototype model fits this data pattern better than the exemplar model, because the prototype model predicts a linear separability constraint. Early in learning, many subjects showed evidence of this linear separability constraint. However, after many practice trials, performance on the exception items improved and the exemplar model tended to fit better than the prototype model. In both of these examples, as well as others (Minda & Smith, 2001), the advantage for the prototype model was strongest when the categories being learned were larger and well-differentiated. The prototype model (and prototype theory in general) continues to influence the field. For example, recent work with the prototype model has shown that it can be augmented with some exemplar memory to account for recognition of specific items (J. D. Smith & Minda, 2000). Other work has shown that subjects learning via inference and prediction, instead of classification, may show stronger prototype effects when compared to classification learners (Chin-Parker & Ross, 2004; Minda & Ross, 2004; Yamauchi & Markman, 1998). Researchers have also demonstrated that the prototype model provides a satisfactory account of category learning in humans and non-human species (J. D. Smith & Minda, 2001; J. D. Smith *et al.*, 2008). Finally, evidence from the field of cognitive neuroscience has suggested that prototype learning may be strongly tied to specific areas in the visual cortex (Ashby & Maddox, 2005; Reber *et al.*, 1998b; Zeithamova, Maddox, & Schnyer, 2008).

Implementation

In this section we show how the basic prototype model can be used to create specific predictions for individual stimuli in a category set, and how simulations can reveal basic properties of prototype-based categorization. We also describe how the model can be fit to observed data.

Generating predictions with the prototype model

The prototype model can be used to make predictions about what kind of performance is expected for some category set, or it can be used to fit the data collected from experimental studies. In either case, the fitting work is done by the attentional weight parameters and the scaling parameter c. The power metric r also plays a role in how the model works, but is typically set before any model fitting is done. We do not consider its use here, because we examine only separable dimension stimuli and we set $r = 1$.

To understand how the prototype model generates predictions for the stimuli in a categorization task, consider the influential category set used by Medin and Schaffer (1978) and shown in Table 3.1. Category A has five training items and Category B has four training items. Each item is made up of four binary dimensions that correspond to features. In the table, these are shown as 0s and 1s but they can be instantiated in an experiment as colours, shapes, sizes, orientations, and so forth. In addition to the nine training items, the category set also has seven transfer items. In an experiment, subjects would be trained on the nine training stimuli (usually trial by trial with feedback after each response) and would then enter the transfer phase in which they would make a classification decision for all the old and new items. Because there are two categories, the prototype model assumes that there are two prototypes. For Category A, we can define the prototype as 1 1 1 1, because those values will represent the most frequently occurring features in Category A. Notice that the Category A prototype appears as stimulus 12. The prototype for Category B can be defined as 0 0 0 0, because this is the item opposite to the prototype for Category A, and closely matches the most frequently occurring values for that category. Alternatively, Category B can be defined as 0 ? 0 0, because the 0-value of the second dimension has low category validity for Category B. Notice that the Category B prototype appears as stimulus 9.

Because the model assumes that the prototypes are the only reference standards, items that are closer to the prototype will generally receive a stronger endorsement. For example, stimulus 1 (1 1 1 0) shares three

Table 3.1 *Category set from Medin and Schaffer (1978)*

Stimulus	d1	d2	d3	d4
Category A				
1	1	1	1	0
2	1	0	1	0
3	1	0	1	1
4	1	1	0	1
5	0	1	1	1
Category B				
6	1	1	0	0
7	0	1	1	0
8	0	0	0	1
9	0	0	0	0
Transfer				
10	1	0	0	1
11	1	0	0	0
12	1	1	1	1
13	0	0	1	0
14	0	1	0	1
15	0	0	1	1
16	0	1	0	0

of four features with its prototype (1 1 1 1) and only one feature with the Category B prototype. As a result, the prototype model assumes that this item will tend to be classified as a Category A member. On the other hand, stimulus 2 (1 0 1 0) shares one half of its features with the Category A prototype (and it shares as many features with the prototype for Category B). As a result, the prototype model will predict lower performance on stimulus 2 relative to stimulus 1 (or equal performance if no attention is paid to dimension 2). Regardless of how the attention is allocated, the arrangement of these two stimuli and their relationship to their respective prototypes ensure that stimulus 2 can never be endorsed as a Category A member more strongly than stimulus 1. This result is a by-product of prototype-based responding.

As an example of how the model makes a prediction, assume first that the model adopts a homogenous attentional profile such that each attentional weight is 0.25 (0.25 for each of the four dimensions, summing to 1.0). This is just an example, because any attentional configuration is allowed as long as the weights sum to 1.0. The model compares each stimulus to the A and B prototype. For example, stimulus 1 is 1 1 1 0 and the prototype for A is 1 1 1 1. Equation 1 results in dimensional distances of 0, 0, 0, and 1, which are multiplied by the weights to arrive at

0, 0, 0, and 0.25. These are summed to get a distance of 0.25. Equation 2 multiplies the distance by the scaling parameter (assume 2.0 for now) and calculates the similarity between stimulus 1 and the Category A prototype as being 0.61. The same procedure calculates the similarity of stimulus 1 to the B prototype (0 0 0 0) as 0.22. The model then uses Equation 3 to generate the probability of Category A membership as being 0.73. This is intuitive, since the item shares 3/4 features with its own prototype and 1/4 features with the prototype in the opposite category. A different configuration of attentional weights produces a different result. If the weights 0.50, 0.20, 0.20, 0.10 are used, the similarity of the items to the A prototype is 0.82 and the similarity of the item to the Category B prototype is 0.16. The model calculates the probability of Category A membership as 0.83, once again an intuitive value because now the discrepant fourth feature has been relatively underweighted in attention.

A simple way to simulate performance on a given category set is to choose a large number of attentional weights and scaling parameter values and to generate a prediction for each set. For example, using the category set in Table 3.1, we can select 50,000 configurations of the standard prototype model. Each configuration is a set of four attention weights and a value of the scaling parameter. For this simulation, we bounded the c parameter between 1.00 and 10.00, though in principle higher values are possible. Averaging across the 50,000 sets of predictions will give a general prediction for each stimulus. The resulting predictions for a simulation like this are shown in Figure 3.3.

Figure 3.3 can also be used to illustrate two points about the prototype model. First, notice that each of the stimuli is classified in accordance with its family resemblance to its prototype. This results in strong typicality effects. Regarding Category B, notice that stimulus 9 (0 0 0 0, the Category B prototype) is categorized as A only 0.035 of the time – that is, it is correctly assigned to Category B 0.965 of the time. In contrast, stimuli 6 and 7 (1 1 0 0 and 0 1 1 0, each with only two features characteristic of Category B) are only correctly assigned to Category B 0.499 and 0.501 of the time, respectively. This is a typicality gradient of about 46%. Regarding Category A, the obedience of the prototype model to family resemblance also results in the predicted advantage for stimulus 1 over stimulus 2 (Medin & Schaffer, 1978; J. D. Smith & Minda, 2000). Stimulus 1 is more prototypical than stimulus 2 and, across thousands of configurations of the prototype model, it receives a stronger Category A prediction. This is a fundamental prediction of the prototype model and it comes about because of the model's basic assumptions about category representation. Any model with a prototype as the representational core and comparison standard must make this prediction. A model that

Simulated Performance

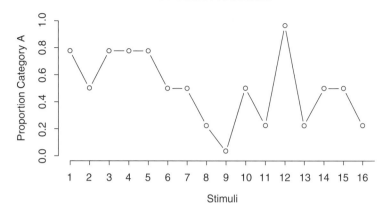

Figure 3.3 The prediction of simulated prototype-based participants for the Medin and Schaffer (1978) category set. Each point represents the average prediction of 50,000 configurations of the prototype model.

assumes an alternative kind of representation (exemplar based, rule and exception, or clustering) is not required to make this prediction.

The second main point concerns the predictions for stimuli 9 and 12. Both are prototypes for their categories (B and A), and they receive the lowest and highest Category A predictions, respectively. The prototype enhancement effect is another core prediction of the prototype model (see also J. D. Smith & Minda, 2000). Again, this prediction comes about because of the assumptions of the model and the fact that only prototypes are referenced for categorization decisions (i.e., presented prototypes will have perfect similarity to their prototype category representations). Together, the strength of typicality gradients and the size of prototype-enhancement effects have become critical diagnostic tools in analysing whether, and when, humans and non-human animals abstract prototypes in category learning.

The effects of the scaling parameter

Simulations can also reveal other properties and predictions of the model. For example, recall from the earlier section that the model makes use of a similarity scaling parameter c. This scaling parameter is a freely estimated parameter that can take on values from 1 to ∞ and reflects how discriminable each prototype is from the other prototypes in psychological space. Low values of c indicate that the prototypes are not distinct from each other; higher values of the sensitivity parameter magnify the psychological

The Effects of the Scaling Parameter

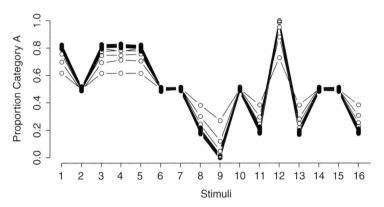

Figure 3.4 The results of 15 simulations of the prototype model on the Medin and Schaffer (1978) category set. Each line represents the performance profile of 2000 configurations of the prototype model with c increasing from 1.00 to 15.00. Performance increases with higher values of c for prototypical items but not for the less prototypical items.

space and increase the steepness of the similarity gradient around the prototypes. We can illustrate the effects of different values of c by conducting the following simulations. Again we use the stimuli from Medin and Schaffer (1978) shown in Table 3.1. We can select 30,000 configurations of the standard prototype model. Each configuration is a set of four attentional weights and a value of the scaling parameter. For the first 2000 configurations, we set the value of c at 1.00 and then we average across the resulting 2000 sets of predictions to find the average prediction for the prototype model with $c = 1.00$. Next we do the same with 2000 configurations and $c = 2.00$ and continue until $c = 15.00$. In this way, we can examine the predictions for 15 increasing values of c (Figure 3.4).

Notice that there is a line of predictions running around the 0.40–0.60 range that corresponds to $c = 1.00$. This is what happens when a category set is represented in a low-sensitivity psychological space in which the prototypes are not very distinct from each other. Though stimuli may be fairly close to one prototype, they will not be that far from the other prototype in a low-sensitivity space, and categorization will remain uncertain with resulting weak category endorsements. However, as the scaling parameter's value increases, so does the differentiation between the prototypes and the typicality gradient around them. For example, performance on stimulus 1 increases to above 0.80. Performance on the prototypes (stimuli 9 and 12) increases even more to 1.0 (or 0.0). On the other hand, for less typical stimuli like stimulus 2, the increases are very small. In other words, increasing the scaling parameter's value increases performance on items proportionally to their prototypicality. Furthermore, increasing c changes the character of performance, but eventually, the model reaches a settling point.

Fitting the model to observed data

This method of using the attention weights and the scaling parameter to run simulations can be used to generate predictions for any stimulus set. However, the model can be used with greater precision to fit observed data. In this case, the researcher has typically collected data from a set of subjects, and wishes to determine whether a model can account for the performance, often in comparison with other models. Model fitting involves estimating and adjusting the model's parameters in order to generate predictions that approximate the observed data. There are several possible algorithms for parameter estimation, but most will find the same set of best-fitting parameters. In this chapter, we discuss a hill-climbing algorithm that minimizes the root mean square deviation (RMSD) between the observed data and the model's predictions (Minda & Smith, 2001; J. D. Smith & Minda, 2000). Other methods of model fitting that have been commonly used with the prototype model are minimizing the sum of squared deviations and maximizing the log likelihood. The model fitting index, the RMSD or another index, can be used to compare and evaluate alternative models (see Myung, 2000, for details on model fitting).[3] To find the best-fitting parameter settings of each model, a single parameter configuration (attention weights and c) is chosen at random and the predicted categorization probabilities for the stimuli in an experiment are calculated according to that configuration. The RMSD is calculated as shown in Equation 4:

$$\text{RMSD} = \sqrt{\frac{\sum_{i=1}^{N}(O_i - P_i)^2}{N}}. \tag{4}$$

---

[3] We use RMSD because it expresses fit in an intuitive way and it allows for comparisons between training sets and transfer sets that have different numbers of items. In general, when the models are fit by minimizing the RMSD or maximizing the log likelihood, the resulting best-fitting parameters and predictions are nearly the same (J. D. Smith & Minda, 2000).

The RMSD between the observed (O_i) and predicted (P_i) probabilities is then minimized with a hill-climbing algorithm that makes a small adjustment to the provisional best-fitting parameter settings and chooses the new settings if they produce a better fit (i.e., a smaller RMSD between predicted and observed performance). During each iteration of the algorithm, a parameter and a directional change are chosen at random. These changes are usually very small, gradations of 1/100, and they always respect the upper and lower bounds of the parameters. To ensure that attentional weights always sum to 1.0, the weight parameters are always adjusted in randomly chosen complementary pairs (e.g., when increasing the weight on dimension 1 by 0.01 the algorithm must decrease the weight on dimension 2 by the same amount). The hill-climbing algorithm continues to adjust the weights and the scaling parameter until no change can produce a better fit. To ensure that local minima are not a problem, the fitting procedure can be repeated by choosing additional starting configurations of the model and hill climbing from there, and choosing the best-fitting parameters of the multiple fittings.[4]

As an example of model fitting, consider again the stimuli shown in Table 3.1. If a classification experiment is conducted using these stimuli, the resulting data can be fit with the prototype model. For example, a hypothetical data[5] set is shown in Figure 3.5. The observed data are graphed as the dark symbols and solid lines and are expressed in terms of Category A performance. The prototype model was fit to this data set using the hill-climbing algorithm described above. The resulting best-fitting profile is shown in open circles on top of the observed data. The prototype model accommodates the data fairly well. For example, it reproduces the prototype-enhancement effect for stimuli 9 and 12 (though, in line with its representational assumption, it actually predicts a stronger enhancement than is shown). In this particular case, the RMSD was 0.05.

A second example illustrates the linear separability constraint of the prototype model. This example uses the category set first used by Smith and colleagues (J. D. Smith & Minda, 1998; J. D. Smith *et al.*, 1997) and

---

[4] Although many statistics and mathematical programs like Matlab, R, and others provide model-fitting routines, we have implemented the model and the fitting procedure in a number of basic computing languages. The simulations and fitting in this chapter were all programmed by the first author in REALbasic for Mac OS.

[5] These data are reflective of the data that have been shown by many actual subjects in some studies. We generated these specific probabilities for this chapter as a way of illustrating the fit of the prototype model to data.

Fitting a 5/4 Data Set

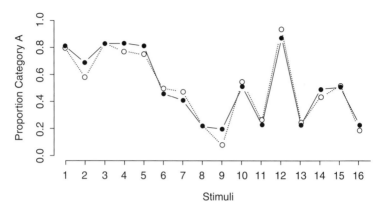

Figure 3.5 This figure shows the fit of the prototype model to a hypothetical set of classification data. The observed data are illustrated with filled circles and solid lines; the predictions of the prototype model are shown with open circles and dotted lines.

shown in Table 3.2. Each exemplar is defined by six binary dimensions, and each category contains seven exemplars. Notice that stimuli 1 and 8 are the actual prototypes for their respective categories. Also notice that stimuli 2–6 and stimuli 9–13 are all high-typicality exemplars that share 5/6 of their features with their own prototype. However, stimulus 7 and stimulus 14 are exception items that only share 1/6 features with their prototype and 5/6 with the opposite category prototype (think of them as BATS in the RODENT category).

Furthermore, there is no combination of attention weights that allows the exception to be correctly classified without making an error on another stimulus. For example, stimuli 5 and 7 in Category A are exact featural opposites. Any attentional allocation that weighted dimension 5 strongly enough to let stimulus 7 be correctly assigned to Category A, would force stimulus 5 to be incorrectly assigned to Category B. The presence of the exceptions along with their respective opposite in the same categories is what breaks the linear separability constraint for these stimuli. As with the previous example, an experiment using this category set would result in a set of classification probabilities. One set of classification probabilities is shown in Figure 3.6A. The solid dots are the Category A probabilities for a hypothetical subject who performed well on the prototypes and high-typicality exemplars, but misclassified the exception items (subjects in J. D. Smith and Minda (1998) did show this

Table 3.2 *Non-linearly separable category set*

Stimulus	d1	d2	d3	d4	d5	d6
Category A						
1	0	0	0	0	0	0
2	1	0	0	0	0	0
3	0	1	0	0	0	0
4	0	0	1	0	0	0
5	0	0	0	0	1	0
6	0	0	0	0	0	1
7	1	1	1	1	0	1
Category B						
8	1	1	1	1	1	1
9	0	1	1	1	1	1
10	1	0	1	1	1	1
11	1	1	0	1	1	1
12	1	1	1	0	1	1
13	1	1	1	1	1	0
14	0	0	0	1	0	0

pattern). The many errors in the data that occur on the exception items suggest a linear separability constraint. As can be seen in the figure, the prototype model accommodates well this pattern (RMSD = 0.06). This is because of the model's assumption that only prototypes serve as the comparison standard. However, as some research has shown, subjects can learn to overcome this linear separability constraint and can learn to classify correctly the exceptions (Medin & Schwanenflugel, 1981; J. D. Smith & Minda, 1998; J. D. Smith *et al.*, 1997). Figure 3.6B shows the data from a hypothetical subject who performed much better on the exception items (and performed well on all the items). In this case, the model did not fit the data as well (RMSD = 0.13), and it made significant under/over prediction errors in the exception items and their complements (stimuli 5 and 7 in Category A; stimuli 12 and 14 in Category B). In this case, the prototype model was still operating under a linearly separable constraint, even while the data did not show this pattern. In other words, prototype models must predict the linear separability constraint as a consequence of their representational assumption.

   To summarize, the basic prototype model can be used to create simulations and to make predictions. These predictions can inform experimenters and can be compared to the outcomes of real experiments. The model can also be configured to fit data collected from experiments. We have also described some fundamental predictions of the prototype model, including the prototype-enhancement effect, the strong typicality

A. Fitting Data with Misclassified Exception Items

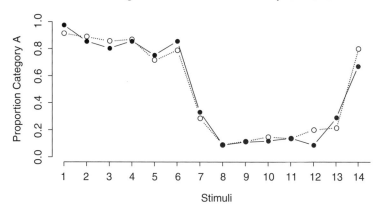

B. Fitting Data with Correctly Classified Exception Items

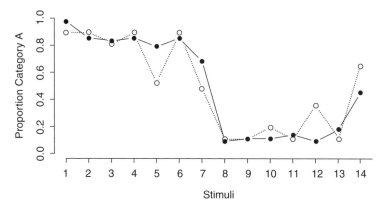

Figure 3.6 This figure shows the fit of the prototype model to two hypothetical sets of classification data. The observed data are illustrated with filled circles and solid lines; the predictions of the prototype model are shown with open circles and dotted lines. Panel A shows observed data that obey a linear separability constraint and panel B shows observed data that do not obey a linear separability constraint.

gradients predicted by prototype-based category representations, the linear separability constraint, and the effect of increasing the value of the scaling parameter. In the next section, we consider the relationship of the prototype model to several other categorization models and also the future of the prototype model.

Relationship to other models

The prototype model is closely related to two classes of models. First, it bears a computational and historical association with the generalized context model (Nosofsky, 1986, 1987), which is also covered in this volume (Chapter 2). Second, the prototype model is related to several models that can assume prototype-based representations, such as SUSTAIN (Love, Medin, & Gureckis, 2004) and KRES (Rehder & Murphy, 2003), both of which have some degree of prototype-based representation and both of which are covered in this volume (Chapters 10 and 12). We cover a number of these relationships, though not all, and we begin with the GCM because of the strong connection between these models.

Relationship with exemplar models

The prototype model that we describe here is a computational partner of the GCM and there are numerous overlaps between these two models, as well as a fundamental difference.[6] First, the GCM and the prototype model rely on the same similarity calculations when deciding category membership (Equations 1 and 2). That is, both models assume that to-be-categorized items are compared to stored representations, that the dimensions can be weighted, and the similarity between items and category representations is an exponential function of distance in psychological space. Furthermore, both models rely on a scaling parameter c to adjust the similarity function. The key difference, of course, is that in the prototype model the to-be-categorized items are compared to stored prototypes whereas in the GCM they are compared to the set of stored exemplar traces. Another similarity between the models is that they make a classification decision in the same way. Once distance and similarity have been computed, the classification choice (Equation 3) is based on the similarity of the items to one category divided by the similarity to all categories. The result is that both of these models produce a decision that corresponds to the probability of category membership. Finally, both models can be fit to subjects' data by the same parameter estimation and minimization/maximization routines (minimizing the RMSD or maximizing the log likelihood). As a result, these two models are well suited

---

[6] Because ALCOVE is a descendant of the GCM, many of the specifics we discuss here will also be true of ALCOVE and KOVE, which are also discussed in this volume.

for comparisons and even for using together to generate predictions about when and how subjects may rely on prototype abstraction and when and how they rely on exemplar learning (Minda & Smith, 2001; J. D. Smith & Minda, 1998).

Given the close correspondence, it should not be surprising that the two models make similar predictions about many categorization phenomena, and indeed both models often provide comparable fits to data sets (J. D. Smith & Minda, 1998, 2000; J. D. Smith et al., 1997). Because of this, researchers have often relied on carefully constructed category sets and experimental designs in order to distinguish these models. Although the literature has several examples of this, including dot patterns and non-linearly separable categories (Medin & Schwanenflugel, 1981; J. D. Smith & Minda, 1998, 2001), we will illustrate our point by discussing the category set shown in Table 3.1. As we mentioned earlier, the prototype model represents each category by storing the prototype (0 0 0 0) of the category. The GCM represents each category by storing the training exemplars (each of the five Category A exemplars). Although the two representational schemes are very different (one involves abstraction, the other does not) the two models often make similar predictions because the prototype is the average of the exemplars that the GCM is storing. It is still possible to differentiate the two models, however. Recall that the prototype model will always predict that stimulus 1 is a better (more typical) member of Category A than stimulus 2, because stimulus 1 shares more features with the prototype. The GCM, however, makes the opposite prediction. Considering exemplar similarities as the GCM does, stimulus 1 is only marginally similar (sharing only 2 of 4 features) to three other members of Category A. In contrast, it is very similar (sharing 3 of 4 features) with two members of Category B. Stimulus 2, on the other hand, has substantial featural overlap with Category A members but not with Category B members. As a result, the GCM predicts stronger Category A assignment for stimulus 2 than for stimulus 1. Although subjects in some of the early experiments showed the pattern predicted by the exemplar model (Medin & Schaffer, 1978), this has not always been the case (Minda & Smith, 2002; J. D. Smith & Minda, 2000). In other words, the category set really does distinguish between prototype and exemplar based categorization, but there is no clear evidence that subjects will learn these categories as prototypes or as exemplars. More recent work with dot patterns, which can also be used to reliably distinguish prototype from exemplar processing, has found more consistent evidence for prototype-based categorization (J. D. Smith, 2005; J. D. Smith & Minda, 2001; J. D. Smith et al., 2008).

Models with prototype assumptions

The prototype model is related to a number of other models discussed in this volume by virtue of the assumption of prototype abstraction. That is, regardless of how classifications are made in other models, and in addition to other assumptions about rules or exemplars, many of the models in this volume contain a mechanism for reproducing prototype-like performance. Take as an example the KRES model (Rehder & Murphy, 2003). This model was originally designed as a prototype-based model and was implemented as a connectionist model that learns direct connections between stimulus features and category labels, amounting to a 'feature list' kind of prototype. As a result, KRES makes many of the same predictions as our standard prototype model, including the assumption about linear separability (Rehder & Murphy, 2003). Of course a key difference between KRES and a basic prototype model is the addition of knowledge to the network (that is the whole point of KRES). Furthermore, the version of KRES discussed in this volume allows for both prototype and exemplar nodes, in order to capture the flexibility and different kinds of knowledge that subjects use.

Another class of models which are discussed in this volume and that make a prototype assumption are the adaptive clustering models, like SUSTAIN (Love & Gureckis, 2007; Love *et al.*, 2004). SUSTAIN is not a prototype model per se but rather, it assumes that categories can be learned as clusters of similar stimuli. A single cluster can represent one or many exemplars. As such, SUSTAIN has the ability to represent categories with a single prototype, several sub-prototypes, or with many single exemplars. Furthermore, SUSTAIN has a mechanism for supervised learning (i.e., explicit, feedback-driven classification) and unsupervised learning (which is important in dot-pattern learning). SUSTAIN has been successfully applied to a broad range of data, suggesting that prototypes may provide the best solution to a classification problem, even when an exemplar-based solution is possible.

Finally, to some degree, the simplicity model (Pothos & Chater, 2002), which is described in this volume (Chapter 9), is likely to find a category description that results in prototype-like classifications. The simplicity model is designed to maximize category coherence and simplicity, though the model itself is not a prototype model. However, like the adaptive clustering models, this model may arrive at a classification that is intuitive, and possibly the result of a prototype representation. Furthermore, like the prototype model, the simplicity model is sensitive to the linear separability constraint.

Future directions

The prototype model has a long history in cognitive psychology and the study of categorization. It is not an understatement to say that the currently rich field of categorization models (as can be seen in this volume) owes some debt to the early success of the prototype model and the various models that were formulated as extensions and counters to it. As an example, consider the debate between the prototype and exemplar models (Blair & Homa, 2001; Medin & Schwanenflugel, 1981; Nosofsky, 1992; Nosofsky & Zaki, 2002; J. D. Smith & Minda, 1998; J. D. Smith et al., 1997). Clearly the GCM benefited from this programme of research at least as much as the prototype model. In fact, one development that came out of that debate was the mixture model (Minda & Smith, 2001; J. D. Smith & Minda, 1998, 2000) that combined a prototype abstraction system with exemplar memorization. This model assumes that although the prototype describes much of subjects' performance, subjects may also try to learn specific exemplars. Other models make the same mixed representational assumption (KRES and ATRIUM, for example).

Clearly the prototype model provides an account of category learning that emphasizes the abstraction and storage of prototypes. Other models do this as well, but the prototype model we have described here is explicit in its assumptions about how these prototypes give rise to performance. As a result, this model makes strong claims about human (and non-human) categorization behaviour. Prototypes must predict a linear separability constraint. This is a strong claim, and clearly not all categories are linearly separable. But there is considerable research, from natural categories, artificial concept learning, comparative work, and computational modelling, suggesting that humans and non-humans may share this constraint. This constraint can be overcome: people can learn exceptions to a well-structured category. But we argue that this linearly separable constraint may be one of the default assumptions about categories that humans and non-humans make when first learning about a new set of categories.

Therefore, we see a constructive future for the prototype model. The prototype model operates via a clear and transparent formalism. Each equation that defines the basic model is intuitive and has strong psychological underpinnings. That is, the assumptions about similarity and psychological space hold up under a variety of circumstances and scenarios. For this reason the prototype model should take a place within a larger understanding of categorization that grants organisms redundant systems and different category representations for different tasks and purposes. This view is not opposed to other categorization models and theories, but rather is inclusive. The minds of humans and non-humans are not unitary in process or representation but diverse and varied in the approaches they take to the fundamental task of forming categories.

REFERENCES

Ashby, F. G., & Maddox, W. T. (2005). Human category learning. *Annual Review of Psychology*, **56**, 149–178.

Blair, M., & Homa, D. (2001). Expanding the search for a linear separability constraint on category learning. *Memory & Cognition*, **29**, 1153–1164.

    (2004). As easy to memorize as they are to classify: the 5-4 categories and the category advantage. *Memory & Cognition*, **31**, 1293–1301.

Chin-Parker, S., & Ross, B. H. (2004). Diagnosticity and prototypicality in category learning: a comparison of inference learning and classification learning. *Journal of Experimental Psychology: Learning, Memory, and Cognition*, **30**, 216–226.

Homa, D., Cross, J., Cornell, D., & Shwartz, S. (1973). Prototype abstraction and classification of new instances as a function of number of instances defining the prototype. *Journal of Experimental Psychology*, **101**, 116–122.

Homa, D., & Cultice, J. C. (1984). Role of feedback, category size, and stimulus distortion on the acquisition and utilization of ill-defined categories. *Journal of Experimental Psychology: Learning, Memory, and Cognition*, **10**, 83–94.

Knowlton, B. J., & Squire, L. R. (1993). The learning of categories: parallel brain systems for item memory and category knowledge. *Science*, **262**, 1747–1749.

Love, B. C., & Gureckis, T. M. (2007). Models in search of a brain. *Cognitive, Affective, & Behavioral Neuroscience*, **7**, 90–108.

Love, B. C., Medin, D. L., & Gureckis, T. M. (2004). SUSTAIN: a network model of category learning. *Psychological Review*, **111**, 309–332.

Medin, D. L., & Schaffer, M. M. (1978). Context theory of classification learning. *Psychological Review*, **85**, 207–238.

Medin, D. L., & Schwanenflugel, P. J. (1981). Linear separability in classification learning. *Journal of Experimental Psychology: Human Learning and Memory*, **7**, 355–368.

Minda, J. P., & Ross, B. H. (2004). Learning categories by making predictions: an investigation of indirect category learning. *Memory & Cognition*, **32**, 1355–1368.

Minda, J. P., & Smith, J. D. (2001). Prototypes in category learning: the effects of category size, category structure, and stimulus complexity. *Journal of Experimental Psychology: Learning, Memory, and Cognition*, **27**, 775–799.

    (2002). Comparing prototype-based and exemplar-based accounts of category learning and attentional allocation. *Journal of Experimental Psychology: Learning, Memory, and Cognition*, **28**, 275–292.

Myung, I. J. (2000). The importance of complexity in model selection. *Journal of Mathematical Psychology*, **44**, 190–204.

Nosofsky, R. M. (1986). Attention, similarity, and the identification-categorization relationship. *Journal of Experimental Psychology: General*, **115**, 39–57.

(1987). Attention and learning processes in the identification and categorization of integral stimuli. *Journal of Experimental Psychology: Learning, Memory, and Cognition*, **13**, 87–108.

(1988). Exemplar-based accounts of relations between classification, recognition, and typicality. *Journal of Experimental Psychology: Learning, Memory, and Cognition*, **14**, 700–708.

(1992). Exemplars, prototypes, and similarity rules. In A. F. Healy, S. M. Kosslyn, & R. M. Shiffrin (eds.), *From Learning Theory to Connectionist Theory: Essays in Honor of William K. Estes* (Vol. 1, pp. 149–167). Hillsdale, NJ: Lawrence Erlbaum.

Nosofsky, R. M., & Zaki, S. R. (2002). Exemplar and prototype models revisited: response strategies, selective attention, and stimulus generalization. *Journal of Experimental Psychology: Learning, Memory, and Cognition*, **28**, 924–940.

Posner, M. I., & Keele, S. W. (1968). On the genesis of abstract ideas. *Journal of Experimental Psychology*, 77, 353–363.

Pothos, E., & Chater, N. (2002). A simplicity principle in unsupervised human categorization. *Cognitive Science*, **26**, 303–343.

Reber, P., Stark, C., & Squire, L. (1998a). Contrasting cortical activity associated with category memory and recognition memory. *Learning & Memory*, 5, 420–428.

(1998b). Cortical areas supporting category learning identified using functional MRI. *Proceedings of the National Academy of Sciences*, **95**, 747–750.

Rehder, B., & Murphy, G. L. (2003). A knowledge-resonance (KRES) model of category learning. *Psychonomic Bulletin & Review*, **10**, 759–784.

Rosch, E., & Mervis, C. B. (1975). Family resemblances: studies in the internal structure of categories. *Cognitive Psychology*, 7, 573–605.

Rosch, E., Mervis, C. B., Gray, W., Johnson, D., & Boyes-Braem, P. (1976). Basic objects in natural categories. *Cognitive Psychology*, **8**, 382–439.

Shepard, R. N. (1987). Toward a universal law of generalization for psychological science. *Science*, 237, 1317–1323.

Smith, E. E., & Medin, D. L. (1981). *Categories and Concepts*. Cambridge, MA: Harvard University Press.

Smith, J. D. (2005). Wanted: a new psychology of exemplars. *Canadian Journal of Experimental Psychology, 2003 Festschrift for Lee R. Brooks*, **59**, 47–53.

Smith, J. D., & Minda, J. P. (1998). Prototypes in the mist: the early epochs of category learning. *Journal of Experimental Psychology: Learning, Memory, and Cognition*, **24**, 1411–1436.

(2000). Thirty categorization results in search of a model. *Journal of Experimental Psychology: Learning, Memory, and Cognition*, **26**, 3–27.

(2001). Journey to the center of the category: the dissociation in amnesia between categorization and recognition. *Journal of Experimental Psychology: Learning, Memory, and Cognition*, **4**, 501–516.

Smith, J. D., Murray, J., Morgan, J., & Minda, J. P. (1997). Straight talk about linear separability. *Journal of Experimental Psychology: Learning, Memory, and Cognition*, **23**, 659–680.

Smith, J. D., Redford, J. S., & Haas, S. M. (2008). Prototype abstraction by monkeys (*Macaca mulatta*). *Journal of Experimental Psychology: General*, **137**, 390–401.

Wittgenstein, L. (1958/2001). *Philosophical Investigations*. New York: Blackwell.

Yamauchi, T., & Markman, A. B. (1998). Category learning by inference and classification. *Journal of Memory & Language*, **39**, 124–148.

Zeithamova, D., Maddox, W. T., & Schnyer, D. M. (2008). Dissociable proto-type learning systems: evidence from brain imaging and behavior. *Journal of Neuroscience*, **28**, 13194–13201.

4 COVIS

F. Gregory Ashby, Erick J. Paul and W. Todd Maddox

Summary

The COVIS model of category learning assumes separate rule-based and procedural-learning categorization systems that compete for access to response production. The rule-based system selects and tests simple verbalizable hypotheses about category membership. The procedural-learning system gradually associates categorization responses with regions of perceptual space via reinforcement learning.

Description and motivation of COVIS

Despite the obvious importance of categorization to survival, and the varied nature of category-learning problems facing every animal, research on category learning has been narrowly focused (e.g., Markman & Ross, 2003). For example, the majority of category-learning studies have focused on situations in which two categories are relevant, the motor response is fixed, the nature and timing of feedback is constant (or ignored), and the only task facing the participant is the relevant categorization problem.

One reason for this narrow focus is that until recently, the goal of most categorization research has been to test predictions from purely cognitive models that assume a single category-learning system. In typical applications, the predictions of two competing single-system models were pitted against each other and simple goodness-of-fit was used to select a winner (Maddox & Ashby, 1993; McKinley & Nosofsky, 1995; Smith & Minda, 1998). During the past decade, however, two developments have begun to alter this landscape.

Preparation of this chapter was supported in part by NIH Grants R01 MH3760-2 (FGA) and R01 MH077708 (WTM) and by support from the U.S. Army Research Office through the Institute for Collaborative Biotechnologies under contract DAAD19-03-D-0004 (FGA).

First, there are now many results suggesting that human categorization is mediated by multiple category-learning systems (Ashby & O'Brien, 2005; Ashby et al., 1998; Erickson & Kruschke, 1998; Love, Medin, & Gureckis, 2004; Reber et al., 2003). These results have profoundly affected the field, partly because no single-system theory has been able to account for more than one or two of these results (described briefly below) simultaneously. One of the earliest multiple-systems approaches was suggested by Brooks and colleagues who argued for separate rule-based and exemplar-based systems (Allen & Brooks, 1991; Brooks, 1978; Regehr & Brooks, 1993). Since then, a number of purely cognitive multiple-systems models have been proposed, with nearly all offering some specific instantiation of Brooks's rule-based and exemplar-based systems (Erickson & Kruschke, 1998; Nosofsky, Palmeri, & McKinley, 1994).

Second, there has been an explosion of new knowledge about the neural basis of category learning (Ashby & Ennis, 2006; Ashby et al., 2003; Filoteo & Maddox, 2007; Maddox & Filoteo, 2005, 2007; Nomura & Reber, 2008; Nomura et al., 2007; Seger, 2008; Seger & Cincotta, 2005, 2006). These new data come from a variety of sources, including fMRI, EEG, single-unit recordings, and behavioural studies with a variety of different neuropsychological patient populations. The purely cognitive models make no predictions about any of these new data. In fact, to date, the only theory of category learning that makes central the constraints imposed by the underlying neurobiology is the COVIS model (Ashby et al., 1998). COVIS postulates two systems that compete throughout learning – an explicit, rule-based system that uses logical reasoning and depends on working memory and executive attention, and an implicit system that uses procedural learning.

The explicit, hypothesis-testing system of COVIS is thought to mediate *rule-based* category learning. Rule-based category-learning tasks are those in which the category structures can be learned via some explicit reasoning process. Frequently, the rule that maximizes accuracy (i.e., the optimal rule) is easy to describe verbally (Ashby et al., 1998). In the most common applications, only one stimulus dimension is relevant, and the observer's task is to discover this relevant dimension and then to map the different dimensional values to the relevant categories. Even so, rule-based tasks can require attention to multiple stimulus dimensions. For example, any task where the optimal strategy is to apply a logical conjunction or disjunction is rule based. The key requirement is that the optimal strategy can be discovered by logical reasoning and is easy for humans to describe verbally.

The implicit procedural-learning system of COVIS is hypothesized to mediate *information-integration* category learning. Information-integration tasks are those in which accuracy is maximized only if information from two or more stimulus components (or dimensions) is integrated at some pre-decisional stage (Ashby & Gott, 1988). Perceptual integration could take many forms – from treating the stimulus as a Gestalt to computing a weighted linear combination of the dimensional values. Typically, the optimal strategy in information-integration tasks is difficult or impossible to describe verbally (Ashby *et al.*, 1998). Rule-based strategies can be applied in information-integration tasks, but they generally lead to sub-optimal levels of accuracy because rule-based strategies make separate decisions about each stimulus component, rather than integrating this information.

While COVIS agrees with the cognitive multiple-systems models that a rule-based system should dominate performance in rule-based tasks, there is disagreement about the nature of the system that should dominate in information-integration tasks. As mentioned above, the cognitive models all assume that an exemplar-similarity-based system should dominate in information-integration tasks, whereas COVIS assumes that a procedural-learning system will dominate. Because procedural learning is associated with motor performance (Hazeltine & Ivry, 2002; Willingham, 1998; Willingham, Nissen, & Bullemer, 1989), a strong prediction of COVIS that differentiates it from the cognitive multiple-systems models is therefore that information-integration category learning should include a motor component – a prediction that has been confirmed by several studies (Ashby, Ell, & Waldron, 2003; Maddox, Bohil, & Ing, 2004; Maddox *et al.*, 2010). No exemplar-based accounts of these motor effects have been offered.

Since its initial publication in 1998, COVIS has generated a huge amount of behavioural research, examining the processing characteristics associated with the explicit and implicit systems by introducing experimental manipulations that should adversely affect processing in one system but not the other, and vice versa, and examining their impact on rule-based and information-integration category learning (see Ashby & Maddox, 2005; Maddox & Ashby, 2004 for a review). COVIS has also inspired a wide range of animal (Smith *et al.*, 2010), neuropsychological (for a review see Filoteo & Maddox, 2007; Maddox & Filoteo, 2005, 2007; Price, Filoteo, & Maddox, 2009) and neuroimaging studies (DeGutis & D'Esposito, 2007; Filoteo *et al.*, 2005; Nomura *et al.*, 2007; Seger & Cincotta, 2005, 2006).

Implementing COVIS

The computational version of COVIS includes three separate components – namely a model of the explicit system, a model of the procedural-learning system, and an algorithm that monitors the output of these two systems and selects a response on each trial. We describe each of these components in turn.

The explicit system

The explicit system in COVIS selects and tests explicit rules that determine category membership. The simplest rule is one-dimensional. More complex rules are constructed from one-dimensional rules via Boolean algebra (e.g., to produce logical conjunctions, disjunctions, etc.). The neural structures that have been implicated in this process include the prefrontal cortex, anterior cingulate, striatum (head of the caudate nucleus), and hippocampus (Ashby & Valentin, 2005; Ashby *et al.*, 1998, 2005). The computational implementation of the COVIS explicit system is a hybrid neural network that includes both symbolic and connectionist components. The model's hybrid character arises from its combination of explicit rule selection and switching and its incremental salience-learning component.

To begin, denote the set of all possible explicit rules by $R = \{R_1, R_2, ..., R_m\}$. In most applications, the set R will include all possible one-dimensional rules, and perhaps a variety of plausible conjunction and/or disjunction rules. On each trial, the model selects one of these rules for application by following an algorithm that is described below. Suppose the stimuli to be categorized vary across trials on r stimulus dimensions. Denote the coordinates of the stimulus on these r dimensions by $\underline{x} = (x_1, x_2, ..., x_r)$. On trials when the active rule is R_j, a response is selected by computing a discriminant value $h_E(\underline{x})$ and using the following decision rule:

Respond A on trial n if $h_E(\underline{x}) < \varepsilon$; respond B if $h_E(\underline{x}) > \varepsilon$,

where ε is a normally distributed random variable with mean 0 and variance σ_E^2. The variance σ_E^2 increases with trial-by-trial variability in the subject's perception of the stimulus and memory of the decision criterion (i.e., perceptual and criterial noise). In the case where R_i is a one-dimensional rule in which the relevant dimension is i, the discriminant function is

$$h_E(\underline{x}) = x_i - C_i, \tag{1}$$

where C_i is a constant that plays the role of a decision criterion. Note that this rule is equivalent to deciding whether the stimulus value on dimension i is greater or less than the criterion C_i. The decision bound is the set of all points for which $x_i - C_i = 0$. Note that $|h_E(\underline{x})|$ increases with the distance between the stimulus and this bound.

Suppose rule R_i is used on trial n. Then the rule selection process proceeds as follows. If the response on trial n is correct, then rule R_i is used again on trial $n + 1$ with probability 1. If the response on trial n is incorrect, then the probability of selecting each rule in the set $\boldsymbol{R}$ for use on trial $n + 1$ is a function of that rule's current weight. The weight associated with each rule is a function of the participant's lifetime history with that rule, the reward history associated with that rule during the current categorization training session, the tendency of the participant to perseverate, and the tendency of the participant to select unusual or creative rules. These factors are all formalized in the following way.

Let $Z_k(n)$ denote the salience of rule R_k on trial n. Therefore, $Z_k(0)$ is the initial salience of rule R_k. Rules that participants have abundant prior experience with have high initial salience, and rules that a participant has rarely used before have low initial salience. In typical applications of COVIS, the initial saliencies of all one-dimensional rules are set equal, whereas the initial saliencies of conjunctive and disjunctive rules are set much lower. The salience of a rule is adjusted after every trial on which it is used, in a manner that depends on whether or not the rule was successful. For example, if rule R_k is used on trial $n - 1$ and a correct response occurs, then

$$Z_k(n) = Z_k(n - 1) + \Delta_C, \tag{2}$$

where Δ_C is some positive constant. If rule R_k is used on trial $n - 1$ and an error occurs, then

$$Z_k(n) = Z_k(n - 1) - \Delta_E, \tag{3}$$

where Δ_E is also a positive constant. The numerical value of Δ_C should depend on the perceived gain associated with a correct response and Δ_E should depend on the perceived cost of an error.

The salience of each rule is then adjusted to produce a weight, Y, according to the following rules.

(1) For the rule R_i that was active on trial n,

$$Y_i(n) = Z_i(n) + \gamma, \tag{4}$$

where the constant γ is a measure of the tendency of the participant to perseverate on the active rule, even though feedback indicates that this rule is incorrect. If γ is small, then switching will be easy, whereas switching is difficult if γ is large. COVIS assumes that switching of executive

attention is mediated within the head of the caudate nucleus, and that the parameter γ is inversely related to basal ganglia dopamine levels.

(2) Choose a rule at random from $\boldsymbol{R}$. Call this rule R_j. The weight for this rule is

$$Y_j(n) = Z_j(n) + \mathbf{X}, \tag{5}$$

where $\mathbf{X}$ is a random variable that has a Poisson distribution with mean λ. Larger values of λ increase the probability that rule R_j will be selected for the next trial, so λ is called the selection parameter. COVIS assumes that selection is mediated by a cortical network that includes the anterior cingulate and the prefrontal cortex, and that λ increases with cortical dopamine levels.

(3) For any other rule R_k (i.e., $R_k \neq R_i$ or R_j),

$$Y_k(n) = Z_k(n). \tag{6}$$

Finally, rule R_k (for all k) is selected for use on trial $n+1$ with probability

$$P_{n+1}(\mathbf{R}_k) = \frac{Y_k(n)}{\displaystyle\sum_{s=1}^{m} Y_s(n)}. \tag{7}$$

This algorithm has a number of attractive properties. First, the more salient the rule, the higher the probability that it will be selected, even after an incorrect trial. Second, after the first trial, feedback is used to adjust the selection probabilities up or down, depending on the success of the rule type. Third, the model has separate selection and switching parameters, reflecting the COVIS assumption that these are separate operations. The random variable $\mathbf{X}$ models the selection operation. The greater the mean of $\mathbf{X}$ (i.e., λ) in Equation 5, the greater the probability that the selected rule (R_j) will become active. In contrast, the parameter γ from Equation 4 models switching, because when γ is large, it is unlikely that the system will switch to the selected rule R_j. It is important to note, however, that with both parameters (i.e., λ and γ), optimal performance occurs at intermediate numerical values. For example, note that if λ is too large, some extremely low salience rules will be selected, and if γ is too low then a single incorrect response could cause a participant to switch away from an otherwise successful rule.

COVIS assumes that selection and switching both depend on brain dopamine levels. In particular, selection should improve as levels of dopamine rise in the frontal cortex (up to some optimal level), and switching should improve if levels of dopamine rise in the striatum (i.e., head of the caudate nucleus). Thus, the parameter λ should increase with dopamine levels in the frontal cortex, and γ is assumed to decrease with dopamine levels in the caudate. Although we currently have no methods for directly measuring brain dopamine levels in humans (microdialysis can be used in animals), many factors are known to affect these levels, including age, mood, genetic predisposition, drug-taking history, and neuropsychological patient status. For example, brain dopamine levels are known to decrease by approximately 7% per decade of life, and Parkinson's disease patients are thought to have lost at least 70% of their birth dopamine levels. Even so, early in the disease, this reduction is thought to be most severe in the striatum. Thus COVIS predicts that early Parkinson's disease patients should have special difficulty switching attention away from an inappropriate rule. In fact, perseveration is a well-known symptom of the disease (Gotham, Brown, & Marsden, 1988; Lees & Smith, 1983).

Each one-dimensional rule has an associated decision criterion (e.g., the C_i in Equation 1) and each conjunction rule has two. These are not free parameters. Rather they are learned using a conventional gradient-descent process with learning rate δ. Thus, the full COVIS explicit system has six free parameters, σ_E^2 (noise variance), γ (perseveration), λ (selection), Δ_C (salience increment when correct), Δ_E (salience increment when incorrect), and δ (gradient-descent learning rate).

The procedural-learning system

In the original version of COVIS (i.e., Ashby *et al.*, 1998), the procedural-learning system was implemented as a perceptron that learned parameters of a linear or quadratic decision bound. Ashby and Waldron (1999) reported evidence that people do not learn decision bounds, and as an alternative they proposed a model called the striatal pattern classifier (SPC), which ever since has been used to implement the procedural-learning system of COVIS. The SPC was further elaborated by Ashby, Ennis, and Spiering (2007). The version we describe here is a simplification of this latter model.

Rather than learn decision bounds, the SPC learns to assign responses to regions of perceptual space. In such models, a decision bound could be defined as the set of all points that separate regions assigned to different responses, but it is important to note that in the SPC, the decision bound has no psychological meaning. As the name suggests, the SPC assumes the key site of learning is at cortical-striatal synapses within the striatum.

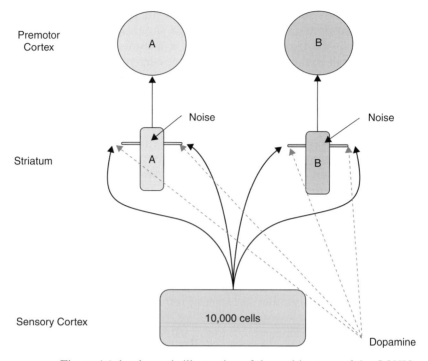

Figure 4.1 A schematic illustration of the architecture of the COVIS procedural system.

The SPC architecture is shown in Figure 4.1 for an application to a categorization task with two contrasting categories. This is a straight-forward three-layer feed-forward network with up to 10,000 units in the input layer and two units each in the hidden and output layers. The only modifiable synapses are between the input and hidden layers. The more biologically detailed version of this model proposed by Ashby *et al.* (2007) included lateral inhibition between striatal units and between cortical units. In the absence of such inhibition, the top motor output layer in Figure 4.1 represents a conceptual place holder for the striatum's projection to premotor areas. This layer is not included in the following computational description.

The key structure in the model is the striatum (body and tail of the caudate nucleus and the posterior putamen), which is a major input region of the basal ganglia. In humans and other primates, all of the extra-striate cortex projects directly to the striatum and these projec-tions are characterized by massive convergence, with the dendritic field of each medium spiny cell innervated by the axons of approximately

380,000 cortical pyramidal cells (Kincaid, Zheng, & Wilson, 1998). COVIS assumes that, through a procedural-learning process, each striatal unit associates an abstract motor programme with a large group of sensory cortical cells (i.e., all that project strongly to it).

The dendrites of striatal medium spiny cells are covered in protuberances called spines. These play a critical role in the model because glutamate projections from the sensory cortex and dopamine projections from the substantia nigra (pars compacta) converge (i.e., synapse) on the dendritic spines of the medium spiny cells (e.g., Smiley *et al.*, 1994). COVIS assumes that these synapses are a critical site of procedural learning.

Activation equations The sensory cortex is modelled as an ordered array of up to 10,000 units, each tuned to a different stimulus. The model assumes that each unit responds maximally when its preferred stimulus is presented, and that its response decreases as a Gaussian function of the distance in stimulus space between the stimulus preferred by that unit and the presented stimulus. Specifically, when a stimulus is presented, the activation in sensory cortical unit K on trial n is given by

$$I_K(n) = e^{-\frac{d(K,\text{ stimulus})^2}{\alpha}}, \tag{8}$$

where α is a constant that scales the unit of measurement in stimulus space and $d(K, \text{stimulus})$ is the distance (in stimulus space) between the stimulus preferred by unit K and the presented stimulus. Equation 8, which is an example of a radial basis function, is a popular method for modelling the receptive fields of sensory units in models of many cognitive tasks (e.g., Kruschke, 1992; Riesenhuber & Poggio, 1999).

COVIS assumes that the activation in striatal unit $\mathcal{J}$ (within the middle or hidden layer) on trial n, denoted $S_{\mathcal{J}}(n)$, is determined by the weighted sum of activations in all sensory cortical cells that project to it:

$$S_{\mathcal{J}}(n) = \sum_K w_{K,\mathcal{J}}(n) I_K(n) + \varepsilon \tag{9}$$

where $w_{K,\mathcal{J}}(n)$ is the strength of the synapse between cortical unit K and striatal cell $\mathcal{J}$ on trial n, $I_K(n)$ is the input from visual cortical unit K on trial n, and ε is normally distributed noise (with mean 0 and variance σ_p^2). In a task with two alternative categories, A and B, the decision rule is:

Respond A on trial n if $S_A(n) > S_B(n)$; otherwise respond B.

The synaptic strengths $w_{K,J}(n)$ are adjusted up and down from trial-to-trial via reinforcement learning, which is described below. To run the model, however, initial values must be selected for these weights. This is done by randomly sampling from some uniform distribution. For example, a typical application would set

$$w_{K,J}(0) = 0.001 + 0.0025U,$$

where U is a random sample from a uniform [0,1] distribution. This algorithm guarantees that all initial synaptic strengths are in the range [0.001, 0.0035], and that they are assigned in an unbiased fashion.

Learning equations   The three factors thought to be necessary to strengthen cortical-striatal synapses are (1) strong pre-synaptic activation, (2) strong post-synaptic activation, and (3) dopamine levels above baseline (e.g., Arbuthnott, Ingham, & Wickens, 2000; Calabresi *et al.*, 1996; Reynolds & Wickens, 2002). According to this model, the synapse between a cell in the sensory association cortex and a medium spiny cell in the striatum is strengthened if the cortical cell responds strongly to the presented stimulus (factors 1 and 2 are present) and the participant is rewarded for responding correctly (factor 3). On the other hand, the strength of the synapse will weaken if the participant responds incorrectly (factor 3 is missing), or if the synapse is driven by a cell in the sensory cortex that does not fire strongly to the stimulus (factors 1 and 2 are missing).

Let $w_{K,J}(n)$ denote the strength of the synapse on trial n between cortical unit K and striatal unit J. COVIS models reinforcement learning as follows:

$$
\begin{aligned}
w_{K,J}(n+1) = w_{K,J}(n) &+ \alpha_w I_K(n)\left[S_J(n) - \theta_{\text{NMDA}}\right]^+ \left[D(n) - D_{\text{base}}\right]^+ \left[w_{\text{max}} - w_{K,J}(n)\right] \\
&- \beta_w I_K(n)\left[S_J(n) - \theta_{\text{NMDA}}\right]^+ \left[D_{\text{base}} - D(n)\right]^+ w_{K,J}(n) \\
&- \gamma_w I_K(n)\left\{\left[\theta_{\text{NMDA}} - S_J(n)\right]^+ - \theta_{\text{AMPA}}\right\}^+ w_{K,J}(n).
\end{aligned}
\tag{10}
$$

The function $[g(n)]+ = g(n)$ if $g(n) > 0$, and otherwise $g(n) = 0$. The constant D_{base} is the baseline dopamine level, $D(n)$ is the amount of dopamine released following feedback on trial n, and $\alpha_w, \beta_w, \gamma_w, \theta_{\text{NMDA}},$ and θ_{AMPA} are all constants. The first three of these (i.e., $\alpha_w, \beta_w,$ and γ_w) operate like standard learning rates because they determine the magnitudes of increases and decreases in synaptic strength. The constants θ_{NMDA} and θ_{AMPA} represent the activation thresholds for post-synaptic NMDA and AMPA (more precisely, non-NMDA) glutamate receptors, respectively. The numerical value of $\theta_{\text{NMDA}} > \theta_{\text{AMPA}}$ because NMDA receptors have a higher threshold for activation than AMPA receptors. This is critical because NMDA receptor activation is required to strengthen cortical-striatal synapses (Calabresi *et al.*, 1992).

The first line in Equation 10 describes the conditions under which synapses are strengthened (i.e., striatal activation above the threshold for NMDA receptor activation and dopamine above baseline) and lines two and three describe conditions that cause the synapse to be weakened. The first possibility (line 2) is that post-synaptic activation is above the NMDA threshold but dopamine is below baseline (as on an error trial), and the second possibility is that striatal activation is between the AMPA and NMDA thresholds. Note that synaptic strength does not change if post-synaptic activation is below the AMPA threshold.

Dopamine model   The Equation 10 model of reinforcement learning requires that we specify the amount of dopamine released on every trial in response to the feedback signal (the $D(n)$ term). The key empirical results are (e.g., Schultz, Dayan, & Montague, 1997; Tobler, Dickinson, & Schultz, 2003): (1) midbrain dopamine cells fire spontaneously (i.e., tonically), (2) dopamine release increases above baseline following unexpected reward, and the more unexpected the reward the greater the release, and (3) dopamine release decreases below baseline following unexpected absence of reward, and the more unexpected the absence, the greater the decrease. One common interpretation of these results is that over a wide range, dopamine firing is proportional to the reward prediction error (RPE):

$$\text{RPE} = \text{Obtained Reward} - \text{Predicted Reward.} \qquad (11)$$

A simple model of dopamine release can be built by specifying how to compute Obtained Reward, Predicted Reward, and exactly how the amount of dopamine release is related to the RPE. Our solution to these three problems is as follows.

Computing Obtained Reward   In applications that do not vary the valence of the rewards (for example, as in designs where some correct responses are rewarded more than others), the obtained reward R_n on trial n is defined as $+1$ if correct or reward feedback is received, 0 in the absence of feedback, and -1 if error feedback is received.

Computing Predicted Reward   We use a simplified version of the well-known Rescorla–Wagner model (Rescorla & Wagner, 1972) to compute Predicted Reward. Consider a trial where the participant has just responded for the nth time to some particular stimulus. Then COVIS assumes that the reward the participant expects to receive equals

$$P_n = P_{n-1} + 0.025(R_{n-1} - P_{n-1}).\tag{12}$$

It is well known that when computed in this fashion, P_n converges exponentially to the expected reward value and then fluctuates around this value until reward contingencies change.

Computing dopamine release from the RPE   Bayer and Glimcher (2005) reported activity in midbrain dopamine cells as a function of RPE. A simple model that nicely matches their results is

$$D(n) = \begin{cases} 1 & \text{if RPE} > 1 \\ 0.8\ \text{RPE} + 0.2 & \text{if} -0.25 < \text{RPE} \le 1 \\ 0 & \text{if RPE} \le -0.25. \end{cases}\tag{13}$$

Note that the baseline dopamine level is 0.2 (i.e., when the RPE $= 0$) and that dopamine levels increase linearly with the RPE. However, note also the asymmetry between dopamine increases and decreases (which is evident in the Bayer & Glimcher, 2005, data) – that is, a negative RPE quickly causes dopamine levels to fall to zero, whereas there is a considerable range for dopamine levels to increase in response to positive RPEs.

Resolving the competition between the explicit and procedural-learning systems

Since on any trial the model can make only one response, the final task is to decide which of the two systems will control the observable response. In COVIS, this competition is resolved by combining two factors: the confidence each system has in the accuracy of its response, and how much each system can be trusted. In the case of the explicit system, confidence equals the absolute value of the discriminant function $|\,h_E(n)\,|$. When $|\,h_E(n)\,| = 0$, the stimulus is exactly on the explicit system's decision bound, so the model has no confidence in its ability to predict the correct response. When $|\,h_E(n)\,|$ is large, the stimulus is far from the bound and confidence is high. In the procedural-learning system, confidence is defined as the absolute value of the difference between the activation values in the two striatal units:

$$|\,h_P(n)\,| = |\,S_A(n) - S_B(n)\,|.\tag{14}$$

The logic is similar. When $|\,h_P(n)\,| = 0$, the stimulus is equally activating both striatal units, so the procedural system has no confidence in its ability to predict the correct response, and when $| h_P(n) |$ is large, the evidence strongly favours one response over the other.

One problem with this approach is that $| h_E(n) |$ and $| h_P(n) |$ will typically have different upper limits, which makes them difficult to compare. For this reason, these values are normalized to a $[0,1]$ scale on every trial. This is done by dividing each discriminant value by its maximum possible value.[1]

The amount of trust that is placed in each system is a function of an initial bias toward the explicit system, and the previous success history of each system. On trial n, the trust in each system increases with the system weights, $\theta_E(n)$ and $\theta_P(n)$, where it is assumed that $\theta_E(n) + \theta_P(n) = 1$. In typical applications, COVIS assumes that the initial trust in the explicit system is much higher than in the procedural system, partly because initially there is no procedural learning to use. A common assumption is that $\theta_E(1) = 0.99$ and $\theta_P(1) = 0.01$. As the experiment progresses, feedback is used to adjust the two system weights up or down depending on the success of the relevant component system. This is done in the following way. If the explicit system suggests the correct response on trial n then

$$\theta_E(n + 1) = \theta_E(n) + \Delta_{OC}[1 - \theta_E(n)], \tag{15}$$

where Δ_{OC} is a parameter. If instead, the explicit system suggests an incorrect response then

$$\theta_E(n + 1) = \theta_E(n) - \Delta_{OE}\theta_E(n), \tag{16}$$

where Δ_{OE} is another parameter. The two regulatory terms on the end of Equations 15 and 16 restrict $\theta_E(n)$ to the range $0 \leq \theta_E(n) \leq 1$. Finally, on every trial, $\theta_P(n + 1) = 1 - \theta_E(n + 1)$. Thus, Equations 15 and 16 also guarantee that $\theta_P(n)$ falls in the range $0 \leq \theta_P(n) \leq 1$.

The last step is to combine confidence and trust. This is done multiplicatively, so the overall system decision rule is:

> Emit the response suggested by the explicit system if
> $\theta_E(n) | h_E(n) | > \theta_P(n) | h_P(n) |$,

otherwise emit the response suggested by the procedural system.

An empirical application

As an example application of COVIS, we apply it to the category-learning data of Waldron and Ashby (2001). In this experiment, participants

---

[1] In the case of the explicit system, this maximum can be computed analytically. For the procedural system, the maximum is computed numerically by simply keeping a record on each trial of the largest previous value of $| h_P(n) |$.

learned either rule-based or information-integration categories, either with or without a simultaneous dual task that required working memory and executive attention. Results showed that the dual-task massively interfered with learning of the rule-based categories, even though the optimal strategy in this task was a simple one-dimensional rule. In contrast, there was no significant interference in the information-integration condition. Similar results were later reported by Zeithamova and Maddox (2006). These results are theoretically important because the only version of ALCOVE (Kruschke, 1992) that can account for these results assumes no attentional learning (Nosofsky & Kruschke, 2002), and therefore, that in the presence of the dual task, participants in the rule-based condition should have no idea that only one dimension was relevant at the end of learning. Ashby and Ell (2002) reported evidence that strongly disconfirmed this prediction.

The stimuli in the Waldron and Ashby (2001) experiment varied across trials on four binary-valued dimensions: background colour (blue or yellow), symbol colour (red or green), symbol shape (circle or square), and symbol number (one or two). Thus, there were 16 stimuli in total. In the rule-based condition, only one dimension was relevant. In the information-integration condition, three dimensions were relevant and one was irrelevant. For each relevant dimension, one stimulus level was assigned a numerical value of 1 and the other level was assigned a numerical value of 0. The optimal rule was to respond A if the sum of the values on the three relevant dimensions exceeded 1.5, and otherwise to respond B. The top panel of Figure 4.2 summarizes the Waldron and Ashby (2001) results (where the learning criterion was eight correct responses in a row).

The version of COVIS used to simulate these data was the same as described above, except for the following modifications. In the procedural-learning system, we assumed that the radial basis function in Equation 8 was narrow enough (i.e., α was small) so that each stimulus only activated a single unit in the visual cortex. For the explicit system, no criterial learning was required because of the binary-valued nature of the dimensions. Also, because the stimuli were not confusable, we set $\sigma_E^2 = 0$. We assumed that the dual task would only affect the perseveration and selection parameters. In other words, because the dual task reduces the capacity of working memory and executive attention, we assumed that participants would therefore be less adept at selecting appropriate new rules to try, and at switching attention away from ineffective rules. The exact parameter values used in the simulations are listed in Table 4.1. No explicit optimization process was employed; rather, parameter values were adjusted manually in a

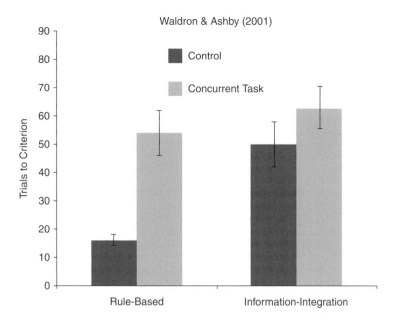

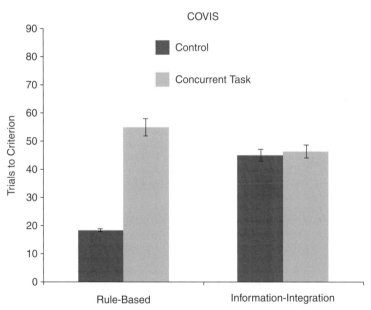

Figure 4.2 Top panel: data from the dual-task experiment of Waldron and Ashby (2001). Bottom panel: data from simulations of COVIS in the Waldron and Ashby (2001) experiment. (From Waldron & Ashby, 2001. Copyright 2001 by the Psychonomic Society. Adapted with permission.)

Table 4.1 *COVIS parameter values used in the simulations of Figure 4.2*

Component	Parameter	Control	Dual-task
Explicit system	Δ_C	0.0025	same
	Δ_E	0.02	same
	γ	1	20
	λ	5	0.5
	$Z_k(0)$, for $k = 1, ..., 4$	0.25	same
Procedural system	D_{base}	0.20	same
	α_w (Eq. 10)	0.65	same
	β_w (Eq. 10)	0.19	same
	γ_w (Eq. 10)	0.02	same
	θ_{NMDA} (Eq. 10)	0.0022	same
	θ_{AMPA} (Eq. 10)	0.01	same
	w_{max} (Eq. 10)	1	same
	σ_P	0.0125	same
Competition	Δ_{OC}	0.01	same
	Δ_{OE}	0.04	same

crude search to match the empirical results. All parameter values were constrained between [0, 1] except for γ and λ, which were constrained to be positive valued.

Results are shown in the bottom panel of Figure 4.2. Note that the model successfully captures the major qualitative properties of the data. In particular, the model predicts that in the absence of a dual task, the information-integration condition is much more difficult than the rule-based condition, and that the dual task disrupts performance in the rule-based condition much more than in the information-integration condition.

Future directions

The version of COVIS described in this chapter makes many neuroscience-related predictions. First, it makes detailed predictions about the effects of varying dopamine levels in different brain areas. Specifically, the model predicts that increasing levels of cortical dopamine should improve rule selection in rule-based tasks, increasing levels of dopamine in the anterior striatum should improve rule switching, and increasing levels of dopamine in the posterior striatum should facilitate learning in information-integration tasks. Second, the model makes specific predictions about the effects of a variety of brain lesions on category learning. For example, the model predicts that prefrontal cortex lesions should significantly impair rule-based learning, but have little effect on information-integration learning.

On the other hand, the version of COVIS described here is not biologically detailed enough to make predictions about single-unit recording data. A future goal is to develop a version of the model with enough biological detail so that it can be tested against single-unit recording data from any of the many brain areas implicated by the theory. Using the methods of Ashby and Waldschmidt (2008), this would also allow the model to be tested against fMRI data. Some progress has already been made toward this goal. For example, Ashby *et al.* (2007) developed a more detailed version of the procedural-learning system that accurately accounts for single-unit recording data from the striatum and premotor cortex in a variety of different tasks. In addition, a biologically detailed version of the explicit system minus the rule-selection module was developed by Ashby *et al.* (2005). This model gave accurate descriptions of single-unit recording data collected from a variety of brain areas in monkeys during a working memory task; these areas included prefrontal cortex, posterior parietal cortex, thalamus (medial dorsal nucleus), striatum (head of the caudate nucleus), and globus pallidus (internal segment). At present, there are only two remaining theoretical barriers that prevent the construction of a more biologically detailed version of the entire COVIS network. The first is to model the neurobiology of rule selection in the explicit system and the second is to model the competition between the two systems.

COVIS currently only accounts for initial category learning. A second goal is to extend the model so that it is also able to account for categorization responses that have been so highly practised that they are executed automatically. Again, considerable progress toward this goal has already been made. Ashby *et al.* (2007) extended the COVIS procedural system to account for the development of automaticity in information-integration tasks by adding cortical-cortical projections from the sensory cortex directly to the relevant areas of the premotor cortex. They argued that a major role of the subcortical path through the striatum is to train these cortical-cortical projections. Thus, they hypothesized that the development of automaticity is a gradual transfer of control from the subcortical path shown in Figure 4.1 to the cortex. This generalization could easily be incorporated into future versions of COVIS. The remaining theoretical challenge would then be to account for the development of automaticity in rule-based tasks.

Relations to other models

Within this volume, COVIS is unique since it is the only model that is rooted in neuroscience. Compared to purely cognitive models, neuroscience-based models have several important advantages. First, whereas cognitive models are limited to making predictions about purely behavioural dependent measures (i.e., accuracy and response time), neuroscience-based models should also be able to make predictions about other types of data. Included in this list are data collected using fMRI, EEG, TMS, and single-unit recordings. In addition, neuroscience models can often make predictions about how drugs, genes, and focal lesions affect behaviour.

Second, grounding a model in neuroscience adds a huge number of constraints that can be used to rapidly confirm or falsify the model, and therefore quickly improve our understanding of the scientific domain under study. For example, as described above, COVIS assumes information-integration learning is mediated largely by reinforcement learning at cortical-striatal synapses, and that dopamine serves as the reinforcement signal. However, it is known that dopamine levels in the striatum increase after reward delivery, which occurs some time after the cortical-striatal synapses are active. Even so, the trace of this activation (i.e., partially phosphorylated CaMKII) is known to persist for several seconds after the striatal cell fires (e.g., Lisman, Schulman & Cline, 2002). Thus, COVIS makes a strong prediction that would be impossible with a purely cognitive model – namely, that information-integration learning should be impaired if the feedback signal is delayed by more than a few seconds (i.e., because then the trace would be gone when the dopamine levels increase), but such delays should not affect rule-based learning (which has access to working memory). This prediction has been supported in several studies (Maddox, Ashby, & Bohil, 2003; Maddox & Ing, 2005), which found that delays as short as 2.5 seconds severely interfered with information-integration learning, but delays as long as 10 seconds had no effect on learning in rule-based tasks of equal difficulty.

With only behavioural results to supply constraints, cognitive models are difficult to differentiate. For example, many studies have shown that people are exquisitely sensitive to correlations between features across category exemplars. This result is so well accepted that it must be predicted by any complete theory of human categorization. The problem is that there are many alternative computational architectures that can account for this result. The same is true for many other purely behavioural results. For this reason, when the major theories in a field attend only to behavioural phenomena, it seems likely that there will be alternative models that seem almost equally viable. In such an unsettled world, it can be difficult to see progress. For example, prototype theory was developed more than 40 years ago (Posner & Keele, 1968), and exemplar theory was developed more than 30 years ago (Medin & Schaffer, 1978).

Yet despite the ensuing decades and numerous empirical tests, neither theory is universally recognized as superior to the other, and as this volume attests, new cognitive models are still being proposed.

In contrast, by building models that are based in neuroscience, cumulative progress may become easier. For example, many studies have shown that the striatum is critical to category learning. This result is now so well established that any theory of category learning that attends to neuroscience must assign some key role to the striatum. Since the neuroanatomy of the striatum (and basal ganglia) is well understood, along with its major inputs and outputs, this means that any neuroscience-sensitive theory of category learning must include some architecture like the one shown in Figure 4.1. More details will be added, and a somewhat different computational role might be assigned to certain components, but it is unlikely that this basic architecture will disappear from any future theory. Continuity of this type can facilitate progress.

REFERENCES

Allen, S. W., & Brooks, L. R. (1991). Specializing the operation of an explicit rule. *Journal of Experimental Psychology: General*, **120**, 3–19.

Arbuthnott, G. W., Ingham, C. A., & Wickens, J. R. (2000). Dopamine and synaptic plasticity in the neostriatum. *Journal of Anatomy*, **196**, 587–596.

Ashby, F. G., Alfonso-Reese, L. A., Turken, A. U., & Waldron, E. M. (1998). A neuropsychological theory of multiple systems in category learning. *Psychological Review*, **105**, 442–481.

Ashby, F. G., & Ell, S. W. (2002). Single versus multiple systems of category learning: reply to Nosofsky and Kruschke (2002). *Psychonomic Bulletin & Review*, **9**, 175–180.

Ashby, F. G., Ell, S. W., Valentin, V., & Casale, M. B. (2005). FROST: a distributed neurocomputational model of working memory maintenance. *Journal of Cognitive Neuroscience*, **17**, 1728–1743.

Ashby, F. G., Ell, S. W., & Waldron, E. M. (2003). Procedural learning in perceptual categorization. *Memory & Cognition*, **31**, 1114–1125.

Ashby, F. G., & Ennis, J. M. (2006). The role of the basal ganglia in category learning. *The Psychology of Learning and Motivation*, **47**, 1–36.

Ashby, F. G., Ennis, J. M., & Spiering, B. J. (2007). A neurobiological theory of automaticity in perceptual categorization. *Psychological Review*, **114**, 632–656.

Ashby, F. G., & Gott, R. E. (1988). Decision rules in the perception and categorization of multidimensional stimuli. *Journal of Experimental Psychology: Learning, Memory, and Cognition*, **14**, 33–53.

Ashby, F. G., & Maddox, W. T. (2005). Human category learning. *Annual Review of Psychology*, **56**, 149–178.

Ashby, F. G., Noble, S., Filoteo, J. V., Waldron, E. M., & Ell, S. W. (2003). Category learning deficits in Parkinson's disease. *Neuropsychology*, **17**, 115–124.

Ashby, F. G., & O'Brien, J. B. (2005). Category learning and multiple memory systems. *Trends in Cognitive Sciences*, **9**, 83–89.

Ashby, F. G., & Valentin, V. V. (2005). Multiple systems of perceptual category learning: theory and cognitive tests. In H. Cohen & C. Lefebvre (eds.), *Categorization in Cognitive Science*. New York: Elsevier.

Ashby, F. G., & Waldron, E. M. (1999). On the nature of implicit categorization. *Psychonomic Bulletin & Review*, **6**, 363–378.

Ashby, F. G., & Waldschmidt, J. G. (2008). Fitting computational models to fMRI data. *Behavior Research Methods*, **40**, 713–721.

Bayer, H. M., & Glimcher, P. W. (2005). Midbrain dopamine neurons encode a quantitative reward prediction error signal. *Neuron*, **47**, 129–141.

Brooks, L. (1978). *Nonanalytic Concept Formation and Memory for Instances.* Hillsdale, NJ: Erlbaum.

Calabresi, P., Pisani, A., Mercuri, N. B., & Bernardi, G. (1992). Long-term potentiation in the striatum is unmasked by removing the voltage-dependent magnesium block of NMDA receptor channels. *European Journal of Neuroscience*, **4**, 929–935.

(1996). The corticostriatal projection: from synaptic plasticity to dysfunctions of the basal ganglia. *Trends in Neurosciences*, **19**, 19–24.

DeGutis, J., & D'Esposito, M. (2007). Distinct mechanisms in visual category learning. *Cognitive, Affective, & Behavioral Neuroscience*, 7 (3), 251–259.

Erickson, M. A., & Kruschke, J. K. (1998). Rules and exemplars in category learning. *Journal of Experimental Psychology: Learning, Memory, and Cognition*, **127**, 107–140.

Filoteo, J. V., & Maddox, W. T. (2007). Category learning in Parkinson's disease. In M. K. Sun (ed.), *Research Progress in Alzheimer's Disease and Dementia* (pp. 339–365). Nova Sciences Publishers.

Filoteo, J. V., Maddox, W. T., Simmons, A. N., Ing, A. D., Cagigas, X. E., Matthews, S., *et al.* (2005). Cortical and subcortical brain regions involved in rule-based category learning. *NeuroReport*, **16** (2), 111–115.

Gotham, A. M., Brown, R. G., & Marsden, C. D. (1988). 'Frontal' cognitive function in patients with Parkinson's disease 'ON' and 'OFF' Levodopa. *Brain*, **111**, 299–321.

Hazeltine, E., & Ivry, R. (2002). Motor skill. In V. Ramachandran (ed.), *Encyclopedia of the Human Brain* (pp. 183–200). San Diego, CA: Academic Press.

Kincaid, A. E., Zheng, T., & Wilson, C. J. (1998). Connectivity and convergence of single corticostriatal axons. *Journal of Neuroscience*, **18**, 4722–4731.

Kruschke, J. K. (1992). ALCOVE: an exemplar-based connectionist model of category learning. *Psychological Review*, **99**, 22–44.

Lees, A. J., & Smith, F. (1983). Cognitive deficits in the early stages of Parkinson's disease. *Brain*, **106**, 257–270.

Lisman, J., Schulman, H., & Cline, H. (2002). The molecular basis of CaMKII function in synaptic and behavioural memory. *Nature Reviews Neuroscience*, **3**, 175–190.

Love, B. C., Medin, D. L., & Gureckis, T. M. (2004). SUSTAIN: a network model of category learning. *Psychological Review*, **111** (2), 309–332.

Maddox, W. T., & Ashby, F. G. (1993). Comparing decision bound and exemplar models of categorization. *Perception & Psychophysics*, **53**, 49–70.

(2004). Dissociating explicit and procedural-learning based systems of perceptual category learning. *Behavioural Processes*, **66** (3), 309–332.

Maddox, W.T., Ashby, F. G., & Bohil, C. J. (2003). Delayed feedback effects on rule-based and information-integration category learning. *Journal of Experimental Psychology: Learning, Memory, and Cognition*, **29**, 650–662.

Maddox, W. T., Bohil, C. J., & Ing, A. D. (2004). Evidence for a procedural-learning-based system in perceptual category learning. *Psychonomic Bulletin & Review*, **11** (5), 945–952.

Maddox, W.T., & Filoteo, J. V. (2005). The neuropsychology of perceptual category learning. In H. Cohen & C. Lefebvre (eds.), *Handbook of Categorization in Cognitive Science* (pp. 573–599). Amsterdam: Elsevier.

(2007). Modeling visual attention and category learning in amnesiacs, striatal-damaged patients and normal aging. In R. W. J. Neufeld (ed.), *Advances in Clinical Cognitive Science: Formal Modeling and Assessment of Processes and Symptoms* (pp. 113–146). Washington DC: American Psychological Association.

Maddox, W. T., Glass, B. D., O'Brien, J. B., Filoteo, J. V., & Ashby, F. G. (2010). Category label and response location shifts in category learning. *Psychological Research*, **74**, 219–236.

Maddox, W. T., & Ing, A. D. (2005). Delayed feedback disrupts the procedural-learning system but not the hypothesis-testing system in perceptual category learning. *Journal of Experimental Psychology: Learning, Memory, and Cognition*, **31**, 100–107.

Markman, A. B., & Ross, B. H. (2003). Category use and category learning. *Psychological Bulletin*, **129** (4), 592–613.

McKinley, S. C., & Nosofsky, R. M. (1995). Investigations of exemplar and decision bound models in large, ill-defined category structures. *Journal of Experimental Psychology: Human Perception and Performance*, **21**, 128–148.

Medin, D. L., & Schaffer, M. M. (1978). Context theory of classification learning. *Psychological Review*, **85**, 207–238.

Nomura, E. M., Maddox, W. T., Filoteo, J. V., Ing, A. D., Gitelman, D. R., Parrish, T. B., *et al.* (2007). Neural correlates of rule-based and information-integration visual category learning. *Cerebral Cortex*, **17** (1), 37–43.

Nomura, E. M., & Reber, P. J. (2008). A review of medial temporal lobe and caudate contributions to visual category learning. *Neuroscience and Biobehavioral Reviews*, **32** (2), 279–291.

Nosofsky, R. M., & Kruschke, J. K. (2002). Single-system models and interference in category learning: commentary on Waldron and Ashby (2001). *Psychonomic Bulletin & Review*, **9**, 169–174.

Nosofsky, R. M., Palmeri, T. J., & McKinley, S. C. (1994). A rule-plus-exception model of classification learning. *Psychological Review*, **101**, 53–79.

Posner, M. I., & Keele, S. W. (1968). On the genesis of abstract ideas. *Journal of Experimental Psychology*, **77**, 353–363.

Price, A., Filoteo, J. V., & Maddox, W. T. (2009). Rule-based category learning in patients with Parkinson's disease. *Neuropsychologia*, **47** (5), 1213–1226.

Reber, P. J., Gitelman, D. R., Parrish, T. B., & Mesulam, M. M. (2003). Dissociating explicit and implicit category knowledge with fMRI. *Journal of Cognitive Neuroscience*, **15** (4), 574–583.

Regehr, G., & Brooks, L. R. (1993). Perceptual manifestations of an analytic structure: the priority of holistic individuation. *Journal of Experimental Psychology: General*, **122** (1), 92–114.

Rescorla, R. A., & Wagner, A. R. (1972). A theory of Pavlovian conditioning: variations in the effectiveness of reinforcement and nonreinforcement. In A. H. Black & W. F. Prokasy (eds.), *Classical Conditioning II: Current Research and Theory* (pp. 64–99). New York: Appleton-Century-Crofts.

Reynolds, J. N. J., & Wickens, J. R. (2002). Dopamine-dependent plasticity of corticostriatal synapses. *Neural Networks*, **15**, 507–521.

Riesenhuber, M., & Poggio, T. (1999). Hierarchical models of object recognition in cortex. *Nature Neuroscience*, **2**, 1019–1025.

Schultz, W., Dayan, P., & Montague, P. R. (1997). A neural substrate of prediction and reward. *Science*, **275**, 1593–1599.

Seger, C. A. (2008). How do the basal ganglia contribute to categorization? Their roles in generalization, response selection, and learning via feedback. *Neuroscience and Biobehavioral Review*, **32** (2), 265–278.

Seger, C. A., & Cincotta, C. M. (2005). The roles of the caudate nucleus in human classification learning. *Journal of Neuroscience*, **25** (11), 2941–2951.

(2006). Dynamics of frontal, striatal, and hippocampal systems during rule learning. *Cerebral Cortex*, **16** (11), 1546–1555.

Smiley, J. F., Levey, A. I., Ciliax, B. J., & Goldman-Rakic, P. S. (1994). D1 dopamine receptor immunoreactivity in human and monkey cerebral cortex: predominant and extrasynaptic localization in dendritic spines. *Proceedings of the National Academy of Sciences*, **91**, 5720–5724.

Smith, J. D., Beran, M. J., Crossley, M., Boomer, J., & Ashby, F. G. (2010). Implicit and explicit category learning by macaques (*Macaca mulatta*) and humans (*Homo sapiens*). *Journal of Experimental Psychology: Animal Behavior Processes*, **36**, 54–65.

Smith, J. D., & Minda, J. P. (1998). Prototypes in the mist: the early epochs of category learning. *Journal of Experimental Psychology: Learning, Memory, and Cognition*, **24**, 1411–1436.

Tobler, P. N., Dickinson, A., & Schultz, W. (2003). Coding of predicted reward omission by dopamine neurons in a conditioned inhibition paradigm. *Journal of Neuroscience*, **23**, 10402–10410.

Waldron, E. M., & Ashby, F. G. (2001). The effects of concurrent task interference on category learning: evidence for multiple category learning systems. *Psychonomic Bulletin & Review*, **8**, 168–176.

Willingham, D. B. (1998). A neuropsychological theory of motor skill learning. *Psychological Review*, **105**, 558–584.

Willingham, D. B., Nissen, M. J., & Bullemer, P. (1989). On the development of procedural knowledge. *Journal of Experimental Psychology: Learning, Memory, and Cognition,* **15** (6), 1047–1060.

Zeithamova, D., & Maddox, W. T. (2006). Dual task interference in perceptual category learning. *Memory & Cognition,* **34** (2), 387–398.

5   Semantics without categorization

Timothy T. Rogers and James L. McClelland

Human beings have a remarkable ability to attribute meaning to the objects and events around them. Without much conscious effort, we are able to recognize the items in our environment as familiar 'kinds' of things, and to attribute to them properties that have not been observed directly. We know, for instance, that the banana on the kitchen counter has a skin that easily peels off, and that beneath the peel we will find a soft yellow-white interior. We know that the banana is meant to be eaten, and can anticipate what it will taste like. Such inferences spring readily to mind whether we observe the banana itself or, as with this paragraph, simply read or hear statements referring to bananas. The cognitive faculty that supports these abilities is sometimes referred to as 'semantic memory', and a key goal of much research in cognitive psychology is to understand the processes that support this aspect of human cognition.

One long-standing hypothesis places categorization at the heart of human semantic abilities. The motivation for this view is that categorization can provide an efficient mechanism for storing and generalizing knowledge about the world. As Rosch (1978) put it, '...what one wishes to gain from one's categories is a great deal of information about the environment while conserving finite resources as much as possible.' Thus categorization-based theories propose that knowledge about the world is stored in a set of discrete category representations, each encoding or providing access to information about the properties that characterize members of the class. New items are assigned to stored categories through a process that is sensitive to the similarity between the item and the stored representations; and once the item has been categorized, it is attributed the properties known to typify the category. There are a great many different hypotheses about and models of the processes by which items are assigned to categories and subsequently are attributed properties (Anderson, 1991; Ashby & Alfonso-Reese, 1995; Kruschke, 1992; Love, Medin, & Gureckis, 2004; Nosofsky, 1984; Pothos & Chater, 2002), but these share commitment to the idea that categorization is the engine that drives storage and generalization of knowledge about the world. Indeed, the idea that semantic abilities are supported by categorization processes is so pervasive that it is seldom treated as a hypothesis. In the preceding quotation, for instance, Rosch inquires only what one wants from one's categories – as though the question of whether our semantic memory system actually employs category representations is itself beyond question.

Still, the idea that categorization is the core mechanism supporting semantic abilities brings with it a series of challenges and puzzles that have yet to be solved. We briefly summarize some of the challenges that have motivated our work; a more extensive discussion of these issues is presented in the first chapter of *Semantic Cognition: A Parallel Distributed Processing Approach* (Rogers & McClelland, 2004).

Multiple category representation

As has long been known, objects in the world usually belong simultaneously to many different categories (Barsalou, 1993; Collins & Quillian, 1969; Murphy & Lassaline, 1997; Rosch *et al.*, 1976). Lassie, for instance, belongs to the categories *collie, dog, pet, animal* and *movie star*. Chickens belong to the categories *bird, animal, poultry* and *livestock*; bulldozers are both *vehicles* and *construction equipment*; and so on. Moreover, the different categories to which an item belongs can license different conclusions about the item's unobserved properties. If the chicken is categorized as an *animal*, this might license the conclusion that it cannot fly, since most animals are flightless. If classified as a *bird*, the reverse conclusion is warranted (most birds can fly); and if classified as a *chicken*, the original conclusion holds (chickens cannot fly). The notion that semantic knowledge resides in or is accessible from a set of stored category representations thus raises the question of how the different competing categories are 'selected' as the appropriate ones for governing generalization in a given context. This in turn seems to require involvement of some additional representational structure or processing mechanism that governs the selection of and interaction among category representations. For instance, the 'spreading activation' theories of the 1970s proposed that different category representations were connected in a graph structure that facilitated the 'flow of activation' between categories that are 'linked' in memory (Collins & Loftus, 1975; Collins & Quillian, 1969).

Category coherence

The problem of multiple category representation highlights a second more general challenge for prototype-like theories where semantic knowledge is thought to be stored in summary representations of categories.

Specifically, how does the semantic system 'know' for which groupings of items it should form a stored category representation (Murphy & Medin, 1985)? Some groupings of items seem to form coherent sets that are useful for governing generalization (e.g. 'birds', 'dogs', 'cars'), whereas other groupings seem less coherent and useful (e.g. 'things that are either blue or orange', 'things that have corners', 'things that could fit in the trunk of my car'). How does the system 'know' that it should store a summary representation of the class of dogs, but should not store a summary representation of the class of things that are blue and orange?

Primacy of different category structures in development, maturity, and dissolution

The general question of how the semantic system 'knows' which categories to store is further constrained by empirical evidence regarding the acquisition of conceptual distinctions over infancy and early childhood, the primacy of certain kinds of category structures in healthy adult cognition, and the dissolution of conceptual knowledge in some forms of dementia. Together, these sources of evidence generally support two seemingly contradictory conclusions about which kinds of categories are easiest to learn and most robustly represented in memory.

First, a large body of research generally suggests that infants and children differentiate quite gross conceptual distinctions (such as the distinction between animals and manmade objects) earlier in life than more fine-grained distinctions (such as the distinction between birds and fish; Keil, 1979; Mandler, 2000; Mandler & McDonough, 1996; Pauen, 2002a, 2002b). A complementary body of work in neuropsychology has shown that the progressive dissolution of conceptual knowledge observed for the degenerative syndrome semantic dementia (SD) follows a reverse path: patients with SD first lose the ability to differentiate quite fine-grained conceptual distinctions (for example, they cannot tell a robin from a canary, but know both are birds), then gradually lose the distinctions among increasingly more general categories as the disease progresses (Patterson & Hodges, 2000; Patterson, Nestor, & Rogers, 2007; Rogers & Patterson, 2007; Rogers *et al.*, 2004). Together, these literatures suggest that more general or global conceptual distinctions are both the first to be acquired and the most robust in the face of global semantic impairment.

Seemingly in contrast to this conclusion, however, are long-standing observations about children's lexical development and the categorization behaviour of healthy adults, both of which seem to suggest that categories at an intermediate level of specificity are primal in both acquisition and adult performance. For instance, a long tradition of research convincingly demonstrates that children learn to name objects at an intermediate or *basic* level of specificity (e.g. 'bird', 'fish'), prior to learning more general (e.g. 'animal', 'vehicle') or specific (e.g. 'robin', 'trout') names (Brown, 1958; Mervis, 1987; Mervis & Crisafi, 1982); and seminal work by Rosch and others (Jolicoeur, Gluck, & Kosslyn, 1984; Mervis & Rosch, 1981; Murphy & Smith, 1982; Rosch *et al.*, 1976) demonstrated that adults (i) usually produce basic-level names in free-naming tasks and (ii) are faster and more accurate at categorizing typical objects at the basic level relative to more general or more specific levels. This body of research seems to suggest that basic-level categories are acquired earlier and are more robustly represented in the semantic system than are more general or more specific representations.

Thus to the general question 'How does the semantic system know which categories should be stored in memory', categorization-based approaches face several further questions pertaining to acquisition and dissolution. Why are more general category distinctions acquired earlier by pre-verbal infants? Why are intermediate-level names learned earliest in development, and why are they so robust in healthy adults? Why are the more general distinctions also more robust to semantic impairment?

Domain-specific patterns of inductive projection

Finally, classic research in the study of children's inductive inferences has found that different kinds of properties tend to generalize from a reference item in quite different ways, at least in older children and adults (Carey, 1985; Gelman & Coley, 1990; Gelman & Wellman, 1991; Gelman & Williams, 1998; Jones, Smith, & Landau, 1991; Macario, 1991; Massey & Gelman, 1988). For instance, when told that a robin 'has an omentum inside', older children and adults generalize the property strongly to the class of birds, but if told that a robin 'likes to live in an omentum', they generalize the property much more narrowly – for instance, only to small birds that build nests in trees. One puzzle for categorization-based theories is how to explain these different patterns of inductive projection for different kinds of properties. If generalization is governed by an item's similarity to stored category representations, how can new learning about a given item generalize in quite different ways, depending upon the 'kind' of information? A further challenge is that patterns of inductive projection for a given property can also vary substantially depending upon the item in question. Thus, for instance, children weight shared shape more heavily than shared colour when generalizing new knowledge in the domain of toys, but show the reverse pattern in the domain of foods (Macario, 1991). Such patterns pose a chicken-and-egg problem for categorization-based theories: a new item cannot be categorized until one knows how to weight its properties, but because these weights depend upon the category, they cannot be determined until the item has been categorized (Gelman & Williams, 1998).

One response to these challenges, of course, is the further development of categorization-based approaches to semantic knowledge. The current volume attests that there are many interesting new developments in this vein. Our own work, however, is motivated by the observation that categorization is not the only efficient mechanism for storing and generalizing knowledge about the world. A tradition of work extending back to the distributed memory model of McClelland and Rumelhart (1986) and the semantic memory models of Rumelhart (Rumelhart, 1990; Rumelhart & Todd, 1993) and Hinton (1981, 1986) provides an alternative mechanism that, like categorization, is efficient in that it does not require addition of a new representational element for every new class or learning event, and that also promotes semantic generalization – all without requiring any internal process of categorization. The internal representations employed in our approach do not correspond to explicit, discrete representations of different classes of objects, and the processes that govern generalization of knowledge to new items do not involve the assignment of the item to one of a finite number of discrete equivalence classes. Consequently, questions about which categories are stored in memory, or how the system determines which category to use when generalizing, are moot in this framework. Furthermore, our framework suggests potential mechanisms that account for the variety of phenomena summarized above, and also provides some clues as to how the semantic system may be organized in the brain. Thus we believe that our approach – semantics without categorization – can resolve many of the puzzles faced by categorization-based approaches to semantic knowledge.

Assumptions of the approach

Our approach adopts the basic assumptions of the connectionist or parallel distributed processing (PDP) approach to cognition generally (Rumelhart, McClelland, & the PDP Research Group, 1986b).

(1) Cognitive phenomena arise from the propagation of activation amongst simple, neuron-like *processing units*, each of which adopts, at any point in time, an activation state analogous to the mean firing rate of a population of neurons. 'Input' units explicitly encode the state of the environment via direct 'sensory' inputs; 'output'

units explicitly encode representations of potential responses; and 'hidden' units mediate the flow of activation between inputs and outputs.

(2) Propagation of activation is constrained by weighted synapse-like *connections* between units. At any given time, the activation of a unit depends on (a) the states of the other units from which it received incoming connections, (b) the values of the weights on the incoming connections, and (c) a transfer function that is typically non-linear and differentiable.

(3) Input and output representations are directly assigned by the theorist and are intended to capture aspects of structure existing in the environment as encoded by sensory and motor systems. Internal representations of the environment take the form of distributed patterns of activation across subsets of hidden units, and information processing involves the updating of unit activations over time in response to some direct input from the environment, which has the effect of transforming input representations into internal representations that are useful for generating appropriate output patterns.

(4) The internal representations generated by inputs depend upon the architecture, that is, the gross pattern of connectivity among units in the network, as well as the particular values of the weights on these connections. Learning – defined as a change in processing prompted by previous experience – arises from experience-dependent changes to the values of the weights on these connections.

In addition to these general principles of parallel distributed processing, our approach adopts further assumptions specific to the domain of semantic cognition.

(1) The function of the semantic system is to generate context- and item-appropriate inferences about the properties of objects (either perceived directly or referred to in speech) that are not directly observed in the current situation.

(2) The semantic system adopts a 'convergent' architecture in which all different kinds of information, regardless of the semantic domain or the modality of input or output, are processed through the same set of units and weights. This architecture permits the model to exploit high-order patterns of covariation in the sets of visual, tactile, auditory, haptic, functional, and linguistic properties that characterize objects.

(3) Changes to weights in the system are generated by a process of predictive error-driven learning. The key idea is that, upon encountering a given object in a particular situation, the semantic system

generates implicit predictions about what will happen next, which are either confirmed or disconfirmed by subsequent experience. Learning involves adjustment of weights throughout the system so as to reduce the discrepancy between observed and expected outcomes over a broad set of experiences with different objects and situations.

(4) Weights are initially very small and random, so that all different kinds of inputs generate very similar internal representations.

(5) Acquisition of new semantic knowledge proceeds slowly and gradually. To promote generalization, our model assumes that semantic representations are distributed and overlapping. To prevent catastrophic interference in such a system, learning must proceed in a slow and interleaved manner, so that new learning does not 'overwrite' useful weight configurations built up over past experience.

(6) The semantic system interacts with a fast-learning episodic memory system (McClelland, McNaughton, & O'Reilly, 1995). Of course, human beings are capable of rapidly acquiring new facts about objects and generalizing them appropriately. Our theory proposes that this ability is supported by a fast-learning system in the medial temporal lobes, consistent with a long history of research in the neural basis of episodic memory (McClelland *et al.*, 1995). The fast-learning system employs sparse representations so that even very similar objects and events are represented with non-overlapping patterns. Consequently, the fast-learning system can learn rapidly without catastrophic interference, but cannot generalize well. We assume that the fast-learning MTL system interacts with the slow-learning semantic system to support the immediate generalization of newly learned information. Our model implements the slow-learning semantic system only.

(7) Internal representations are shaped by the situation or context. We assume that the internal representations that guide semantic cognition are shaped, not only by the current object of interest, but also by learned representations of the situation or task-context in which the item is experienced. So, for instance, the same object – say, a chicken – can evoke different internal representations, depending on whether the current situation demands retrieval of the item's name, function, expected behaviour, shape, and so on. In the models reported here, the *Relation* inputs provide information about the context that influences the *Hidden* unit activations directly; however, in other work, we have investigated models that must learn distributed internal representations that capture similarity structure across relation contexts (Rogers & McClelland, 2008).

These are the core assumptions adopted by our approach. In the next section we describe a simple feed-forward model that conforms to these assumptions, and illustrate how it offers leverage on the challenges faced by categorization-based approaches raised earlier.

A simple model implementation

The model architecture is based on that described by Rumelhart (1990) and shown in Figure 5.1. It consists of five layers of units connected in a feed-forward manner as indicated in the illustration. Units in the *Item* input layer directly encode localist representations of individual items that may be encountered in the environment. In the original model employed by Rumelhart, these included eight items taken from the classic hierarchical spreading-activation model of Collins and Quillian (1969). In the simulations we will discuss, we extended this simple corpus to include eight plants (four different flowers and four different trees) and 13 animals (four birds, four fish, and five mammals). Units in the *Relation* input layer directly encode localist representations of different relational contexts in which the various items might be encountered. The relation context constrains which of the item's various properties are immediately relevant to the current situation. For instance, the 'can' context indicates a situation in which the system must anticipate or report the item's expected behaviour; the 'has' context indicates a situation in which the system must anticipate or report its component parts; the 'is' situation indicates contexts in which the item's visual appearance is relevant; and so on. Of course, in the real world there exist many more potential items and potential contexts. In this model, the items and the relation contexts both represent a simple elaboration of the subordinate concepts and relation terms employed by Collins and Quillian (1969) and by Rumelhart (1990).

Whereas the activations of *Item* and *Relation* units are directly set by the environment, all other unit activations are determined by the inputs they receive from the units to which they are connected. The net input to a receiving unit is the inner product of the activations of the units from which it receives projections and the values of the weights on those projections, plus a fixed bias constant of −2 that serves to turn units off in the absence of input. Unit activations are set by passing the net input through a sigmoidal activation function:

$$a_i = 1/(1 + e^{-net_i}) \qquad (1)$$

where a_i is the activation of unit i and net_i is the net input to unit i. This function is bounded between 0 and 1 and increases smoothly and

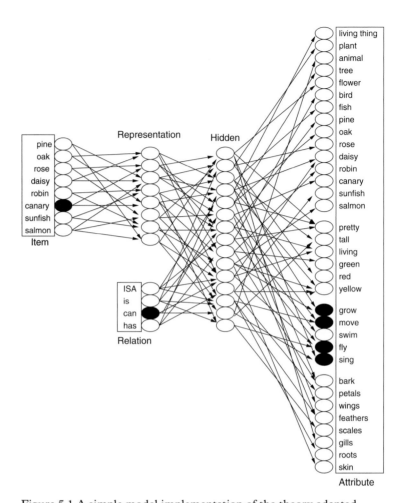

Figure 5.1 A simple model implementation of the theory adapted
from Rumelhart and Todd (1993), used to learn all the propositions
true of the specific concepts (pine, oak, etc.) in the classic
hierarchical spreading activation model of Collins and Quillian
(1969). Input units are shown on the left, and activation propagates
from the left to the right. Where connections are indicated, every
unit in the pool on the left is connected to every unit in the pool to
the right. Each unit in the *Item* layer corresponds to an individual
item in the environment. Each unit in the *Relation* layer represents
contextual constraints on the kind of information to be retrieved.
Thus, the input pair *canary can* corresponds to a situation in which
the network is shown a picture of a canary and asked what it can
do. The network is trained to turn on all those units that represent
correct completions of the input query. In the example shown, the
correct units to activate are *grow*, *move*, *fly*, and *sing*. All simulations
discussed were conducted with variants of this model.

monotonically, but non-linearly, in this range. The sigmoid activation function is important for learning in multi-layer networks because it is non-linear and differentiable, and so allows gradient-descent learning to form internal representations capable of supporting essentially any input-output mapping (Rumelhart, Hinton, & Williams, 1986a; Rumelhart *et al.*, 1995). It is extensively used in connectionist modelling, partly because it has a comparatively simple derivative for use in gradient-descent learning, and partly because it approximates the expected firing rate for a population of integrate-and-fire neurons given the same net input (Movellan & McClelland, 1993).

Units in the *Item* layer project forward to the layer labelled *Representation*. Activation of a single unit in the *Item* layer thus provokes a distributed pattern of activation across the *Representation* units. This pattern depends upon the values of the weights projecting from input to *Representation* layers, and these weights are shaped by learning and experience – so that the patterns produced in the trained model are distributed learned internal representations of the inputs.

These distributed representations in turn send connections forward to the *Hidden* layer, which also receives inputs from the *Relation* input units. The distributed patterns that arise here are therefore influenced by both the internal representation of the current item and by the current relation – so that the same item can give rise to quite different internal representations, depending upon the particular relation context in which it is encountered. Thus, whereas the *Representation* layer encodes a context-independent internal representation of the current item that is the same across all relation contexts, the *Hidden* layer encodes a context-dependent representation that varies across different contexts.

A final set of weights projects forward from the *Hidden* layer to the *Attribute* layer. Units in this layer correspond to explicit properties that can be attributed to objects, including their perceptual properties, their names and other verbal statements about them, their behaviours, or the motor responses one might generate when interacting with them. In general we view these as directly capturing properties that can in principle be directly experienced from the environment, though all the properties may not be present in any given situation. For instance, there is an *Attribute* unit corresponding to the property 'can move', which may be directly available from the environment whenever an item is observed to be moving, but which can also be inferred by the knowledgeable observer even if the item is currently stationary.

The model is 'queried' by presenting inputs to the *Item* and *Relation* units, corresponding to the observation of a given item in a particular situation, and computing activations for all units in a forward pass, based on the values of the interconnecting weights and the sigmoidal activation function of the units. When the configuration of weights is such that the model activates all and only the appropriate responses for all the various possible queries – for instance, when it activates the units 'grow', 'move', 'fly', and 'sing' for the canary – the model can be said to 'know' the domain.

To find such a configuration of weights, the model is trained with the backpropagation learning algorithm (Rumelhart *et al.*, 1986a). In backpropagation learning, the output generated by the network for a given input is compared to the desired output, and the difference is converted to a measure of error. The derivative of this error with respect to each weight in the network is then computed, and all weights are adjusted by a small amount in the direction that reduces the error for the given training item. In our simulations, we employed the sum-squared error: for each output unit, the squared difference between the target and the actual output is computed, and this is summed across output units to provide a total error signal to guide gradient-descent learning for each pattern. Though error propagation is thought by some to be a biologically implausible mechanism for learning, it is possible for error-like signals to be carried in unit activation states, and hence to drive learning, in networks with bidirectional connectivity (Hinton & McClelland, 1988; O'Reilly, 1996). We take backpropagation to be a simple way of approximating this kind of learning in a feed-forward network, and as a simple and direct instantiation of the general assumption stated earlier that learning takes place via a process of predictive error-driven learning.

In keeping with the assumption that learning in the semantic system is slow and gradual, the weight changes for any given event are small and incremental. As a consequence, changes that improve prediction for a single item-pair, but hurt performance for other item-relation pairs, are soon reversed by subsequent learning, whereas changes that improve prediction for many different item-relation pairs accrete over time, allowing the model to discover a set of weights that 'work' well for all of the items in the training environment simultaneously. This slow and gradual learning process thus provides a mechanism for developmental change in knowledge acquisition. The internal representations and outputs generated by any given input depend upon the configuration of weights at the time of testing. These weights – and consequently the internal representations and responses – evolve in interesting ways over the course of training with a fixed environment, providing a means of understanding patterns of behaviour in different age groups and across different tasks.

After training, the patterns that arise over the *Representation* layer capture similarity structure apparent in the output patterns describing each individual item. Items that have many properties in common across the different relation contexts are represented with similar patterns in this layer, whereas those with few properties in common are represented with quite different patterns. Because semantically related items tend to have many properties in common, these internal patterns come to capture the semantic or conceptual similarity relations among items – so they can serve as a basis for semantic generalization.

The *Representation* units, because they receive inputs from *Item* but not from *Relation*, must find representational structure that works well across all different relation contexts. This structure will, however, not be useful for governing generalization in every individual relation context, because different 'kinds' of properties can capture quite different similarity relations among the items. The representations that evolve on the *Hidden* units are constrained by input from the *Relation* units, and so, as elaborated below, can 'reshape' the deeper similarity structure encoded in the *Representation* units. Feed-forward networks with different internal architectures – for instance, networks that connect inputs directly to outputs, or connect via a single hidden layer – are not obliged to simultaneously find both context-neutral and context-specific levels of representation, and so do not show many of the interesting behaviours of the Rumelhart network (see Chapter 9 of Rogers & McClelland, 2004, for further discussion). The five-layer architecture of this model is therefore very important to its functioning.

Recommended implementation

Simulations reported in Rogers and McClelland (2004) were conducted using the pdp++ software package. The latest version of this software, now called Emergent, can be found on the Web at http://grey.colorado.edu/emergent/index.php/Main_Page. Use of this software requires, however, somewhat specialized knowledge and training. For those without this expertise, we therefore recommend implementing the model in Matlab using PDPTool.

PDPTool is a fully functional re-implementation, in Matlab, of the original software released with the PDP handbook (McClelland & Rumelhart, 1988), coupled with an intuitive graphical user interface. It takes the form of a library of object-types, functions, and graphical display objects that can be loaded in the Matlab environment or can be run as a stand-alone application. Currently the library includes objects and functions that implement feed-forward, simple recurrent, and fully recurrent backpropagation, interactive activation and competition networks, and competitive learning. The library, including instructions for installing the software, a user's manual, a short tutorial, and an online version of the PDP handbook, can be downloaded from the Web at www. stanford.edu/group/pdplab/resources.html. A brief article describing the aims and utility of PDPTool was published in the Academic Edition of the Matlab Digest in October 2009.

The PDPTool release comes with a set of pre-built network, template, and environment files, some for use with the handbook and tutorials, and others providing implementations of classic PDP networks from the literature. These example files include an implementation of the original eight-item Rumelhart network. A picture of the PDPTool display for this network is shown in Figure 5.2.

We further note that, in order to replicate simulation results reported in Rogers and McClelland (2004), including those reviewed below, the user will need to build and parameterize networks as described in the source material. The original work develops a series of increasingly elaborate model implementations. The architecture, training patterns, and model parameters for each implementation are, however, documented in the appendices to the book and these should be sufficient for the reader to replicate the original work in PDPTool.

Addressing the core phenomena

In this section we revisit the core phenomena motivating the approach and briefly indicate how the model addresses these.

Multiple category representation

In our framework, the internal representations that govern how knowledge generalizes are not discrete category representations, but are patterns of activation across continuous-valued units in the *Representation* and *Hidden* layers of the network. Each pattern can be viewed as a point in a continuous high-dimensional space, with each individual unit encoding one dimension. In this sense our model is similar to exemplar-based models, except that (i) the dimensions of the space do not correspond to interpretable semantic features and (ii) there is no 'database' of stored exemplars. Instead each exemplar leaves its 'trace' on the values of the interconnecting weights. Categories have no real existence in the model's internal representations, but correspond roughly to densely occupied regions of the representation space. For instance, the four individual fish are all represented as somewhat similar to one another, and as quite different from the birds and mammals, and so form a fairly tight cluster that corresponds roughly to the category *fish*. More general categories correspond to more

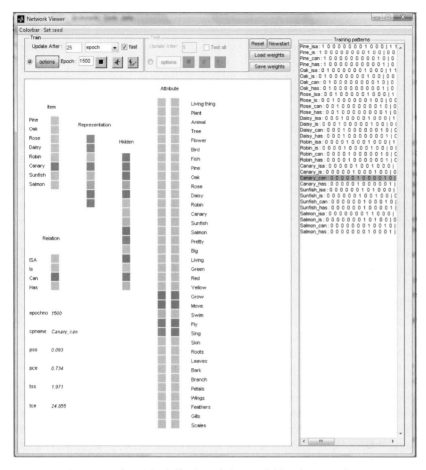

Figure 5.2 Graphical display of the model implemented as a part
of the standard release of the PDPTool Matlab application. Input
units appear on the left, and activation flows rightward toward
the attribute unit on the right. The rightmost column of units
displays the target values used to train the model. The figure shows
activation of unit states when the trained model is queried with the
input *canary can*. The model correctly activates all correct responses
in the output, including the attributes *grow*, *move*, *fly*, and *sing*.

inclusive clusters in the space, and more specific categories to less inclusive
clusters. Because there are no direct internal category representations in
the model, there is no problem of deciding which categories are 'stored' by
the semantic system, or of adjudicating which category structures should
be used to govern generalization for a given task.

Nevertheless, the model can categorize in its overt behaviour. Each output unit can be viewed as a probabilistic categorical response to a given input. For instance, the output unit corresponding to the name 'bird' can be viewed as indicating the likelihood that a given item belongs to the class of things that are labelled 'bird'. Such judgments depend upon the configuration of the weights that project from the *Hidden* units to the *bird* name unit, which will strongly activate this unit for a subvolume of the representation space defined by the units in this layer. Whenever the model's internal representation occupies a point in this subspace, it will generate the overt judgment that the represented item is called a 'bird'. The precise location and extent of this volume depends upon the values of the weights projecting from *Hidden* to *Output* layers, which are acquired through the learning rule. Thus the model, like people, can generate explicit category judgments in its outputs, but it does not employ an internal categorization process to do so. It is also the case that explicit categorization labels may or may not align well with the organization of the model's internal representations. Though labels like 'salmon', 'fish', and 'animal' may align well with clusters at different levels of granularity, nothing prevents the model from learning other labels that cross-cut this structure. For instance, a name like 'pet' might apply to the canary, dog, and cat, but not to the other birds or mammals in the corpus.

Category coherence

Because the model does not store overt category representations, there is no question about why some categories (like 'dog') are stored and others (like 'blue-and-orange things') are not. Beyond this, however, the model suggests one reason why some groupings of items seem to provide good candidates for naming and for inductive generalization whereas others do not. Specifically, the model's internal representations are strongly shaped by the covariance structure of the properties of objects in the environment. Sets of items that tend to share many properties in common with one another are represented as quite similar to one another. Consequently, learning about the properties of one such item tends to generalize strongly to all other similarly represented items. This in turn means that the properties common to most items within such a cluster are learned very rapidly, whereas the properties that individuate items within a cluster will be somewhat more difficult to learn. On this view, coherent categories – sets of items that provide good vehicles for induction and are likely to receive names in the language – are those groups of items sharing properties that themselves reliably covary with many other properties. We note that this conception of coherence does not necessarily just reflect raw overall similarity amongst items: sets of items that share many properties will not be represented as similar if the properties they happen to share do not themselves covary strongly with many other properties in the set (see Chapter 3 of Rogers & McClelland, 2004).

Primacy of superordinate structure in development and dementia

Although the fully trained model finds internal representations that capture the similarity structure of the training patterns, the network does not discover this organization of internal representations all at once. Instead, the representations undergo a progressive non-linear process of differentiation – first discriminating items from grossly different conceptual domains (e.g., plants and animals) without any apparent fine-grained structure; then capturing intermediate distinctions (e.g., birds versus fish) without further subordinate organization; and finally pulling apart individual items. Figure 5.3 shows a multidimensional scaling diagram of the model's internal representations taken at evenly spaced points throughout training. Each line shows the trajectory of a single item's representation throughout learning. Initially, all items are represented as similar to one another, because the network is initialized with small, random values. Very quickly, however, the plants become differentiated from the animals, while within these coarse categories we see very little differentiation. Some time later, the network begins to differentiate more intermediate clusters (birds and fish, flowers and trees) but with little differentiation of the individual items. In the last phase, the individual items begin to pull apart from one another. A full explanation of the reasons for this phenomenon is beyond the scope of this chapter but was provided in Chapter 2 of Rogers and McClelland (2004). This progressive coarse-to-fine discrimination of internal representations mirrors the pattern of conceptual development observed in carefully controlled studies of pre-verbal infants in the work of Mandler (2000), Pauen (2002b) and others.

Figure 5.3 suggests why more general or superordinate-level information tends to be more robust in progressive semantic syndromes like semantic dementia. In its fully trained state, the network has learned to map out from its internal representations (coded in *Representation* and *Hidden* layers) to explicit representations of overt responses. For properties that are only true of very specific concepts – for instance, the name 'canary', or the property 'can sing' (true only of the canary) – the network has learned to activate the corresponding unit only from the internal state corresponding to the represented item. Thus there is a relatively narrow subvolume of the representation state space from

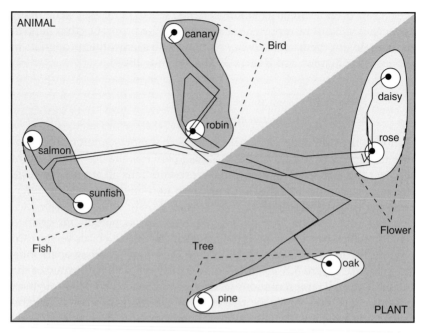

Figure 5.3 Progressive differentiation of concepts and preservation of superordinate information in the model. The labelled endpoints show a multidimensional scaling diagram of the model's internal representations of eight items after it has correctly learned all properties of all items. The lines show a multidimensional scaling of the trajectory of these representations over the course of learning. Though representations begin very similar to one another, animals and plants quickly differentiate from one another, followed by more intermediate categories, and finally the individual items are pulled apart. This 'coarse-to-fine' differentiation of concepts mirrors patterns of conceptual differentiation observed in child development. The shading provides a conceptual illustration of the reason why superordinate information tends to be preserved: properties shared by animals, for instance, are true of all birds and fish, and so tend to be activated by points within a broad region of the representation space (light grey shading in upper-left). Properties shared only by the birds, in contrast, are activated by points in a comparatively narrower volume of the space (dark shading around canary and robin representations), whereas properties true of individual items are only activated for a very narrow volume of space (the white 'bubbles' around each individual item representation).

which the network will activate the units corresponding to very specific properties. For properties that characterize more general classes – properties like has wings (true of all birds) or can move (true of all animals) – the network has learned to activate the corresponding output units for a wider set of items, all of which are represented as somewhat similar to one another. The consequence is that, for these items, there is a broader subvolume of the representation state space from which the model has learned to generate the corresponding response. When the system degrades with disease, the internal representations generated by a given input become distorted – some of the connections that encode the representation are no longer present. For very specific properties, small distortions can move the representation out of the relatively narrow subvolume from which the model can generate the appropriate response. For more general properties, small distortions to the correct pattern will not move the representation out of this subvolume, and the model will continue to generate the appropriate response. Thus, the more general the category to which the property applies, the more robust knowledge of the property will be to semantic impairment.

The left panel of Figure 5.4 shows the ability of the network to activate subordinate, basic, and superordinate-level names for items in its environment as the patterns of activation in the *Representation* layer are subject to increasing amounts of noise (simulating the degradation of semantic representations arising from progressive brain damage). Whereas basic-level names are initially the most strongly active labels, activation of these units declines more sharply than the activation of the more superordinate name units, producing a 'cross-over' effect where general-level responses are more active than basic-level responses when the network is subject to moderate to severe semantic impairment. The right side of Figure 5.4 shows analogous data from patients with semantic dementia performing a category-verification task (Rogers & Patterson, 2007).

Primacy of the basic level in lexical acquisition and adult categorization and naming

If more general concepts are the first to be differentiated in acquisition and are the most robust to semantic impairment, why do categories at the more intermediate or 'basic' level appear to be 'privileged' in lexical acquisition and in adult categorization? Our approach suggests an answer to this seeming paradox, which stems from the observation that the coarse-to-fine differentiation of concepts is observed fairly early in development, before children have begun to speak. By the time children have begun to name objects, they are also able to differentiate concepts at

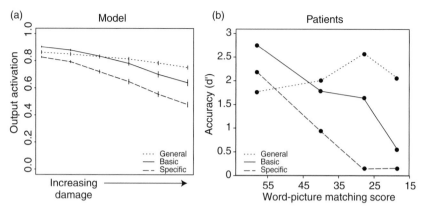

Figure 5.4 Left: activation of correct name units for names at
general (e.g. 'animal'), basic (e.g. 'fish'), and specific (e.g. 'salmon')
levels in a variant of the model trained with 21 items, when the
model's internal representations are subject to increasing amounts
of noise. Whereas the basic-level name is initially the most active
unit, this activation declines more rapidly than the more general
name unit, so that the network performs better when naming at
more general levels. Right: smoothed data from eight patients with
SD performing a category-verification task in which they must
decide whether a picture matches a name at either the general,
basic, or specific level. Like the model, performance is initially
better for basic-level names, but declines with increasing semantic
impairment, so that the more impaired patients show an advantage
for categorizing at the most general level. (Panels reprinted with
permission from Rogers and McClelland (2004), Figure 5.4, p. 196,
and from Rogers and Patterson (2007), Figure 2, p. 455.)

the basic level (Mandler, 2000; Mandler & Bauer, 1988; Pauen, 2002a,
2002b). Once the semantic system has begun to differentiate basic clusters within some more general domain, it is actually at a disadvantage in
learning superordinate relative to basic-level names.

To see this, consider teaching the Rumelhart model to name at a point
in its development such that the birds have been differentiated from
the fish, but the individual birds and fish are still quite similar to one
another. For each item, there are three different names that might be
appropriate – for instance, for the canary, the network could name it as
an 'animal', a 'bird', or a 'canary'. Suppose further that all of the different
names occurred equally frequently in the environment – say, four times
per epoch of training. Which names would the network learn first?

First consider the name 'animal'. When the model learns that the
canary is an animal, this response will tend to generalize strongly to

the robin (which is represented as quite similar) but less strongly to the salmon and the sunfish (which are now somewhat distinct). Similarly when the network learns that the salmon is an animal, this response will generalize strongly to the sunfish but less strongly to the canary. So each time the name appears for one of the four animals, only half of the items that share the name benefit strongly from the learning.

When learning to call the canary a 'bird', the same pattern is observed: the response generalizes strongly to the robin and not to either of the fish. This time, however, the name bird is only *ever* applied to one of the two individual birds. If it occurs four times per epoch, then it occurs twice with the canary and twice with the robin. So *every* time the name appears it benefits *all* of the items to which it applies. On these grounds, this intermediate-level name should be learned more rapidly than the more general name.

What about specific names? In our scenario, the word 'canary' appears four times per epoch, always with the *canary* item. As before, this response will have a strong tendency to generalize to the *robin*. In this case, however, the generalization is detrimental – the name 'canary' does not apply to the robin. So, when the model encounters the robin, it must reverse the weight changes, to turn off the name unit corresponding to 'canary' and turn on the unit corresponding to 'robin'. This similarity-based interference will prevent the network from rapidly learning this more specific name. Only when the robin and canary are sufficiently differentiated from one another will the system easily learn to generate different subordinate names for them.

In other words, when word-frequency is controlled, then at any given point in development, the network will best be able to learn those words that demarcate items within a relatively tight cluster. More general names will be learned more slowly because they apply to items that are dispersed in the space and so do not promote strong cross-item generalization; more specific names will be learned more slowly because they apply to items with similar representations and so suffer from strong cross-item interference. Since children learn to name only after they have differentiated intermediate concepts, they are most likely to learn intermediate-level names. And because basic-level clusters continue to be 'tight' and well separated into adulthood, adults are likely to show similar advantages in basic-level categorization and naming.

Basic-level advantages arise in our model for largely the same reasons proposed by Rosch and others (Murphy & Brownell, 1985; Rosch et al., 1976; Tanaka & Taylor, 1991). A key difference is that, on the PDP theory, the representational similarity structure that promotes basic-level advantages is not present initially, but only emerges after coarser conceptual distinctions have been acquired. Thus the primacy of the basic level in lexical acquisition and adult categorization co-exists with the coarse-to-fine differentiation of concepts in pre-verbal infants and the preservation of general-level information in semantic impairment. For instance, in the simulation results shown in the left panel of Figure 5.4, the undamaged model activates basic-level names more strongly than either superordinate or subordinate names – but nevertheless, superordinate-level information is more robust when the network is damaged and, though not shown here, the internal representations still differentiate in a coarse-to-fine manner in the same simulation (Rogers & McClelland, 2004).

Domain-specific patterns of inductive projection

Finally, the basic architecture of the network in Figure 5.1 suggests one answer to the puzzle of domain-specific inductive projection. Recall that, in classic studies of inductive projection – where children are taught a new property of a familiar item, and are then asked what other objects likely share the property – the pattern of inductive projection can differ depending upon the kind of property in question. For instance, if the property is understood to be a biological trait, it may generalize to one subset of items, but if it is understood to be a physical trait, it may generalize to a very different subset (Carey, 1985; Gelman & Markman, 1986). If categorization is the process that supports inductive projection, then how can new learning about a given item show very different patterns of generalization?

In our framework, the internal representations that constrain generalization of new learning are shaped, not only by the item in question, but also by information about the current task context. Specifically, the patterns of activation arising across *Hidden* units in the model depend partly upon inputs from the *Representation* units, but also on inputs from the *Context* units. Weights projecting out from the *Relation* units, like the weights projecting out from the *Item* units, are shaped by learning – so the network must learn how to treat items in different relation contexts, just as it learns how to represent the items themselves.

A natural consequence of this architecture is that, when the properties associated with two different relations capture quite different aspects of similarity among a set of items, then the similarity structure arising across *Hidden* units can be quite different, depending on the relation context. To see this, consider Figure 5.5, which shows a multi-dimensional scaling of the model's internal representations of 16 different items in different contexts. The middle plot shows the similarity of

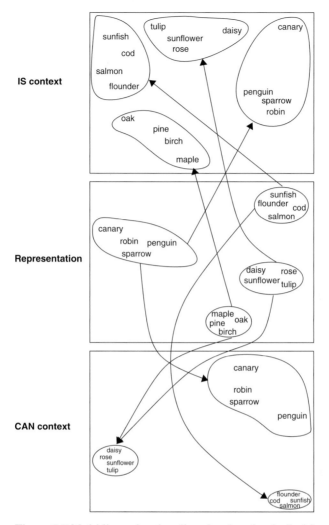

Figure 5.5 Multidimensional scaling showing the similarities
represented by the model for objects in different relation contexts.
The middle plot shows the similarities among object representations
in the *Representation* layer. The top graph shows the similarities
among the same objects in the *Hidden* layer, when the *is* relation unit
is activated. The bottom graph shows the similarities across these
same units when the *can* relation unit is activated. The *is* relation
context exaggerates differences among related objects; for example,
relative to the similarities in the *Representation* layer, the trees are
fairly well spread out in the *is* context. Moreover, similarities in object
appearances are preserved in these representations; for example, the
canary is as close to the flowers as to the other birds in the *is* context,
by virtue of being pretty. By contrast, the *can* context collapses
differences among the plants, because in the network's world, all
plants can do only one thing: grow.

the 16 items as encoded in the *Representation* layer of a trained model. The top panel shows the same 16 items as encoded by the *Hidden* layer when the *is* context is activated in the input, whereas the bottom panel shows *Hidden* layer patterns for these items when the *can* context is activated in the input. In the network's environment, all of the plants can do only one thing: grow. In the *can* context, then, the model has learned to represent all eight plants as nearly identical to one another. The birds and the fish, because they can do different things, remain well differentiated from one another. In the *is* context, in contrast, all of the various items have quite different and somewhat random properties (mostly colours and idiosyncratic visual traits; note that the *is* relation is separate from the class inclusion relation denoted by *isa* in both our model and Collins and Quillian's original work). Consequently the 16 individual items are all fairly well differentiated from one another, although the deeper similarity structure present in the base representation can still be observed (for instance, the fish are all more similar to one another than they are to the birds).

It seems that the inputs from the *Relation* layer can 're-shape' the base similarity structure encoded by *Representation* units, to better capture structure suited to the context at hand. Because this is so, the model will show quite different patterns of inductive projection for the exact same reference item, depending upon the relation context in which the property is learned. For instance, Figure 5.6 shows what happens when the model is taught a new fact about the maple tree: that it *can queem*, *has a queem*, or *is queem*. Depending upon the relation, the model generalizes this new fact in quite different ways: to all of the plants if 'queem' is a kind of behaviour (the *can* context), to just the trees if 'queem' is a part (the *has* context), and to an idiosyncratic set of items if 'queem' is a superficial appearance property (the *is* context).

In summary, an important aspect of our theory is the idea that internal semantic representations capture knowledge, not just about the item in question, but also about the context in which the task is being performed. This context can capture information about the particular kind of information that the system is being asked to retrieve – consequently the kinds of generalization behaviours exhibited by the system can vary depending upon this information.

Relation to other approaches

Our theory addresses a series of empirical and theoretical issues that have proven challenging for some categorization-based approaches. We are not aware of other computational approaches which have tackled

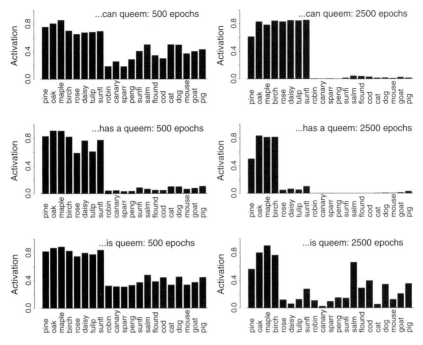

Figure 5.6 Barplot showing activation of the nonsense property 'queem' in an extended version of the model when the network is queried with various inputs, after it has learned that the maple 'can queem', 'has a queem', or 'is queem'. If the network learns the new property after 500 epochs of training, the property generalizes across the entire superordinate category, regardless of the relation context. When the network is taught the novel property after 2500 epochs of training, it shows different patterns of generalization depending on whether 'queem' is understood to be a behaviour, a part, or a physical attribute.

precisely the same set of motivating phenomena as has our work. In particular, our focus on core issues in child development and in neuropsychology makes it difficult to compare our approach to others in this volume, since these approaches are, by and large, targeted at explaining detailed observations about adult categorization behaviour, mostly with reference to new category-learning experiments. With regard to the nature of semantic representations and the mechanisms that support semantic generalization, however, our approach does share some commonalities and some differences with other computational approaches to categorization.

Exemplar theories/nonparametric density estimation

Our framework shares some characteristics with exemplar-based approaches to categorization (Kruschke, 1992; Medin & Schaffer, 1978; Nosofsky, 1986), some of which may be viewed as similar in many ways to nonparametric density estimation (Griffiths *et al.*, 2008). In these approaches, as in our work, categorization behaviour is viewed, not as reflecting the internal mechanism that governs knowledge generalization, but as a probabilistic response generated from a continuous internal representation space. The approaches differ in their conception of the nature of the underlying representations and the processes that govern generalization.

In exemplar theories, the elements are a vast set of stored discrete representations of previous learning events, each typically construed as a point in a high-dimensional feature space. Learning involves adding new representations to this set with each learning episode. From these representations, a continuous probability density function is estimated for the full space, and generalization is then governed by maximum likelihood estimates given the observed features of a new item and the estimated probability density. In our theory, the dimensions of the representation space do not correspond to interpretable semantic features, nothing is added with new learning, and there is no store of discrete events in memory. Instead what is 'stored' is a single matrix of connection weights, and each learning event leaves a 'trace' through its influence on the values of these weights.

Exemplar theories have mainly focused on learning to assign items to a single set of mutually exclusive categories, and it is not clear to what extent the best known theories (such as Nosofsky's generalized context model, Chapter 2, or Kruschke's ALCOVE model, Chapter 6) fare when required to learn assignment of items to multiple different categorization schemes (Palmeri, 1999; Verheyen *et al.*, 2008). Our approach assumes that there is no single categorization scheme that is always employed for all items, but that the semantic system is capable of categorizing items according to a variety of different schemes.

Finally, some exemplar theories have focused on understanding how people weight the different properties of objects when categorizing them (Kruschke, 1992; Nosofsky, 1986). The PDP theory also suggests a mechanism for feature-weighting – specifically, it suggests that sets of properties that covary coherently with many other properties will receive greater weight in determining an item's internal representation, and consequently will strongly shape the similarity structure that governs generalization in the system. Understanding the similarities and differences between this approach to feature weighting and that offered by other computational approaches remains a goal for future research.

Prototype theories/parametric density estimation

In some respects, our approach may seem to be more similar to parametric approaches to density estimation (Ashby & Alfonso-Reese, 1995). In these approaches, the probability density in some feature space is computed, not by retaining a full record of all previous events, but by fitting some set of n parameterizable distributions to the observed data. For instance, such an approach might assume that each cluster in a multi-dimensional feature space has been generated from some Gaussian distribution, that the probability distribution for the full space can be approximated by a mixture of such Gaussians, and that 'categories' correspond either to individual Gaussians or to some set of Gaussians in the mixture. On this view, learning serves to help determine how many 'clusters' (Gaussians) there are, and what the parameters of the distributions are (i.e., the location of their modes in the feature space, the height of the mode and the variance of the distribution). Prototype theories (Chapter 3) can be viewed as a special case of parametric density estimation in which there exists one distribution ('prototype') for each known category.

Our approach is similar to parametric density estimation in that knowledge is stored in a fixed set of parameterizable elements – namely the weights – so that learning does not 'add' new elements into a memory store. We believe this analogy to be somewhat misleading, however, because in most parametric approaches to density estimation, the basic representational elements are the distributions that need to be parameterized. That is, there is typically a one-to-one or a many-to-one correspondence between the individual distributions and the categories stored in memory. This is not the case in the PDP model – there is no sense in which either the weights or units in our model correspond directly to some explicit category. The internal representations generated for various inputs always depend on the full set of weights, and each weight contributes to the representation of all categories and items.

Structured probabilistic models

Under structured probabilistic approaches (Kemp & Tenenbaum, 2008; Tenenbaum & Griffiths, 2001; Tenenbaum, Griffiths, & Kemp, 2006), semantic cognition is viewed as the inductive problem of deciding which of a vast number of conceptual structures is most likely to have generated the observed properties of a set of items in a domain. The relationship between such approaches and the PDP approach is the subject of much current debate beyond the scope of this chapter; the interested reader can find recent commentary in (Griffiths *et al.*, 2010; McClelland *et al.*, 2010; Rogers & McClelland, 2008). Here we simply wish to note some key commonalities and differences between the approaches.

Briefly, both views emphasize that the function of the semantic system is to promote inductive inference; both propose that inductive inference is probabilistic; and both situate the problem of learning within an optimization framework. The key differences lie in basic assumptions about representation and mechanism. Structured probabilistic approaches assume that the semantic system approximates optimal probabilistic inference – so that any method and any representational assumption that allows the theorist to compute the true probability distribution over some set of outcomes may be employed to understand how the system is working. In practice the representations often involve discrete category representations embedded in graph structures, with probability distributions computed over all possible categories and all possible graphs. The approach also requires specification of initial biases for all categories and graph structures, and so presupposes considerable initial knowledge. Learning involves using observed data to select the most probable set of categories and graph structures governing some behaviour, and then updating prior beliefs about the likelihood of these different structures.

On the PDP approach, representations must take the form of distributed patterns of activity across processing units – hence there is no analogy to the graphical structures often employed in structured probabilistic approaches. Also, there are no discrete internal category representations, no explicit 'hypotheses' about categories and structures, and no explicit biases attached to different hypotheses and category structures. The internal representations and outputs generated by objects and relations depend upon the particular configuration of weights instantiated in the network at a given point in time. This configuration itself can be viewed as a point in a fully continuous multidimensional weight space. The weight space determines the full set of input-output mappings that can be expressed by the network, and in this sense is similar to the 'hypothesis space' (the set of all possible concepts and graph structures) presupposed by the probabilistic framework. There are, however, several key differences. First, unlike the structured probabilistic approach, there is no enumerated set of possible structure types (or constructors for such structure types). Second, there is never a sense of comparative evaluation of alternative possible structure types – at any given point in time, the system has a single configuration of weights, capturing a single input-output mapping. Third, learning occurs quite differently in the connectionist framework: each new experience results in a slight adjustment of the connection weights, gradually leading, through an ongoing developmental process, to elaboration of a structured knowledge representation. While the structured probabilistic approach can be applied in such an 'on-line' method, it is typical to view each new experience as adding to the corpus of stored experiences from which the best possible structure will be inferred using arbitrary computational methods. Thus, the connectionist framework imposes strong constraints on the learning process not considered within structured probabilistic approaches.

Conclusion

In summary, we believe it is fruitful to investigate approaches to semantic cognition that do not invoke an internal categorization mechanism as the primary vehicle for knowledge storage and generalization. The PDP approach to semantic cognition provides an alternative set of mechanisms for efficient storage and generalization of semantic information. Although our framework shares some characteristics with other computational approaches, it also differs in several key respects. In particular, the applicability of the framework to phenomena in cognitive development and disordered semantic cognition allows the theory to address a comparatively broad range of empirical findings.

REFERENCES

Anderson, J.R. (1991). The adaptive nature of human categorization. *Psychological Review*, **98** (3), 409–426.

Ashby, F.G., & Alfonso-Reese, L.A. (1995). Categorization as probability density estimation. *Journal of Mathematical Psychology*, **39** (2), 216–233.

Barsalou, L. (1993). Flexibility, structure, and linguistic vagary in concepts: manifestations of a compositional system of perceptual symbols. In A.F. Collins, S.E. Gathercole, M.A. Conway, & P.E. Morris (eds.), *Theories of Memory*. Hillsdale, NJ: Lawrence Erlbaum Associates.

Brown, R. (1958). How shall a thing be called? *Psychological Review*, **65**, 14–21.

Carey, S. (1985). *Conceptual Change in Childhood*. Cambridge, MA: MIT Press.

Collins, A.M., & Loftus, E.F. (1975). A spreading-activation theory of semantic processing. *Psychological Review*, **82**, 407–428.

Collins, A.M., & Quillian, M.R. (1969). Retrieval time from semantic memory. *Journal of Verbal Learning and Verbal Behavior*, **8**, 240–247.

Gelman, R., & Williams, E.M. (1998). Enabling constraints for cognitive development and learning: a domain-specific epigenetic theory. In W. Damon (ed.), *Handbook of Child Psychology, Vol. II: Cognition, Perception and Development* (pp. 575–630). New York: John Wiley and Sons.

Gelman, S., & Coley, J.D. (1990). The importance of knowing a dodo is a bird: categories and inferences in 2-year-old children. *Developmental Psychology*, **26**, 796–804.

Gelman, S.A., & Markman, E.M. (1986). Categories and induction in young children. *Cognition*, **23**, 183–209.

Gelman, S.A., & Wellman, H.M. (1991). Insides and essences: early understandings of the nonobvious. *Cognition*, **38**, 213–244.

Griffiths, T.L., Chater, N., Kemp, C., Perfors, A., & Tenenbaum, J.B. (2010). Probabilistic models of cognition: exploring representations and inductive biases. *Trends in Cognitive Sciences*, **14** (8), 357–364.

Griffiths, T.L., Sanborn, A.N., Canini, D.J., & Navarro, D.J. (2008). Categorization as nonparametric Bayesian density estimation. In N. Chater & M. Oaksford (eds.), *The Probabilistic Mind: Prospects for a Bayesian Cognitive Science*. Oxford: Oxford University Press.

Hinton, G.E. (1981). Implementing semantic networks in parallel hardware. In G.E. Hinton & J.A. Anderson (eds.), *Parallel Models of Associative Memory* (pp. 161–187). Hillsdale, NJ: Erlbaum.

(1986). Learning distributed representations of concepts. In *Proceedings of the Cognitive Science Society* (pp. 1–12). Hillsdale, NJ: LEA.

Hinton, G.E., & McClelland, J.L. (1988). Learning representations by recirculation. In D.Z. Anderson (ed.), *Neural Information Processing Systems* (pp. 358–366). New York: American Institute of Physics.

Jolicoeur, P., Gluck, M., & Kosslyn, S.M. (1984). Pictures and names: making the connection. *Cognitive Psychology*, **19**, 31–53.

Jones, S.S., Smith, L.B., & Landau, B. (1991). Object properties and knowledge in early lexical learning. *Child Development*, **62** (3), 499–516.

Keil, F. (1979). *Semantic and Conceptual Development: an Ontological Perspective*. Cambridge, MA: Harvard University Press.

Kemp, C., & Tenenbaum, J.B. (2008). The discovery of structural form. *Proceedings of the National Academy of Sciences*, **105** (31), 10687–10692.

Kruschke, J.K. (1992). ALCOVE: an exemplar-based connectionist model of category learning. *Psychological Review*, **99** (1), 22–44.

Love, B.C., Medin, D.L., & Gureckis, T.M. (2004). SUSTAIN: a network model of category learning. *Psychological Review*, **111** (2), 3009–3332.

Macario, J.F. (1991). Young children's use of color in classification: foods and canonically colored objects. *Cognitive Development*, **6**, 17–46.

Mandler, J.M. (2000). Perceptual and conceptual processes in infancy. *Journal of Cognition and Development*, **1**, 3–36.

Mandler, J.M., & Bauer, P.J. (1988). The cradle of categorization: is the basic level basic? *Cognitive Development*, **3**, 247–264.

Mandler, J.M., & McDonough, L. (1996). Drinking and driving don't mix: inductive generalization in infancy. *Cognition*, **59**, 307–355.

Massey, C.M., & Gelman, R. (1988). Preschooler's ability to decide whether a photographed unfamiliar object can move by itself. *Developmental Psychology*, **24** (3), 307–317.

McClelland, J.L., Botvinick, M.B., Noelle, D., Plaut, D.C., Rogers, T.T., Seidenberg, M., & Smith, L. (2010). Letting structure emerge: connectionist

and dynamical systems approaches to cognition. *Trends in Cognitive Sciences*, **14** (8), 348–356.

McClelland, J.L., McNaughton, B.L., & O'Reilly, R.C. (1995). Why there are complementary learning-systems in the hippocampus and neocortex – insights from the successes and failures of connectionist models of learning and memory. *Psychological Review*, **102** (3), 419–457.

McClelland, J.L., & Rumelhart, D.E. (1986). A distributed model of human learning and memory. In J.L. McClelland, D.E. Rumelhart & the PDP Research Group (eds.), *Parallel Distributed Processing: Explorations in the Microstructure of Cognition* (Vol. 2, pp. 170–215). Cambridge, MA: MIT Press.

(1988). *Explorations in Parallel Distributed Processing: A Handbook of Models, Programs, and Exercises*. Cambridge, MA: MIT Press.

Medin, D.L., & Schaffer, M.M. (1978). Context theory of classification learning. *Psychological Review*, **85**, 207–238.

Mervis, C.B. (1987). Child basic object categories and early lexical development. In U. Neisser (ed.), *Concepts and Conceptual Development: Ecological and Intellectual Factors in Categorization*. Cambridge: Cambridge University Press.

Mervis, C.A., & Crisafi, M.A. (1982). Order of acquisition of subordinate-, basic-, and superordinate-level categories. *Child Development*, **53** (1), 258–266.

Mervis, C.B., & Rosch, E. (1981). Categorization of natural objects. *Annual Review of Psychology*, **32**, 89–115.

Movellan, J.R., & McClelland, J.L. (1993). Learning continuous probability distributions with symmetric diffusion networks. *Cognitive Science*, **17**, 463–496.

Murphy, G.L., & Brownell, H.H. (1985). Category differentiation in object recognition: typicality constraints on the basic category advantage. *Journal of Experimental Psychology: Learning, Memory, and Cognition*, **11** (1), 70–84.

Murphy, G.L., & Lassaline, M.E. (1997). Hierarchical structure in concepts and the basic level of categorization. In K. Lamberts & D. Shanks (eds.), *Knowledge, Concepts and Categories* (pp. 93–131). Hove: Psychology Press.

Murphy, G.L., & Medin, D.L. (1985). The role of theories in conceptual coherence. *Psychological Review*, **92**, 289–316.

Murphy, G.L., & Smith, E.E. (1982). Basic level superiority in picture categorization. *Journal of Verbal Learning and Verbal Behavior*, **21**, 1–20.

Nosofsky, R. (1984). Choice, similarity, and the context theory of classification. *Journal of Experimental Psychology: Learning, Memory, and Cognition*, **10**, 104–110.

Nosofsky, R.M. (1986). Attention, similarity and the identification-categorization relationship. *Journal of Experimental Psychology: Learning, Memory, and Cognition*, **115** (1), 39–57.

O'Reilly, R.C. (1996). Biologically plausible error-driven learning using local activation differences: the generalized recirculation algorithm. *Neural Computation*, **8**, 895–938.

Palmeri, T.J. (1999). Learning categories at different hierarchical levels: a comparison of category learning models. *Psychonomic Bulletin & Review*, **6**, 495–503.

Patterson, K., & Hodges, J. (2000). Semantic dementia: one window on the structure and organisation of semantic memory. In J. Cermak (ed.), *Handbook of Neuropsychology, Vol. 2: Memory and its Disorders* (pp. 313–333). Amsterdam: Elsevier Science.

Patterson, K., Nestor, P.J., & Rogers, T. (2007). Where do you know what you know? The representation of semantic knowledge in the human brain. *Nature Reviews Neuroscience*, **8**, 976–987.

Pauen, S. (2002a). Evidence for knowledge-based category discrimination in infancy. *Child Development*, **73** (4), 1016–1033.

(2002b). The global-to-basic shift in infants' categorical thinking: first evidence from a longitudinal study. *International Journal of Behavioural Development*, **26** (6), 492–499.

Pothos, E.M., & Chater, N. (2002). A simplicity principle in unsupervised human categorization. *Cognitive Science*, **26**, 303–343.

Rogers, T.T., Lambon Ralph, M.A., Garrard, P., Bozeat, S., McClelland, J.L., Hodges, J.R., *et al.* (2004). The structure and deterioration of semantic memory: a computational and neuropsychological investigation. *Psychological Review*, **111** (1), 205–235.

Rogers, T.T., & McClelland, J.L. (2004). *Semantic Cognition: A Parallel Distributed Processing Approach*. Cambridge, MA: MIT Press.

(2008). A simple model from a powerful framework that spans levels of analysis. *Behavioral and Brain Sciences*, **31**, 729–749.

Rogers, T.T., & Patterson, K. (2007). Object categorization: reversals and explanations of the basic-level advantage. *Journal of Experimental Psychology: General*, **136** (3), 451–469.

Rosch, E. (1978). Principles of categorization. In E. Rosch & B. Lloyd (eds.), *Cognition and Categorization*. Hillsdale, NJ: Lawrence Erlbaum Associates.

Rosch, E., Mervis, C.B., Gray, W., Johnson, D., & Boyes-Braem, P. (1976). Basic objects in natural categories. *Cognitive Psychology*, **8**, 382–439.

Rumelhart, D.E. (1990). Brain style computation: learning and generalization. In S.F. Zornetzer, J.C. Davis, & C. Lau (eds.), *An Introduction to Neural and Electronic Networks* (pp. 405–420). San Diego, CA: Academic Press.

Rumelhart, D.E., Durbin, R., Golden, R., & Chauvin, Y. (1995). Back-propagation: the basic theory. In Y. Chauvin & D.E. Rumelhart (eds.), *Back-Propagation: Theory, Architectures, and Applications* (pp. 1–34). Hillsdale, NJ: Erlbaum.

Rumelhart, D.E., Hinton, G.E., & Williams, R.J. (1986a). Learning representations by back-propagating errors. *Nature*, **323** (9), 533–536.

Rumelhart, D.E., McClelland, J.L., & the PDP Research Group (1986b). *Parallel Distributed Processing: Explorations in the Microstructure of Cognition, Vol. I: Foundations & Vol. II: Psychological and Biological Models*. Cambridge, MA: MIT Press.

Rumelhart, D.E., & Todd, P.M. (1993). Learning and connectionist representations. In D.E. Meyer & S. Kornblum (eds.), *Attention and Performance*

XIV: Synergies in Experimental Psychology, Artificial Intelligence, and Cognitive Neuroscience (pp. 3–30). Cambridge, MA: MIT Press.

Tanaka, J., & Taylor, M. (1991). Object categories and expertise: is the basic level in the eye of the beholder? *Cognitive Psychology*, **23**, 457–482.

Tenenbaum, J.B., & Griffiths, T.L. (2001). Generalization, similarity, and Bayesian inference. *Behavioral and Brain Sciences*, **24**, 629–640.

Tenenbaum, J.B., Griffiths, T.L., & Kemp, C. (2006). Theory-based Bayesian models of inductive learning and reasoning. *Trends in Cognitive Sciences*, **10** (7), 309–318.

Verheyen, S., Ameel, E., Rogers, T.T., & Storms, G. (2008). *Learning a hierarchical organization of categories.* Paper presented at the Proceedings of the Cognitive Science Society, Amsterdam, the Netherlands.

6   Models of attentional learning

John K. Kruschke

Many theories of learning provide no role for learned selective attention (e.g., Anderson, 1991; Pearce, 1994; Rehder & Murphy, 2003). Selective attention is crucial, however, for explaining many phenomena in learning. The mechanism of selective attention in learning is also well motivated by its ability to minimize proactive interference and enhance generalization, thereby accelerating learning. Therefore, not only does the mechanism help explain behavioural phenomena, it makes sense that it should have evolved (Kruschke & Hullinger, 2010).

The phrase 'learned selective attention' denotes three qualities. First, 'attention' means the amplification or attenuation of the processing of stimuli. Second, 'selective' refers to differentially amplifying and/or attenuating a subset of the components of the stimulus. This selectivity within a stimulus is different from attenuating or amplifying all aspects of a stimulus simultaneously (cf. Larrauri & Schmajuk, 2008). Third, 'learned' denotes the idea that the allocation of selective processing is retained for future use. The allocation may be context sensitive, so that attention is allocated differently in different contexts.

There are many phenomena in human and animal learning that suggest the involvement of learned selective attention. The first part of this chapter briefly reviews some of those phenomena. The emphasis of the chapter is not the empirical phenomena, however. Instead, the focus is on a collection of models that formally express theories of learned attention. These models will be surveyed subsequently.

Phenomena suggestive of selective attention in learning

There are many phenomena in human and animal learning that suggest that learning involves allocating attention to informative cues, while ignoring uninformative cues. The following subsections indicate the

The author thanks Michael A. Erickson for discussion regarding ATRIUM and COVIS.

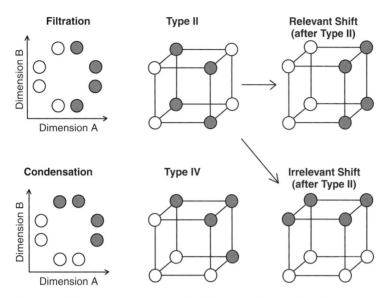

Figure 6.1 Category structures that illustrate the benefits of selective attention. Axes denote stimulus dimensions. Disks denote stimuli, with the shading of the disk denoting the correct category label. The structures in the upper row are easier to learn than the corresponding structures in the lower row.

benefits of selective allocation of attention, and illustrate the benefits with particular findings.

Attentional shifts facilitate learning

Learning can be faster when selective attention is able to enhance the relevant cues and suppress the irrelevant cues. As an example, consider the upper-left panel of Figure 6.1, labelled 'Filtration'. It shows a two-dimensional stimulus space, wherein each point represents a stimulus with corresponding values on the two dimensions. For example, dimension B could be the height of a rectangle, and dimension A could be the horizontal position of an interior line segment. The disks indicate the stimuli that were used on different training trials, and the shading of the disk indicates the correct category label. Notice that for the Filtration structure, the correct category label can be inferred from dimension A alone; dimension B can be ignored. The lower-left panel shows a very similar structure labelled 'Condensation'. The only difference is in which stimuli belong to which category. Notice that for the Condensation structure, the correct category label can be inferred only by using information from both dimensions.

When people are trained on the Filtration and Condensation structures, the Filtration structure is learned much faster than the Condensation structure (Kruschke, 1993). This difference obtains despite the fact that both structures are linearly separable, and the clustering of instances is actually slightly better for the Condensation structure than for the Filtration structure. The Filtration advantage can be naturally explained by positing selective attention. In the Filtration structure, people learn to pay attention to the relevant dimension and they learn to ignore the irrelevant dimension. The selective attention enhances discriminability along the relevant dimension and greatly enhances generalization across values of the irrelevant dimension.

Another example is shown in the middle column of Figure 6.1. These structures involve stimuli with three binary dimensions, e.g., big/small, red/blue, triangle/square. Inspection of the upper-middle structure, labelled 'Type II', reveals that the vertical dimension is irrelevant, i.e., it can be ignored without loss of accuracy. The remaining two dimensions are relevant, and the categorization is a non-linearly separable, exclusive-OR on those dimensions. The lower-middle structure, labelled 'Type IV', merely rearranges the category assignments of the exemplars. In this structure, no dimension can be ignored if perfect accuracy is to be attained. The structure is linearly separable, however, and comprises two prototypes in opposite corners of the stimulus space.

When people are trained on Type II and Type IV, Type II is learned faster, despite the fact that it involves a non-linearly separable categorization (Nosofsky *et al.*, 1994; Shepard, Hovland, & Jenkins, 1961). Again this difference can be explained by the action of selective attention. When learning Type II, people learn to ignore the irrelevant dimension, thereby quickly generalizing across that dimension.

Attentional shifting protects previous learning and accelerates new learning

Consider a situation in which a new response is to be learned. In this situation, the stimuli that occur for the new response have some new components but also some components that have been previously associated with old responses. The old components could cause proactive interference when the new response is being learned. However, if the old components could be selectively suppressed when learning the new response, learning of the new response would be accelerated, while the previously learned association would be protected.

Table 6.1 *Training designs for blocking and highlighting*

Phase	Blocking		Highlighting	
Early	A→X	F→Y	I.PE→E	
Late	A.B→X	C.D→Y	I.PE→E	I.PL→L
Test	B.D→? (Y)		I→? (E)	
	A.C→? (X)		PE.PL→? (L)	

Each cell indicates Cues→Correct Response. In the test phase, typical response tendencies are shown in parentheses.

This sort of phenomenon has been observed in a training design referred to as 'highlighting', and displayed in the right side of Table 6.1. The stimuli consist of selectively attendable cues, such as spatially separated words displayed on a computer screen. In the early phase of training, two cues, denoted I and PE, occur with outcome E. This case is denoted I.PE→E. In the late phase of training, these cases continue, interspersed with cases of a new correspondence: I.PL→L. The total number of trials of I.PE→E equals the total number of trials of I.PL→L; there is merely a front-loading of the I.PE→E cases to assure that they are learned first. Notice that the two cases are symmetric. The early outcome E is indicated by a perfect predictor PE and an imperfect predictor I, while the late outcome L is indicated by a perfect predictor PL and the imperfect predictor I. If people learn this simple symmetry, then cue I should be equally associated with outcomes E and L. In fact, people strongly prefer to respond with E when tested on cue I. This preference cannot be trivially explained as a mere primacy effect, however, because when people are presented with the cue pair PE.PL, they strongly prefer the outcome L (for a review, see Kruschke, 2010). This 'torsion' in the response preferences, whereby E is preferred for one ambiguous cue but L is preferred for another ambiguous cue, is called the highlighting effect.

The highlighting effect can be explained by the action of selective attention during learning. During the early phase, people build moderate-strength associations from cues I and PE to outcome E. During the later phase, when learning I.PL→L, attention shifts away from I to PL, because attending to I yields the wrong outcome. With PL attended, and I ignored, people then learn a strong association for PL to L. Notice that the learned attentional allocation depends on context. In the context of PE, attention is not shifted away from I, but in the context of PL, attention is shifted away from I.

Individual differences in selective attention

The magnitude of the highlighting effect varies across individuals. If the magnitude corresponds with the degree of attentional shifting, and if the degree of attentional shifting is a fairly stable individual characteristic, then the magnitude of highlighting ought to correlate with the magnitude of other phenomena attributed to selective attention in learning.

This prediction has been confirmed for two other measures of attention (Kruschke, Kappenman, & Hetrick, 2005). One measure is the magnitude of 'blocking', which is another sort of response preference in associative learning. The left side of Table 6.1 shows that in blocking, late training consists of an equal number of cases of A.B→X and C.D→Y. The only difference between them is training in the previous, early phase. A.B→X is preceded by cases of A→X, wherein A by itself predicts X. This previous training with A alone apparently blocks learning about B, as assayed by subsequent tests with the conflicting cues B.D, for which people strongly prefer outcome Y. This weakened association from B can be explained, at least in part, by learned inattention to B. When learning A.B→X, the person already knows that A indicates X, so it is helpful to learn to suppress the distracting cue B. Now that blocking has been described, here is the point: across individuals, the magnitude of blocking is correlated with the magnitude of highlighting. Moreover, eye tracking reveals that the magnitude of differential gaze at the cues, during testing, is correlated with the magnitudes of highlighting and blocking (Kruschke *et al.*, 2005; Wills *et al.*, 2007).

Learned attention perseverates into subsequent learning

If people learn to attend to some cues or dimensions while suppressing attention to other cues or dimensions, then it is natural to suppose that the learned attention should perseverate into subsequent training even if the dimension values and/or the category assignments change. In particular, if the same dimension remains relevant after the change, then re-learning should be easier than if a different dimension becomes relevant. This prediction, that an intra-dimensional shift should be easier than an extra-dimensional shift, has been well established in classical discrimination learning, especially in situations in which the cue values change when the relevance shifts (for a review, see, e.g., Slamecka, 1968).

Figure 6.1 shows a type of shift design that is quite different from traditional designs and solves some of their problems. Instead of changing the stimuli or outcomes when the relevance changes, all the stimuli and outcomes stay the same; only the mapping between them changes.

Therefore there is no novelty in the stimuli or outcomes to indicate a change across which knowledge must be transferred. Specifically, learners first were trained on the Type II structure shown in the upper middle of Figure 6.1. Then they were seamlessly shifted to one of the structures shown in the right column of Figure 6.1. Both of the right structures have only a single relevant dimension. In the upper right (labelled 'Relevant Shift'), the newly relevant dimension is one of the dimensions that was previously relevant for the Type II structure. In the lower right (labelled 'Irrelevant Shift'), the newly relevant dimension is the dimension that was irrelevant in the previous Type II structure. Notice that in both shifts there are exactly four stimuli that change their outcomes, and therefore any difference in difficulty of shift cannot be attributed to how many stimulus-outcome correspondences must be re-learned. Finally, notice that the Type II structure of the initial phase makes all the dimensions have zero correlation with the outcome. In other words, for any single dimension, there is 50% probability of both outcomes at both values of the dimension. Therefore, any difference in difficulty of shift cannot be attributed to the correlation between the dimension and the outcome in the initial phase. This type of structure has been used in subsequent studies by George and Pearce (1999) and by Oswald et al. (2001).

Results from human learners showed that the relevant shift was much easier to learn than the irrelevant shift (Kruschke, 1996b). This result is naturally explained by positing learned attention: people learned to attend to the two relevant dimensions for the Type II structure, and to ignore its irrelevant dimension. Therefore, in subsequent training, it was relatively difficult to learn to attend to the previously irrelevant dimension. Analogous results have been obtained for learning after highlighting and after blocking. When trained on new associations involving previously highlighted cues, learning is faster (Kruschke, 2005). When trained on new associations involving previously blocked cues, learning is slower (Kruschke, 2005; Kruschke & Blair, 2000; Le Pelley & McLaren, 2003; Le Pelley et al., 2005). Again, these results are naturally explained in terms of learned selective attention.

Competition for attention explains effects of cue salience

If attention has a role in associative learning, then cue salience should have an effect in learning, because salience connotes attraction of attention. The term 'salience' has no generally accepted definition, but salience is defined here as the relatively long-lived ability of a cue to attract attention. A cue's salience might be assessed by its initial attentional allocation at the beginning of an experiment, before additional learning has shifted attention. The salience of a cue is always relative to the saliences of other cues that are present at the same time.

As one example, consider a situation in which words presented on a computer screen must be associated with corresponding key presses. The word 'peek' might indicate pressing the F key, while the word 'toll' indicates pressing the J key. The correspondence is probabilistic, however. Suppose that in addition to those words that are correlated with the correct key press, the screen also displays other words that are not correlated with the correct key press. The learner does not know in advance which words are correlated or uncorrelated with the correct answer. If the words compete for attention during learning, then learning about the relevant cues should be influenced by the relative salience of the irrelevant words. If the irrelevant words are highly salient, such as 'boy' and 'cat', then learning about the relevant words should be relatively difficult. If the irrelevant words are obscure and not salient, such as 'nabob' and 'witan', then learning about the relevant words should be relatively easy. This prediction, which is novel from a specific attentional theory of associative learning, was confirmed in Experiment 4 of Kruschke and Johansen (1999). For this example, involving words, salience refers to the encodability (e.g., concreteness) and associability (e.g., meaningfulness). In other applications, salience has been instantiated as the intensity or quantity of the cue. For example, when the cue is the colour red, then the cue salience might be manipulated by the amount or density of red pixels on the computer screen (Denton & Kruschke, 2006).

As another example, recall the training procedure for blocking (left side of Table 6.1). The redundant cue B, added to the already-learned cue A, was learned to be ignored because it (cue B) distracted attention from the diagnostic cue. Thus, blocking is caused, at least in part, by learned inattention to the blocked cue. This theory predicts that the degree of blocking should be modulated by the relative salience of the to-be-blocked cue. In particular, if cue B is highly salient, then it should be difficult to block. Indeed, when cue B is highly salient, it might even dominate learning in the second phase, actually robbing cue A of some control over responding. This prediction has been confirmed in humans and animals (Denton & Kruschke, 2006; Hall *et al.*, 1977).

Attention can shift between representations

The previous sections have assumed that attention can be allocated to present/absent cues, such as the word 'cat', or to values of dimensions, such as the specific colours blue and red, or to entire dimensions, such as height. But attention can also be allocated to representational systems, such as a rule system or an exemplar system. The idea is that learners can associate stimuli with outcomes via a variety of different types of mappings. Some mappings might be mediated by exemplars. In an exemplar system, if a stimulus is similar to exemplars in memory, then the system anticipates the outcome stored in those exemplars. Other mappings might be mediated by rules. In a rule system, if a stimulus satisfies a specific condition, then the system anticipates the corresponding outcome. The condition for a rule typically spans a much larger area of stimulus space than an exemplar. For example, a rule might have as its condition 'anything taller than 3 cm', whereas an exemplar might have as its condition 'something very nearly 3 cm tall and 2 cm wide and coloured green and weighing more than a kilogram'. As another example, in learning to map continuous cues to continuous outcomes (i.e., in so-called function learning), an exemplar system would map a cue value near $x = 3.0$ (say) to an outcome of $y = 6.0$ (say), but a rule system could map any value of x to $y = 2x$. Learners should allocate attention to the different types of mappings according to how efficiently and accurately the mappings accommodate the training items. The allocation of attention among representational systems is learned, and the tuning of the mappings within the systems is learned.

Empirical evidence for this sort of attentional allocation has come from a series of experiments in category learning. The stimuli for these experiments had two continuous dimensions, like the Filtration and Condensation stimuli on the left of Figure 6.1. The structure of the categories was much like the Filtration structure, for which the stimuli were accurately classified by a simple rule: if the stimulus has dimension A value left of centre, then the stimulus is in category 1. But the structure was more involved than the simple Filtration structure, because it also had exceptions to the rule. The exceptions were arranged so that extrapolation beyond the training cases could be tested. The attentional theory predicts that for test cases that are fairly far from the exceptions, but even farther from the trained rule cases, responses should nevertheless favour the rule-predicted outcomes. This prediction stems from how attention is allocated to the systems. Attention goes to the exemplar system especially when the stimulus is highly similar to a known exception, but otherwise attention may prefer the rule system, which accommodates most of the training items. This prediction and many others have been confirmed in a series of experiments (Denton, Kruschke, & Erickson, 2008; Erickson & Kruschke, 1998, 2002; Kruschke & Erickson, 1994). Additional evidence comes from the theory predicting switch costs, i.e., response time increases, when stimuli switch across trials from being rule mapped to being exemplar mapped, and vice versa (Erickson, 2008). Other category learning experiments, using various other structures and stimuli, along with extensive explorations of models, have bolstered interpretations in terms of distinct representational subsystems that are allocated attention in different circumstances (Lewandowsky, Roberts, &Yang, 2006; Little & Lewandowsky, 2009; Yang & Lewandowsky, 2003, 2004).

General framework for models of attentional learning

The phenomena reviewed in the previous section share an explanatory framework in which attention is rapidly reallocated across cues, dimensions, or representations. The learning of associations depends on the reallocation of attention, and the reallocation is itself learned. Figure 6.2

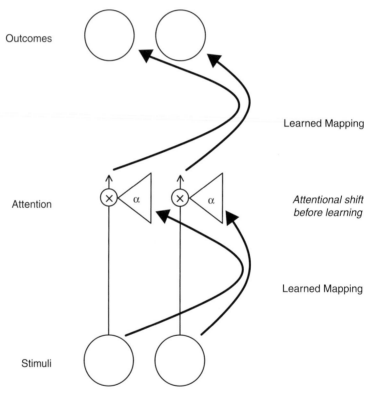

Figure 6.2 General framework for models of attentional learning. The stimuli are represented at the bottom of the diagram by activations of corresponding nodes. Thick curved arrows denote learned associative mappings. Attention is denoted by α in the middle layer and acts as a multiplier on the stimuli. On a given trial of learning, attention is shifted before the mappings are learned.

shows this general framework as an associative architecture. Associations feed forward from the stimuli at the bottom of the diagram to the outcomes at the top of the diagram.

In the general framework of Figure 6.2, attention is thought of as multiplicative gates on the stimulus components. The attentional gate on a stimulus component is indicated in Figure 6.2 by the multiplication sign and the α symbol accompanying each stimulus component. The attentional values are shifted in response to feedback regarding correct outcomes. Attention is shifted away from stimulus components that generate error, toward stimulus components that reduce error. The reallocated attention values are then learned, as associations from the stimuli. The outcomes are learned as associations from the attentionally filtered stimuli.

The general framework can be instantiated with different specific formalisms, depending on the situation to be modelled and the complexity demanded by the data. For example, the mappings between layers might be accomplished by simple linear associators if the domain and behaviour are simple enough. But a more general model would need more complex representational options to accommodate more complex, nonlinear mappings. The remainder of the chapter reviews several specific formal instantiations of the general framework in Figure 6.2.

Particular instantiations

Learned attention across exemplars: RASHNL and ALCOVE Figure 6.3 shows the RASHNL model (Kruschke & Johansen, 1999), successor to the ALCOVE model (Kruschke, 1992). ALCOVE was a connectionist implementation of the generalized context model (GCM; Nosofsky, 1986), which in turn was a generalization of the context model (Medin & Schaffer, 1978). RASHNL is an acronym for 'Rapid Attention SHifts aNd Learning'. The name is a play on the word 'rational' because the model mechanisms are all driven by the rational goal of error reduction, even though the behavioural results are rash attentional shifts and seemingly irrational generalization behaviours. The name also gives a nod to the rational model of categorization of Anderson (1991).

In the RASHNL model (and ALCOVE), stimuli are represented by values on psychological dimensions, as denoted at the bottom of Figure 6.3. For example, the stimulus might have a height of 27 and a brightness of 12. The stimulus coordinates, for example (27, 12), are compared to the coordinates of exemplars in memory. The memory exemplars are activated to the extent that they are similar to the presented stimulus. Thus, memory exemplars that are very similar to the stimulus are

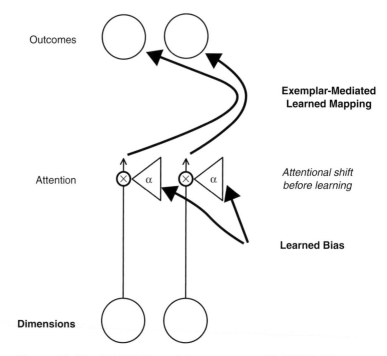

Figure 6.3 The RASHNL model, successor to ALCOVE. The
stimuli are assumed to be values on dimensions, and attention
is allocated to dimensions. The learned attentional allocation is
simplistically assumed to be a bias that applies equally to all stimuli,
unlike the general framework which allows stimulus-specific
attentional mappings. The mapping from attended stimuli to
outcomes is mediated by exemplars.

strongly activated, but memory exemplars that are highly dissimilar to
the stimulus are only weakly activated. The exemplars then propagate
their activation to the outcome nodes along weighted connections. The
weights encode the learned degree of association between each exemplar
and the outcomes. This exemplar mediation of the mapping to outcomes
from stimulus dimensions is indicated in the upper right of Figure 6.3.

The key role for attention is how much each stimulus dimension is
used in the calculation of similarity. In the Filtration structure of Figure
6.1, for example, dimension A will be strongly emphasized when determining the similarity of the stimulus to the exemplars, while dimension
B will be mostly disregarded as irrelevant.

When a stimulus is first presented, attention is allocated to its dimensions according to previously learned biases, as shown in the lower right

of Figure 6.3. Activation is propagated up to the outcome nodes, to determine a predicted outcome. The prediction is a magnitude of preference for each outcome. Then corrective feedback is supplied, and the discrepancy between the predicted outcome and the actual outcome is computed. This prediction error is used to drive all learning in the model.

The first response to the error is a rapid reallocation of attention. This rapid shift is denoted in the middle right of Figure 6.3. Attention is shifted toward dimensions that reduce error, and away from dimensions that cause error. For example, when learning the Filtration structure of Figure 6.1, error is reduced by decreasing attention on dimension B, because the collapsing of dimension B brings closer together the exemplars that map to the same outcome, whereby learning about one exemplar enhances generalization to other exemplars.

After the attention to dimensions has been reallocated, then the model attempts to retain the reallocation for future use. This learning of the reallocation is stored in the bias weights. This learning is error driven, just like the initial rapid reallocation. The bias weights are adjusted to reduce the discrepancy between the initial attentional allocation and the reallocation demanded by the actual outcome. It is important to understand that the rapid shift of attention, in response to corrective feedback, is distinct from the learning of that shift. The shift might be large, but the large shift might not be retained to the next trial if the shift is not learned. Figure 6.3, like the general framework in Figure 6.2, points out this distinction by the label, 'attentional shift before learning'. The ALCOVE model, which was the precursor to RASHNL, does not have a rapid reallocation of attention before the learning of attention.

At the same time that the attentional shift is learned, the model attempts to learn the correct outcomes, by adjusting associations between the activated exemplars and the outcome nodes. An associative weight between an outcome and an exemplar is adjusted only to the extent that the exemplar is activated and there is error at the outcome node.

This sort of model has been shown to accurately fit learning performance and generalization behaviour in a number of situations. For example, when applied to the Filtration and Condensation structures in Figure 6.1, ALCOVE shows a robust advantage for Filtration (Kruschke, 1993). When applied to the Type II and Type IV structures in Figure 6.1, ALCOVE again shows accurate fits to human learning data (Kruschke, 1992; Nosofsky et al., 1994). When applied to the Relevant and Irrelevant shifts in Figure 6.1, ALCOVE exhibits a strong advantage for the Relevant shift (Kruschke, 1996b). When applied to situations in which irrelevant cues have different saliences, as with the words 'cat', 'toll', and 'witan' described earlier, the RASHNL model nicely captures human utilizations of the cues (Kruschke & Johansen, 1999). The RASHNL model, with its rapid shifts of attention, also qualitatively mimics the large individual differences in attentional allocation seen in human learners (Kruschke & Johansen, 1999). RASHNL has also been used in clinical assessment. For example, men's attention to women's facial affect or body exposure, and other socially relevant cues, were studied by Treat and colleagues (Treat *et al.*, 2001, 2007, 2010). Male participants learned arbitrary category labels assigned to photos of women. Fits of RASHNL to the learning data revealed that these two stimulus dimensions were difficult to selectively attend, and, in particular, that learning to reallocate attention away from the initial individual biases was very difficult.

Although RASHNL is a successor to ALCOVE, RASHNL has not yet been tested on all the data sets for which ALCOVE has been tested. ALCOVE is nearly (but not exactly) a special case of RASHNL for which the magnitude of rapid attention shifting is set to zero, so in that sense RASHNL might trivially be able to reproduce the behaviours of ALCOVE. More challenging, however, would be to simultaneously fit the data that motivated the creation of RASHNL and the data that have been successfully fit by ALCOVE. For example, it is not known whether RASHNL could reproduce the advantage of Relevant over Irrelevant shifts that ALCOVE shows robustly. Presumably it could, because attentional learning can be slow even when initial shifts are large, but simulations have yet to be conducted.

Context-specific learned attention: EXIT and ADIT   Figure 6.4 shows the EXIT model (Denton & Kruschke, 2006; Kruschke, 2001a, 2001b; Kruschke *et al.*, 2005), successor to ADIT (Kruschke, 1996a). Ideas similar to those formalized by ADIT were previously described informally by Medin and Edelson (1988). The name ADIT is an acronym for Attention to Distinctive InpuT. The word 'adit' refers to an entrance to a place that is mined, and so the play on words is that the model is an entrance to the mind. The successor model, EXIT, was so named because an exit can come after an adit.

EXIT is another instantiation of the general framework of Figure 6.2. The EXIT model assumes that stimuli are represented as present/absent cues (instead of values on dimensions, as in RASHNL). Most importantly, EXIT assumes that the learned attentional allocation can be exemplar specific. Thus, attention might be allocated one way for some stimuli, but a different way for other stimuli. RASHNL and ALCOVE do not have this flexibility. The allocation of attention in EXIT is a learned mapping from stimulus cues to attentional values, mediated

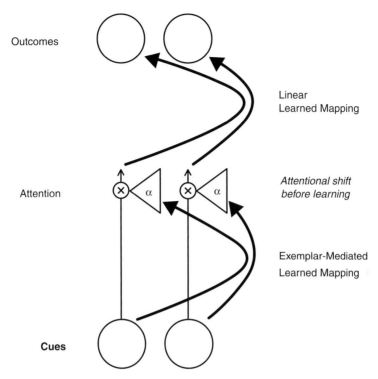

Figure 6.4 The EXIT model, successor to ADIT. The stimuli are assumed to be present/absent cues. The mapping from cues to attention is exemplar mediated, whereas the mapping from attentionally gated cues to outcomes is simplistically assumed to be linear.

by exemplars. A comparison of EXIT in Figure 6.4 and RASHNL in Figure 6.3 shows this contrast in the associative weights going into the attention gates.

Because EXIT has been applied to relatively simple mappings of stimuli to outcomes, the model incorporates only a linear associator to outcomes from attended cues. This use of a linear associator on the outcome layer is merely for simplicity and reduction of parameters. If the model were applied to more complex situations, a more complex associator would have to be used, such as the exemplar-mediated associator used in RASHNL. This option is discussed more in a later section.

Aside from the representational differences just described, processing in EXIT proceeds much like processing in RASHNL. When a stimulus appears, activation is propagated up the network and an outcome is predicted. Corrective feedback is provided, and the degree of error is computed. At this point, attention is rapidly reallocated across the cues, away from cues that cause error, to cues that reduce error. This reallocated attention serves as a target for error-driven subsequent learning of associations from stimulus cues to attentional allocation. As in RASHNL, attention shifting and attention learning are two distinct steps of processing. In particular, it is possible to have shifting without learning of the shifts, as was assumed in the ADIT model.

EXIT (and ADIT) have been shown to fit many complex data sets from human learning experiments, including the highlighting and blocking designs in Table 6.1 (Denton & Kruschke, 2006; Kruschke, 1996a, 2001a, 2001b, 2005; Kruschke *et al.*, 2005). EXIT is especially good at capturing detailed choice preferences for a variety of cue combinations tested after highlighting. EXIT accomplishes this mimicry of human responding by the way the model shifts and learns attentional allocation to cues, especially during learning of the late-phase cases of I.PL→L (see Table 6.1). When a case of I.PL→L appears, attention is allocated away from cue I, because it is already associated with the other outcome E, and attention is shifted toward cue PL, because it does not conflict with the correct outcome. The attentional reallocation is then learned, specific to the cue combination I.PL. In other words, EXIT learns that when stimuli I.PL are presented, suppress attention to I and attend to PL, but when stimuli I.PE are presented, maintain some attention to both cues.

Because EXIT has learned an attentional allocation for particular cues, this learning will persist into subsequent phases of training. In particular, if subsequent phases of training have stimulus-outcome mappings with the same relevant cues, then subsequent learning should be easy. But if subsequent training has a stimulus-outcome mapping with different relevant cues, then the subsequent learning should be relatively difficult. These predictions have been confirmed and modelled by EXIT (Kruschke, 2005). For example, after highlighting, participants continued into subsequent training for which two novel outcomes were perfectly predicted by two cues that played the roles of the imperfect predictors in the previous highlighting phases. For some participants, the I cues were accompanied by the PE cues from the previous highlighting phases. When accompanied by PE, the I cues should receive some attention, and therefore the new learning should be relatively easy. Other participants learned about the I cues accompanied by PL cues from the previous highlighting phases. When accompanied by PL, the I cues should receive less attention, and therefore the new learning should be relatively difficult. This prediction was confirmed, and modelled by EXIT. Analogous results have been shown and modelled for blocking (Kruschke, 2001b, 2005; Kruschke & Blair, 2000).

EXIT and ADIT have also been shown to accurately fit human choice preferences for a variety of probabilistic mappings, and structures involving differential base rates of the categories. One of the benefits of the attentional interpretation provided by the models is that some of the empirical phenomena can be better understood. In particular, some findings regarding differential base rates could be re-interpreted in terms of attention shifts caused by the induced order of learning (Kruschke, 1996a, 2010). When two categories have very different base rates, the high-frequency category is learned first. The low-frequency category is subsequently learned, and attention is reallocated during learning of the low-frequency category. The attentional reallocation accounts for many choice preferences that are otherwise theoretically perplexing.

In general, attentional reallocation is beneficial for fast learning. For example, when learning I.PL→L in the late phase of highlighting, the shift of attention away from cue I protects the previously learned association from I to E, thereby retaining that association for accurate future prediction of outcome E. Learning of the shift also prevents subsequent errors when I.PL are presented again, because attention is allocated away from cue I. Thus, attentional allocation is a mechanism by which an organism can accelerate learning of new items while retaining knowledge of old items. This argument has been suggested in several previous publications (e.g., Kruschke, 2003c; Kruschke & Johansen, 1999). Recently it has been shown that when connectionist architectures are evolved using simulated genetic algorithms, the optimal architectures are those, like EXIT, that have the ability to rapidly reallocate attention across cues (Kruschke & Hullinger, 2010). In the simulated evolution, the only adaptive pressure put on the evolving learners was to learn fast, i.e., to have as little total error as possible during the lifetime of the organism. One of the key structural aspects of the training environment was that some cues changed less frequently than others. The slowly changing cues formed the context for the rapidly changing cues, and the attentional reallocation took advantage of the relevances of changing cues in different contexts.

Attentionally modulated exemplars and exemplar-mediated attention A comparison of RASHNL (Figure 6.3) and EXIT (Figure 6.4) invites two natural generalizations. First, the present/absent cues assumed by EXIT might be generalized to dimensions, as assumed in RASHNL. Such a generalization has been explored, wherein a dimensional value is represented by thermometer-style encoding of present/absent elements that represent levels on the dimension (Kalish, 2001; Kalish & Kruschke, 2000). In these models, attention can be allocated to different dimensions, and also to different values within dimensions. It remains to be seen whether or not this approach will be useful as a general solution to representing stimuli and selective attention to their components.

Second, a general model would allow exemplar-mediated mapping at both the attentional and outcome levels. Such a generalization has been developed and reported at conferences (Kruschke, 2003a, 2003b), but not yet published. In this generalized model, the exemplars that mediate the outcome mapping are attentionally modulated, as in RASHNL. In addition, there are exemplars that mediate the attention mapping, as in EXIT. Hence the model has attentionally modulated exemplars and exemplar-mediated attention. The attentional modulation on the exemplars also determines whether or not new exemplars are recruited during learning: if attention shifts away from candidate exemplars, they are not retained.

A key aspect of this generalization is that exemplars for the outcome-mapping encode both the cues and the attention paid to them. This is different than the type of exemplars used in RASHNL and ALCOVE. Instead, these generalized exemplars record the cues and their attentional gating. In other words, an exemplar for the outcome mapping contains not only the stimulus coordinates, but also the attentional allocation when that stimulus is processed. An interesting consequence of this representation is that the attentional values that are stored in the exemplars can be adjusted to reduce error, and this error-driven adjustment of exemplar-specific attention accounts for so-called 'retrospective revaluation' effects. Retrospective revaluation occurs when new learning occurs for a cue even when it is not present in the stimulus. In the generalized model, an exemplar node that encodes a present cue can retrospectively reduce or increase its stored attention to that cue, even when that cue is not present in the current stimulus. This approach to retrospective revaluation is promising, but was eclipsed by Bayesian approaches, discussed in a subsequent section. Nevertheless, the generalized exemplar approach deserves renewed attention in the future.

Mixture of experts: ATRIUM and POLE   As mentioned in the introduction, attention can be allocated to representational systems, in addition to cues or dimensions or values on dimensions. For example, one representational system may map stimuli to outcomes via exemplar memory, while another representational system may map stimuli to outcomes via condition-consequent rules.

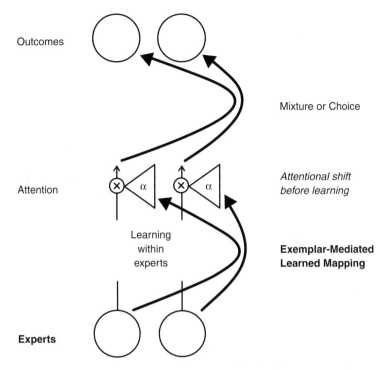

Figure 6.5 The ATRIUM and POLE models, both instances of a mixture-of-experts architecture. Attention is allocated to 'experts', each of which constitutes a complete learning system from stimuli to outcomes. The mapping from stimuli to attention is exemplar mediated, so that different experts can dominate in different contexts. The internal details of the experts are not shown. The final outcome is a mixture or choice from among the attended experts.

Figure 6.5 shows the basic structure of models that learn to allocate attention among 'expert' subsystems. Each expert learns its own mapping from stimuli to outcomes, using its own form of representation. Which expert takes responsibility, for learning and responding to any particular stimulus, is determined by a gating network. The gating network is indicated in Figure 6.5 as an exemplar-mediated, learned mapping. As is the case for all the models described so far, the allocation of responsibility to experts is driven by error reduction. Attention is allocated to experts that accommodate the current training case, and attention is allocated away from experts that cause error. These models are cases of a mixture-of-experts architecture (Jacobs, Jordan, & Barto, 1991; Jacobs et al., 1991).

The ATRIUM model has been used to model learning of categories in which the structure can be intuitively described as a rule with exceptions (Erickson & Kruschke, 1998; Kruschke & Erickson, 1994). As mentioned in the introduction, one of the key findings is that when people are tested with novel cases that demand extrapolation away from the training cases, responses are usually consistent with the rule, despite the fact that the nearest training case was an exception to the rule. Although some researchers have challenged the generality of the findings or shown that a variation of an exemplar-only model can capture some aspects of the findings (Nosofsky & Johansen, 2000; Rodrigues & Murre, 2007), follow-up experiments have repeatedly demonstrated that the effect is robust and that exemplar-only models cannot accommodate extrapolation of rules with exceptions, while the mixture-of-experts ATRIUM model can (Denton *et al.*, 2008; Erickson & Kruschke, 2002). Thus, rule and exception learning continues to challenge exemplar-only models, and mixture-of-expert models continue to fit the data better. Results from other category structures also point to the utility of mixture-of-expert models (Lewandowsky *et al.*, 2006; Little & Lewandowsky, 2009; Yang & Lewandowsky, 2003, 2004).

Analogous findings have been found in function learning. In function learning, instead of mapping stimuli to categorical outcomes, both the stimuli and outcomes are metric. Typically some simple function relates the input to output values, such as a linear or low-order polynomial. Consider a situation in which most of the training cases follow a simple linear function, but a few exceptions deviate from the line. In particular, one of the exceptions is the most extreme of the trained stimulus values. When tested for extrapolation beyond this last training case, people tend to revert to the rule, rather than respond according to the nearest (exception) exemplar. Several cases of this sort of behaviour were reported and modelled by Kalish, Lewandowsky, and Kruschke (2004). The model was a mixture-of-experts architecture called POLE (Population Of Linear Experts) in which expert modules for simple linear functions were gated along with exemplar-based experts. The model learned to allocate responsibility to the linear expert except when the stimulus was very similar to one of the learned exceptions.

Finally, the classic attentional model of Mackintosh (1975) can be generalized and re-expressed in a mixture-of-experts framework (Kruschke, 2001b). Each expert consists of a single distinct cue, trying to learn on its own to predict the presence or absence of the single outcome (i.e., the unconditioned stimulus in animal conditioning experiments). The attentional gate allocates responsibility to the cues to the extent that they successfully predict the outcome.

Locally Bayesian learning The previous instantiations of the general framework have all relied on error-driven learning, i.e., gradient descent on error as in backpropagation (Rumelhart, Hinton, & Williams, 1986). In all those models, the knowledge of the model at any time consists of a single specific combination of associative weights. There is no representation of other weight combinations that might be nearly as good.

An alternative formalization of learning comes from a Bayesian approach. In a Bayesian learner, multiple possible hypotheses are entertained simultaneously, each with a learned degree of credibility. For example, consider a situation with two cues, labelled A and B, and a single outcome X. The Bayesian learner might entertain three possible hypotheses. $H_{A(\neg B)}$: A, but not B, indicates X. $H_{B(\neg A)}$: B, but not A, indicates X. $H_{A \lor B}$: A or B indicate X. If the Bayesian learner experiences training cases of A→X, then the credibilities of $H_{A(\neg B)}$ and $H_{A \lor B}$ increase, while the credibility of $H_{B(\neg A)}$ decreases. 'Hypotheses' need not be expressed as logical rules. Indeed, most Bayesian models involve hypotheses about mappings that have continuous values, and the hypothesis space consists of the infinite space of all possible combinations of the continuous values. The fact that the hypothesis space is infinite does not mean that a Bayesian learner needs an infinite-capacity mind. On the contrary, the credibility of the infinite hypotheses can be summarized by just a few values, as, for example, the mean and standard deviation summarize an infinitely wide normal distribution. An infinite distribution can also be summarized approximately by a large representative sample.

Bayesian learning models have many attractions, both in terms of their general computational abilities and as models of mind. There is not space here to review their many applications, but an overview is provided by Chater, Tenenbaum, and Yuille (2006), and a tutorial of their application to associative models is provided by Kruschke (2008). One learning phenomenon that is easily explained by Bayesian models, but that is challenging for many non-Bayesian associative models, is backward blocking. In backward blocking the training phases of the blocking procedure in Table 6.1 are run in backward order. Curiously, the blocking effect is still exhibited by human learners (e.g., Dickinson & Burke, 1996; Kruschke & Blair, 2000; Shanks, 1985). In Bayesian accounts of backward blocking, different combinations of associative weights are considered simultaneously, with more belief allocated to the combination that is most consistent with the training items. Because the cases of A→X decrease the credibility of $H_{B(\neg A)}$, as explained in the previous paragraph, cue B is effectively blocked regardless of when the cases of A→X occur (Dayan & Kakade, 2001; Tenenbaum & Griffiths, 2003).

A theoretical framework that combines the attentional and Bayesian approaches is called 'locally Bayesian learning' (LBL, Kruschke, 2006b). The overall LBL framework is quite general and does not rely on any notion of attention. The general LBL framework is based on the idea that a learning system may consist of a sequence of subsystems in a feed-forward chain, each of which is a (locally) Bayesian learner. The argument for locally learning layers was as follows. First, Bayesian learning is very attractive for explaining retrospective revaluation effects such as backward blocking, among many other phenomena (Chater *et al.*, 2006). Second, Bayesian learning may also be unattractive for a number of reasons. In highly complex hypothesis spaces, it may be extremely difficult to accomplish even approximate Bayesian learning. In other words, keeping track of all viable hypotheses, even approximately, may be computationally intractable. Furthermore, many globally Bayesian models do not explain learning phenomena such as highlighting (Table 6.1) that depend on training order, because the models treat all training items as equally representative of the world to be learned, regardless of when the items occurred. Finally, the level of analysis for theories of learning is arbitrary: learning occurs simultaneously at the levels of neurons, brain regions, functional components, individuals, committees, institutions, and societies, all of which may be modelled (in principle) as Bayesian learners. Therefore, a system of locally Bayesian learning components may retain some attractions of Bayesian models while also implementing Bayesian learning in smaller, tractable hypothesis spaces.

The general framework for locally Bayesian learning has been instantiated in a particular two-layer model, wherein one layer learns how to allocate attention to cues, and a second layer learns how to associate attended cues with outcomes (Kruschke, 2006a, 2006b). Figure 6.6 shows the structure of the model. When a stimulus is presented, the model generates a predicted outcome as follows. The mapping, from stimuli to attention allocation, comprises many candidate hypotheses regarding how to allocate attention.

Each hypothesis has a degree of credibility at that point in training. The actual allocation of attention is taken to be the average allocation across all the hypotheses, weighted by their credibilities. The attentionally gated stimulus is then delivered to the next layer, which maps the stimulus to outcomes. This layer again consists of many candidate hypotheses, each with a degree of credibility. The predicted outcome is the average of the predicted outcomes across all the hypotheses, weighted by their credibilities.

Outcomes

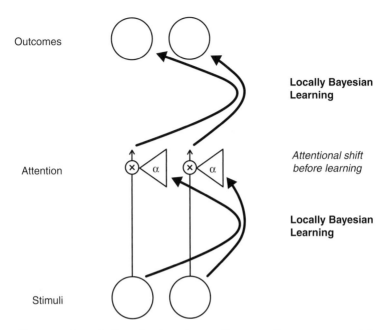

Locally Bayesian Learning

Attentional shift before learning

Attention

Locally Bayesian Learning

Stimuli

Figure 6.6 Locally Bayesian learning applies generally to componential models. Here it is applied to the case in which the first layer learns to allocate attention, and the second layer learns to generate an outcome, given the attended stimuli.

When corrective feedback is presented, learning occurs. (There are different possible learning dynamics. The one described here is the one that most closely mimics the processing of previously described attentional models.) First, the topmost layer determines which allocation of attention would best match the actual correct outcome. In other words, the system finds the allocation of attention that would be most consistent with the currently credible hypotheses of the outcome layer. This is the 'rapid shift of attention before learning'. This best allocation of attention is treated as the target for the lower layer. With the attention reallocated, both layers then learn according to standard Bayesian inference. In the attentional layer, credibilities are shifted toward hypotheses that are consistent with the current stimulus being mapped to the target allocation of attention. In the outcome layer, credibilities are shifted toward hypotheses that are consistent with the attended components being mapped to the correct outcomes.

This locally Bayesian learning generates behaviour that depends on training trial order. The reason that learning depends on trial order is that the internal attentional target depends on the current beliefs in the outcome layer. In other words, a particular stimulus and actual outcome will be given different internal attentional targets, depending on the current credibilities of outcome hypotheses.

The highlighting effect (recall Table 6.1) is a trial-order effect. Highlighting occurs robustly even when the total frequency of each category is the same (Kruschke, 2010). Highlighting occurs in the LBL model because of how attention is allocated in the late-training phase. By the time the late-training phase has occurred, the model's outcome layer has established some credibility in associations from cue I to outcome E. When the training case I.PL→L occurs, the model reallocates attention away from cue I, because leaving attention on I violates its current beliefs. Then the model learns, in its lower layer, that when I.PL occurs, it should allocate attention away from I toward PL. The model's upper layer retains its belief that cue I is associated with outcome E.

Whereas it is difficult for many globally Bayesian models to account for highlighting, LBL can. In addition, unlike the non-Bayesian models such as EXIT, LBL can also account for backward blocking, as mentioned earlier. Backward blocking is accommodated by the upper layer in LBL, but backward blocking of cues to outcomes does not require Bayesian learning in the lower layer. Recent empirical work has provided suggestive evidence that there can also be backward blocking of cues that are themselves uncorrelated with the outcomes, but which indicate what other cues are relevant to the outcome. This backward blocking of cues to relevance can be accommodated by Bayesian learning in the lower layer of the LBL architecture (Kruschke & Denton, 2010).

The description of LBL has been informal, because the exact mathematical expression can take different forms. For example, Kruschke (2006b) implemented LBL with a small finite set of weight combinations in a non-linear mapping. On the other hand, Kruschke and Denton (2010) implemented LBL with layers of Kalman filters, which represent infinite spaces of possible associative weight combinations in linear mappings. (An introduction to Kalman filters is provided in Kruschke, 2008.) Both approaches show the same qualitative behaviour.

In summary, LBL in general alleviates some of the computational problems of globally Bayesian learning, yet retains the attraction that learning may be Bayesian at some levels of analysis. LBL as specifically applied to attentional learning exhibits many human learning phenomena that are challenging to globally Bayesian models or to non-Bayesian models.

Relations to other models, and possible generalizations

The general attentional framework described in the previous sections has emphasized how attention shifts toward representational components (such as cues, dimensions, or expert modules) that accommodate the goal (such as accurately predicting the outcome), and how attention shifts away from representational components that conflict with, or are irrelevant to, the goal. In other words, the attentional mechanism pays attention to information that is useful, and ignores information that is useless. Attentional mechanisms effectively compress out redundancies in the stimulus encoding, simplifying the encoding of information, and minimizing the description length of conditions for generating responses. Attentional shifting might be construed as a mechanism for on-the-fly discovery of minimal encoding. Thus, the attentional approach has conceptual affinity with the simplicity model of Pothos and Chater (2002), as summarized by Pothos, Chater and Hines (Chapter 9 of this volume). Further suggestive of a close relation between attention and encoding simplicity is the fact that ALCOVE, which dynamically reallocates attention, predicts the relative difficulties of different category structures much like (but not always exactly the same as) the ordering predicted by the theory of structural complexity and categorical invariance by Vigo (2006, 2009). Attention might also be construed as a mechanism that mimics or implements prior beliefs about candidate rule structures, as formalized in some Bayesian approaches to category learning (Goodman *et al.*, 2008).

All of the instantiations of the general attentional framework in Figure 6.2 have intellectual ancestors and cousins. The ALCOVE model, in particular, is a direct connectionist implementation of the generalized context model (GCM; Nosofsky, 1986), which is summarized by Nosofsky (Chapter 2 of this volume). ALCOVE extends the GCM by providing a mechanism whereby the dimensional attention strengths are learned (rather than freely estimated to fit data at different points in training) and the exemplar-to-outcome associations are learned (rather than set equal to co-occurrence frequencies). One advantage of ALCOVE over the GCM is that ALCOVE provides a simple and intellectually appealing learning mechanism, with only two learning rate parameters (on attention and association weights) instead of several dimensional attention parameters. Some disadvantages of ALCOVE are that the learning mechanism might not mimic actual learning performance, and that predictions of ALCOVE can only be ascertained via trial-by-trial simulations of entire training sequences whereas predictions of the GCM do not require trial-by-trial training.

Exemplars in ALCOVE and RASHNL were, for convenience, assumed to be either (1) preloaded as a random covering of the stimulus space, or (2) preloaded because of prior exposure to, or inference about, the range of possible stimuli, or (3) recruited on-the-fly when novel stimuli occurred. A different mechanism for recruiting exemplars was used in the model described in the section on attentionally modulated exemplars and exemplar-mediated attention in this chapter. In that section it was mentioned that exemplars can mediate the mappings in both layers of the general framework, and the exemplar activations can themselves be attentionally modulated. When attention modulates the exemplars, the attentional modulation can govern whether candidate exemplars, elicited by stimuli on every trial, are retained for future learning or retired after that trial. Specifically, if attention is shifted toward a candidate exemplar (because previously learned exemplars cause error), it is retained, but if attention is shifted away from a candidate exemplar (because previously learned exemplars are already performing well), it is retired. Notice that this mechanism constitutes an error-driven attentionally based exemplar recruitment mechanism. This recruitment mechanism may be similar in spirit to cluster recruitment in the supervised mode of the SUSTAIN model (Love, Medin, & Gureckis, 2004), summarized by McDonnell and Gureckis (Chapter 10 of this volume), but SUSTAIN uses an error threshold for recruitment instead of an attentional mechanism. SUSTAIN also recruits clusters during unsupervised learning, using a novelty threshold, which might be mimicked in the proposed model by attentional shifts in an auto-encoding architecture (in which the outcome layer includes a copy of the cues). The ability of SUSTAIN to create adjustable clusters is a representational advantage over exemplar-only models. Future models may benefit from combining the clustering ideas of SUSTAIN with other mechanisms of cluster recruitment.

Exemplar representation has also been the subject of extensive investigation by animal-learning researchers, albeit under the rubric of 'configural' versus 'elemental' representations. A prominent configural model in animal learning was created by Pearce (1994). The configural model is analogous to ALCOVE in many ways, such as having error-driven learning of associative weights between configural units and outcomes. But it differs from ALCOVE significantly by having no selective attention to cues, whereby different cues within a stimulus are selectively amplified or attenuated. Configural models are contrasted with elemental models, which attempt to account for learning by using stimulus representations only of individual cues, instead of combinations of cues. A prominent example of an elemental approach is the basic version of the Rescorla–Wagner model (without configural cues; Rescorla & Wagner, 1972), upon which the ADIT model is based. Other elemental models include the one by McLaren and Mackintosh (2000, 2002) which uses a representation akin to stimulus-sampling theory (SST; Atkinson & Estes, 1963; Estes, 1962) and is summarized by Livesey and McLaren (Chapter 7 of this volume). Another intriguing elemental model has been reported by Harris (2006), also based on SST but which includes a limited-capacity attention buffer. These elemental models, like Pearce's configural model, have no learned selective attention to cues. Future generalizations might profitably combine SST-like cue representations with learnable, selective attentional shifting, perhaps not unlike the manner explored by Kalish and Kruschke (2000).

The notion of learned selective attention to specific cues has a long heritage, however, in both animal and human learning research. As just one example from human-learning research, Medin and Edelson (1988) informally expressed ideas about attention shifting that were subsequently formalized in the ADIT and EXIT models. In the animal learning literature, the model of Mackintosh (1975) described how cue associabilities may adapt through training. Mackintosh's heuristic formalism was shown subsequently to be closely related to a mixture-of-experts model in which each expert is a single cue acting individually to predict the outcome (Kruschke, 2001b). The EXIT model instead sums the influences of the cues, thereby generating different behaviours (such as conditioned inhibition, see Kruschke, 2001b).

Both EXIT and ATRIUM use exemplars to mediate the mapping from input to attentional allocation. This allows the models to learn stimulus-specific attentional allocation. EXIT has stimulus-specific attention to cues, whereas ATRIUM has stimulus-specific attention to representational modules. Another prominent model that uses distinct representational modules is the COVIS model of Ashby *et al.* (1998), summarized in its current form by Ashby, Paul and Maddox (Chapter 4 of this volume). ATRIUM and COVIS are analogous insofar as they both have rule-like and exemplar-like subsystems. Although both models are founded on the idea that people can learn category mappings via different representational subsystems, the formalizations of the idea have different motivations in the two models. ATRIUM was motivated by a unifying mathematical aesthetic, whereby the rule module and the exemplar module and the gating between them are all driven by the same mechanism: gradient descent on the overall error. COVIS was motivated by neuropsychological considerations, such that the rule (i.e., explicit verbal) subsystem has formalisms motivated by hypothesis testing, and the exemplar-like (i.e., procedural) system has formalisms motivated by neural mechanisms, and the competition between the subsystems is driven by a separate heuristic that combines the long-term accuracies of the modules (i.e., their 'trust') with the decisiveness of each module regarding the current stimulus (i.e., their 'confidence'). The module-combination rule in COVIS is not stimulus specific, but the module-gating mechanism in ATRIUM is stimulus specific. This difference between the models generates different predictions for the category structure used by Erickson (2008).[1] That structure combined a one-dimensional rule, similar to the Filtration structure in Figure 6.1, with an 'information integration' structure, similar to the Condensation structure in Figure 6.1, simultaneously in different regions of stimulus space. Consider stimuli that are near the boundary of the information-integration (i.e., Condensation) training items, which are simultaneously far from any of the one-dimensional rule (i.e., Filtration) training items. In ATRIUM, these stimuli will be given responses from information-integration categories, because the gating mechanism is stimulus specific and therefore allocates attention to the exemplar module. In COVIS, on the other hand, these stimuli will be given responses corresponding to the one-dimensional rule, because the exemplar-like (procedural) module has very low confidence but the rule module has very high confidence. There are many other differences in details of the models, which future research may explore. Insights from the two models, and the phenomena to which they have been applied, might profitably be merged in a future generalization.

Essentially all the models mentioned in the preceding paragraphs learn by some form of error reduction. None of the models learns by applying Bayes's rule to the space of possible representations that could be learned. In a previous section of the chapter, the method of locally Bayesian learning (LBL) was described, wherein the learned attentional allocation and the learned mapping from (attentionally filtered) stimuli to outcomes are learned in a Bayesian fashion. The implementation of each layer in LBL can be any Bayesian associator. For example, Kruschke (2006b) used linear sigmoids with a finite space of weight combinations, but Kruschke and Denton (2010) used Kalman filters. Kruschke (2006b) suggested that the layers could instead be implemented by the (approximately Bayesian) rational model of Anderson (1991). Indeed, the fully

---

[1] This implication was pointed out by Michael A. Erickson (personal communication, October 10, 2009).

Bayesian nonparametric approach of Sanborn, Griffiths, and Navarro (2006), summarized in its developed form by Griffiths *et al.* (Chapter 8 of this volume), could be used instead. Alternatively, the layers could learn about latent causes in a sigmoid-belief network, as proposed by Courville, Daw, and Touretzky (2006). All of these different representations incorporate the intellectual appeal of Bayesian rationality for local learning, along with the benefit of accounting for complex learning phenomena such as backward blocking, and the explanatory power of attentional learning.

Finally, the last few Bayesian models that were mentioned, such as nonparametric clustering and latent causes, are non-directional models. Unlike the feed-forward prediction of outcomes from stimuli, assumed by the diagrams throughout this chapter, these models simultaneously generate stimulus features and outcome features, and predict missing values from any other present values. (In the Bayesian literature, such models are referred to as 'generative' as opposed to 'discriminative'.) Non-Bayesian connectionist models can also be designed to allow prediction of any missing features. Such models could involve feedback connections, as in the KRES model of Rehder and Murphy (2003) (cf. the model's recent generalization summarized by Harris and Rehder in Chapter 12 of this volume), or the models could instead use auto-encoder-style architectures that have the complete stimulus pattern included in the output pattern to be predicted. This space of modelling possibilities is huge, but it is likely that accurate models of human learning will involve mechanisms for learned selective attention.

REFERENCES

Anderson, J. R. (1991). The adaptive nature of human categorization. *Psychological Review*, **98** (3), 409–429.

Ashby, F. G., Alfonso-Reese, L. A., Turken, A. U., & Waldron, E. M. (1998). A neuropsychological theory of multiple systems in category learning. *Psychological Review*, **105** (3), 442–481.

Atkinson, R. C., & Estes, W. K. (1963). Stimulus sampling theory. In R. D. Luce, R. R. Bush, & E. Galanter (eds.), *Handbook of Mathematical Psychology*. New York: Wiley.

Chater, N., Tenenbaum, J. B., & Yuille, A. (eds.) (2006). Special issue: probabilistic models of cognition. *Trends in Cognitive Sciences*, **10** (7), 287–344.

Courville, A. C., Daw, N. D., & Touretzky, D. S. (2006). Bayesian theories of conditioning in a changing world. *Trends in Cognitive Sciences*, **10** (7), 294–300.

Dayan, P., & Kakade, S. (2001). Explaining away in weight space. In T. Leen, T. Dietterich, & V. Tresp (eds.), *Advances in Neural Information Processing Systems* (Vol. 13, pp. 451–457). Cambridge, MA: MIT Press.

Denton, S.E., & Kruschke, J.K. (2006). Attention and salience in associative blocking. *Learning & Behavior*, **34** (3), 285–304.

Denton, S.E., Kruschke, J.K., & Erickson, M.A. (2008). Rule-based extrapolation: a continuing challenge for exemplar models. *Psychonomic Bulletin & Review*, **15** (4), 780–786.

Dickinson, A., & Burke, J. (1996). Within-compound associations mediate the retrospective revaluation of causality judgements. *Quarterly Journal of Experimental Psychology: Comparative & Physiological Psychology*, **49B**, 60–80.

Erickson, M.A. (2008). Executive attention and task switching in category learning: evidence for stimulus-dependent representation. *Memory & Cognition*, **36** (4), 749–761.

Erickson, M.A., & Kruschke, J.K. (1998). Rules and exemplars in category learning. *Journal of Experimental Psychology: General*, **127** (2), 107–140.

(2002). Rule-based extrapolation in perceptual categorization. *Psychonomic Bulletin & Review*, **9** (1), 160–168.

Estes, W.K. (1962). Learning theory. *Annual Review of Psychology*, **13** (1), 107–144.

George, D.N., & Pearce, J.M. (1999). Acquired distinctiveness is controlled by stimulus relevance not correlation with reward. *Journal of Experimental Psychology: Animal Behavior Processes*, **25** (3), 363–373.

Goodman, N.D., Tenenbaum, J.B., Feldman, J., & Griffiths, T.L. (2008). A rational analysis of rule-based concept learning. *Cognitive Science*, **32** (1), 108–154.

Hall, G., Mackintosh, N.J., Goodall, G., & Dal Martello, M. (1977). Loss of control by a less valid or by a less salient stimulus compounded with a better predictor of reinforcement. *Learning and Motivation*, **8**, 145–158.

Harris, J.A. (2006). Elemental representations of stimuli in associative learning. *Psychological Review*, **113** (3), 584–605.

Jacobs, R.A., Jordan, M.I., & Barto, A. (1991). Task decomposition through competition in a modular connectionist architecture: the what and where vision tasks. *Cognitive Science*, **15**, 219–250.

Jacobs, R.A., Jordan, M.I., Nowlan, S.J., & Hinton, G.E. (1991). Adaptive mixtures of local experts. *Neural Computation*, **3**, 79–87.

Kalish, M.L. (2001). An inverse base rate effect with continuously valued stimuli. *Memory & Cognition*, **29** (4), 587–597.

Kalish, M.L., & Kruschke, J.K. (2000). The role of attention shifts in the categorization of continuous dimensioned stimuli. *Psychological Research*, **64**, 105–116.

Kalish, M.L., Lewandowsky, S., & Kruschke, J.K. (2004). Population of linear experts: knowledge partitioning and function learning. *Psychological Review*, **111** (4), 1072–1099.

Kruschke, J.K. (1992). ALCOVE: an exemplar-based connectionist model of category learning. *Psychological Review*, **99**, 22–44.

(1993). Human category learning: implications for backpropagation models. *Connection Science*, **5**, 3–36.

(1996a). Base rates in category learning. *Journal of Experimental Psychology: Learning, Memory, and Cognition*, **22**, 3–26.

(1996b). Dimensional relevance shifts in category learning. *Connection Science*, **8**, 201–223.

(2001a). The inverse base rate effect is not explained by eliminative inference. *Journal of Experimental Psychology: Learning, Memory, and Cognition*, **27**, 1385–1400.

(2001b). Toward a unified model of attention in associative learning. *Journal of Mathematical Psychology*, **45**, 812–863.

(2003a). *Attentionally modulated exemplars and exemplar mediated attention.* Invited talk at the Seventh International Conference on Cognitive and Neural Systems, Boston University, May 28–31.

(2003b). *Attentionally modulated exemplars and exemplar mediated attention.* Keynote Address to the Associative Learning Conference, Gregynog (University of Cardiff) Wales, April 15–17.

(2003c). Attentional theory is a viable explanation of the inverse base rate effect: a reply to Winman, Wennerholm, and Juslin (2003). *Journal of Experimental Psychology: Learning, Memory, and Cognition*, **29**, 1396–1400.

(2005). Learning involves attention. In G. Houghton (ed.), *Connectionist Models in Cognitive Psychology* (pp. 113–140). Hove: Psychology Press.

(2006a). Locally Bayesian learning. In R. Sun (ed.), *Proceedings of the 28th Annual Conference of the Cognitive Science Society* (pp. 453–458). Mahwah, NJ: Erlbaum.

(2006b). Locally Bayesian learning with applications to retrospective revaluation and highlighting. *Psychological Review*, **113** (4), 677–699.

(2008). Bayesian approaches to associative learning: from passive to active learning. *Learning & Behavior*, **36** (3), 210–226.

(2010). Highlighting: a canonical experiment. In B. Ross (ed.), *The Psychology of Learning and Motivation*, **51**, 153–185.

Kruschke, J. K., & Blair, N. J. (2000). Blocking and backward blocking involve learned inattention. *Psychonomic Bulletin & Review*, 7, 636–645.

Kruschke, J. K., & Denton, S. E. (2010). Backward blocking of relevance-indicating cues: evidence for locally Bayesian learning. In C. J. Mitchell & M. E. Le Pelley (eds.), *Attention and Associative Learning.* New York: Oxford University Press.

Kruschke, J. K., & Erickson, M. A. (1994). Learning of rules that have high-frequency exceptions: New empirical data and a hybrid connectionist model. In *The Proceedings of the Sixteenth Annual Conference of the Cognitive Science Society* (pp. 514–519). Hillsdale, NJ: Erlbaum.

Kruschke, J. K., & Hullinger, R. A. (2010). The evolution of learned attention. In N. Schmajuk (ed.), *Computational Models of Conditioning.* Cambridge: Cambridge University Press.

Kruschke, J. K., & Johansen, M. K. (1999). A model of probabilistic category learning. *Journal of Experimental Psychology: Learning, Memory, and Cognition*, **25** (5), 1083–1119.

Kruschke, J. K., Kappenman, E. S., & Hetrick, W. P. (2005). Eye gaze and individual differences consistent with learned attention in associative blocking and highlighting. *Journal of Experimental Psychology: Learning, Memory, and Cognition*, **31**, 830–845.

Larrauri, J. A., & Schmajuk, N. A. (2008). Attentional, associative, and configural mechanisms in extinction. *Psychological Review*, **115** (3), 640–675.

Le Pelley, M. E., & McLaren, I. P. L. (2003). Learned associability and associative change in human causal learning. *The Quarterly Journal of Experimental Psychology Section B*, **56** (1), 68–79.

Le Pelley, M. E., Oakeshott, S. M., Wills, A. J., & McLaren, I. P. L. (2005). The outcome specificity of learned predictiveness effects: parallels between human causal learning and animal conditioning. *Journal of Experimental Psychology: Animal Behavior Processes*, **31** (2), 226–236.

Lewandowsky, S., Roberts, L., & Yang, L. X. (2006). Knowledge partitioning in categorization: boundary conditions. *Memory & Cognition*, **34** (8), 1676–1688.

Little, D. R., & Lewandowsky, S. (2009). Beyond non-utilization: irrelevant cues can gate learning in probabilistic categorization. *Journal of Experimental Psychology: Human Perception and Performance*, **35** (2), 530–550.

Love, B. C., Medin, D. L., & Gureckis, T. M. (2004). SUSTAIN: a network model of category learning. *Psychological Review*, **111** (2), 309–332.

Mackintosh, N. J. (1975). A theory of attention: variations in the associability of stimuli with reinforcement. *Psychological Review*, **82**, 276–298.

McLaren, I. P. L., & Mackintosh, N. J. (2000). An elemental model of associative learning: I. Latent inhibition and perceptual learning. *Animal Learning and Behavior*, **28** (3), 211–246.

(2002). An elemental model of associative learning: II. Generalization and discrimination. *Animal Learning and Behavior*, **30**, 177–200.

Medin, D. L., & Edelson, S. M. (1988). Problem structure and the use of base-rate information from experience. *Journal of Experimental Psychology: General*, **117**, 68–85.

Medin, D. L., & Schaffer, M. M. (1978). Context theory of classification learning. *Psychological Review*, **85**, 207–238.

Nosofsky, R. M. (1986). Attention, similarity, and the identification-categorization relationship. *Journal of Experimental Psychology*, **115**, 39–57.

Nosofsky, R. M., Gluck, M. A., Palmeri, T. J., McKinley, S. C., & Glauthier, P. (1994). Comparing models of rule-based classification learning: a replication of Shepard, Hovland, and Jenkins (1961). *Memory & Cognition*, **22**, 352–369.

Nosofsky, R. M., & Johansen, M. K. (2000). Exemplar-based accounts of 'multiple-system' phenomena in perceptual categorization. *Psychonomic Bulletin & Review*, **7** (3), 375–402.

Oswald, C. J. P., Yee, B. K., Rawlins, J. N. P., Bannerman, D. B., Good, M., & Honey, R. C. (2001). Involvement of the entorhinal cortex in a process of attentional modulation: evidence from a novel variant of an IDS/EDS procedure. *Behavioral Neuroscience*, **115** (4), 841–849.

Pearce, J. M. (1994). Similarity and discrimination: a selective review and a connectionist model. *Psychological Review*, **101**, 587–607.

Pothos, E. M., & Chater, N. (2002). A simplicity principle in unsupervised human categorization. *Cognitive Science*, **26**, 303–343.

Rehder, B., & Murphy, G. L. (2003). A knowledge-resonance (KRES) model of category learning. *Psychonomic Bulletin & Review*, **10** (4), 759–784.

Rescorla, R. A., & Wagner, A. R. (1972). A theory of Pavlovian conditioning: variations in the effectiveness of reinforcement and non-reinforcement. In A. H. Black & W. F. Prokasy (eds.), *Classical Conditioning II: Current Research and Theory* (pp. 64–99). New York: Appleton-Century-Crofts.

Rodrigues, P. M., & Murre, J. M. J. (2007). Rules-plus-exception tasks: a problem for exemplar models? *Psychonomic Bulletin & Review*, **14**, 640–646.

Rumelhart, D. E., Hinton, G. E., & Williams, R. J. (1986). Learning internal representations by back-propagating errors. In D. E. Rumelhart & J. L. McClelland (eds.), *Parallel Distributed Processing* (Vol. 1). Cambridge, MA: MIT Press.

Sanborn, A. N., Griffiths, T. L., & Navarro, D. (2006). A more rational model of categorization. In R. Sun & N. Miyake (eds.), *Proceedings of the 28th Annual Conference of the Cognitive Science Society*. Mahwah, NJ: Erlbaum.

Shanks, D. R. (1985). Forward and backward blocking in human contingency judgement. *Quarterly Journal of Experimental Psychology: Comparative & Physiological Psychology*, **37B**, 1–21.

Shepard, R. N., Hovland, C. L., & Jenkins, H. M. (1961). Learning and memorization of classifications. *Psychological Monographs*, **75** (13), Whole No. 517.

Slamecka, N. J. (1968). A methodological analysis of shift paradigms in human discrimination learning. *Psychological Bulletin*, **69**, 423–438.

Tenenbaum, J. B., & Griffiths, T. L. (2003). Theory-based causal inference. In S. Becker, S. Thrun, & K. Obermayer (eds.), *Advances in Neural Information Processing Systems* (Vol. 15, pp. 35–42). Cambridge, MA: MIT Press.

Treat, T. A., Kruschke, J. K., Viken, R. J., & McFall, R. M. (2010). Application of associative learning paradigms to clinically relevant individual differences in cognitive processing. In T. R. Schachtman & S. Reilly (eds.), *Conditioning and Animal Learning: Human and non-Human Animal Applications*. Oxford: Oxford University Press.

Treat, T. A., McFall, R. M., Viken, R. J., & Kruschke, J. K. (2001). Using cognitive science methods to assess the role of social information processing in sexually coercive behavior. *Psychological Assessment*, **13** (4), 549–565.

Treat, T. A., McFall, R. M., Viken, R. J., Kruschke, J. K., Nosofsky, R. M., & Wang, S. S. (2007). Clinical cognitive science: applying quantitative models of cognitive processing to examine cognitive aspects of psychopathology. In R. W. J. Neufeld (ed.), *Advances in Clinical Cognitive Science: Formal Modeling of Processes and Symptoms* (pp. 179–205). Washington, DC: American Psychological Association.

Vigo, R. (2006). A note on the complexity of Boolean concepts. *Journal of Mathematical Psychology*, **50**, 501–510.

(2009). Categorical invariance and structural complexity in human concept learning. *Journal of Mathematical Psychology*, **53**, 203–221.

Wills, A. J., Lavric, A., Croft, G. S., & Hodgson, T. L. (2007). Predictive learning, prediction errors, and attention: evidence from event-related potentials and eye tracking. *Journal of Cognitive Neuroscience*, **19** (5), 843–854.

Yang, L.-X., & Lewandowsky, S. (2003). Context-gated knowledge partitioning in categorization. *Journal of Experimental Psychology: Learning, Memory, & Cognition*, **29** (4), 663–679.

(2004). Knowledge partitioning in categorization: constraints on exemplar models. *Journal of Experimental Psychology: Learning, Memory, & Cognition*, **30** (5), 1045–1064.

7 An elemental model of associative learning and memory

Evan Livesey and Ian McLaren

The aim of this chapter is to demonstrate that an elemental model, using a relatively simple error correcting learning algorithm, can prove remarkably resourceful when it comes to simulating human and infrahuman learning and memory. The basic premise behind all elemental models of category learning is that the representation of any stimulus comprises multiple components which can individually enter into associations with designated category labels or responses. Used to its full potential, this approach captures the strengths of both prototype- and exemplar-based approaches to categorization. The full range of resources that elemental associative theories have to offer are rarely taken into account in comparisons with models that use other forms of representation, such as the configural theories offered by Pearce (1987, 1994) in the animal domain and Nosofsky (1991) in the human domain. We are by no means the only theorists to adopt this position, and the reader will find considerable overlap between our approach and that of several others (Brandon, Vogel, & Wagner, 2000; Harris, 2006; Wagner & Brandon, 2001).

We first set out the formal details of a model that implements elemental representation within an associative network employing a modified delta rule (following McClelland & Rumelhart, 1985). The modifications transform the delta rule into the basic real-time learning algorithm used by McLaren, Kaye, and Mackintosh (1989). For simplicity, some of the complexities of the latter model (e.g., weight decay and salience modulation) will not be considered here. We then implement the approach taken in McLaren and Mackintosh (2000, 2002) of using a sophisticated form of elemental representation and examine its effectiveness against results that have been thought to compel an analysis in terms of a configural model. Our chosen test domain will be that of dimensional classification, whereby stimuli on a dimension have to be categorized into two or more groups.

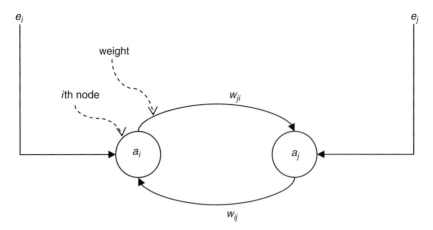

Figure 7.1 The standard components of a connectionist system employing the delta rule; *a* stands for activation, *w* for weight and *e* for external input.

The delta rule algorithm

Figure 7.1 shows two elements or nodes interconnected by associative links. The strength of the link between any two nodes may vary and this link strength or weight (w) dictates to what degree the activation (a) of one element can influence the activation of the other. The activation of the emitting node is multiplied by the weight for the link from that node to the recipient to give the resultant input along that link; hence a weight of zero prevents any activation from passing. Note that links are unidirectional.

Typically, nodes themselves can have an activation of between +1 and −1. This activation is the result of external input (e_i, e_j) and internal input, the latter simply being the input received by a node from other nodes via the links. The summed external input for a given node will be termed e, and the summed internal input i. The latter is given by Equation 1:

$$i_i = \Sigma \, w_{ij} \, a_j \qquad\qquad (1)$$

where i_i is the summed internal input to the ith node, w_{ij} is the weight from node j to node i, and a_j is the activation of the jth node.

When input is applied to a node, its activation changes, and when the input ends, the level of activation in the node reverts to its original level. The time course of these changes in activation is described by Equation 2:

$$da_i/dt = E(e_i + i_i)(1 - a_i) - Da_i \qquad \text{for } a_i > 0$$

$$da_i/dt = E(e_i + i_i)(1 + a_i) - Da_i \qquad \text{otherwise}$$

(2)

where E and D are the (positive) constants for excitation and decay respectively. Broadly speaking these equations ensure that the level of activation changes until the excitation, $E(e + i)(1 - a)$ for $a > 0$, equals the decay, Da, at which point the rate of change of activation is zero and the node is in equilibrium. For example, if e and i are positive and a is small then excitation will prevail over decay and activation will rise, but this decreases the excitation and increases the decay, hence the rate of increase of activation slows and activation settles towards some equilibrium level. If the input to the node is now terminated, then the decay term smoothly reduces the activation to zero.

However, activation is not the only quantity varying over time; the weights change as well, in a manner which gives the delta rule its name and reveals it to be of the Widrow–Hoff (1960) error correcting type. Whilst activation is controlled by the sum of e and i, the weights vary in a manner controlled by the difference between e and i, the rule being given in Equation 3:

$$dw_{ij}/dt = S(e_i - i_i)a_j$$

(3)

where S is a positive constant. The term $(e - i)$ is often referred to as delta (Δ). The effect of this rule is that on successive learning trials the weights into a node are changed until e and i are equal, that is, until the external input is matched by the internal input. In doing this the weights from the more active nodes are changed the most.

The account of the delta rule given up to this point has been the standard one as used in simulations of categorization (see McClelland & Rumelhart, 1985). Typically, models employing this rule would be simulated by treating the differential equations given as difference equations, with each of the model's processes dealt with in a self-contained or ad-hoc manner. The network would be allowed to settle to an equilibrium state before any of the weights were changed, dividing processing on a 'trial' into discrete stages dealing with activation and learning. The next section introduces some modifications of the basic rule that will allow a more realistic approach to simulation.

Modification of the delta rule

All the processes discussed in this treatment now act on-line and continuously: for example there is no waiting for the system to settle before changing the weights as is common in simulations employing the delta rule. This represents a rather more realistic and efficient state of affairs than the standard technique of dividing the learning cycle up into discrete phases. It also allows some modelling of the temporal processes governing learning and performance in the model, for example predictions of reaction time to categorize a stimulus.

For present purposes our main modification is to restrict the range of activation values to $0 \leq a \leq 1$, i.e. to forbid negative activations, and to constrain e to be positive. Thus Equation 2 becomes

$$da_i/dt = E(e_i + i_i)(1 - a_i) - Da_i \qquad \text{for } a_i \geq 0$$

$$da_i/dt = 0 \qquad \text{otherwise.}$$

(4)

This modification has important implications for the model architecture and representational scheme we use later. Essentially, it allows for the existence of a range of representational units, which we call elements, that are sensitive to the degree of co-occurrence of features. For example, a unit that generally receives inhibitory input, but has strong positive connections from two other units representing features in the environment, may only come on when both those features are present, thus detecting that configuration. If it had been able to take negative activations, then the non-linearity inherent in its being off all the time except when both features co-occur would, to some degree, be lost. The fact that the units also have an asymptotic level of activation (set at 1) also provides another source of non-linearity. Two features, either of which will activate a unit strongly, will in combination make little difference to this unit. We call this type of unit one that represents features as a non-additive element, in that its activation does not reflect the sum of the individual effects that each feature has on it. We have used the fact that this rule coupled with appropriate architectures can produce representational elements of this type to explain a number of phenomena in associative learning (see McLaren & Mackintosh, 2000, 2002). As already mentioned, it proves crucial in constraining the behaviour of the model of dimensional classification that we introduce in the next section.

The equations governing this system can now be summarized as (with all constants positive)

$$da_i/dt = E(e_i + i_i)(1 - a_i) - Da_i \qquad \text{for } a_i \geq 0$$

$$da_i/dt = 0 \qquad \text{otherwise}$$

$$\Delta_i = e_i - i_i \qquad a_i > 0 \qquad (5)$$

$$dw_{ij}/dt = S\Delta_i a_j \qquad \text{where } S \text{ is a positive constant}$$

$$e_i \geq 0 : a_i \geq 0 \qquad \text{at all times.}$$

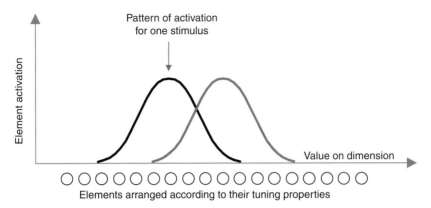

Figure 7.2 Representation of a stimulus dimension in a connectionist system.

Stimulus representation as distributed elemental activation

In this model, a stimulus is represented as the distributed activation of many elements. Variations among stimuli are achieved by manipulating which elements are activated by each stimulus and by how much. The manner in which these variations are implemented may depend on how the stimuli in question vary from one another. For instance, the McLaren *et al.* (1989) model assumed that variation along a stimulus dimension such as brightness was represented by different elements corresponding to different values on the dimension, rather than the activation level of an individual element being the *primary* indicator of value on the dimension (cf. Thompson, 1965). Figure 7.2 represents this idea schematically. Each element had a 'tuning curve' such that it responded most strongly to a certain value on the dimension and this response dropped off fairly rapidly with 'distance' from this optimal value. The advantage of this scheme was that it permitted relatively independent coding of values on a dimension: for example, the brightness of a stimulus could take low or high values, which could easily be associated with opposing categories or responses. But at the same time, the graded activation over neighbouring elements provided an intrinsic mechanism for generalization to stimuli with similar attributes.

This scheme was further developed in McLaren and Mackintosh's (2000, 2002) general theory of elemental associative learning by implementing an architecture (shown in Figure 7.3) that produced the same scheme from basic representational features without making any

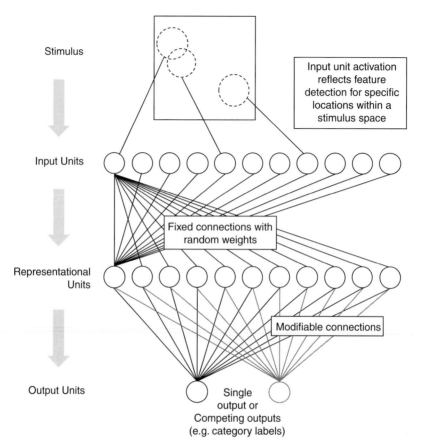

Stimulus

Input unit activation
reflects feature
detection for specific
locations within a
stimulus space

Input Units

Fixed connections with
random weights

Representational
Units

Modifiable connections

Output Units

Single
output or
Competing outputs
(e.g. category labels)

Figure 7.3 A model architecture based on McLaren and Mackintosh (2000, 2002).

assumptions about dimensionality at all. Instead, these factors *emerge* from the stimulus properties themselves. The mechanism through which learning proceeds is the modified delta rule that we have already introduced acting to link a large number of representational units with the output units. The representational units can be thought of as the 'elements' described in the McLaren and Mackintosh model, and can be implemented using some fairly simple assumptions.

Local feature coding

A stimulus is first encoded as activation of multiple input units. As a matter of convenience, here we will use a relatively simple form of local coding whereby each feature in each specific location activates a single input node. Thus feature A in position 1 would be represented as activation in one input unit, while feature A in position 2 (or feature B in position 1) would be represented as activation in another. Thus input unit i is fully activated ($A_i = 1$) when that location-specific feature is present and not activated at all ($A_i = 0$) otherwise. These input units are connected to the representational elements and provide their source of external input. The weights connecting inputs and elements are set with a high degree of random variation and are fixed throughout each simulation. We will describe two ways of implementing this scheme in a fashion that preserves localist information about features in specific configurations while also representing information about the presence or absence of features irrespective of their location (allowing generalization, for instance, between feature A in position 1 and feature A in position 2).

Hyper-localist versus feature-specific elements   Weights are specified in one of two ways, depending on which representational unit is involved. For most of the representational units, all incoming weights are allowed to vary randomly between −1 and +1, irrespective of which feature type and which spatial location the connected input is representing. But for a subset of the representational units, positive weights varying randomly from 0 to +1 connect the unit with each of the location-specific inputs that represent one particular feature, while the connections to all other input units have small, random negative weights.

Feature-biased elements   The absolute strength of all weights between input units and representational units is allowed to vary randomly. However, each representational unit is slightly biased towards those weights being positive for inputs representing some features and negative for inputs representing other features. In other words, the probability (p) of a weight being greater than 0 is 0.5 overall, but $p > 0.5$ for some input feature types and $p < 0.5$ for other feature types.

Importantly, there are no assumptions of dimensionality inherent in this system of representation – the elements are activated via a series of random weights with *all* of the activated inputs such that input $I = \Sigma A_i W_{ij}$ where A_i is the activation of input unit i and W_{ij} is the random fixed weight between input unit i and second layer unit j. If this input is negative then unit j has no activation ($A_j = 0$), otherwise if I is positive then activation of unit j will settle to $A_j = E.I/(D + E.I)$ where E and D are constants. This latter equation simply gives the equilibrium value that will result from implementing the activation function given in Equation set 5. In effect, this means that on presentation of any specific stimulus, roughly half of the second layer units will have an activation of zero as their summed input will be negative, while the activation of the other half will vary between 0 and 1, the distribution of which is affected by the values of the constants D and E.

Each of the elements is then connected to output units that mediate responding in the model. In the example given here (used for simulation of human associative learning) there are two output units, one corresponding to each response (left and right key presses). These weights are initially set to zero and vary according to the delta rule already given. During training, the output unit corresponding to the correct response is given an external input of 1 while the incorrect response output has an external input of 0.

Response unit activations are then transformed into response probabilities by using an exponential form of the ratio rule. For instance, the probability of a left response, $P(left\ response) = e^{kL} / (e^{kL} + e^{kR})$ where L and R are the summed inputs to the units corresponding to left response and right response respectively, and k is a constant. This ratio rule can be considered a standard method of calculating response probabilities from two competing response tendencies (see for example Wills *et al.*, 2000).

The next section considers an example of the application of this model to peak shift in discrimination learning, and focuses on a case study which at first sight seems to demand an explanation in terms of elemental and configural processing. We then go on to compare our model to other models of dimensional classification based on Nosofsky's (1986) GCM.

Peak shift with an artificial dimension

Peak shift is a well-documented consequence of stimulus discrimination and generalization and continues to stimulate interesting research half a century after its discovery (for reviews see Ghirlanda & Enquist, 2003; Honig & Urcuioli, 1981). Typically, subjects will be trained to discriminate between two very similar stimuli, usually by learning to respond to one (S+) and not the other (S–). Subjects are then presented with a range of stimuli that lie at successive points along the same dimension to test for stimulus generalization. Peak shift takes place when the peak response strength or accuracy occurs not for S+ but for a similar stimulus that is further away from S–.

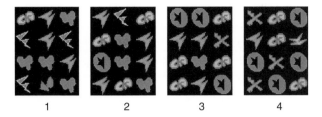

Figure 7.4 Examples of 'icon' stimuli. A possible set of generalization test stimuli used here.

Elemental theories that implement stimulus representation as graded activation (as described above for McLaren *et al.*, 1989, but see also Blough, 1975) can easily model peak shift effects because of the dimensional properties of the elements. By its very nature, peak shift can only be observed over a series of stimuli that have a systematic relationship with one another. While very simple stimuli with characteristics that lie along a physical dimension such as wavelength of light obviously fit this requirement, some experiments have used much more complex stimuli including morphed faces (Spetch, Cheng, & Clifford, 2004) and patterns of small abstract shapes commonly referred to as 'icons' (Oakeshott, 2002; Wills & Mackintosh, 1998). The latter generally employ a range of icons organized so that a logical sequence of patterns is produced, akin to a series of points along a dimension. The frequency of occurrence of each type of icon is systematically varied from one stimulus to the next so that shifting one 'step' along the artificial dimension means replacing some icons with new ones but still retaining a proportion from the original. Figure 7.4 demonstrates one hypothetical set of four stimuli of this nature (see Table 7.1 below for further explanation of the dimensional design).

Peak shift along an artificial dimension has been of particular interest to proponents of elemental associative learning, because it provides a degree of control over the similarity between stimuli and the pattern of activation across units that they might stimulate (Wills & Mackintosh, 1998). Indeed, peak shift effects with icon stimuli have now been shown with both human and pigeon subjects under a variety of experimental conditions (Jones & McLaren, 1999; Livesey, 2006; Oakeshott, 2002; Wills & Mackintosh, 1998). Although elemental models have no trouble accounting for peak shift, in this particular case it seems less tenable to rely on dimensional assumptions about overlapping patterns of element activation when the test dimension itself is artificially contrived. Indeed, a recent finding by Oakeshott (2002) has highlighted the inadequacy of this approach.

Table 7.1 *Stimulus dimension used by Oakeshott (2002)*

| Stimulus | Frequency of occurrence of icons A to I in each stimulus | | | | | | | | |
	A	B	C	D	E	F	G	H	I
F+	1	3	4	3	1				
		1	3	4	3	1			
N+			1	3	4	3	1		
S+				1	3	4	3	1	
S–					1	3	4	3	1

F+, N+, S+, and S– refer to the test stimuli presented to subjects. Numbers refer to the number of copies of each icon A–I embedded in each stimulus. Pigeons were initially trained using one reinforced (S+) and one non-reinforced (S–) stimulus.

The effect of spatial variability

Oakeshott (2002) found that the level of spatial variability across successive presentations of these complex patterns of icons significantly affects the post-discrimination generalization gradient. This poses an interesting problem for elemental associative models which assume that the relative position of the icons should make little or no difference to the overall pattern of generalization. Icon experiments that have produced strong peak shift effects have typically allowed the positions of each icon within the pattern to vary randomly from one trial to the next, and many experiments have also allowed the exact number of each type of icon to vary stochastically, averaging to a given frequency over multiple trials (e.g., Livesey, 2006; Wills & Mackintosh, 1998). Looking at peak shift with pigeons, Oakeshott (2002) demonstrated that when spatial and frequency variations are removed so that the position and number of each icon for a given stimulus remains fixed throughout the experiment, the peak shift effect seems to disappear. Using the design shown in Table 7.1, Oakeshott trained pigeons to discriminate between S+ and S–, under either fixed or variable spatial organization. When tested across several stimuli, pigeons in the variable group showed evidence of a peak shift, with highest response rates for N+, one step removed from S+, and declining response rates further along the dimension at F+. However, pigeons in the fixed group did not show any evidence of peak shift, with highest response rates at S+, declining steadily to N+ and F+. Oakeshott (2002) found that the varied generalization gradient mirrors the predictions of an elemental model while the fixed gradient resembles that predicted by a configural model such as Pearce (1987, 1994). As Oakeshott (2002) noted, the result taken as a whole appears to be irreconcilable with either type of model. Hence it

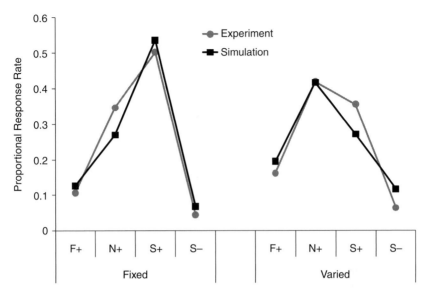

Figure 7.5 Experimental data from Oakeshott (2002) and results from simulation.

poses a significant problem for the associative models that seek to explain post-discrimination generalization gradients in experiments with artificial dimensions. However, the more sophisticated elemental model discussed above can in fact account for both of these results.

For the purposes of modelling this result, the elements in the model are connected to a single output unit corresponding to the key-peck response required for reinforcement. Since Oakeshott (2002) reported proportional response rates to each of four test stimuli (F+, N+, S+, S–), for this model the summed input to the single response output was also converted to proportional values of e^{kI} for the same four stimuli, where k is a constant held at a single value for all subjects and I is the summed input to the response output unit. The results of these simulations can be seen in Figure 7.5, plotted against the proportional response rates reported by Oakeshott (2002). It is quite clear that the model predicts a peak shift for the varied condition but not for the fixed condition, and gives a good fit to Oakeshott's data.

The key aspect of the model that allows it to capture the difference between the two conditions is the interaction between the pattern of activation of the elements and weight change based on a summed error term. The system of representation, with random fixed weights between the inputs and hidden units, allows the expression of both general frequency of occurrence of icons and also location-specific configurations of icons. In the fixed condition, the units that are activated by configurations of position-specific icons present in S+ but not S– gradually accrue the strongest weights to the response output unit. As soon as some icons change, as happens when presenting N+, the configurations change and the activation of the units governing the discrimination may change considerably. In contrast, in the varied condition, the hidden units that will gradually come to govern the discrimination are those that are *generally* activated by icons occurring more frequently in S+ than S–, irrespective of the position of these icons. This involves a more gradual and variable process of weight change, which seems to fit with the observation that varied conditions are typically more difficult and are learnt more slowly than fixed conditions (Livesey, 2006; Oakeshott, 2002). In this case, N+ will contain many of the icons predictive of S+ (and relatively few of those predicting S–) and will result in a high level of activation of the units with associative control, leading to peak shift.

The fixed versus varied effect in human categorization

Peak shift with icon stimuli has been found with human subjects in a categorization paradigm (Wills & Mackintosh, 1998) and the current model can quite readily be applied to human categorization as well as animal conditioning. Using the same architecture but with two response output units rather than one (as shown in Figure 7.3), we simulated a very similar experiment in which the task was to learn to respond with a left key press for one training stimulus (S_L) and with a right key press for another training stimulus (S_R). The system of representation expressed through the input units and random fixed weights to the second-layer units was identical to the animal model.

Not surprisingly, this model predicted very similar results to the animal model, with a peak shift evident for the varied condition but not for the fixed. An experiment with human subjects was run as further confirmation of the predictions of the model and to replicate Oakeshott's (2002) effect of spatial variability (Livesey, Pearson & McLaren, 2005). The post-discrimination generalization gradients for the test phase of this experiment are shown in Figure 7.6.

The model gives a reasonably good fit to the data. In the fixed group, post-discrimination generalization decreases rapidly as the test stimuli become systematically more dissimilar to the training stimuli. In the varied group, the generalization gradient resembles a negatively

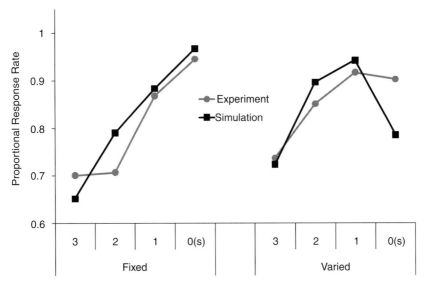

Figure 7.6 Experimental data and simulation results. Data are expressed as accuracy as a function of distance from the pair of training stimuli (S). A distance of 3 steps corresponds to Oakeshott's F+ stimulus, while a distance of 1 step corresponds to N+.

accelerating curve as accuracy peaks for test stimuli that are one step removed from S. The major discrepancy between model and data occurs at S in the varied group, but even here the model fit cannot be rejected because of variability in the data at this point. Subsequent studies (Livesey, 2006) have produced a stronger peak shift due to relatively low accuracy for S, which confirms the predictions of the model for the varied group.

The simulation data predict a very similar difference in post-discrimination generalization gradients between fixed and varied groups, under the conditions run in the current experiment and under conditions more closely resembling the pigeon experiments reported by Oakeshott (2002). This implementation of the McLaren and Mackintosh model accounts for the effect of spatial variability on stimulus categorization without resorting to the assumption that the stimuli have dimensional properties of any sort. Instead, the dimension-like qualities of the generalization gradients and the peak shift effect emerge as a consequence of the process of associative learning. There is also no need to posit any shift from elemental to configural processing of the stimuli to explain the different post-discrimination gradients observed in the fixed and varied cases, an explanation that was suggested by Oakeshott (2002).

Model comparison

This is not the first time that we have addressed the issue of dimensional classification and peak shift. McLaren *et al.* (1995) used chequerboard stimuli constructed so as to define two categories in terms of prototypes, and then to construct exemplars of these categories that varied along a dimension from one category to the other (and beyond). McLaren *et al.* were able to garner evidence for both prototype and peak shift effects with these stimuli, and offered an elemental analysis of the results. This analysis relied on representation of individual squares in specific locations and representation of configurations of squares as well. It should by now come as no surprise that the model we have just presented is ideally placed to implement this elemental account of the McLaren *et al.* (1995) results.

This earlier study was also motivated by a desire to test exemplar-based theories derived from Nosofsky's (1991) GCM model that would apply to the same data. McLaren *et al.* were able to show, by a process of MDS followed by model fitting, that the GCM based account had difficulty in generating the correct pattern of results in this experiment. This conclusion provoked two types of response from exemplar theorists. Lamberts (1996) was able to show that by picking the correct parameters and using a 256-dimensional space (not an entirely arbitrary number, the stimuli were 16 × 16 chequerboards) to represent our stimuli the GCM could produce our pattern of results. Some years later Palmeri and Nosofsky (2001) carried out some similar experiments and obtained a different MDS solution to their data than ours, which also allowed the GCM to produce the correct pattern of results. It should be noted at this point that the reliable effect they obtained was only part of the full pattern of results obtained by McLaren *et al.* (1995), but the advantage for prototypes over far exemplars (exemplars generated to be a member of a category and more distant from the other category prototype than their own category prototype) which was the main cause for the GCM's difficulty in modelling the data was replicated. The MDS solution they used was obtained after categorization (another major difference between this study and ours).

Taking Lamberts's contribution first there is no doubt that it is good to be reminded that these theories have considerable resources available to them, and that a solution can often be found if sufficient ingenuity is applied. We had tried to use what we took to be a 'standard' approach to modelling using the GCM; Lamberts's 256-dimensional alternative went well beyond this. It may be that by helping itself to 256 dimensions, this variant essentially mimicked the elemental model that made use of location-specific representations of squares. In any case, the later work by Palmeri and Nosofsky supersedes this approach as they settle on an MDS solution that employs only six dimensions. Clearly then, the 256-dimensional solution is of theoretical interest, but simply not the case in practice.

The Palmeri and Nosofsky approach requires a different critique. Our approach is to move towards a model that makes minimal assumptions, and then tries to generate the observed learning. The initial inputs are simple, and do not vary if the same stimuli are used. The effects of training are to be captured via learning in the model, and if this produces the wrong results then the model is wrong. In using the MDS solution derived from participants' responses after they had participated in the experiment, Palmeri and Nosofsky may be building into the representations they deploy prior to implementing the GCM the very learning that they wish to explain. It is not hard to model a result if your inputs have that result already in them. Our view is that this element of inevitable circularity is unwelcome, and undermines this type of model fitting. If they were to return to capturing the MDS solution before training, then we speculate that they would arrive at a solution similar to ours that does not enable the GCM to generate the correct pattern of results.

This brings us to the present paradigm and dataset. The reason we have laboured to convey our principled objection to the Palmeri and Nosofsky approach is that we suspect that the same technique could be employed to explain the very different post-discrimination gradients obtained after fixed and varied training regimes. If an MDS solution were obtained before training then it is hard to see the required pattern of results emerging from the GCM. If an MDS solution were obtained after training, then it might well contain something of the impact that that training had had on the ability to discriminate between stimuli from these categories, and so would lend itself to producing that pattern of results when plugged into the GCM. Our approach does not do this; it explains the effect in a non-circular fashion rather than using the effect to explain itself, as we believe Palmeri and Nosofsky have done. In fairness, we should point out that Palmeri and Nosofsky do consider this point, and the reader is invited to consult the paper for their treatment of this issue. We, however, are convinced that the elemental approach is better placed to explain (rather than just fit) the findings reviewed in this chapter. Part of the appeal of the elemental learning approach is that it provides a principled mechanism for generalization and stimulus similarity that is based on the elements that different stimuli share in common.

Future directions

Here, we have provided a very simple exposition of the elemental learning approach, and there are clearly a number of key processes and phenomena that it does not speak to. Some of these have been addressed in detail elsewhere, such as the effect of stimulus exposure on learning (perceptual learning and latent inhibition, see McLaren & Mackintosh, 2000). Others will require closer examination in the future. Two current theoretical concerns are the way elemental learning should interact with (a) selective attention mechanisms and (b) reasoning, rules and propositional learning.

An elemental approach to selective attention?

Selective attention broadly refers to the preferential processing of information from certain stimulus features or dimensions, potentially at the expense of processing other (ignored) stimuli. In category learning, selective attention is usually equated with biases in *associability*, that is the rate at which the various aspects of a stimulus are associated with new categories or outcomes. In both human category learning and animal conditioning, selective changes in stimulus associability seem to be influenced by the relative usefulness of each stimulus in predicting relevant outcomes on previous learning episodes. For instance, in a learning task with novel categories, stimulus features which were good predictors of category membership in a previous task will generally be learned about faster than features that were poor predictors in a previous task: the so-called learned predictiveness effect (Le Pelley & McLaren, 2003; Lochman & Wills, 2003). Although selective attention is often implemented at a dimensional level in models of category learning, effects such as learned predictiveness lend themselves readily to an explanation in terms of elemental changes in associability for specific features. Indeed, we have previously argued that learned predictiveness in categorization is demonstrably elemental in its operation (Livesey & McLaren, 2007).

Therefore one important step for this approach is to implement mechanisms for selective attention within an elemental framework. Such mechanisms need to address results that suggest attention can be feature specific in some circumstances and dimension specific in others. There are several ways in which such a problem could be addressed (e.g. see Suret & McLaren, 2005) and the most appropriate implementation may depend on the link between associability and other aspects of stimulus processing, as recent studies suggest that learning is accompanied by a range of performance-related changes in attention (e.g. Le Pelley, Suret, & Beesley, 2009; Livesey, Harris, & Harris, 2009).

Reasoning and higher level cognition

The current model is aimed squarely at feature-level learning: the processes by which one remembers that stimuli of a certain physical appearance belong to a certain category or require a certain response. Humans are clearly also capable of learning rules about abstract relations between stimuli, relations which are not necessarily grounded in the representation of physical properties (e.g. 'brighter than' or 'larger than'). We have argued elsewhere that relational rule learning can sometimes result in a very different pattern of categorization and stimulus generalization (Livesey & McLaren, 2009). Similarly, learning a *strategic* rule can in some circumstances be clearly distinguished from associative category learning. For instance, negative patterning, where a compound of two stimuli (A+B) must be treated differently to both of the constituent single stimuli (A or B alone), can be solved by elemental learning or by learning a strategy to handle the compound ('Choose the opposite category when they appear together'). However, the latter results in *new* compound stimuli being categorized quite differently because the strategic rule generalizes in ways that feature-level learning does not (Harris & Livesey, 2008; Shanks & Darby, 1998).

A comprehensive model of categorization needs to take into account how explicit rule use can change category judgements and in what circumstances they do so. In this case the relationship between elemental learning and explicit rule use will need to be characterized in detail. This is an ambitious goal and one which will require a larger test-bed of category learning tasks in which the difficulty of identifying and using appropriate rules can be manipulated. The hybrid approach used by Jones and McLaren (2009) (following Spiegel & McLaren, 2003) might then serve as a basis for a possible integration of dual associative and rule-based systems for learning and performance that would allow us to model the categorization data this programme of research produced.

REFERENCES

Blough, D. S. (1975). Steady state data and a quantitative model of operant generalization and discrimination. *Journal of Experimental Psychology: Animal Behavior Processes*, 1, 3–21.

Brandon, S. E., Vogel, E. H., & Wagner, A. R. (2000). A componential view of configural cues in generalization and discrimination in Pavlovian conditioning. *Behavioral Brain Research*, 110, 67–72.

Ghirlanda, S., & Enquist, M. (2003). A century of generalization. *Animal Behaviour*, **66**, 15–36.

Harris, J. A. (2006). Elemental representations of stimuli in associative learning. *Psychological Review*, **113**, 584–605.

Harris, J. A. & Livesey, E. J. (2008). Comparing patterning and biconditional discriminations in humans. *Journal of Experimental Psychology: Animal Behavior Processes*, **34**, 144–154.

Honig, W.K., & Urcuioli, P.J. (1981). The legacy of Guttman and Kalish (1956): 25 years of research on stimulus generalization. *Journal of the Experimental Analysis of Behavior*, **36**, 405–445.

Jones, F., & McLaren, I.P.L. (1999). Rules and associations. In *Proceedings of the Twenty-First Annual Conference of the Cognitive Science Society*. Mahwah, NJ: Erlbaum.

Jones, F. W., & McLaren, I.P.L. (2009). Human sequence learning under incidental and intentional conditions. *Journal of Experimental Psychology: Animal Behavior Processes*, **35**, 538–553.

Lamberts, K. (1996). Exemplar models and prototype effects in similarity-based categorization. *Journal of Experimental Psychology: Learning, Memory, and Cognition*, **22**, 1503–1507.

Le Pelley, M.E., & McLaren, I.P.L. (2003). Learned associability and associative change in human causal learning. *Quarterly Journal of Experimental Psychology*, **56B**, 56–67.

Le Pelley, M.E., Suret, M. B., & Beesley, T. (2009). Learned predictiveness effects in humans: a function of learning, performance, or both? *Journal of Experimental Psychology: Animal Behavior Processes*, **35** (3), 312–327.

Livesey, E.J. (2006). *Discrimination learning and stimulus representation.* Unpublished PhD thesis, University of Cambridge, Cambridge.

Livesey, E.J., Harris, I.M., & Harris, J.A. (2009). Attentional changes during implicit learning: signal validity protects a target stimulus from the attentional blink. *Journal of Experimental Psychology: Learning, Memory, and Cognition*, **35**, 408–422.

Livesey, E.J., & McLaren, I.P.L. (2007). Elemental associability changes in human discrimination learning. *Journal of Experimental Psychology: Animal Behavior Processes*, **33**, 148–159.

(2009). Discrimination and generalization along a simple dimension: peak shift and rule-governed responding. *Journal of Experimental Psychology: Animal Behavior Processes*, **35**, 554–565.

Livesey, E.J., Pearson, L.S., & McLaren, I.P.L. (2005). Spatial variability and peak shift: a challenge for elemental associative learning? In *Proceedings of the Twenty-Seventh Annual Conference of the Cognitive Science Society* (pp. 1302–1307). Mahwah, NJ: Erlbaum.

Lochman, T., & Wills, A.J. (2003). Predictive history in an allergy prediction task. In *Proceedings of EuroCogSci 03: The European Conference of the Cognitive Science Society* (pp. 217–222).

McClelland, J.L., & Rumelhart, D.E. (1985). Distributed memory and the representation of general and specific information. *Journal of Experimental Psychology: General*, **114**, 159–188.

McLaren, I.P.L., Bennett, C.H., Guttman-Nahir, T., Kim, K., & Mackintosh, N. J. (1995). Prototype effects and peak-shift in categorisation. *Journal of Experimental Psychology: Learning, Memory, and Cognition*, 21, 662–673.

McLaren, I.P.L., Kaye, H., & Mackintosh, N.J. (1989). An associative theory of the representation of stimuli: applications to perceptual learning and latent inhibition. In R. G. M. Morris (ed.), *Parallel Distributed Processing: Implications for Psychology and Neurobiology* (pp. 102–130). Oxford: Oxford University Press, Clarendon Press.

McLaren, I.P.L., & Mackintosh, N.J. (2000). An elemental model of associative learning: I. Latent inhibition and perceptual learning. *Animal Learning and Behavior*, 28, 211–246.

(2002). Associative learning and elemental representation: II. Generalization and discrimination. *Animal Learning and Behavior*, 30, 177–200.

Nosofsky, R.M. (1986). Attention, similarity, and the identification-categorization relationship. *Journal of Experimental Psychology: General*, 115, 39–57.

(1991). Typicality in logically defined categories: exemplar-similarity versus rule instantiation. *Memory & Cognition*, 19, 131–150.

Oakeshott, S.M. (2002). *Peak shift: an elemental vs a configural analysis*. Unpublished PhD thesis, University of Cambridge, Cambridge.

Palmeri, T.J., & Nosofsky, R.M. (2001). Central tendencies, extreme points, and prototype enhancement effects in ill-defined perceptual categorization. *Quarterly Journal of Experimental Psychology*, 54A, 197–235.

Pearce, J.M. (1987). A model of stimulus generalisation for Pavlovian conditioning. *Psychological Review*, 94, 61–73.

(1994). Similarity and discrimination: a selective review and a connectionist model. *Psychological Review*, 101, 587–607.

Shanks, D.R., & Darby, R.J. (1998). Feature- and rule-based generalization in human associative learning. *Journal of Experimental Psychology: Animal Behavior Processes*, 24, 405–415.

Spetch, M.L., Cheng, K., & Clifford, C.W.G. (2004). Peak shift but not range effects in recognition of faces. *Learning and Motivation*, 35 (3), 221–241.

Spiegel, R. & McLaren, I.P.L. (2003). Abstract and associatively-based representations in human sequence learning. *Philosophical Transactions of the Royal Society of London, Series B*, 358, 1277–1283.

Suret, M.B., & McLaren, I.P.L. (2005). Elemental representation and associability: an integrated model. In A.J. Wills (ed.), *New Directions in Human Associative Learning*. Mahwah, NJ: Lawrence Erlbaum.

Thompson, R.F. (1965). The neural basis of stimulus generalization. In D.I. Mostofsky (ed.), *Stimulus Generalization* (pp. 154–178). Stanford, CA: Stanford University Press.

Wagner, A.R., & Brandon, S.E. (2001). A componential theory of Pavlovian conditioning. In R.R. Mowrer & S.B. Klein (eds.), *Handbook of Contemporary Learning Theories* (pp. 23–64). Mahwah, NJ: Erlbaum.

Widrow, G., & Hoff, M.E. (1960). Adaptive switching circuits. *Institute of Radio Engineers, Western Electronic Show and Convention Record*, 4, 96–104.

Wills, A. J., Reimers, S., Stewart, N., Suret, M., & McLaren, I. P. L. (2000). Tests of the ratio rule in categorization. *Quarterly Journal of Experimental Psychology*, **53A** (4), 983–1011.

Wills, S., & Mackintosh, N. J. (1998). Peak shift on an artificial dimension. *Quarterly Journal of Experimental Psychology*, **51B** (1), 1–32.

8 Nonparametric Bayesian models of categorization

Thomas L. Griffiths, Adam N. Sanborn,
Kevin R. Canini, Daniel J. Navarro
and Joshua B. Tenenbaum

Motivation

Models of human categorization often focus on the psychological processes by which people form and use knowledge of categories, appealing to concepts such as memory traces, activation, and similarity. An alternative approach is to take a step back from these psychological processes, and instead consider the abstract computational problem being solved when we learn categories, exploring how ideal solutions to that problem might shed light on human behaviour. This kind of investigation – conducted at Marr's (1982) computational level, or via Anderson's (1990) principles of rational analysis – has been particularly successful for categorization, identifying some surprising connections between psychological process models and methods used in machine learning and statistics. This chapter explores some of these connections in detail, and may present technical ideas that are new to many readers. Those who are interested in the mathematical details can find readable introductions from the perspectives of machine learning and cognitive science in Bishop (2006) and Griffiths, Kemp, and Tenenbaum (2008a) respectively.

Categorization is an instance of an inductive problem, requiring category membership to be inferred from the limited information provided by the features of a stimulus. As such, an ideal solution to this problem is provided by Bayesian inference, and in particular by computing a probability distribution over categories given the stimulus. If the joint

TLG and KRC were supported by grant number FA9550-07-1-0351 from the Air Force Office of Scientific Research. ANS was supported by a Royal Society Fellowship and the Gatsby Charitable Foundation. DJN was supported by an Australian Research Fellowship (ARC grant DP-0773794). This chapter summarizes and expands on material previously presented in Griffiths *et al.* (2008).

probability of the features x and category label c of a stimulus is $p(x, c)$, then the probability that x belongs to category c is given by

$$p(c|x) = \frac{p(x,c)}{\sum_{c'} p(x,c')} \tag{1}$$

where the sum in the denominator ranges over all categories. From this perspective, learning a category reduces to estimating the joint probability distribution $p(x, c)$, indicating the probability of observing an object x that belongs to category c. Rational analyses of category learning thus agree that it is fundamentally a problem of *density estimation*, although they differ in whether they focus on estimating the joint distribution $p(x, c)$ directly (e.g., Anderson, 1990) or they consider how conditional distributions $p(x|c)$ could be estimated for each category separately (e.g., Ashby & Alfonso-Reese, 1995; Nosofsky, 1998; Rosseel, 2002).

Traditional statistical solutions to the problem of density estimation are of two types: parametric and nonparametric (Silverman, 1986). In parametric density estimation, a probability distribution is assumed to be of a known form, such as a Gaussian, and density estimation consists of determining the parameters of that distribution. In traditional nonparametric density estimation schemes, a probability distribution is approximated as the sum of a set of 'kernels' – functions that fall off with distance from a central point – where the kernels are centred on points sampled from the distribution. When used to estimate the conditional distribution on features associated with each category, $p(x|c)$, these two approaches correspond to the two main classes of psychological process models: prototype and exemplar models (Ashby & Alfonso-Reese, 1995). Prototype models, corresponding to parametric density estimation, assume that a category is associated with a single prototype and that categorization involves comparing new stimuli to these prototypes (e.g., Reed, 1972). Exemplar models, corresponding to kernel-based nonparametric density estimation, assume that a category is represented by a set of stored exemplars and that categorizing new stimuli involves comparing these stimuli to the set of exemplars in each category (e.g., Medin & Schaffer, 1978; Nosofsky, 1986).

Traditional parametric and nonparametric density estimation methods have different advantages and disadvantages: the greater flexibility of nonparametric methods comes at the cost of requiring more data to estimate a distribution. Consequently, there is not a clear argument in favour of one of these approaches from rational grounds, and statisticians have begun to explore more sophisticated density estimation techniques that combine the strengths of both approaches by supporting representations that interpolate between using a single parametric distribution and having a kernel associated with each stimulus. Many of these approaches are based on *mixture models*, in which a distribution is assumed to be a mixture of a set of parametric densities (McLachlan & Basford, 1988). This is an idea that resonates with work in psychology that has explored process models in which categories are represented using clusters of several exemplars, with each cluster having its own prototype (e.g., Love, Medin, & Gureckis, 2004; Vanpaemel & Storms, 2008). The potential for mixture models to capture representations that lie between prototypes and exemplars has been recognized in the psychological literature (Anderson, 1990; Rosseel, 2002).

Recently, models of human categorization have begun to draw on another basic advance in density estimation techniques from statistics and machine learning. *Nonparametric Bayesian* methods for density estimation (e.g., Escobar & West, 1995; Neal, 1998) provide ways to adaptively select the effective number of clusters to use in representing a distribution, while allowing the number of possible clusters to remain unbounded. These models are particularly interesting in the context of understanding human category learning, as they offer an alternative to the idea that a single fixed representational strategy (such as forming prototypes or remembering exemplars) is necessary. Nonparametric Bayesian models illustrate how a rational learner could adaptively form a representation based on the distributional properties of the observed stimuli.

The most basic nonparametric Bayesian density estimation method is based on the *Dirichlet process mixture model* (DPMM; Antoniak, 1974). The DPMM assumes that a probability distribution can be represented as an infinite mixture of parametric densities, where the parameters of those densities are generated from a stochastic process known as the Dirichlet process (Ferguson, 1973). While the mathematical definition of the Dirichlet process is complex (for details, see Navarro *et al.*, 2006), its implications are straightforward. When the first stimulus is observed, a cluster (with an associated parametric distribution) is created to represent that stimulus. Each subsequent stimulus is then assigned to either an existing cluster (with probability proportional to the number of stimuli already assigned to that density), or is represented by a new cluster. The result of this process is a probability distribution over partitions of the stimuli into clusters that are each modelled with a single parametric density. This partitioning of the data is equivalent to the assumption in psychological process models that people might represent categories in terms of several clusters that can each be summarized by a prototype (e.g., Kruschke, 1990; Love *et al.*, 2004; Vanpaemel & Storms, 2008).

As with other density estimation methods, the DPMM has a connection to a psychological model. However, in this case the connection is not to a process model, but to a rational model: Anderson's (1990, 1991) rational model of categorization. Anderson considered how the probability distribution associated with a set of categories could be estimated, and independently developed a solution to this problem that was equivalent to the DPMM (the equivalence was first pointed out by Neal, 1998). Recognizing this equivalence makes it possible to use algorithms developed for the DPMM to better approximate optimal performance in Anderson's rational model (Sanborn, Griffiths, & Navarro, 2006) and to develop psychological models that draw on recent generalizations of the Dirichlet process that have been developed in machine learning and statistics, such as the hierarchical Dirichlet process (Teh *et al.*, 2004).

The key idea behind nonparametric Bayesian models – that learners can adaptively form a representation that captures the structure expressed in the observed data – is also applicable in cases that go beyond simple clustering of stimuli based on their features. Shafto *et al.* (2006) introduced a model for learning cross-cutting systems of categories in which a similar principle was used to simultaneously decide how many systems of categories might be relevant to understanding the features of stimuli, and which category each stimulus belongs to within each system. Kemp *et al.* (2006) showed how the key ideas behind the DPMM could be extended to data that reflect the relations that exist among a set of stimuli, rather than the features that those stimuli express. This model could discover clusters of stimuli that behaved similarly in relation to other clusters of stimuli, forming abstractions about relational roles that might form a first step towards learning more complex relational systems such as folk theories (Kemp *et al.*, 2010).

Our goal in this chapter is to provide a basic introduction to the ideas behind nonparametric Bayesian models in the context of category learning. To this end, we first give a more formal description of some nonparametric Bayesian models – the Dirichlet process mixture model, the hierarchical Dirichlet process, and related extensions. We then discuss how algorithms for inference in these models can be implemented, describing algorithms proposed both in psychology and in statistics. Finally, we present simple examples illustrating the operation of different algorithms and the prediction of human behaviour.

Description

Our description of nonparametric Bayesian models of categorization begins with the Dirichlet process mixture model, since this model provides the simplest illustration of the principles on which other models are based. We then define the hierarchical Dirichlet process, and summarize some of the other ways in which this model has been extended.

The Dirichlet process mixture model

In order to compute the conditional probability distribution over categories specified in Equation 1, we need to estimate a probability distribution over features x and category labels c, $p(x, c)$. For simplicity, we will drop c, since it can be considered another feature of the stimulus (albeit one that should be given greater weight than other features), and just consider how we can estimate the joint distribution of a sequence of stimuli $\mathbf{x}_N = (x_1, ..., x_N)$.[1] Like other mixture models, the Dirichlet process mixture model assumes that each x_i was generated from a mixture component that is a parametric density. Intuitively, each mixture component corresponds to a cluster of stimuli that go together. We will use z_j to denote the index of the mixture component from which x_i was generated, and $\mathbf{z}_N = (z_1, ..., z_N)$ to indicate the vector of component assignments for all stimuli. Each z_j is just a nominal variable picking out the cluster to which x_i belongs, so $\mathbf{z}_N$ partitions the stimuli into clusters. A simple example helps to clarify the notation. In Figure 8.1, we have three stimuli that are observed sequentially. Each stimulus has three binary features, but their features will not be important for now. Let us assume that an observer has already seen the first two stimuli, but has not yet seen the third stimulus. x_2 is thus the set of the first two stimuli, x_1 and x_2. If these stimuli are assigned to the same component, the z_j values will be equal, for example $z_1 = z_2 = 1$. The only other alternative for two stimuli is that they are assigned to different components, in which case $z_1 = 1$ and $z_2 = 2$.

Usually, we just observe the stimuli x_N without being told which clusters they belong to. The joint distribution $p(\mathbf{x}_N)$ is thus obtained by averaging over all possible assignments of stimuli to clusters, with

$$p(\mathbf{x}_N) = \sum_{\mathbf{z}_N} p(\mathbf{x}_N \mid \mathbf{z}_N) p(\mathbf{z}_N) \tag{2}$$

where $p(\mathbf{x}_N \mid \mathbf{z}_N)$ indicates the probability of the stimuli under the assignments $\mathbf{z}_N$, and $p(\mathbf{z}_N)$ is a distribution that reflects our ignorance about the cluster assignments. If $p(\mathbf{x}_N \mid \mathbf{z}_N)$ depends only on which stimuli are

---

[1] Throughout this chapter, we use boldface to indicate that a variable is a vector (e.g., $\mathbf{x}_N$), and italics to indicate that a variable is a scalar (e.g., x_i).

Trial   I   II   III

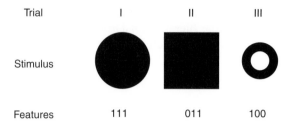

Stimulus

Features   111   011   100

Figure 8.1 Example stimuli for a categorization experiment. Each stimulus is presented on one of three trials, and possesses three binary features.

assigned to the same clusters, then all vectors of assignments z_N that result in the same partition of the stimuli will give the same probability to $\mathbf{x}_N$. Consequently, we can define $p(\mathbf{z}_N)$ by specifying a probability distribution over partitions of N objects.

In the DPMM, this distribution over partitions corresponds to a stochastic process known as the *Chinese restaurant process* (CRP; Aldous, 1985; Pitman, 2002). The CRP defines a distribution that has two desirable properties: it makes it possible for any number of clusters to appear in the data, and it gives each partition that has clusters of the same sizes the same probability. Under this process, we imagine that stimuli are assigned to clusters one after another and the probability that stimulus $i + 1$ is assigned to cluster k is

$$P\left(z_i = k \mid \mathbf{z}_{i-1} \right) = \begin{cases} \dfrac{M_k}{i-1+\alpha} & \text{if } M_k > 0 \ \left(\text{i.e., } k \text{ is old} \right) \\[2ex] \dfrac{\alpha}{i-1+\alpha} & \text{if } M_k = 0 \ \left(\text{i.e., } k \text{ is old} \right) \end{cases} \tag{3}$$

where M_k is the number of stimuli that have already been assigned to cluster k, and α is a parameter of the process that determines the probability of generating new clusters. The process gets its unusual name from thinking of stimuli as customers entering a large Chinese restaurant, where the table they choose to sit at corresponds to their cluster assignment. Following this process for all N stimuli results in a distribution $p(\mathbf{z}_N)$ that has an interesting property: the probability of a partition $\mathbf{z}_N$ does not depend on the order in which we assigned stimuli to clusters. This property is known as *exchangeability* (Aldous, 1985).

To illustrate the use of the CRP, assume that the first two stimuli shown in Figure 8.1 are assigned to the same cluster, $\mathbf{z}_2 = (1,1)$, when the third stimulus, x_3, is observed. We can then use the CRP to calculate the prior distribution over the cluster assignment for that object, z_3. The CRP gives the prior probability of x_3 belonging to the cluster with the other two stimuli and the prior probability that it is assigned to its own cluster. If $\alpha = 0.5$, then

$$P\left(z_3 = 1 \mid \mathbf{z}_2\right) = \frac{2}{3 - 1 + 0.5} = 0.8 \text{ and } P\left(z_3 = 2 \mid \mathbf{z}_2\right) = \frac{0.5}{3 - 1 + 0.5} = 0.2.$$

The probability of a new cluster being created increases as α increases.

Up until this point, the features of the stimuli have been unimportant, but to fully specify the DPMM, we also need to define the distribution $p(\mathbf{x}_N \mid \mathbf{z}_N)$ that links partitions to stimuli (often referred to as the *likelihood*, with the Dirichlet process providing the *prior* on partitions z_N). This is done by assuming that each cluster is associated with a probability distribution over stimuli. The choice of this distribution depends on the properties of the data: with continuous features, a Gaussian distribution may be appropriate, capturing the mean and variance of those features in each cluster; with discrete features, a multinomial distribution can be used to specify the probability of each feature value in each cluster. The distribution for each cluster is characterized by a set of parameters that can be estimated from the stimuli assigned to that cluster, or simply integrated out of the probabilistic model. The stimuli in the simple example shown in Figure 8.1 are parameterized by three binary features and the likelihoods $p(\mathbf{x}_3 \mid \mathbf{z}_3)$ are calculated using separate multinomial distributions for each cluster. These multinomial distributions are independent for each feature (for details, see Anderson, 1990; Neal, 1998; Sanborn *et al.*, 2006).

When using the DPMM for categorization, we need to be able to compute the probability distribution over features (including the category label) for a novel object. The distribution $p(x, c)$ required to apply Equation 1 is taken to be the *posterior predictive distribution* generated by the DPMM. This distribution is used because we do not know what the appropriate cluster assignments $\mathbf{z}_N$ are, so we have to average over the posterior distribution on cluster assignments, just as we averaged over the prior in computing $p(\mathbf{x}_N)$ in Equation 2. The posterior predictive distribution is obtained by computing the posterior probability of each partition $\mathbf{z}_N$ of the stimuli $\mathbf{x}_N$ that belong to the category, and then averaging the probability of a new stimulus x over the resulting distribution. More formally, dropping c again for convenience, we have

$$p(x \mid \mathbf{x}_N) = \sum_{\mathbf{z}_N} \sum_{z} p(x \mid z, \mathbf{z}_N, \mathbf{x}_N) p(z \mid \mathbf{z}_N) p(\mathbf{z}_N \mid \mathbf{x}_N) \tag{4}$$

where $p(x|z, Z_N, X_N)$ is the probability of the stimulus x under the distribution associated with cluster z given the other stimuli in x_N assigned to z by the partition z_N, $p(z|\mathbf{z}_N)$ is the probability of a stimulus being generated from cluster z given the partition z_N, and $p(\mathbf{z}_N|\mathbf{x}_N)$ is the posterior probability of the partition z_N given the stimuli x_N. Of the quantities on the right hand side of this equation, $p(x|z, \mathbf{z}_N, \mathbf{x}_N)$ can be computed directly from the specification of the distribution associated with each cluster. The quantity $p(z|\mathbf{z}_N)$ follows directly from the CRP.

In the example shown in Figure 8.1, computing the posterior predictive distribution $p(x_3|\mathbf{x}_2)$ requires summing over all possible partitions $\mathbf{z}_2$ which are $\mathbf{z}_2 = (1,1)$ and $\mathbf{z}_2 = (1,2)$ and summing over all possible assignments of x_3 to clusters given z_2. Though this is straightforward in this case, computing the posterior predictive distribution is computationally expensive for larger numbers of stimuli. The main challenge of performing probabilistic inference using the DPMM is calculating the posterior distribution over partitions $\mathbf{z}_N$ given $\mathbf{x}_N$, because the number of partitions increases rapidly with N. We return to this problem later in the chapter.

The hierarchical Dirichlet process

In Anderson's (1990, 1991) original presentation of his rational model, category labels were taken to be just another feature of the stimuli, as in our presentation of the DPMM. However, other rational analyses of categorization have focused on estimating the conditional distribution over features x for each category c, $p(x|c)$ (e.g., Ashby & Alfonso-Reese, 1995; Nosofsky, 1998; Rosseel, 2002). It is straightforward to use a DPMM to estimate these conditional distributions, but taking a separate mixture model for each category means that the clusters that comprise those categories are taken to be completely disjoint. However, in some cases it may make sense to share those clusters between categories, providing a common vocabulary at a higher level than raw stimuli in which the structure of categories can be expressed. For example, a cluster of tabby cats might be useful in learning the categories of both cats and striped objects. This kind of sharing of clusters between categories can be achieved using the hierarchical Dirichlet process (HDP).

The HDP, introduced by Teh *et al.* (2004), is a straightforward generalization of the basic Dirichlet process. Stimuli are divided into categories, and each category is modelled using a Dirichlet process mixture model (with parameter α). A new stimulus is first compared to all of the clusters in its category, with the prior probability of each cluster determined by Equation 3. If the stimulus is to be assigned to a new cluster, the new cluster is drawn from a second Dirichlet process that compares

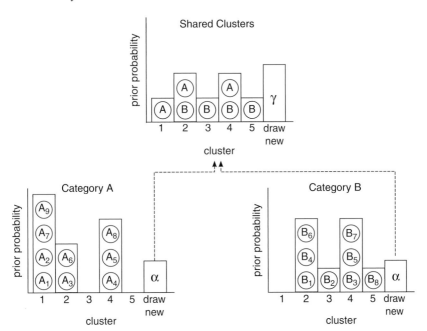

Figure 8.2 Illustration of the hierarchical Dirichlet process. The prior probability for each cluster at the lower level is based on the number of category examples in that cluster. If a cluster is selected from the higher level, the prior probability of clusters is based on the number of categories by which they have been selected. Completely new clusters can only be created at the higher level. (Reproduced from Griffiths *et al.* (2008b) with permission from Oxford University Press.)

the stimulus to all of the clusters that have been created across groups. The probability of generating a new cluster in this higher-level Dirichlet process is governed by the parameter γ, analogous to α, and the prior probability of each cluster is proportional to the number of times that cluster has been selected by any category, instead of the number of stimuli in each cluster. The new stimulus is only assigned to a completely new cluster if both Dirichlet processes select a new cluster. In this manner, stimuli in different categories can end up belonging to the same mixture component, simply by being drawn from the same partition in the higher level. An illustration of this is shown in Figure 8.2.

The HDP provides a way to model probability distributions across categories. Each distribution is a mixture of an unbounded number of clusters, but the clusters can be shared between categories. Shared clusters allow the model to leverage examples from across categories to better estimate cluster parameters. A priori expectations about the number of clusters in a category and the extent to which clusters are shared between categories are determined by the parameters α and γ. When α is small, each category will have few clusters, but when α is large, the number of clusters will be closer to the number of stimuli. When γ is small, categories are likely to share clusters, but when γ is large, the clusters in each category are likely to be unique.

The extra flexibility provided by the capacity to share clusters between categories means that the HDP can be used to characterize a variety of different schemes for representing the structure of categories as α and γ are varied. When $\alpha \to \infty$ and $\gamma \to \infty$ we obtain an exemplar model, with one cluster per stimulus and no sharing of clusters. When $\alpha \to 0$ and $\gamma \to \infty$ we obtain a prototype model, with one cluster per category and no sharing of clusters. When $\alpha \to 0$ and γ is free to vary, we obtain a model where each stimulus comes from its own cluster but those clusters are drawn from a Dirichlet process shared between categories, similar to the original scheme for representing categories introduced by Anderson (1990, 1991). The hierarchical Dirichlet process has thus been proposed as a unifying rational model of categorization, containing these other models as special cases and allowing the learner to adaptively select an appropriate representation through estimation of α and γ in a given domain (Griffiths *et al.*, 2007).

Other nonparametric Bayesian models

The basic principles behind the nonparametric Bayesian models outlined in this section can be used in any probabilistic model in which categories can be represented in terms of underlying clusters. This means that the nonparametric Bayesian approach can be extended to capture learning from different kinds of data, and forming richer representations of category structure. We will briefly summarize two models that provide examples of such extensions: learning from relations, and learning cross-cutting systems of categories.

Learning cross-cutting categories   Most approaches to categorization, including the methods we describe above, assume that there is one best way to organize the entities in a given semantic domain. Most natural domains, however, can be represented in multiple ways: animals may be thought of in terms of their taxonomic groupings or their ecological niches, foods may be thought of in terms of their nutritional content or social role; products may be thought of in terms of function or brand;

movies may be thought of in terms of their genre or star quality. Another nonparametric Bayesian model, CrossCat (Shafto *et al.*, 2006), discovers multiple systems of categories given information about a domain of entities and their attributes. Each system of entity-categories accounts for a distinct and coherent subset of the observed attributes.

As with the other models we have discussed, CrossCat uses Dirichlet processes as priors on how to partition entities into categories within each system, and how to allocate attributes across systems. The nonparametric formulation allows CrossCat to find appropriate tradeoffs between two kinds of simplicity that are both desirable in a domain theory but tend to compete with each other: minimizing the number of category systems, and minimizing the number of categories within each system. Building an overly simplified model at either of these levels will lead to an overly complex model at the other. CrossCat naturally prefers the theory that is most compact overall, splitting up a category system into two if it will lead to many fewer categories per system, or splitting up a category within a system if it will substantially increase the number of attributes that system can explain.

CrossCat has been shown to discover meaningful semantic concepts in several kinds of data. For instance, given a data set of animal species and their attributes, CrossCat finds three ways to categorize the species: a system of taxonomic classes that accounts for anatomical and physiological properties, a system of ecological classes that accounts for behavioural features (relevant to being a predator or prey, or living in the land, air or sea), and a third system in which almost all species belong to the same class and which explains features that do not vary much, or vary idiosyncratically over this domain (e.g., the colour or size of an animal). The model also finds cross-cutting systems of categories that match those identified by human learners in laboratory experiments (Shafto *et al.*, 2006).

Learning from relations   Traditional approaches to categorization treat each entity individually, simply in terms of the features it has. Richer semantic structure can be found if we can develop methods for effectively learning from complex forms of relational data, where categories are defined in terms of the relations between one another. Nonparametric Bayesian models can be used to solve this problem, discovering systems of related concepts from heterogeneous data sources. One such model, the infinite relational model (Kemp *et al.*, 2006), identifies clusters of objects that not only share similar features, but also participate in similar relations. Given data involving one or more types of entities, their attributes, and relations among them, this model can discover the kinds of entities in each set and the relations between kinds that are possible or likely. For instance, a data set for consumer choice could be characterized in terms of these relations: which consumers bought which products, which features are present in which products, which demographic attributes characterize which users, and so on. The model simultaneously discovers how to cluster each type of entity as well as the regularities in how these clusters are related (for example, consumers in class X tend to buy products in class Y).

The nonparametric nature of the infinite relational model allows it to automatically discover the appropriate number of categories to be used in describing each type of entity, and to increase the complexity of these categorization systems as new data warrant. This ability to grow representations of appropriate complexity as the observed data grow is especially important in relational settings. When the data concern how entities of different types interact, a choice about how finely to group entities of one type interacts with the analogous choices for all other types those entities interact with. For example, grouping one type too coarsely may lead to overly fine-grained representation of another type it interacts with. The automatic discovery of clusters of the appropriate granularity produced by this model also provides a way to explain how people might form categories of objects based on the causal relations that hold between them, providing a basic step towards learning a more sophisticated relational theory of a domain (Kemp *et al.*, 2010).

Implementation

Nonparametric Bayesian models present a basic challenge for the learner and the modeller: performing probabilistic inference about the values of the latent variables in the model (such as the partitions of stimuli used in the DPMM). Psychological research using these models has explored three algorithms for probabilistic inference. One algorithm, which we call the *local MAP* algorithm, was introduced by Anderson (1990) and motivated by psychological considerations. The two other algorithms – *Gibbs sampling* and *particle filtering* – draw on the statistics literature, and were first applied in a psychological setting by Sanborn *et al.* (2006). For simplicity, we present these three algorithms just for the DPMM, but the same principles apply when they are used with other models.

The local MAP algorithm

The local MAP algorithm (short for local maximum a posteriori probability) approximates the sum in Equation 4 with just a single partition of the N objects, z_N. This partition is selected by assigning each object to the highest probability cluster as it is observed. The posterior probability that stimulus i was generated from cluster k given the features of all stimuli, along with the cluster assignments $\mathbf{z}_{i-1}$ for the previous $i-1$ stimuli, is

$$p(z_i = k \,|\, x_i, \mathbf{z}_{i-1}, \mathbf{x}_{i-1}) \propto p(x_i \,|\, z_i = k, \mathbf{z}_{i-1}, \mathbf{x}_{i-1}) p(z_i = k \,|\, \mathbf{z}_{i-1}) \qquad (5)$$

where $p(z_i = k \,|\, \mathbf{z}_{i-1})$ is given by Equation 3. Under the local MAP algorithm, x_i is assigned to the cluster k that maximizes Equation 5. Iterating this process results in a single partition of a set of N objects. The local MAP algorithm approximates the complete joint distribution using only this partition.

To illustrate the local MAP algorithm, we applied it to the simple example of sequentially presented stimuli in Figure 8.1. As mentioned above, each stimulus is parameterized by three binary features and the likelihood $p(\mathbf{x} \,|\, \mathbf{z})$ is calculated using multinomial distributions that are independent for each feature, which is the standard approach for modelling binary data (for details, see Anderson, 1990; Neal, 1998; Sanborn et al., 2006). The local MAP algorithm initially assigns the first observed stimulus to its own cluster (Figure 8.3). When the second stimulus is observed, the algorithm generates each possible partition: either it is assigned to the same cluster as the first stimulus or to a new cluster. The posterior probability of each of these partitions is calculated and the partition with the highest posterior probability is always chosen as the representation. After the third stimulus is observed, the algorithm produces all possible partitions involving the third stimulus, assuming that the first two stimuli are part of the same cluster. Note that not all possible partitions of the three stimuli are considered, because the algorithm makes an irrevocable choice for the partition of the first two stimuli and the possible partitions on later trials have to be consistent with this choice. The local MAP algorithm will always produce the same final partition for a given sequential order of the stimuli, assuming there are no ties in the posterior probability.

Unfortunately, although this approach is fast and simple, the local MAP algorithm has some odd characteristics. In particular, the quality of the approximation is often poor, and the algorithm violates the principle of exchangeability discussed above. Figure 8.4 shows that the posterior distribution over partitions produced by the local MAP is very different from the distribution it attempts to approximate. The local MAP results in a single outcome, while the exact posterior distribution has some non-zero probability for every outcome. The partition the local MAP selects depends on the order in which the stimuli are observed, and this order

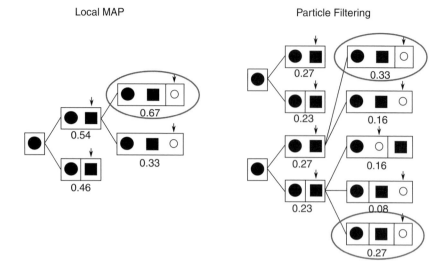

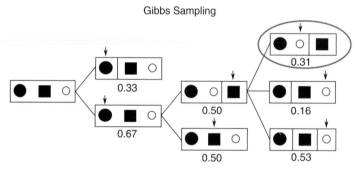

Figure 8.3 Illustration of the local MAP, particle filtering, and Gibbs sampling approximation algorithms. All three algorithms are applied to the stimuli shown in Figure 8.1. Each algorithm starts on the left side with an initial partition of the stimuli. Each box is a partition that contains one or more stimuli and the presence of a separating vertical line indicates that the stimuli belong to different clusters. The children of the initial (leftmost) partition are the partitions under consideration in the next step of each algorithm. These children partitions are all the possible reassignments of the stimulus marked by the arrow. Numbers underneath each partition show the posterior probability of that partition. Not all possible paths are followed, with Gibbs sampling and particle filtering choosing partitions to continue stochastically, while local MAP always chooses the partition with the maximum posterior probability. The circled partitions are the outcomes of the algorithms.

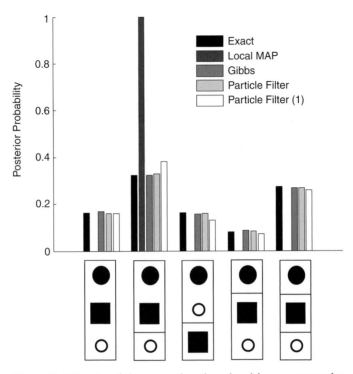

Figure 8.4 Results of the approximation algorithms compared to the exact posterior. The five bar groupings correspond to the five possible partitions of the three stimuli in Figure 8.3. The bars within each grouping correspond to the approximation algorithms outlined in the text. Standard error bars are provided for the Gibbs sampling, particle filter, and single-particle particle filter algorithms.

dependence is perhaps stronger than the order dependence displayed by human participants (see Sanborn *et al.*, 2006).

Gibbs sampling

The approximate inference algorithm most commonly used with the DPMM is Gibbs sampling, a Markov chain Monte Carlo (MCMC) method (see Gilks, Richardson, & Spiegelhalter, 1996). This algorithm involves constructing a Markov chain that will converge to the distribution from which we want to sample, in this case the posterior distribution over partitions. The state space of the Markov chain is the set of partitions, and transitions between states are produced by sampling the cluster assignment of each stimulus from its conditional distribution, given the current assignments of all other stimuli. The algorithm thus moves from state to state by sequentially sampling each z_i from the distribution

$$p(z_i = k \,|\, x_i, \mathbf{z}_{-i}, \mathbf{x}_{-i}) \propto p(x_i \,|\, z_i = k, \mathbf{z}_{-i}, \mathbf{x}_{-i}) p(z_i = k \,|\, \mathbf{z}_{-i}) \qquad (6)$$

where $\mathbf{z}_{-i}$ refers to all cluster assignments except for the ith.

Equation 6 is very similar to Equation 5, although it gives the probability of a cluster based on all of the trials in the entire experiment except for the current trial, instead of just the previous trials. Exchangeability means that these probabilities are actually computed in exactly the same way: the order of the stimuli can be rearranged so that any particular stimulus is considered the last stimulus. Hence, we can use Equation 3 to compute $p(z_i \,|\, \mathbf{z}_{-i})$, with old clusters receiving probability in proportion to their popularity, and a new cluster being chosen with probability determined by α. The other terms reflect the probability of the features and category label of stimulus i under the partition that results from this choice of z_i, and depend on the nature of the features.

The Gibbs sampling algorithm for the DPMM is straightforward (Neal, 1998) and is illustrated for the simple example in Figure 8.1. First, an initial assignment of stimuli to clusters is chosen, with a convenient choice being all stimuli assigned to a single cluster. Unlike the local MAP algorithm, Gibbs sampling is not a sequential algorithm; all stimuli must be observed before it can be used. Next, we choose a single stimulus and consider all possible reassignments of that stimulus to clusters, including not making a change in assignments or assigning the stimulus to a new cluster. Equation 6 gives the probability of each partition and one of the partitions is sampled based on its posterior probability, making this algorithm stochastic, unlike the local MAP. The stochastic nature of the algorithm is evident in the example in Figure 8.3, because the final circled assignment has lower probability than the alternatives. The example shows a single iteration of Gibbs sampling, in which each stimulus is cycled through and reassigned. The algorithm goes through many iterations, with the output of one iteration the input to the next. Since the probability of obtaining a particular partition after each iteration depends only on the partition produced on the previous iteration, this is a Markov chain.

After enough iterations for the Markov chain to converge, we begin to save the partitions it produces. The partition produced on one iteration is not independent of the next, so the results of some iterations are discarded to approximate independence. The partitions generated by the Gibbs sampler can be used in the same way as samples from the posterior distribution $p(\mathbf{z}_N \,|\, \mathbf{x}_N)$. Averaging over these samples thus provides a way to approximate the sum over $\mathbf{z}_N$ in Equation 4 without needing to calculate the posterior probability of all partitions. Over 10,000 iterations the Gibbs sampler produces a good approximation to the exact posterior, as shown in Figure 8.4.

Particle filtering

Particle filtering is a sequential Monte Carlo technique that can be used to provide a discrete approximation to a posterior distribution that can be updated with new data (Doucet, de Freitas, & Gordon, 2001). Each 'particle' is a partition Z_i^l of the stimuli from the first i trials, where l is the index of the particle. Unlike the local MAP algorithm, in which the posterior distribution is approximated with a single partition, the particle filter uses m partitions. Summing over these particles gives us an approximation to the posterior distribution over partitions:

$$p\left(\mathbf{z}_i \mid \mathbf{x}_i\right) \approx \frac{1}{m} \sum_{l=1}^{m} \delta\left(\mathbf{z}_i, \mathbf{z}_i^{(l)}\right) \tag{7}$$

where $\delta(\mathbf{z},\mathbf{z}')$ is 1 when $\mathbf{z} = \mathbf{z}'$, and 0 otherwise. If Equation 7 is used as an approximation to the posterior distribution over partitions $\mathbf{z}_i$ after the first i trials, then we can approximate the distribution of $\mathbf{z}_{i+1}$ given the stimuli x_i in the following manner:

$$\begin{aligned} p\left(\mathbf{z}_{i+1} \mid \mathbf{x}_i\right) &= \sum_{\mathbf{z}_i} p(\mathbf{z}_{i+1} \mid \mathbf{z}_i) p(\mathbf{z}_i \mid \mathbf{x}_i) \\ &\approx \sum_{\mathbf{z}_i} p\left(\mathbf{z}_{i+1} \mid \mathbf{z}_i\right) \frac{1}{m} \sum_{l=1}^{m} \delta\left(\mathbf{z}_i, \mathbf{z}_i^{(l)}\right) \\ &= \frac{1}{m} \sum_{l=1}^{m} p\left(\mathbf{z}_{i+1} \mid \mathbf{z}_i^{(l)}\right) \end{aligned} \tag{8}$$

where $p(\mathbf{z}_{i+1} \mid \mathbf{z}_i)$ is given by Equation 3. We can then incorporate the information conveyed by the features and label of stimulus $i + 1$, arriving at the approximate posterior probability

$$\begin{aligned} p\left(\mathbf{z}_{i+1} \mid \mathbf{x}_{i+1}\right) &= p(x_{i+1} \mid \mathbf{z}_{i+1}, \mathbf{x}_i) p(\mathbf{z}_{i+1} \mid \mathbf{x}_i) \\ &\approx \frac{1}{m} \sum_{l=1}^{m} p\left(x_{i+1} \mid \mathbf{z}_{i+1}, \mathbf{x}_i\right) p\left(\mathbf{z}_{i+1} \mid \mathbf{z}_i^{(l)}\right). \end{aligned} \tag{9}$$

The result is a discrete distribution over all the previous particle assignments and all possible assignments for the current stimulus. Drawing m samples from this distribution provides us with our new set of particles.

The particle filter for the simple example from Figure 8.1 is illustrated in Figure 8.3. The particle filter for the DPMM is initialized with the first stimulus assigned to the first cluster for all m particles, in this case $m = 2$. On observing each new stimulus, the distribution in Equation 9 is calculated, based on the particles sampled in the last trial. Like the local MAP, the particle filter updates the partition as each new stimulus is observed, and like the local MAP, only new partitions that are consistent with the previous choices made by the algorithm are considered. This consistency can be seen in the potential partitions when the third stimulus is observed in Figure 8.3: each descendant is consistent with the partition choices made by its ancestor. The particle filter differs in two ways from the local MAP algorithm. The first is that the choice of new partitions is stochastic instead of deterministic. The particle filter algorithm samples new partitions based on their posterior probabilities instead of always selecting the partition with the maximum probability. Stochastic selection generally produces more accurate approximation of the exact distribution, which can be seen in Figure 8.4. A particle filter with $m = 1$ particles is equivalent to the local MAP algorithm, except that the new partition is sampled instead of deterministically selected. Over 1000 runs of the algorithm, the single-particle particle filter produces a far closer approximation to the exact distribution than the local MAP. The second difference is that multiple particles means that multiple partitions can be used instead of the single partition passed forward by the local MAP. The m partitions are selected without regard for ancestry, allowing a partition that was selected for the early observations to die out as the descendants of other partitions replace it. A large enough set of particles will prevent this algorithm from being sent down the wrong track, which is a danger for the local MAP. The particle filter in Figure 8.4 used 10 particles with 1000 repetitions. The results of this algorithm are indistinguishable from the exact solution, and are both a better approximation than the local MAP or the single-particle particle filter.

Example

We present the following example to demonstrate how nonparametric models can capture certain aspects of human categorization that are not well explained by either prototype or exemplar models. A more detailed analysis of this example can be found in Griffiths *et al.* (2007). In an experiment conducted by Smith and Minda (1998), a prototype model

Table 8.1 *Categories A and B from Smith and Minda (1998)*

Category	Stimuli
A	000000, 100000, 010000, 001000, 000010, 000001, 111101
B	111111, 011111, 101111, 110111, 111011, 111110, 000100

was found to provide a better explanation for human performance on a categorization task during the early stages of learning, while an exemplar model was found to be a better fit to the later stages. The authors presented these findings to dispute the sentiment that exemplar models provided a dominant account of human categorization over prototype models. Instead, they argued, people seemed to use strategies corresponding to both of these models, perhaps shifting between them over time. Due to the natural ability of the HDP to interpolate between exemplar- and prototype-style representations as warranted by the observed data, it seems a natural candidate to explain the results found by Smith and Minda.

We focus on the non-linearly separable structure explored in Experiment 2 of Smith and Minda (1998). The experiment consisted of a series of trials in which 16 participants were asked to guess whether six-letter nonsense words belonged to Category A or Category B. Each letter of the words took on one of two possible values, producing the binary feature representations of the two categories shown in Table 8.1.

Each category contains one prototypical stimulus (000000 versus 111111), five stimuli with five features in common with the prototype, and one stimulus with only one feature in common, which we refer to as an 'exception'. No linear function of the features can correctly classify every stimulus, meaning that a prototype model will not be able to distinguish between the categories exactly. Participants received feedback after each trial and were tested a total of 40 times on each of the 14 stimuli. The trials were split into 10 segments, each consisting of 4 trials of each of the 10 stimuli. The results of the experiment are shown in Figure 8.5. The exceptions were initially identified as belonging to the wrong category, with performance improving over time.

As in the previous example, in applying the computational models, we can use a Beta prior distribution for each dimension of each cluster, allowing us to integrate out the parameters of each cluster to obtain a tractable distribution for $p(x \mid z)$. The three models that were tested, a prototype model, an exemplar model, and the DPMM, were exposed to the same training stimuli as the human participants and used to categorize each

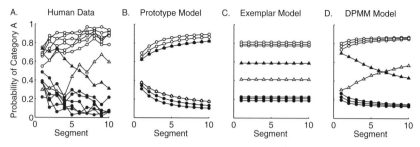

Figure 8.5 Human data and model predictions for Smith and Minda (1998, Experiment 2). (A) Human performance, (B) prototype model, (C) exemplar model, (D) DPMM. For all panels, white plot markers are stimuli in Category A, and black symbols are stimuli in Category B. Triangular markers correspond to the exceptions to the prototype structure, i.e., stimuli 111101 and 000100, respectively. (Reproduced from Griffiths *et al.* (2008b) with permission from Oxford University Press.)

stimulus after each segment of four exposures to the stimuli. The inferences of the prototype and exemplar models can be computed exactly, but because the DPMM involves a summation over all the partitions of the stimuli into clusters, we resorted to the Gibbs sampling procedure described above. The results of the three models are plotted in Figure 8.5. Only the DPMM captures the cross-over effect for the exception stimuli, where they are categorized incorrectly at first and are learned gradually over time. This effect is due to the ability of the DPMM to shift its representation between the prototype and exemplar styles. At first, it is more likely to use a single cluster to represent each category, as a prototype model would. After repeated exposure to the stimuli, the DPMM becomes more likely to split the exception stimuli into their own individual clusters, moving closer to an exemplar representation.

Relationship to other models

The relationships between Bayesian and other approaches can be described in terms of a few key concepts. In the first instance, the Bayesian framework described sits at the computational level of analysis. As with the machine learning approach suggested by Iba and Langley (Chapter 11), we chose to phrase the problem in probabilistic language, but the model can be converted into a MDL style description (Chapter 9) without difficulty. The important similarity here is that all three models share the goal of expressing human inferences primarily in terms of the statistical characteristics of the problem to be solved. This is in sharp contrast to Ashby, Paul and Maddox (Chapter 4), for instance, who describe the only model in this volume that has strong ties to the neural implementation level of analysis. However, the majority of the other chapters operate at the algorithmic level, and rely heavily on mechanistic psychological processes. Process assumptions can operate at a representational level, as is the case for prototype abstraction (Chapter 3) and exemplar storage (Chapter 2), but can also describe learning rules such as backpropagation (Chapter 6) and Hebbian learning (Chapter 12). Bayesian theories have typically stayed away from making strong commitments at the algorithmic level, or exploring the cognitive consequences of different algorithms for Bayesian learning and inference, but this is changing. As described in the section on implementation, we suggest that particle filtering and other methods may provide new possibilities for algorithmic-level Bayesian modelling that can bridge the gap between rational analyses and psychological processes.

Several of the contributions relate to our chapter through variations on the theme of hierarchical learning. The HDP model is hierarchical in the sense that it infers a generic clustering of entities in the environment in addition to the various category-specific distributions. It is via this mechanism that the HDP unifies prototypes (Chapter 3) and exemplars (Chapter 2) with the original rational model (Anderson, 1991) and other mixture models, and the clustering of stimuli within categories is similar to other models of categorization such as SUSTAIN (Chapter 10). However, the idea has considerably more generality. In a related line of work, Bayesian theories exploit the fact that the representations learned at the top level act as priors over category distributions at the low level. In this respect, there is a strong link to the learned hierarchies in the Iba and Langley contribution (Chapter 11) and to the prior knowledge constraints described by Harris and Rehder (Chapter 12): there are now several Bayesian models that focus on how such constraints can be learned from experience (e.g., Kemp, Perfors, & Tenenbaum, 2007; Kemp & Tenenbaum, 2008; Shafto et al., 2006). As an example, Kemp et al. (2007) show how hierarchical learning provides an explanation for how children learn inductive biases about object categories. Over shorter time scales, learned selective attention (Chapter 6) can also be considered to exemplify the same kind of learning, insofar as people learn the assignments of items to specific categories, as well as general knowledge about the extensions of categories along different dimensions. Hierarchical learning accounts for standard attentional phenomena such as the condensation-filtration effect (Navarro, 2006), as well as how people can make inferences about entirely novel categories (Perfors & Tenenbaum,

2009). Within the Bayesian framework, these things are all characterized as different examples of hierarchical learning, though defined over different domain sizes, complexities and time scales.

Other contributions raise different issues. The multiple system model described by Ashby, Paul and Maddox (Chapter 4) raises the question of how best to unify rule-based learning with graded, probabilistic categorization models from a computational perspective. The HDP model described here is probabilistic, though other Bayesian models have a rule-like character through their reliance on deterministic 'consequential sets' (Navarro, 2006; Shepard, 1987; Tenenbaum & Griffiths, 2001), and others use formal grammars to place priors over logical rules (Goodman *et al.*, 2008). An open question in this context is how to integrate these different kinds of mental representation, or whether deterministic rules and probabilistic categories should be left as two fundamentally distinct learning systems. Some prospects for unification exist. In a different context Maas and Kemp (2009) use priors constructed to induce a bias towards determinism, while Jaynes (2003) argues that some 'improper' priors mimic the kind of one-shot learning of logical rules that occurs in the physical sciences. Nevertheless, this remains an avenue for future work.

The simplicity model (Chapter 9) raises a different question in relation to the HDP model, regarding the nature of Ockham's razor. The scheme used to index partitions is a two-part code, encoding the number of categories K using the same number of bits regardless of the value of K. Via the equivalence between codelength functions and probability distributions (e.g., Grünwald, 2007) this translates to a uniform prior over the number of categories K. Similarly, all partitions of the same cardinality are equally likely. This is very different to the prior over partitions in the Dirichlet process, which has a bias toward small K, and is non-uniform even for given K. The Dirichlet process supplies an explicit Ockham's razor (simplicity through the prior), whereas the simplicity model prefers fewer categories only to the extent that a simpler clustering provides the better account of the data (simplicity through the likelihood). Although in practice the two approaches often behave similarly (e.g., compare Lee & Navarro, 2005, to Navarro & Griffiths, 2008), there is a deeper theoretical question at stake. Do we possess genuine pre-existing biases to prefer simple categorizations, or do our preferences emerge because simple models just work better? This is another open question for future research.

Future directions

Nonparametric Bayesian models provide a way to analyse how an ideal learner would solve categorization problems that unifies previous models and creates the opportunity to define new models of human category learning. The 'nonparametric' aspect of this approach provides flexibility, making it possible to entertain hypotheses about the structure of categories that have unbounded complexity, while the 'Bayesian' aspect provides a framework for making statistical inferences about how much complexity is warranted given the observed data. We anticipate two important future directions for this approach to category learning, each building on one of these two aspects of the approach.

The first future direction is expanding the scope of nonparametric Bayesian models. Many of the models discussed in this chapter focus on the traditional task of learning to classify objects as belonging to a small number of non-overlapping categories. Despite the long history of research into human categorization, there still exist many behaviours and techniques used by people in category learning settings that have yet to be formally studied and modelled. These include the transfer of information from one category to another to increase learning rate, the automatic inference of hierarchically organized category taxonomies, and the exploitation of logical (AND/OR) relationships between categories. In future work, we intend to experimentally study each of these behaviours and model them using extensions of the nonparametric Bayesian models considered here. For example, the HDP model with both α and γ positive and finite allows each category to be modelled as a Dirichlet process mixture model with the underlying clusters being shared among all categories, serving as a model for transfer learning. Combining a prior distribution over tree structures with the natural formulation of the HDP model on trees could serve as a model for the automatic inference of taxonomies. Finally, we envision an extension of the HDP that allows each category to be algebraically related to the others; this model could capture the effects of telling a learner that categories have certain logical relationships to each other.

The second future direction is capturing the effects of prior knowledge on category learning. Psychological research has shown that people are strongly affected by their knowledge of the world when learning new categories, with categories that are consistent with prior knowledge being easier to learn. These effects are obtained in experiments that use meaningful stimuli that draw on the real-world knowledge of human learners, such as intuitions about the factors that influence the inflation of balloons (Pazzani, 1991), the properties of different types of buildings (Heit & Bott, 2000), the definition of honesty (Wattenmaker et al., 1986), and the properties of vehicles (Murphy & Allopenna, 1994). Only a small number of computational models of knowledge effects in category learning exist (Heit & Bott, 2000; Rehder & Murphy, 2003) and these models have been developed with the more traditional psychological goals of understanding the mechanisms underlying this process. Developing probabilistic models that can account for knowledge effects in category learning provides the opportunity to discover how such knowledge *should* be used, and to generalize the resulting insights to develop better machine learning systems. Thinking about categorization in terms of density estimation lays the foundation for exploring these deeper questions about human cognition, and the opportunity to draw on tools from artificial intelligence and statistics in formalizing the prior knowledge that guides category learning.

REFERENCES

Aldous, D. (1985). Exchangeability and related topics. In *École d'Été de Probabilités de Saint-Flour, XIII – 1983* (pp. 1–198). Berlin: Springer.

Anderson, J. R. (1990). *The Adaptive Character of Thought.* Hillsdale, NJ: Erlbaum.

(1991). The adaptive nature of human categorization. *Psychological Review,* **98** (3), 409–429.

Antoniak, C. (1974). Mixtures of Dirichlet processes with applications to Bayesian nonparametric problems. *The Annals of Statistics,* **2**, 1152–1174.

Ashby, F. G., & Alfonso-Reese, L. A. (1995). Categorization as probability density estimation. *Journal of Mathematical Psychology,* **39**, 216–233.

Bishop, C. M. (2006). *Pattern Recognition and Machine Learning.* New York: Springer.

Doucet, A., de Freitas, N., & Gordon, N. (2001). *Sequential Monte Carlo Methods in Practice.* New York: Springer.

Escobar, M. D., & West, M. (1995). Bayesian density estimation and inference using mixtures. *Journal of the American Statistical Association,* **90**, 577–588.

Ferguson, T. (1973). A Bayesian analysis of some nonparametric problems. *The Annals of Statistics,* **1**, 209–230.

Gilks, W., Richardson, S., & Spiegelhalter, D. J. (eds.) (1996). *Markov Chain Monte Carlo in Practice.* Boca Raton, FL: Chapman and Hall CRC.

Goodman, N. D., Tenenbaum, J. B., Feldman, J., & Griffiths, T. L. (2008). A rational analysis of rule-based concept learning. *Cognitive Science,* **32**, 108–154.

Griffiths, T. L., Canini, K. R., Sanborn, A. N., & Navarro, D. J. (2007). Unifying rational models of categorization via the hierarchical Dirichlet process. In *Proceedings of the Twenty-Ninth Annual Conference of the Cognitive Science Society.* Hillsdale, NJ: Erlbaum.

Griffiths, T. L., Kemp, C., & Tenenbaum, J. B. (2008a). Bayesian models of cognition. In R. Sun (ed.), *Cambridge Handbook of Computational Cognitive Modeling.* Cambridge: Cambridge University Press.

Griffiths, T. L., Sanborn, A. N., Canini, K. R., & Navarro, D. J. (2008b). Categorization as nonparametric Bayesian density estimation. In N. Chater & M. Oaksford (eds.), *The Probabilistic Mind.* Oxford: Oxford University Press.

Grünwald, P. D. (2007). *The Minimum Description Length Principle.* Cambridge, MA: MIT Press.

Heit, E., & Bott, L. (2000). Knowledge selection in category learning. In D. L. Medin (ed.), *The Psychology of Learning and Motivation* (Vol. 39, pp. 163–199). San Diego, CA: Academic Press.

Jaynes, E. T. (2003). *Probability Theory: The Logic of Science.* Cambridge: Cambridge University Press.

Kemp, C., Perfors, A., & Tenenbaum, J. B. (2007). Learning over hypotheses with hierarchical Bayesian models. *Developmental Science*, 10, 307–321.

Kemp, C., & Tenenbaum, J. B. (2008). The discovery of structural form. *Proceedings of the National Academy of Sciences*, 105, 10687–10692.

Kemp, C., Tenenbaum, J. B., Griffiths, T. L., Yamada, T., & Ueda, N. (2006). Learning systems of concepts with an infinite relational model. In *Proceedings of the 21st National Conference on Artificial Intelligence* (pp. 381–388). Boston, MA: AAAI Press.

Kemp, C., Tenenbaum, J. B., Niyogi, S., & Griffiths, T. L. (2010). A probabilistic model of theory formation. *Cognition*, 114, 165–196.

Kruschke, J. K. (1990). *A connectionist model of category learning.* Unpublished doctoral dissertation, University of California, Berkeley, CA.

Lee, M. D., & Navarro, D. J. (2005). Minimum description length and psychological clustering models. In P. D. Grünwald, I. J. Myung, & M. A. Pitt (eds.), *Advances in Minimum Description Length: Theory and Applications* (pp. 355–384). Cambridge, MA: MIT Press.

Love, B. C., Medin, D. L., & Gureckis, T. M. (2004). SUSTAIN: a network model of category learning. *Psychological Review*, 111, 309–332.

Maas, A. L., & Kemp, C. (2009). One-shot learning with Bayesian networks. *Proceedings of the 31st Annual Conference of the Cognitive Science Society.* Austin, TX: Cognitive Science Society.

Marr, D. (1982). *Vision.* San Francisco, CA: W. H. Freeman.

McLachlan, G. J., & Basford, K. E. (1988). *Mixture Models.* New York: Marcel Dekker.

Medin, D. L., & Schaffer, M. M. (1978). Context theory of classification learning. *Psychological Review*, 85, 207–238.

Murphy, G. L., & Allopenna, P. D. (1994). The locus of knowledge effects in concept learning. *Journal of Experimental Psychology: Learning, Memory, and Cognition*, 20, 904–919.

Navarro, D. J. (2006). From natural kinds to complex categories. In *Proceedings of the 28th Annual Conference of the Cognitive Science Society.* Mahwah, NJ: Erlbaum.

Navarro, D. J., & Griffiths, T. L. (2008). Latent features in similarity judgments: a nonparametric Bayesian approach. *Neural Computation*, 20, 2597–2628.

Navarro, D. J., Griffiths, T. L., Steyvers, M., & Lee, M. D. (2006). Modeling individual differences using Dirichlet processes. *Journal of Mathematical Psychology*, 50, 101–122.

Neal, R. M. (1998). *Markov chain sampling methods for Dirichlet process mixture models* (Tech. Rep. No. 9815). Department of Statistics, University of Toronto.

Nosofsky, R. M. (1986). Attention, similarity, and the identification-categorization relationship. *Journal of Experimental Psychology: General*, 115, 39–57.

(1998). Optimal performance and exemplar models of classification. In M. Oaksford & N. Chater (eds.), *Rational Models of Cognition* (pp. 218–247). Oxford: Oxford University Press.

Pazzani, M. J. (1991). Influence of prior knowledge on concept acquisition: experimental and computational results. *Journal of Experimental Psychology: Learning, Memory, and Cognition*, **17**, 416–432.

Perfors, A., & Tenenbaum, J. B. (2009). Learning to learn categories. In *Proceedings of the 31st Annual Conference of the Cognitive Science Society*. Austin, TX: Cognitive Science Society.

Pitman, J. (2002). *Combinatorial stochastic processes*. Notes for Saint Flour Summer School.

Reed, S. K. (1972). Pattern recognition and categorization. *Cognitive Psychology*, **3**, 393–407.

Rehder, B., & Murphy, G. L. (2003). A knowledge-resonance (KRES) model of category learning. *Psychonomic Bulletin & Review*, **10**, 759–784.

Rosseel, Y. (2002). Mixture models of categorization. *Journal of Mathematical Psychology*, **46**, 178–210.

Sanborn, A. N., Griffiths, T. L., & Navarro, D. J. (2006). A more rational model of categorization. In *Proceedings of the 28th Annual Conference of the Cognitive Science Society*. Mahwah, NJ: Erlbaum.

Shafto, P., Kemp, C., Mansinghka, V., Gordon, M., & Tenenbaum, J. B. (2006). Learning cross-cutting systems of categories. In *Proceedings of the 28th Annual Conference of the Cognitive Science Society*. Mahwah, NJ: Erlbaum.

Shepard, R. N. (1987). Toward a universal law of generalization for psychological science. *Science*, **237**, 1317–1323.

Silverman, B. W. (1986). *Density Estimation for Statistics and Data Analysis*. London: Chapman and Hall.

Smith, J. D., & Minda, J. P. (1998). Prototypes in the mist: the early epochs of category learning. *Journal of Experimental Psychology: Learning, Memory, and Cognition*, **24**, 1411–1436.

Teh, Y., Jordan, M., Beal, M., & Blei, D. (2004). Hierarchical Dirichlet processes. In *Advances in Neural Information Processing Systems 17*. Cambridge, MA: MIT Press.

Tenenbaum, J. B., & Griffiths, T. L. (2001). Generalization, similarity, and Bayesian inference. *Behavioral and Brain Sciences*, **24**, 629–641.

Vanpaemel, W., & Storms, G. (2008). In search of abstraction: the varying abstraction model of categorization. *Psychonomic Bulletin & Review*, **15**, 732–749.

Wattenmaker, W. D., Dewey, G. I., Murphy, T. D., & Medin, D. L. (1986). Linear separability and concept learning: context, relational properties, and concept naturalness. *Cognitive Psychology*, **18**, 158–194.

9 The simplicity model of unsupervised categorization

Emmanuel M. Pothos, Nick Chater and Peter Hines

Summary

The main objective of the simplicity model of unsupervised categorization is to predict the relative intuitiveness of different classifications of items, based on their similarity. The model derives from the minimum description length framework, which is an algorithmic formalization of Ockham's razor. It generally prefers classifications which maximize within-category similarity, while minimizing between-category similarity.

Description of the model

The simplicity model of categorization can be viewed as one route to the formalization of Rosch and Mervis's (1975) proposal concerning the nature of 'basic level' categories, that is, the categories with which we prefer to classify objects (as opposed to corresponding superordinate or subordinate categories). According to Rosch and Mervis, basic level categories are those that maximize within-category similarity and minimize between-category similarity. Pothos and Chater (2002) examined whether this proposal may be suitable for predicting category preference generally, within a computational framework based on the simplicity principle.

The application of the simplicity principle in psychology has its origins in theories of perception (e.g., Hochberg & McAlister, 1953; Mach, 1959/1906). Informally, the simplicity principle states that simple explanations should be preferred – here 'explanation' refers to a pattern or structure in the data. The intuition is that the degree to which a pattern is suggested by the data can be quantified by assessing how briefly the data can be encoded, using that pattern. Thus, in the case of perception, an organization of the perceptual input is preferred, according to the simplicity principle (Hochberg & McAlister, 1953; Leeuwenberg, 1969), if it supports a brief encoding of the perceptual input. The simplicity principle often provides a successful strategy for problems of inductive inference, and so many researchers have advocated its suitability for cognitive modelling as well (Chater, 1999; Feldman, 2000; see Chater, 1996, for a discussion of the relation between Bayesian and simplicity approaches). The aim of the simplicity model of unsupervised classification, described here, is to explain how naive observers spontaneously classify a set of items, without any constraints at all.

Pothos and Chater (2002) adopted a particular algorithmic version of the simplicity principle, that of minimum description length (MDL; e.g., Rissanen, 1978, 1986; Wallace & Freeman, 1987). Applying the MDL approach requires specifying a code for some data, D, a code for the data given a particular hypothesis (explanation), $D|H$, and a code for the hypothesis itself, H. Each of these codes will have a certain complexity, which indicates the difficulty with which the code is specified. Then, the preferred hypothesis is the one for which complexity$(D|H)$ + complexity(H) is least (and ideally less than complexity(D)). Clearly, the particular complexity values will depend on the coding scheme that is selected; the selection of coding scheme in MDL approaches is closely analogous to the selection of prior distributions in Bayesian ones.

One justification for the MDL approach comes from the mathematical theory of Kolmogorov complexity, which can, in principle, define values for complexities independent of any particular coding scheme, and provides a rich algorithmic theory of probability, randomness and inductive inference (Li & Vitányi, 1997). While this approach is theoretically appealing, practical applications have been less forthcoming. MDL and related approaches make this 'ideal' measure of simplicity concrete. But in doing so, they require specific assumptions about the class of models to be considered, and how they are represented by a code. While, for data and models of any form, the results of the MDL approach are sensitive to these choices, it is often the case that reasonable choices give similar answers.

A more important theoretical 'degree of freedom' concerns the framing of the learning problem, i.e., what is the nature of the data which must be encoded? A superficially appealing approach would be to represent the items to be classified by a code that captures the specific properties of each object. Such an approach, though, quickly runs into difficulties, since it is very difficult to provide accurate concrete estimates of the complexity of an object. Instead, following Rosch and Mervis (1975), we assume that categorization attempts to capture relations of similarity and dissimilarity between pairs of items. Thus, our basic data correspond to a similarity matrix capturing the pairwise similarities between items. Specifically, in order to apply the MDL approach to categorization, one needs to define the quantities D, H, and $D|H$, in a way that is relevant to categorization, and then to devise a coding scheme for computing the complexity of these codes. D is assumed to correspond to the information about the similarity in a set of items without any categories. This is done by assuming that every pair of stimuli is compared with every other pair to determine relative similarities in terms of which pairs are more similar than which others. For example, suppose that we have four stimuli, labelled by 1,2,3,4. Then, similarity information would be encoded as similarity(1,2) > similarity(1,3), similarity(1,2) < similarity(1,4), etc., with each comparison requiring one bit of information to specify whether the first pair is more similar or less similar than the second. (One bit is the information required to determine the outcome of a binary choice.) Here, it is assumed that equalities in the similarity relations do not exist; that is, it is never the case that, for example, similarity(1,2) = similarity(1,3). The justification for making this assumption is that in general, in real life, one would not expect such equalities to occur. Nonetheless, it is straightforward to modify the model without this assumption.

A further assumption is that similarities obey symmetry and minimality. In other words, similarity(1,2) = similarity(2,1) and similarity(1,1) = maximum similarity. This assumption is justified by considering Tversky's (1977) celebrated findings of when similarity relations are likely to violate symmetry (and the other metric axioms). Tversky found that participants judged the similarity between Korea and China to be high, but the similarity between China and Korea to be low. He explained this asymmetry by pointing out that in the first case participants were comparing a concept about which they knew very little with one about which they knew a lot, and vice versa for the second case. Accordingly, Tversky's results indicate that violations of symmetry (and the other metric axioms) are likely when the concepts/objects compared vary in terms of how much is known about them. By contrast, in situations when the objects compared are meaningless, schematic stimuli, no violations of the metric axioms are expected. All applications of the simplicity model have so far involved meaningless, schematic stimuli. Therefore, the simplicity model has been specified by assuming that similarities obey minimality and symmetry.

Given the above, suppose, for example that we have 10 objects. For 10 objects, there are $10x(10 - 1)/2 = 45$ unique pairs; by unique pairs, we mean that, for example, if pair (1,2) is included, then pair (2,1) will not be included and also pairs like (1,1) are not included. Therefore, there are $45x(45 - 1)/2 = 990$ unique pairs of pairs. By unique pairs of pairs, we mean all relations of the form similarity(1,2) > similarity(1,3), such that if relation similarity(1,2) > similarity(1,3) is included, then relation similarity(1,3) < similarity(1,2) will not be included and that pairs like similarity(1,2) > similarity(1,2) are not included. Therefore, for 10 objects there are 990 pairs of similarity relations, so that 990 bits are required to describe the corresponding information. Hines, Pothos, and Chater (2007) present analytical formulae for computing the complexity of the code for the similarity information of a set of items, with and without the metric axioms (minimality, symmetry, and transitivity). Overall, in all cases, the number of comparisons, and therefore the informational cost of specifying relative similarities in the absence of categories, is a simple polynomial function of the number of items.

Next, consider how to compute the term $D|H$, that is, the code for the similarity information for a set of items, *with* categories. In other words, we have to consider how a categorization may alter (and ideally simplify) the description of similarity information for a set of items. Pothos and Chater (2002) *defined* categories as imposing *constraints* on the similarity relations between pairs of stimuli. Specifically, all similarities within categories are assumed to be greater than all similarities between categories – this is effectively an algorithmic interpretation of Rosch and Mervis's (1975) suggestion for basic level categorization. For example, suppose that we decide to place stimuli 1,2 in one category and stimuli 3,4 in a different category. Then, our definition of categories implies that similarity(1,2) > {similarity(1,3), similarity(1,4)} and that similarity(3,4) > {similarity(1,3), similarity(1,4)}. Thus, the *codelength* for the similarity structure for a set of stimuli can be reduced by using categories, if the constraints specified by the categories are numerous and, generally, correct. If a categorization specifies incorrect constraints, then the MDL approach requires a term to correct them. The way this is done in the simplicity model is by identifying the set of erroneous constraints amongst all constraints. From standard combinatorics, if we have u items in total, then there are $u!/e!(u-e)!$ subsets of e items. Note also that the information required in order to identify a particular element out of n elements is given by $\log_2 n$. Therefore, if in u constraints there are e incorrect ones we require $\log_2(u+1) + \log_2(u!/e!(u-e)!)$ bits of information to correct them (the first term in the cost computation is required because we also need to identify the total number of erroneous constraints we have). A slight problem arises in that this formula predicts that having few errors will be easy to correct, but having many errors will also be easy to correct; the function $\log_2(u!/e!(u-e)!)$ is symmetrical. In other words, from an information-theoretic point of view, it is equally easy to identify a subset with very few errors as it is to identify a subset with many errors. The simplicity model makes the (sensible) assumption that human observers prefer classifications which are associated with few erroneous constraints and that classification for which more than half the constraints are erroneous will rarely, if ever, be observed. Accordingly, the function for correcting errors is inverted when $e = u/2$, so that it is strictly monotonically increasing (Hines *et al.*, 2007).

So far we have specified the codelengths for D and $D|H$. The final term required in a MDL model is the codelength for H. Since the simplicity model aims to describe spontaneous classification of a set of objects without any constraints, for r objects, we have to consider all possible classifications into any possible number of clusters. A classical result on Stirling numbers (as described in Comtet, 1974) gives that the number of distinct partitions of a set of r elements into n subsets is the (Type II) Stirling number

$$\text{Part}(r,n) = \sum_{v=0}^{n-1} (-1)^v \frac{(n-v)^r}{(n-v)!v!}.$$

Note that the summation ranges over all possible numbers of clusters. For a set with r elements, an arbitrary clustering may be specified by first giving a number n of subsets, and then by specifying which clustering into n subsets has been chosen. Hence an arbitrary clustering may be specified with a codelength of $\log_2(\text{Part}(r,n)) + \log_2(n + 1)$ bits. Note that this term will typically be dwarfed by the term required for correcting the erroneous constraints.

Overall, there is a codelength without categories (D) and a codelength with categories ($\{D|H\} + H$). Comparing the two gives a measure of how much a particular classification *simplifies* the description of the similarity structure for a set of objects. The psychological prediction is that the greater this simplification, the more psychologically intuitive the corresponding classification should be. In effect, this is just a formalization of the simplicity principle in the context of categorization. Typically, what is reported is

$$\frac{\text{codelength}\left(\{D|H\} + H\right)}{\text{codelength}(D)},$$

as a percentage, and referred to as just 'codelength'. When there are several, valid constraints, this ratio would be expected to be lower – and participants would be predicted to prefer the corresponding classification.

Motivation

The simplicity model has been designed to achieve two objectives: first, to identify the classification which should be spontaneously preferred by participants (without any constraints at all) and second to produce a number which indicates how much more intuitive a particular classification should be with respect to both alternative classifications for the same objects and alternative classifications of *different* sets of objects. The first objective is not particularly significant, all the more so since the sets of objects typically employed in unsupervised categorization studies have to conform to reasonably naturalistic category structures (cf. Compton & Logan, 1993, 1999; Pothos & Chater, 2002). In other words, if a set of objects approximately conforms to a two-cluster or three-cluster category structure, then naive observers might be expected to produce these classifications (or classifications similar to the intended ones). By contrast, if the intended classification involves a complex, non-linear category boundary, then it is unlikely that naive observers will spontaneously produce it. So, we expect that the classifications predicted by the simplicity model as preferred would be identical to the classifications predicted as intuitive by other clustering algorithms, with broadly similar constraints (e.g., the between-groups linkage method; cf. Fraboni & Cooper, 1989).

The second objective is the significant one. For example, consider a set of objects which conforms to a simple two-cluster category structure and a different set of objects which conforms to a three-cluster category structure. The simplicity model predicts that the first classification should be more intuitive than the second, because the codelength for the first is lower than the codelength for the second. Empirical markers of preference in unsupervised categorization are easy to establish. For example, participants can be said to prefer one classification more than another when the former classification is produced more often than the other and when there is less disagreement as to how a set of objects should be classified compared to another set of objects (in other words, if participants classify a set of stimuli and each one of them produces a different classification, then we can say that the underlying category structure is less intuitive, compared to the converse situation in which all participants agree on how the stimuli should be classified). Note that these two criteria appear similar but, in principle, can be independent (Pothos *et al.*, 2008). So, the main objective of the simplicity model is to produce intuitiveness values for different classifications/sets of objects, which should correspond to participants' preferences in spontaneous categorization tasks.

This second objective of the simplicity model corresponds to a generalization of Rosch and Mervis's (1975) model for basic level categorization. In a hierarchy of concepts, Rosch and Mervis attempted to predict the category level which would be *preferred* by participants – the basic level of categorization. Rosch and Mervis suggested that the basic level of categorization should be the one for which within-category similarity is maximized and between-category similarity minimized. Therefore, there are clear analogues between both the objectives and the formalizations of the simplicity model and Rosch and Mervis's idea. Psychologically, in using Rosch and Mervis's model as a starting point for the simplicity model, it is assumed that the process which allows us to identify a classification for a set of objects as more intuitive than alternatives, is the same process which leads us to prefer the basic categorization level. Whether basic level categorization can be reduced in such a way to a special case of unsupervised categorization is an empirical issue: can models of unsupervised categorization correctly predict the basic categorization level? Preliminary results are encouraging, but more thorough work is needed before this issue can be settled (Gosselin & Schyns, 2001).

A reasonable question at this point is why the simplicity approach is needed at all: that is, why not specify a model of unsupervised categorization by directly implementing Rosch and Mervis's suggestion (compute the average of within-category similarities and compare to the average of between-category similarities, cf. Murphy, 1991). It can be seen, though, that any attempt to formalize Rosch and Mervis's suggestion encounters a number of key problems, such as how to numerically represent similarity, how to compare within-category to between-category similarities, and how to infer categories from this comparison. The simplicity model provides one framework for dealing with these problems. The comparison of within and between similarities is achieved with the MDL framework. The representation of similarity is non-metric and coarse. Regarding the latter assumption, for example, in Figure 9.1, the cluster would be predicted to be equally intuitive by the simplicity model in the two panels, even though in panel B the points in the cluster are better separated from the third point, compared to panel A. By contrast, by comparing within-category similarity (distances) to between-category similarity, the cluster in panel A would be predicted to be less intuitive compared to the one in panel B. The simplicity model assumes that naive observers are not sensitive to such differences, but this is clearly an empirical issue.

In general, the use of the simplicity principle in psychological modelling has been most prominent in perceptual organization. In an influential research tradition, the perceptual system has been argued to prefer the simplest perceptual organization consistent with sensory input (Barlow, 1974; Chater, 1996; Pomerantz & Kubovy, 1986). The use of the simplicity principle in the simplicity model effectively implies an assumption that spontaneous categorization may share some functional similarities with perceptual organization. Intuitively, this is a plausible assumption,

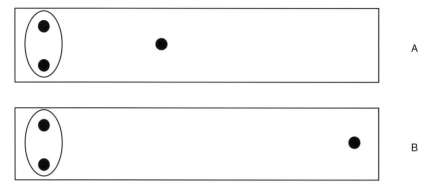

Figure 9.1 According to the simplicity model, the 'intuitiveness' of the shown cluster is the same in panel A and panel B.

in that spontaneous categorization appears to involve a process of recognizing certain groupings as more appropriate than others (although see Milton, Longmore, & Wills, 2008; Milton & Wills, 2004, for a more analytic view of unsupervised categorization). Likewise, perceptual organization is a spontaneous process of recognizing certain interpretations for a distal layout as more appropriate. There is some more direct evidence in favour of this assumption: Pothos and Chater (2002) compared unsupervised categorization performance with two ways of presenting the stimuli. The first way involved diagrams like those in Figure 9.2; participants were presented with such diagrams and were asked to indicate their preferred classifications by drawing curves to enclose the points which should be in the same category (cf. Compton & Logan, 1993, 1999). Such a grouping procedure arguably engages processes of perceptual organization. The second way of presenting the stimuli involved mapping the diagram dimensions into dimensions of physical variation and so creating stimuli which were presented to participants individually (printed on cards). This procedure should correspond more to a generic process of unsupervised categorization. Classification results using the two procedures were very similar, so that we can tentatively accept the assumption in the simplicity model, that it may be possible to understand spontaneous categorization and perceptual organization in the same modelling framework.

More generally, there has been a lot of interest in examining the range of cognitive processes which could be understood in terms of the simplicity principle (Chater, 1999). For example, there have been simplicity models of language (Brent & Cartwright, 1996; Wolff, 1977), decision making (Oaksford & Chater, 1994), similarity (Hahn, Chater, & Richardson,

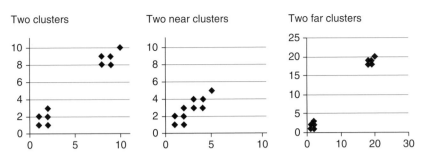

Figure 9.2 The three datasets exploring variations of a simple two-cluster category structure in Table 9.1.

2003), memory (Attneave, 1959; Garner, 1974) and learning (Pothos & Wolff, 2006). The simplicity principle basically provides a general framework for inductive inference. Since most of psychological behaviour involves inductive inference, then the simplicity principle could provide a general framework for understanding cognition. The simplicity model in categorization can be seen as such an attempt to explore the scope of the simplicity principle in modelling cognition. In practice, as with all attempts to provide a general computational framework for cognition, the success of simplicity will depend on the consistency and coherence between individual instantiations of the simplicity principle for particular cognitive models.

Implementation

We describe the implementation of the simplicity model in terms of distances (instead of similarities), even though the model can operate with similarity information which violates all metric axioms. The reason for considering distances is that it simplifies the description of the model.

The simplicity model can be used in either of two modes. In the first mode, the researcher requires the model to identify the best possible classification for a set of items. In the second mode, the researcher is interested in the codelength (intuitiveness) of a particular classification. The two modes can be implemented in an identical way, with the exception of the augmentation of the first mode with an appropriate search algorithm. Both modes require the following functions: first, a function which enumerates all within-category distances and all between-category distances, for a particular classification; second, a function which compares all within-category distances with all between-category distances, and identifies the number of instances for which a between-category distance is less than a within-category distance (these are the erroneous constraints). Note that when a within-category distance is equal to a between-category distance the constraint is true. This is a convention which had to be made in both the implementation and the theory to ensure consistency in counting the erroneous constraints (Hines *et al.*, 2007). Third, they require a function which computes the number of possible classifications for a set of objects. Finally, one needs a function which utilizes the output of the other functions to compute the various information-theoretic terms required by the simplicity model. The problem in the above computations relates to computing the various factorial terms. Because these are typically very large numbers, unless high precision floating arithmetic is used, there is a risk for computation errors to accumulate (we hope to resolve this problem eventually by using lookup tables for the various combinatorics terms).

The most common form of input to the simplicity model is item coordinates, corresponding to a stimulus set participants are asked to spontaneously classify. From these coordinates, one needs to compute information about the relative magnitude of pairs of similarities. Accordingly, a distance metric has to be assumed. Unlike prominent models of supervised categorization (e.g., exemplar or prototype theory, Chapters 2 and 3), in the simplicity model the distance metric has not been systematically examined, with the Euclidean metric typically being the default (we have not identified situations in which choice of metric drastically affects model output). When the input to the simplicity model is distances, then clearly constraints have to be counted in a way which assumes the metric axioms – that is, for example, distance (a,b) and distance (b,a) have to be considered one entity. However, the simplicity model can operate directly on the similarity matrix for a set of objects. Such similarity matrices can correspond to similarity information collected either from an individual participant, or the average similarity information from a group of participants (e.g., Pothos & Chater, 2005). In such a case, transitivity has to be assumed but whether symmetry and minimality are assumed is a choice of the experimenter. Finally, the simplicity model could be applied directly in terms of pairs of similarities, in which case all three metric axioms could be violated. This application has not been systematically explored yet.

When the simplicity model is asked to identify the most intuitive classification for a set of objects, it needs an appropriate search algorithm. The simplicity model employs a variation of the commonly used agglomerative method in clustering. Initially, each item is considered a separate cluster. At each step, all possible cluster pairs are formed and the total codelength that is needed to describe the data is calculated, assuming that a pair is merged and the other clusters are left intact. The cluster pair associated with the greatest reduction in codelength is then merged. This process is iterated until all items are in the same cluster. The algorithm then singles out the level when no more reduction (improvement) in codelength occurs, as the optimal classification according to the simplicity model. This basic procedure can lead to slight variations, which depend on how to select the clusters to merge at each step. One choice is to merge the pair of clusters/items which leads to the greatest reduction in codelength ('absolute' method). Another choice is to favour the merge which minimizes the quantity

$$\frac{costs}{1 + constraints},$$

in which *costs* is the codelength required for encoding the classification and the errors, and *constraints* is how many inequalities are specified by the classification ('ratio' method). Both the ratio and the absolute methods optimize simplicity globally in the sense that the information-theoretic advantage of the entire classification is evaluated at each step. The absolute method tends first to exhaust the possibilities for increasing the size of an already large cluster, while the ratio method initially favours smaller clusters (with very few errors). With well-clustered datasets, both algorithms identify the same classification. Finally, where the algorithms produce different classifications, the one to be preferred is the one associated with the least codelength.

Example of the model's operation

We employ the C++ computer program for the simplicity model created by Peter Hines and Emmanuel Pothos. In running the program, the first choice which needs to be made is regarding the number of decimal places to be used in the simplicity computations (the program uses a special high precision arithmetic package due to W. Wyatt). A typical choice for datasets with 30 objects or less would be 20 decimal places.

We first illustrate the two search algorithms. Using the absolute and ratio methods for the 'two clusters' dataset (Table 9.1, Figure 9.2), both methods identify the optimal classification to be (0 1 2 3 4) (5 6 7 8 9), with a codelength of 51.6%. The codelength for describing the similarity structure of the items is 990 bits, the number of constraints associated with the classification 500, and the number of erroneous constraints 0. The input to the simplicity model program is simply a text file in which the first line is the number of dimensions (2 in this case) and each subsequent line denotes the coordinates of each point. A convenient

Table 9.1 *Three datasets exploring variations of a simple two-cluster category structure*

Item indices	Two clusters		Two near clusters		Two far clusters	
0	1	1	1	1	1	1
1	1	2	1	2	1	2
2	2	1	2	1	2	1
3	2	2	2	2	2	2
4	2	3	2	3	2	3
5	8	9	3	4	18	19
6	9	8	4	3	19	18
7	8	8	3	3	18	18
8	9	9	4	4	19	19
9	10	10	5	5	20	20

convention for describing predicted classifications is to assign a numerical label to each point in a dataset, starting with 0 (so that, for example, in the classification above, point 0 has coordinates 1,1). The number of constraints specified by the classification can be readily computed by noting that there are two clusters of 5 points each, which means that there are 25 between-category distances in total, and $5x \, (5 − 1)/2 = 10$ within-category distances in each cluster. Therefore, the total number of constraints specified by the classification is 10×2 (since we have two clusters) $\times 25 = 500$ (each within-category distance should be greater than all between-category distances). The fact that there are zero erroneous constraints simply means that the clusters are well separated. However, note that the code for the classification still needs to include the information that there are zero erroneous constraints – the associated cost is about 8.9 bits (this cost is $\log_2(500)$, noting that 500 is the total number of constraints). Finally, there is the cost for specifying the classification, which is about 11.9 bits. So, overall, even though the clusters are perfectly well separated, there are still two cost terms. The ratio of bits required to specify the similarity information with the classification divided by the bits required for the similarity information without the classification is, in this case, 510.8/990 = 51.6% (recall that when describing simplicity model results, it is this value which is typically referred to as codelength).

We next employ the two search algorithms in the case of the dataset 'two near clusters'. In this case, the classification should be predicted to be less intuitive, since the clusters are less well separated. The absolute method predicts as optimal the classification (0 1 2 3 4) (5 6 7 8) (9), with a codelength of 71.8%. The ratio method predicts (0 1 2 3 4) (5 6 7 8 9), with a codelength of 76.4%. Therefore, in this case the results from the two methods diverge; the prediction from the simplicity model is the classification with the least codelength. As said, with less well-clustered datasets, it is worth examining both methods. Note that neither method is guaranteed to identify the best possible classification. However, in practice, this is not so much of a problem since the codelength values produced from different methods tend to be similar.

Finally, examining the 'two far clusters' dataset, both methods predict as optimal the classification (0 1 2 3 4) (5 6 7 8 9), with a codelength of 51.6%. In other words, once two clusters are perfectly separated (as is the case in the 'two clusters' dataset), there are no further improvements in codelength if the clusters are pushed further apart. This is an implication of the way in which between-category and within-category similarities are counted by the simplicity model. Note that the simplicity model correctly predicts that datasets 'two clusters' and 'two far clusters' are more intuitive than the dataset 'two near clusters'. Interpreting differences in codelength as differences in predicted psychological intuitiveness for different classifications is the key aspect of the simplicity model (Pothos et al., 2008). One can ask whether 51.6% is the least codelength possible for a dataset of 10 items. We considered cases of two perfectly separated clusters, such that the two cluster sizes were 1 and 9, 2 and 8, 3 and 7, 4 and 6, to obtain codelengths, respectively, of 69.2%, 55.2%, 51.2%, and 51.2%. Thus, the lowest possible codelength is about 51%. Note that this value will somewhat depend on the size of the dataset. For example, if we consider a dataset with 20 points, then the lowest possible codelength value for a classification of two, equally sized, perfectly separated clusters is 50.1% and for 40 points the corresponding value is 49.9% (the current version of the simplicity model code can handle stimulus sets of up to 50 points). Thus, the lowest possible codelength does have a small dependence on the number of points in the dataset; currently, it is unclear whether this dependence should be interpreted psychologically or not (noting, though, that in practice it does not affect predictions for classification performance).

We next consider a 'random' dataset of 10 points such that the points are randomly arranged in psychological space (by random assignment we mean that the points were positioned without any regard to an underlying classification, in an approximately homogeneous way). The best codelength identified for this dataset is 72.4% with the absolute method. This codelength is higher compared to the codelength for any of the structured datasets in Table 9.1 and Figure 9.2 ('two clusters' or 'two far clusters'). The corresponding psychological prediction is that participants spontaneously classifying the 'random' dataset will produce more varied classifications compared to participants spontaneously classifying the structured datasets in Table 9.1 and Figure 9.2. Equally, in the 'random' dataset there would not be any classification which is produced with a frequency as high as that for the optimal classification for the structured datasets of Table 9.1 and Figure 9.2. We can therefore say that the 'random' dataset has little classification structure, while a dataset like the 'two clusters' one has a lot of classification structure. Note that even though the 'random' dataset is associated with a very high codelength, this codelength is still below 100%. In other words, it appears that describing the similarity information in that dataset with a classification still leads to some simplification, even though there are not meant to be any intuitive categories. This is because the codelength computations in the model are subject to a slight bias for finding structure (this bias has little impact on the application of the model to psychological data, although, of course, it is desirable to study it further in future revisions).

Relation to other models

Theoretically, the formulation of the simplicity model shares many key elements with other models. First, the formation of clusters in the simplicity model is guided by a bias to maximize within-category similarity, while minimizing between-category similarity (Rosch & Mervis, 1975). Many models of categorization embody a principle of similarity. Regarding unsupervised categorization, SUSTAIN (Love, Medin, & Gureckis, 2004; Chapter 10) also favours groupings of similar items. In supervised categorization, both the GCM (Chapter 2) and prototype theory (Chapter 3) classify novel instances on the basis of their similarity to either category exemplars or category prototypes. In fact, it is possible to derive an unsupervised version of the GCM (Pothos & Bailey, 2009). However, the GCM and the unsupervised GCM do not directly take into account between-category similarity (cf. Stewart & Brown, 2005). Also, the GCM looks for 'similarity-based' clusters with respect to both the original psychological space and all possible transformations of this space which are possible by attentional weighting of dimensions or overall stretching/compression of the space.

Second, most other models of unsupervised categorization embody a principle of economy, in relation to the creation of new clusters. For example, SUSTAIN will only create new clusters if the current clusters do a poor job of encoding the current stimulus (SUSTAIN is a trial-by-trial model, i.e. it processes stimuli one by one). The likelihood of creating new clusters in SUSTAIN is determined by a parameter (tau). Exactly the same situation applies to the rational model (Anderson, 1991; Sanborn, Griffiths, & Navarro, 2006; Chapter 8) and the unsupervised version of DIVA (DIVA was originally proposed as a connectionist model of supervised categorization; Kurtz, 2007). A difference between the simplicity model and these other models is that the optimal number of clusters arises from the MDL framework of the model (i.e., the information-theoretic cost of specifying a particular classification), while in SUSTAIN, the rational model, and DIVA the number of clusters is determined by a free parameter.

Third, the MDL framework, which has been used to specify the simplicity model, is closely related to the Bayesian probabilistic framework, which is the basis for the rational model. Chater (1996) argued that probabilities can be converted to codelengths if one assumes the so-called 'universal priors'. Broadly speaking, the universal priors for an object correspond to its absolute likelihood of occurrence. Intuitively, simpler objects are more likely to occur in nature.

The unique aspects of the simplicity model relate mostly to the particular characteristics of its MDL implementation, which allows it to be specified in a parameter-free way. In fact, the simplicity model is the only model in this volume which has no free parameters. This immediately raises some problems. For example, empirical work has shown that, depending on the learned categorization, naive observers are able to selectively attend to some stimulus dimensions at the expense of others. There have recently been suggestions that dimensional weighting may occur in unsupervised categorization as well (Gureckis & Goldstone, 2008; Pothos & Chater, 2005). It is therefore an essential extension to the simplicity model to allow it to perform dimensional weighting. Colreavy and Lewandowsky (2008) first suggested that one could compute the 'goodness' of the optimal classification for several different projections of the stimuli onto subspaces of the original psychological space. The classification associated with the best overall codelength would be considered the prediction of the simplicity model; also, the projection associated with this best classification could be used to infer the attentional weights predicted by the model. Pothos and Close (2008) employed a slightly more formal version of the same approach. This idea appears promising, however, more work is needed on how evaluation of classifications along different projections can be implemented in a more efficient way; both Colreavy and Lewandowsky, and Pothos and Close, simply evaluated the codelength for a series of alternative classifications (corresponding to different projections).

In this respect, it is worth noting that the unsupervised GCM can compute the optimal dimensional weighting for a particular stimulus set. In other words, it can figure out automatically which subspace leads to clusters which are maximally cohesive, for a particular stimulus set. While such a property appears very impressive, it is undermined by the fact that, more often than not, the unsupervised GCM finds too many such subspaces, many of which appear psychologically unrealistic (Pothos & Bailey, 2009).

Another unique aspect of the simplicity model is the fact that it is non-metric. The model receives as input similarity information in the form of relative similarity relations (of course, it is trivial to compute relative similarity relations from stimulus coordinates). As discussed above (e.g., see Figure 9.1), this non-metricity implies a certain 'coarseness' in how similarity information is considered by the model. It is currently not clear whether this assumption is psychologically accurate or not. The relevant empirical question concerns the degree of specificity with which similarity information is considered by naive observers, when it comes to categorizing a set of stimuli. The GCM (and equivalent formulations of the prototype theory) incorporates a parameter which corresponds to an analogous issue, the sensitivity parameter. When this parameter is large, a new instance is categorized on the basis of its nearest neighbours in psychological space; when it is small it is categorized on the basis of most available exemplars. In the current formulation of the simplicity model, however, it is currently not clear how one could move from a more coarse representation of similarity (as in Figure 9.1) to a more specific one – the current working assumption of the model is that, when it comes to unsupervised categorization, only the former is relevant.

Direct computational comparisons between the simplicity model and other models have been carried out by Pothos (2007) and Pothos and Bailey (2009). The first study compared the simplicity model and the continuous version of the rational model against a series of simple, artificial stimulus sets. The predictions of the two models were very similar, despite the fact that the simplicity model is specified in terms of similarity and the rational model in terms of (a function of) category/feature utility. However, the strength of this conclusion is undermined by the limited range of the considered stimulus sets. Pothos and Bailey (2009) compared the simplicity model with the rational model and the unsupervised GCM against datasets from supervised categorization (e.g., if a classification was more difficult to teach, they inferred that this classification was less intuitive). No model emerged as clearly superior.

Perhaps the most significant aspect of the simplicity model is that it raised the profile of a new dependent variable in the study of categorization, category intuitiveness. As supervised categorization had dominated the categorization literature, so it has been the case that the dependent variable considered was the classification probability of novel instances. But, clearly, such a dependent variable is not relevant in unsupervised categorization. The simplicity model is the first model which was specifically designed to make predictions about category intuitiveness and so has helped the development of novel approaches in the comparison of models of unsupervised categorization and corresponding empirical studies.

Future directions

In the previous section we discussed some of the implementational shortcomings of the simplicity model, particularly in relation to attentional weighting and the specificity of similarity information. However, on the whole, information theory (still) appears a promising framework for specifying a categorization model. This is because information theory provides a natural language for talking about the utility of different classifications, a theme which has been taken up by many other approaches (e.g., the rational model, Chapter 8, or the category utility model, Chapter 11). Therefore, we do not envisage any major departure in the formalism of the model, even if certain aspects of its implementation have to be improved. Note, however, some researchers have recently argued that quantum probability is a better framework within which to study cognitive processes, compared to classical probability, so that it is possible that future revisions of the simplicity model may be more suitably specified in the framework of quantum information theory (e.g., Busemeyer, Matthew, & Wang, 2006; Nielsen & Chuang, 2000).

The most obvious shortcoming of the model is that it entirely fails to provide any insight into the relevant neuroscience of unsupervised categorization. Other modelling approaches, such as the COVIS model (Ashby *et al.*, 1998; Chapter 4), increasingly integrate their computational specification with brain neuroscience. A difficulty in this respect is that there is hardly any research in the neuroscience of unsupervised categorization with the entirely unconstrained categorization tasks employed by, for example, Pothos and Chater (2002). Brain structures which have been implicated in supervised categorization, such as the prefrontal cortex and anterior cingulate cortex in the explicit learning system of COVIS, or the basal ganglia in passive learning, do not appear relevant in unsupervised categorization. One possibility is that unsupervised categorization simply involves the organization of the shown stimuli according to their similarity, in higher visual areas, such as the lateral occipital cortex (Op de Beeck, Torfs, & Wagemans, 2008; but cf. Milton,

Wills, & Hodgson, 2009). Indeed, such an approach would fit well with the general assumption of the simplicity model, that unsupervised categorization is like perceptual organization. However, we are immediately faced with the problem of whether perceptual organization may be all there is to unsupervised categorization. This is a complicated issue which is unlikely to be resolved soon.

Another important shortcoming in the simplicity model is that it has yet to provide a convincing hypothesis for how general knowledge could affect classification. Empirically, this is an important issue, since we often (spontaneously) categorize meaningful stimuli. Pothos and Chater (2002) suggested that the term for the codelength of a classification could be modified to take into account whether a classification is plausible or not, in terms of our general knowledge. There are two problems with this suggestion. First, computationally it is not clear how it can be implemented. Second, the effect of this term on the overall computation is rather minor. However, we know from related research in supervised categorization (e.g., Murphy & Allopenna, 1994; see also Chapter 12) that general knowledge manipulations can often have dramatic effects in people's categorizations.

There are other, more straightforward challenges, such as the adaptation of the model for application with trial-by-trial categorization data. Ultimately, the development of the simplicity model has to be guided by a more careful appreciation of its relation to alternative models (such as the rational model and SUSTAIN). Unfortunately, the detailed model comparisons which have informed the development of supervised models of categorization have yet to be carried out in unsupervised categorization. We are currently in the process of conducting such a comparison, which will hopefully further illuminate the specific strengths and weaknesses of the simplicity model and so guide its development.

REFERENCES

Anderson, J. R. (1991). The adaptive nature of human categorization. *Psychological Review*, **98**, 409–429.

Ashby, G. F., Alfonso-Reese, L. A., Turken, A. U., & Waldron, E. M. (1998). A neuropsychological theory of multiple systems in category learning. *Psychological Review*, **105**, 442–481.

Attneave, F. (1959). *Applications of Information Theory to Psychology*. New York: Holt, Rinehart & Winston.

Barlow, B. H. (1974). Inductive inference, coding, perception, and language. *Perception*, **3**, 123–134.

Brent, M. R., & Cartwright, T. A. (1996). Distributional regularity and phonotactic constraints are useful for segmentation. *Cognition*, **61**, 93–125.

Busemeyer, J. R., Matthew, M., & Wang, Z. A. (2006). Quantum game theory explanation of disjunction effects. In R. Sun & N. Miyake (eds.), *Proceedings of the 28th Annual Conference of the Cognitive Science Society* (pp. 131–135). Mahwah, NJ: Erlbaum.

Chater, N. (1996). Reconciling simplicity and likelihood principles in perceptual organization. *Psychological Review*, **103**, 566–591.

  (1999). The search for simplicity: a fundamental cognitive principle? *Quarterly Journal of Experimental Psychology*, **52A**, 273–302.

Colreavy, E., & Lewandowsky, S. (2008). Strategy development and learning differences in supervised and unsupervised categorization. *Memory & Cognition*, **36**, 762–775.

Compton, B. J., & Logan, G. D. (1993). Evaluating a computational model of perceptual grouping. *Perception & Psychophysics*, **53**, 403–421.

Compton, B. J. & Logan, G. D. (1999). Judgments of perceptual groups: reliability and sensitivity to stimulus transformation. *Perception & Psychophysics*, **61**, 1320–1335.

Comtet, L. (1974). *Advanced Combinatorics, the Art of Finite and Infinite Expansions*. Dordrecht: Reidel.

Feldman, J. (2000). Minimization of Boolean complexity in human concept learning. *Nature*, **407**, 630–633.

Fraboni, M., & Cooper, D. (1989). Six clustering algorithms applied to the WAIS-R: the problem of dissimilar cluster analysis. *Journal of Clinical Psychology*, **45**, 932–935.

Garner, W. R. (1974). *The Processing of Information and Structure*. Potomac, MD: LEA.

Gosselin, F. & Schyns, P. G. (2001). Why do we SLIP to the basic-level? Computational constraints and their implementation. *Psychological Review*, **108**, 735–758.

Gureckis, T. M., & Goldstone, R. L. (2008). The effect of the internal structure of categories on perception. In *Proceedings of the 30th Annual Meeting of the Cognitive Science Society*. Mahwah, NJ: Lawrence Erlbaum.

Hahn, U., Chater, N., & Richardson, L. B. C. (2003). Similarity as transformation. *Cognition*, **87**, 1–32.

Hines, P., Pothos, E. M., & Chater, N. (2007). A non-parametric approach to simplicity clustering. *Applied Artificial Intelligence*, **21**, 729–752.

Hochberg, J. E., & McAlister, E. (1953). A quantitative approach to figural goodness. *Journal of Experimental Psychology*, **46**, 361–364.

Kurtz, K. J. (2007). The divergent autoencoder (DIVA) model of category learning. *Psychonomic Bulletin & Review*, **14**, 560–576.

Leeuwenberg, E. (1969). Quantitative specification of information in sequential patterns. *Psychological Review*, **76**, 216–220.

Li, M., & Vitányi, P. (1997). *An Introduction to Kolmogorov Complexity and its Applications* (2nd edition). Berlin: Springer-Verlag.

Love, B. C., Medin, D. L., & Gureckis, T. M. (2004). SUSTAIN: a network model of category learning. *Psychological Review*, **111**, 309–332.

Mach, E. (1959/1906). *The Analysis of Sensations and the Relation of the Physical to the Psychical*. New York: Dover Publications.

Milton, F., Longmore, C. A., & Wills, A. J. (2008). Processes of overall similarity sorting in free classification. *Journal of Experimental Psychology: Human Perception and Performance*, **34**, 676–692.

Milton, F., & Wills, A. J. (2004). The influence of stimulus properties on category construction. *Journal of Experimental Psychology: Learning, Memory, and Cognition*, **30**, 407–415.

Milton, F., Wills, A. J., & Hodgson, T. L. (2009). The neural basis of overall similarity sorting. *NeuroImage*, **46**, 319–326.

Murphy, G. L. (1991). Parts in object concepts: experiments with artificial categories. *Memory & Cognition*, **19**, 423–438.

Murphy, G. L., & Allopenna, P. D. (1994). The locus of knowledge effects in concept learning. *Journal of Experimental Psychology: Learning, Memory, and Cognition*, **20**, 904–919.

Nielsen, M. A., & Chuang, L. L. (2000). *Quantum Computation and Quantum Information*. Cambridge: Cambridge University Press.

Oaksford, M., & Chater, N. (1994). A rational analysis of the selection task as optimal data selection. *Psychological Review*, **101**, 608–631.

Op de Beeck, H., Torfs, K., & Wagemans, J. (2008). Perceived shape similarity among unfamiliar objects and the organization of the human object vision pathway. *Journal of Neuroscience*, **28**, 10111–10123.

Pomerantz, J. R., & Kubovy, M. (1986). Theoretical approaches to perceptual organization: simplicity and likelihood principles. In K. R. Boff, L. Kaufman, & J. P. Thomas (Eds.), *Handbook of Perception and Human Performance, Vol. II: Cognitive Processes and Performance* (pp. 1–45). New York: Wiley.

Pothos, E. M. (2007). Occam and Bayes in predicting category intuitiveness. *Artificial Intelligence Review*, **21** (8), 729–752.

Pothos, E. M., & Bailey, T. M. (2009). Predicting category intuitiveness with the rational model, the simplicity model, and the Generalized Context Model. *Journal of Experimental Psychology: Learning, Memory, and Cognition*, **35**, 1062–1080.

Pothos, E. M., & Chater, N. (2002). A simplicity principle in unsupervised human categorization. *Cognitive Science*, **26**, 303–343.

(2005). Unsupervised categorization and category learning. *Quarterly Journal of Experimental Psychology*, **58A**, 733–752.

Pothos, E. M., & Close, J. (2008). One or two dimensions in spontaneous classification: a simplicity approach. *Cognition*, **107**, 581–602.

Pothos, E. M., Perlman, A., Edwards, D. J., Gureckis, T. M., Hines, P. M., & Chater, N. (2008). Modeling category intuitiveness. In *Proceedings of the 30th Annual Conference of the Cognitive Science Society*. Mahwah, NJ: LEA.

Pothos, E. M., & Wolff, J. G. (2006). The simplicity and power model for inductive inference. *Artificial Intelligence Review*, **26**, 211–225.

Rissanen, J. (1978). Modeling by shortest data description. *Automatica*, **14**, 465–471.

(1986). Stochastic complexity and modeling. *Annals of Statistics*, **14**, 1080–1100.

Rosch, E., & Mervis, C. B. (1975). Family resemblances: studies in the internal structure of categories. *Cognitive Psychology*, 7, 573–605.

Sanborn, A. N., Griffiths, T. L., & Navarro, D. (2006). A more rational model of categorization. In R. Sun & N. Miyake (eds.), *Proceedings of the 28th Annual Conference of the Cognitive Science Society*. Mahwah, NJ: Erlbaum.

Stewart, N., & Brown, G. D. A. (2005). Similarity and dissimilarity as evidence in perceptual categorization. *Journal of Mathematical Psychology*, **49**, 403–409.

Tversky, A. (1977). Features of similarity. *Psychological Review*, **84**, 327–352.

Wallace, C. S., & Freeman, P. R. (1987). Estimation and inference by compact coding. *Journal of the Royal Statistical Society, Series B*, **49**, 240–251.

Wolff, J. G. (1977). The discovery of segmentation in natural language. *British Journal of Psychology*, **67**, 377–390.

10 Adaptive clustering models of categorization

John V. McDonnell and Todd M. Gureckis

Summary

Numerous proposals have been put forward concerning the nature of human category representations, ranging from rules to exemplars to prototypes. However, it is unlikely that a single, fixed form of representation is sufficient to account for the flexibility of human categories. In this chapter, we describe an alternative to these fixed-representation accounts based on the principle of adaptive clustering. The specific model we consider, SUSTAIN, represents categories in terms of feature bundles called clusters which are adaptively recruited in response to task demands. In some cases, SUSTAIN acts like an exemplar model, storing each category instance as a separate memory trace, while in others it appears more like a prototype model, extracting only the central tendency of a number of items. In addition, selective attention in the model allows it to mimic many of the behaviours associated with rule-based systems. We review a variety of evidence in support of the clustering principle, including studies of the relationship between categorization and recognition memory, changes in unsupervised category learning abilities across development, and the influence of category learning on perceptual discrimination. In each case, we show how the nature of human category representations is best accounted for using an adaptive clustering scheme. SUSTAIN is just one example of a system that casts category learning in terms of adaptive clustering, and future directions for the approach are discussed.

Introduction

Debates concerning the representational primitives underlying our ability to categorize information in our environment have played a central role in models of category learning. Traditionally, there have been three main proposals for how people might represent categories: rules (Bruner, Goodnow, & Austin, 1956; Nosofsky, Palmeri, & McKinley, 1994), prototypes (Rosch & Mervis, 1975; Smith & Minda, 2000), and exemplars

(Kruschke, 1992; Medin & Schaffer, 1978; Nosofsky, 1984). Each of these accounts makes strong, testable predictions about the nature of human categories which have driven considerable progress in the field. However, one feature common to all of these proposals is that they are somewhat static and inflexible. Each category the learner acquires is assumed to be represented in exactly the same way. For example, prototype theories hold that all categories are represented in terms of a central tendency, while in exemplar theories categories are based on memories for individual experiences or episodes. In addition, the representation that the learner adopts is assumed to be invariant to the structure of the material, the learner's goals, or the way in which the learner interacts with the stimuli while learning.

In this chapter, we describe an alternative to these fixed-representation accounts based on the principle of adaptive clustering. Clusters are a way of representing particular subsets of category items or experiences in a way that captures the similarity structure of the items. A key feature of clusters is that they can vary in how abstract or specific they are. Models based on clustering share a common view of human memory as an adaptive process that coordinates the recollection and encoding of both highly specific, detailed information, and more abstract generalizations. In everyday life, it is clear that we sometimes need to remember distinct, individual memories (such as recognizing a particular face) while at other times we need to combine information across a number of distinct experiences to abstract the underlying commonalities (such as when categorizing objects like chairs). However, the type of encoding we need may vary greatly depending on task and context. The central idea behind most clustering models is that the 'grain-size' of the representation that the learner adopts should flexibly adapt depending on the demands of the learning task and the structure of the environment.

Numerous models of human learning have been proposed that instantiate this idea in different ways, including adaptive resonance theory (Carpenter & Grossberg, 1988), the rational model (Anderson, 1991), the 'more rational' model (Sanborn, Griffiths, & Navarro, 2006), the Simplicity Model (Pothos & Chater, 2002), the varying abstraction model (Vanpaemel, Storms, & Ons, 2005), and CLUSTER (Love & Jones, 2006). In this chapter, we focus our discussion on a single example which is representative of this broad class, the Supervised and Unsupervised STratified Adaptive Incremental Network (SUSTAIN, Love, Medin, & Gureckis, 2004). We begin by describing the operation of the model in qualitative terms and identify its key psychological principles. We then discuss the formal implementation of the model and give some guidance for researchers interested in applying SUSTAIN to their own research.

Next, we review a number of empirical and simulation studies which highlight the key mechanisms in the model. We conclude with a discussion of the relationship between SUSTAIN and other models, along with future directions for models based on the principle of adaptive clustering.

Motivation

SUSTAIN is a computational model of human category learning. The central psychological principle guiding SUSTAIN is that the representation that a learner adopts may be determined by a variety of factors including the learner's goals and the structure of the task environment (Love, 2005). In SUSTAIN, categories are represented by clusters which are adaptively recruited in response to task demands. Clusters in the model are essentially 'bundles of features' that capture important regularities in the environment. Clusters begin their existence centred over a single stimulus item, but can evolve over time to become more abstract and prototype-like, capturing the central tendency of a number of items. The model starts with the simplest possible clustering scheme (a single cluster encoding the first stimulus item presented) and incrementally adds new clusters in response to task demands. Thus, the representation that the learner adopts is assumed to grow in complexity as needed to solve the task. Interestingly, the emergent properties of SUSTAIN's clustering scheme allow it to subsume many of the properties of systems that assume 'fixed' category representations. For example, when SUSTAIN recruits only a single cluster to represent a category, it reduces to a prototype model. In other cases, it can act as an exemplar model by recruiting a separate cluster for each individual member of a category. Finally, the interaction between SUSTAIN's clustering scheme and selective attention processes allows it to mimic the behaviour of rule-based models.

One of the key contributions of SUSTAIN is that it has helped to expand the range of category learning tasks that can be addressed with formal models. SUSTAIN has been used to model a variety of induction tasks including classification learning (Love *et al.*, 2004), inference learning (Love *et al.*, 2004), unsupervised category learning (Gureckis & Love, 2002, 2003), probabilistic categorization (McDonnell & Gureckis, 2009), the relationship between categorization and recognition memory (Sakamoto & Love, 2004), and the influence of categorization on perceptual discrimination (Gureckis & Goldstone, 2008). In addition, the model has successfully accounted for changes in categorization and recognition memory performance as a function of disease and brain damage (Love & Gureckis, 2007), declines in categorization performance with aging (Love & Gureckis, 2007), changes in categorization abilities throughout development (Gureckis & Love, 2004), and cross-cultural differences in categorization (Love & Gureckis, 2005). More recently, SUSTAIN has been integrated into a neurobiological theory of how an interactive circuit involving the hippocampus, perirhinal cortex, and pre-frontal cortex (PFC) contribute to category learning and recognition memory (Love & Gureckis, 2007).

An overview of the operation of SUSTAIN

The core principles of SUSTAIN are formally instantiated in a connec-tionist network. Figure 10.1 shows a graphical overview of the model. Like people, the model acquires knowledge about categories on a trial-by-trial basis. On each learning episode, the model takes as input a description of the current stimulus item represented as a set of values along a set of perceptual feature dimensions. Like other models of cat-egory learning (e.g., Anderson, 1991), SUSTAIN treats the category membership (or category label) of a stimulus item as an additional stimu-lus feature dimension. The input units in the model feed into a selective attention mechanism which allows the model to differentially weight stimulus dimensions that are more or less useful for the current categor-ization task (Kruschke, 1992). In Figure 10.1, this attentional mechan-ism is illustrated by the exponentially shaped receptive fields positioned above each input dimension.

The internal representations in the model consist of a set of clusters (denoted by the circles in the centre of Figure 10.1) which inhabit the multidimensional psychological space defined by the stimulus dimen-sions. Categories are represented in the model as one or more clusters. Likewise, clusters can belong to one or more categories. Initially, the network has only one cluster, centred on the first input pattern. As new stimulus items are presented, the model attempts to assign these new items to an existing cluster. This assignment is done through an unsuper-vised procedure based on the similarity of the new item to the stored clusters. When a new item is assigned to a cluster, the cluster updates its internal representation to move closer to the average of all items assigned to the cluster so far.

New clusters are recruited under the principle of 'adaptation to sur-prise' (Gureckis & Love, 2003). In supervised learning, SUSTAIN cre-ates a new cluster in response to a surprising misclassification, whereas in unsupervised learning, a new cluster is created when the model encounters a surprisingly novel stimulus item (as determined by a sin-gle parameter in the model). In addition, clusters compete with each other to respond to the current stimulus item. The cluster that wins

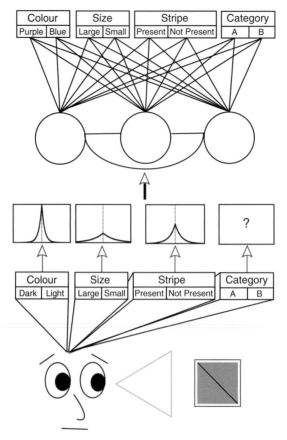

Figure 10.1 Schematic illustration of SUSTAIN. Stimuli are encoded as a set of values of individual stimulus dimensions. Attentional weighting determines the specificity of each of these values, and the weighted signal activates each of the clusters. The clusters compete with one another to explain the input such that the activation of the winning cluster is reduced in the presence of plausible competitors. The winning cluster then activates the output nodes, which correspond exactly to the input nodes. Predictions about missing features or the category label are based on these output unit activations.

this competition passes its activation over connection weights to a set of output units in a winner-take-self fashion. In this sense, clusters can be seen as competing explanations of the current input. The output units replicate the structure of the input dimensions (illustrated at the top of Figure 10.1) making the model formally an auto-encoder (see also Gluck & Myers, 1993). Because SUSTAIN learns to recreate its input at its output, it can easily model tasks such as inference learning, where participants are given the category label and a subset of features for an item and asked to predict a missing feature (Yamauchi, Love, & Markman, 2002). The connection weights between the clusters and output units are adjusted over the course of learning so that the association between each cluster and the appropriate response for members of that cluster is strengthened. SUSTAIN's ultimate response is biased towards the most activated output unit for a queried dimension. In this way, classification decisions are ultimately based on the cluster to which an instance is assigned.

The short description just provided gives an overview of the mechanistic operation of the model. However, the construction of SUSTAIN's learning algorithm is not arbitrary, and each component of the model is motivated by a corresponding psychological principle (Gureckis & Love, 2002).

> *Principle 1: SUSTAIN is representationally biased towards simple solutions.* SUSTAIN begins learning with only a single cluster, and adds new clusters as needed, based on the demands of the task. Thus, the model is biased towards simpler task representations, and revises these representations dynamically as the task unfolds. SUSTAIN also learns to weight its attention to feature dimensions that prove to be more informative, further reducing the complexity of its solutions by focusing only on a relevant subset of dimensions.
>
> *Principle 2: Similar stimulus items tend to cluster together in memory.* SUSTAIN assigns new items to clusters based on the overall similarity between the target item and each cluster. For example, when classifying different types of animals, SUSTAIN might group certain species such as whales and dolphins together in a single cluster. This ensures that the knowledge structures in the model (i.e., clusters) naturally capture the similarity structure of items that occur in the task or environment.
>
> *Principle 3: SUSTAIN can learn in both a supervised and unsupervised fashion.* Without feedback about the 'true' identity of the stimuli, SUSTAIN will form clusters based on the apparent clustering of stimuli in the environment. New clusters are recruited to capture items that are surprisingly novel in the sense that they do not fit well with existing clusters. This process is unsupervised, in that it only depends on the similarity between new items and existing clusters.

In supervised learning contexts (where a teacher is available to provide corrective feedback), additional processes intervene to structure learning. Under supervision, feedback that the model has given an incorrect classification response causes the model to recruit a new cluster to capture the incorrectly classified item. Thus, inaccurate predictions encourage an increase in the complexity of the representation that the model adopts (particularly when stimuli that appear to belong in one cluster turn out to belong to another). For example, consider the situation where the model has been trained on a set of animals and formed two clusters, one representing animals with four legs and warm blood (i.e., mammals) and another representing animals with wings (i.e., birds). According to this clustering strategy, a novel example of a bat might initially be grouped with birds on the basis of overall similarity. However, in a supervised learning context, SUSTAIN will receive feedback that bats are actually mammals, and recruit a new cluster centred on bats to capture this new exception to the bird cluster. This example also demonstrates SUSTAIN's bias towards simple solutions combined with an ability to entertain more complex solutions when the structure of the task demands it.

Principle 4: The exact pattern of feedback and stimuli matters. SUSTAIN will often create different cluster representations based on the order in which it learns about a set of stimuli. For example, imagine a category that has three members, arranged along a single dimension. If SUSTAIN sees the middle member first, and then the others, it might be inclined to represent them all under a single cluster. But if it sees one of the extreme examples first, followed by the opposite extreme, it might be surprised enough to recruit a new cluster for the opposite extremity, resulting in two clusters instead of one. This allows SUSTAIN to make strong predictions about how the order of stimulus presentation in a task influences learning. This property can also allow SUSTAIN to predict different learning patterns for tasks that offer identical information but vary in their pattern of feedback (such as inference learning and classification learning).

Principle 5: Cluster competition. Clusters can be seen as competing ways of explaining a given observation. The strength of the response of the winning cluster is attenuated in the presence of other clusters that are somewhat similar to the current stimulus. This principle has implications for the relationship between SUSTAIN's acquired clusters and recognition memory for studied items, as strong competition can reduce the strength of memory for particular items.

Implementation

With these key principles in mind, the following section describes the formal implementation of the model.

Input representation

Inputs to SUSTAIN are represented as vector frames where the dimensionality of the vector is equal to the number of dimensions along which the stimuli can vary. In addition, the category label is considered to be a stimulus dimension for the purposes of encoding. Thus, a stimulus that varied along three dimensions, along with a category label, would be represented as a vector frame with four slots (or dimensions), such as 121?, where '?' represents the queried dimension (i.e., the dimension the learner is being asked to predict). Typically, the category label is treated as the right-most slot in the vector frame. This input representation is quite flexible and allows SUSTAIN to model alternative induction tasks such as inference learning where dimensions other than the category label are queried. Thus, a classification learning trial would take the form 121?→1211, while an inference trial might take the form 12?1→1211 (the second pattern being the full stimulus after feedback), since a dimension other than the category label is queried.

To represent a single stimulus dimension that can display multiple values, SUSTAIN uses multiple input units which are organized within each slot. For example, the disjunctive feature 'marital status' has three possible values (*single, married, divorced*). In order to represent this information to the model, a bit vector with three values is used. The value of the vector is set to 1 for the encoded feature value and 0 at all other locations. Thus, a single person would be represented by the bit vector [100], a married person as [010], etc. A complete stimulus is represented by a vector frame $I^{pos_{ik}}$, where i indexes the stimulus dimension (or slot) and k indexes the nominal values within that dimension i. Figure 10.2A provides an illustrative example. Here, the shape of the stimulus can take on one of three values: square, triangle, or circle. Because the displayed item is triangular, $I^{pos_{12}}$ is valued at 1 while $I^{pos_{11}}$ and $I^{pos_{13}}$ are 0. The pos in I^{pos} denotes that the current stimulus is located in a certain position in the multidimensional stimulus space.

As Figure 10.2B shows, the same basic representational framework is used to represent clusters as well. However, the position of a cluster often has values other than 1 or 0 which can be interpreted as the probability of displaying a value given that an item is a member of the cluster. For

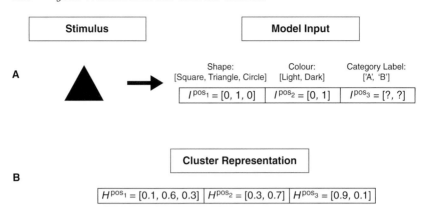

Figure 10.2 A visualization of the stimulus encoding process, and analogous cluster representation. In A, the stimulus is presented, and two features are visible. The queried category label is hidden. Note that because there are three possible shapes, shape is represented as a slot in the vector frame with three different values, one for 'square', 'triangle', and 'circle' respectively. Because the stimulus is a triangle, the value for triangle is 1 while the value for the other shapes is 0. In B, a possible cluster representation is shown. The cluster is represented by a vector frame corresponding exactly to the stimulus structure. However, because clusters often lie between actual stimulus values, they often take on intermediate values. For example, the majority of stimuli that have fit this cluster have had a dark colour, but a few have had a light colour, which is why SUSTAIN's value for H^{pos} is [0.3, 0.7] rather than [0, 1].

example, in the cluster shown in Figure 10.2B, none of the values in the cluster are 0 or 1. This is because this example cluster has moved towards the central tendency of the items which have been assigned to it. Over the course of learning, the location of a cluster eventually converges to indicate the proportion of items bearing each stimulus value that have been assigned to that cluster. For example, if over the course of many trials 10% of its members are squares, 60% are triangles, and 30% are circles, the values of the bit vector for the colour dimension would be expected to converge to [.1.6.3].

Calculating the psychological distance between internal units and the current pattern

Psychological distance in SUSTAIN is measured via a city-block metric. Here, the distance μ_{ij} between the current stimulus and cluster j along the ith feature dimension is:

$$\mu_{ij} = \frac{1}{2} \sum_{k=1}^{v_i} |I^{\text{pos}_{ik}} - H_j^{\text{pos}_{ik}}|, \tag{1}$$

where v_i is the number of different nominal values on the ith dimension, I is the current stimulus representation presented to SUSTAIN, and $H_j^{\text{pos}_{ik}}$ is cluster j's position on the ith dimension for value k. Along any given dimension, the sum of all k units is 1.

Receptive fields

Each cluster has a receptive field which falls off exponentially with distance from the centre. The activation on each dimension is described as:

$$\alpha(\mu) = \lambda e^{-\lambda\mu} \tag{2}$$

where λ is the specificity of the receptive field, μ is the eccentricity of the stimulus with respect to the field's centre, and $\alpha(\mu)$ is the response generated by the receptive field to a stimulus falling μ units from the centre of the field.

Although receptive fields with different λ have different shapes (ranging from a broad to a peaked exponential), for any λ the area underneath a receptive field is constant:

$$\int_0^\infty \alpha(\mu)d\mu = \int_0^\infty \lambda e^{-\lambda\mu}d\mu = 1. \tag{3}$$

Equation 3 enforces the property that the wider the receptive field, the less the activation at the centre of the field. This ensures that broad tuning comes at the expense of specificity.

Given a particular value for μ, λ can be adjusted to maximize $\alpha(\mu)$ based on the following derivative:

$$\frac{\partial\alpha}{\partial\lambda} = e^{-\lambda\mu}(1-\lambda\mu). \tag{4}$$

This provides the basis for allocating attention in the model. SUSTAIN's means of updating attention is different from that found in models such as ALCOVE. Rather than using a top-down gradient descent learning rule to minimize error, SUSTAIN increases attention to dimensions that effectively segregate clusters (i.e., those with a small average value of μ). If dimensions vary across clusters irregularly (and thus μ is larger), attention is down-weighted. The actual updating rule is given below by Equation 12.

Cluster activation

Combining the previous two sections, the activation for each cluster when a stimulus is presented is given by:

$$H_j^{\text{act}} = \frac{\sum_{i=1}^{m} (\lambda_i)^r e^{-\lambda_i \mu_{ij}}}{\sum_{i=1}^{m} (\lambda_i)^r} \tag{5}$$

where H_j^{act} is the activation of the jth cluster, m is the number of stimulus dimensions, λ_i is the tuning of the receptive field for the ith input dimension, and r is an always non-negative attentional parameter. Increasing r accentuates attentional effects, causing dimensions with larger λ to dominate the activation function. If r is set to zero, every dimension receives equal attention. Equation 5 sums the responses of the receptive fields for each input dimension and normalizes the sum. Unknown stimulus dimensions (e.g., the category label in a classification trial) are not included in the above calculation.

Competition

In SUSTAIN, clusters competing to explain the input stimulus inhibit one another. This competition is implemented via a lateral inhibition mechanism that causes highly activated clusters to dampen the output of the winning cluster (H_j^{out}):

for the winning H_j with the greatest H^{act},

$$H_j^{\text{out}} = \frac{(H_j^{\text{act}})^\beta}{\sum_{i=1}^{n} (H_j^{\text{act}})^\beta} H_j^{\text{act}}, \tag{6}$$

$$H_j^{\text{out}} = 0,$$

where n is the number of clusters and β is the lateral inhibition parameter that determines the degree of cluster competition (always non-negative). A smaller value for β causes a stronger lateral inhibition effect. The lateral inhibition effect only impacts the winner, because the activation of all losing clusters is set to zero. Equation 6 thus describes a process which might be explained in psychological terms as a reduction in confidence in a choice when there are likely alternatives available.

Choice rule

Activation is spread from the winning cluster to the output layer, where units represent each possible value of the queried dimension z. Once a winning cluster is chosen, it spreads its activation to the output layer. The activation of each possible response k for the queried stimulus dimension z is given by:

$$C_{zk}^{\text{out}} = \sum_{j=1}^{n} w_{j,zk} H_j^{\text{out}} \tag{7}$$

where C_{zk}^{out} is the output of the output unit representing the kth nominal value of the queried (unknown) zth dimension, n is the number of clusters, and $w_{j,zk}$ is the weight from cluster j to category unit C_{zk}.

Activation on the response units then determines the probability of making each response, with the probability for each response k given by:

$$\Pr(k) = \frac{e^{(d \cdot C_{zk}^{\text{out}})}}{\sum_{j=1}^{v_z} e^{(d \cdot C_{zj}^{\text{out}})}} \tag{8}$$

where d is a non-negative response parameter and v_z is the number of nominal units (i.e., possible responses) forming the queried dimension z. This is analogous to the Luce choice rule (Luce, 1959), giving a weighted probability to each response, and becoming more deterministic as d increases.

Learning

In supervised learning, after a choice is made, feedback is provided to SUSTAIN. The target value for the kth category unit of the queried dimension z is:

$$t_{zk} = \begin{cases} \max(C_{zk}^{\text{out}}, 1) & \text{if } I^{\text{pos}_{zk}} = 1 \\ \min(C_{zk}^{\text{out}}, 0) & \text{if } I^{\text{pos}_{zk}} = 0 \end{cases} \tag{9}$$

This sort of teaching signal was incorporated into ALCOVE by Kruschke (1992), who referred to it as a 'humble teacher'. Kruschke (1992) explains the assumptions behind it and the contexts in which its use is appropriate. With a humble teacher, the model is not penalized for predicting the correct response more strongly than is necessary. This is a reasonable assumption in a case where actual feedback given to participants is nominal rather than indicating a degree of correctness.

New cluster recruitment   If a new stimulus is 'surprising' enough, a new cluster will be recruited to represent it (Gureckis & Love, 2003).

Cluster recruitment proceeds differently depending on whether the task involves supervised or unsupervised learning. In the case of supervised learning, a new cluster is recruited if the winning cluster predicts an incorrect response. For the response to be considered correct, the output unit representing the correct nominal value must be the most activated of all the output units forming the queried stimulus dimension. In the case of an unsupervised learning situation, SUSTAIN is self-supervising and recruits a cluster when the most activated cluster has activation below the threshold τ.

In both supervised and unsupervised learning situations, when a new cluster is recruited it is centred on the misclassified input pattern. That is to say, the input frame is copied to become the frame representing the new cluster. The clusters' activations and outputs are then recalculated. The new cluster necessarily becomes the winner because it will be the most highly activated cluster (all μ_{ij} will be zero).

Output weight adjustment.   Weights from the units of a new cluster to the output units are initialized at zero. On each trial, the weights from the winning cluster to the queried output units are then adjusted according to the one-layer delta learning rule (Widrow & Hoff, 1960):

$$\Delta w_{j,zk} = \eta(t_{zk} - C_{zk}^{\text{out}})H_j^{\text{out}} \tag{10}$$

where z is the queried dimension. Because the output of the non-winning clusters has been set to zero, only the weights of the winning cluster will be adjusted.

Cluster adjustment   In cases where a new cluster is not recruited, the position of the winner is adjusted to accommodate the new input pattern according to the following rule:

For the winning H_j,
$$\Delta H_j^{\text{pos}_{ik}} = \eta(I^{\text{pos}_{ik}} - H_j^{\text{pos}_{ik}}), \tag{11}$$

where η is the learning rate. This rule move causes the centres of the winning cluster's receptive fields to move incrementally towards the current input pattern, via the Kohonen learning rule (Kohonen, 1982). This method of adjustment will slowly cause the cluster to become centred amidst its members.

Attention learning Attention is adjusted by altering receptive field tunings on the basis of our result from Equation 4:

$$\Delta\lambda_i = \eta e^{-\lambda_i \mu_{ij}}(1 - \lambda_i \mu_{ij}), \tag{12}$$

where j is the index of the winning cluster. This equation explains how SUSTAIN modulates attention on a trial-by-trial basis. The intuition is that attention, which is represented in terms of the peakedness of the receptive field for each input dimension, is increased along stimulus dimensions which effectively discriminate among clusters, and reduced along stimulus dimensions which are less indicative of cluster membership. Equation 12 adjusts the peakedness of the receptive field. Initially, λ_i is set to be broadly tuned with a value of 1. The value of 1 is chosen because the maximal distance μ_{ij} is 1 and the optimal setting of λ_i for this case is 1 (i.e., Equation 12 equals zero). Under this scheme, λ_i cannot become less than 1, but can become more narrowly tuned. Note that only the winning cluster updates the value of λ_i.

Parameter fitting and optimization

One advantage of SUSTAIN is that it is designed to be directly comparable to human performance in categorization tasks. This includes learning in the same number of trials as human participants. Predictions from the model are typically derived by running the model thousands of times on different stimulus orderings and comparing the average results to patterns of human data.

As described in the previous section, SUSTAIN has a number of free parameters which can be fit to human performance in any particular data set. Although these parameters can be fit to each individual study, previous work with the model has identified a single set of parameters which qualitatively fit a large number of studies (Love *et al.*, 2004). These parameters, shown in Table 10.1, provide an excellent starting point for applying the model in a new context. Two parameters of the model which are relatively sensitive to the nature of the experiment being modelled are λ and τ. The λ parameter governs the initial attentional weight, so its best-fit value is often strongly influenced by the task (for example if there is reason to believe that one dimension is a priori more salient than others). The τ parameter governs the tendency of the model to form new clusters in response to surprise or novelty. The τ parameter is of particular interest, since it governs the complexity of representations SUSTAIN creates. Love and Gureckis (2007) provide evidence that individual

Table 10.1 *Best fit parameters from Love* et al. *(2004)*

Function	Symbol	Global best fit
Attentional focus	*r*	2.844642
Cluster competition	*β*	2.386305
Learning rate	η	0.09361126
Decision consistency	*d*	12.0

Love *et al.* (2004) conducted a series of global parameter fits to a variety of empirical data concerning both supervised and unsupervised category learning. Presented here are the 'global' best fit parameters which are a good starting point for investigations with the model (as described in the text, τ and λ are often fit for individual studies depending on the nature of the stimuli).

differences in this parameter may relate to differences in memory capacity between individuals and populations.

On-line resources

SUSTAIN is fairly straightforward to implement. However, to assist researchers interested in applying SUSTAIN to their own data, we have created a website where a simple implementation of SUSTAIN in the Python scripting language can be downloaded (http://smash.psych.nyu.edu/sustain.php). The website explains how to check out an up-to-date version.

Example studies

As described before, SUSTAIN has been successfully applied to a large number of human learning studies. In the following section, we discuss three example studies that illustrate the key principles of adaptive clustering as instantiated by SUSTAIN.

Recognition memory for category exceptions

One of SUSTAIN's key predictions is that people's representations of categories can have internal structure of varying complexity. In the simplest case, a category may be represented by a single cluster which captures the central tendency of all category members (akin to a prototype model). In other cases, each exemplar of the category might have its own cluster (akin to an exemplar model). However, in intermediate cases, some subsets of stimuli may be clustered together, while others are captured separately with item-specific clusters. One way to study this latter type of 'hybrid' representation is to test learning and memory for categories which are defined by a salient rule but contain exceptions that violate the rule.

For example, Palmeri and Nosofsky (1995) examine category learning and recognition memory for so-called 'rule-plus-exception' categories. In their task, participants learned to classify a set of items into two mutually exclusive categories. Category membership was determined by a simple rule along a single dimension. For example, all small items might be in category 'A' and all large items in category 'B'. However, there were exceptions: one 'A' exception (e.g., a big item in category 'A') and one 'B' exception (e.g., a small item in category 'B'). Following categorization training, recognition memory for the studied items along with novel test items was assessed. Palmeri and Nosofsky found a memory advantage for items that were exceptions to the category rule. Strict exemplar models cannot account for the exception item memory advantage because they represent all items the same way. RULEX can explain the memory advantage for exception items, but does not predict a memory advantage for previously viewed items as opposed to novel rule-following items. The authors explained the results by means of a complex hybrid model that combined the rule-learning components of RULEX (Nosofsky *et al.*, 1994) with a separate exemplar memory system based on the generalized context model (GCM) (Nosofsky, 1984).

SUSTAIN is able to account for these results without modification using a single principle: adaptive clustering (Sakamoto & Love, 2004). As in the hybrid representation case described above, SUSTAIN creates one or two clusters to capture the rule-following items. In contrast, the exception items are accounted for by single item-specific clusters which foster improved recognition memory for these items. Interestingly, due to cluster competition, SUSTAIN predicts increased recognition memory for exception items that are exceptions to rules with a larger number of rule-following items, a prediction which was confirmed in human participants by Sakamoto and Love (2004). This is something that is not expected via the traditional rule learning account, since a rule, once learned, should apply equally well regardless of the number of specific items that follow that rule.

Overall, studies of rule-plus-exception categories provide an excellent example of how the complexity of the representation that learners adopt can be adapted to match the demands of the task. Rule-like representations in SUSTAIN are an emergent property of clustered representations, but are not given a privileged status. Instead, SUSTAIN's clustering principle focuses on the key distinction of how specific or general a representation is rather than by assuming a completely different type of representation or learning mechanism.

How do developmental changes in perceptual or cognitive capacities influence concept acquisition?

Adaptive clustering models are particularly compelling when used to model individual differences in categorization and memory. For example, in SUSTAIN, differences in memory ability can be neatly operationalized as changes in the ability to recruit new clusters, which is controlled by the τ parameter (Love & Gureckis, 2007). As described in the Implementation section, the τ parameter controls SUSTAIN's threshold for recruiting new clusters in response to surprising events (i.e., how novel an item has to be to invoke cluster recruitment). When τ is high, learners will show a fine-grained sensitivity to differences between items and will construct many distinct clusters in memory. In contrast, with a low value of τ the model has trouble recruiting clusters in response to novel items, and thus tends to adopt more prototype-like representations. Thus, γ effectively controls the 'grain size' of SUSTAIN's clustered representations. Using this principle, SUSTAIN has successfully accounted for the category learning and memory deficits associated with a number of memory-impaired populations including medial-temporal lobe (MTL) amnesics, older adults, and infants (Love & Gureckis, 2007). Here we focus on a set of simulations reported by Gureckis and Love (2004) which examined how changes in memory or perceptual abilities might account for changes in categorization across development.

Younger and Cohen (1986) reported a developmental study examining changes in categorization abilities across infancy in a looking-time habituation task. Infants were tested at 4, 7, and 10 months. They were presented with imaginary animals created out of different combinations of parts. For example, a stimulus could have an elephant head, horse tail, and webbed feet. During the training phase, the infants were habituated to a set of stimuli that had a correlation between two stimulus features. That is, certain body parts only appeared with particular other body parts, for example, an elephant head might have always appeared with a horse tail. In the test phase, novel animals were presented that either broke or preserved the correlational structure established in the previous phase. Evidence that infants had learned the correlation between the attributes was assessed through the preferential looking time method. If infants looked equally at both the 'correlated' test item and the novel 'uncorrelated' item, it would be evidence that they did not learn the correlation. In contrast, if looking times increased to the novel uncorrelated

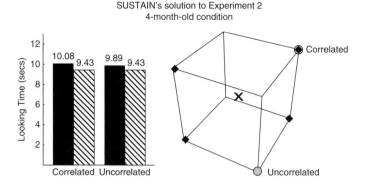

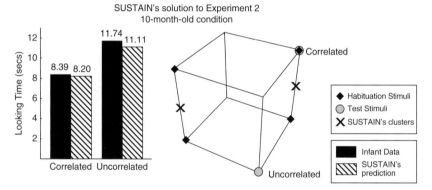

Figure 10.3 The clustering results from Gureckis and Love
(2004) for Experiment 2 in Younger and Cohen (1986). As shown
on the left, SUSTAIN was able to accurately predict looking
times for 4-month-old and 10-month-old infants. To the right
are SUSTAIN's clustering solutions for the two cohorts. The
performance of 4-month-olds could be captured by one cluster
centred in the centre of the stimulus space, whereas the performance
of 10-month-olds was captured by two clusters on opposite ends of
the stimulus space.

item, it would indicate that infants had learned the correlation structure
and noticed that it was broken in this item. The results showed that at
4 months of age, infants were not sensitive to the correlational structure,
but by 10 months, infants did show dishabituation to the novel uncorrelated stimulus configurations, as evidenced by increased looking times
(compare Figure 10.3, left top and left bottom).

Gureckis and Love (2004) modelled these results with SUSTAIN
by assuming that younger infants have reduced memory capacity (i.e.,

cluster recruitment abilities), which gradually increases along with development. Thus, younger infants were simulated with a lower setting of τ compared to older infants. The final clustering solution for this problem is depicted graphically in Figure 10.3. The lower setting of τ in the simulated 4-month-olds caused SUSTAIN to solve the task using only one cluster (located in the centre of the multidimensional stimulus space). Under the assumption that the infant looking time is linearly related to the perceived novelty of test items with respect to the acquired category representation, SUSTAIN predicts that 4-month-old infants will be indifferent to the test pairs (i.e., insensitive to the correlational structure among the stimuli). As Figure 10.3 (top right) shows, with only one cluster located at the centre of the space, all test and study items are equally familiar/novel since they are equidistant from the acquired representation. This means that, like infants, the model over-generalizes to the novel test patterns that break the correlation between the first two stimulus dimensions. SUSTAIN's one-cluster explanation is further bolstered by the findings of Younger (1985), who showed that infants at 4 months of age appear to habituate to the mean stimulus of a set of items, which is where SUSTAIN predicts the only cluster to be centred. By contrast, in the 10-month-old simulations (Figure 10.3, bottom), SUSTAIN created two clusters. This causes the correlated test item to be judged more familiar than the uncorrelated item, since the uncorrelated test items are now further away from the nearest cluster compared to the correlated test items. Thus the model correctly predicts that the 10-month-olds should show different looking time to the test pairs.

Love and Gureckis (2007) extend this account to explain differences in categorization performance for a wide group of memory-impaired individuals including MTL amnesics and older adults. Together, these results show how SUSTAIN can provide mechanistic explanations for differences in performance between different population groups. The adaptive clustering principle suggests that different groups actually learn different representations of the task, which then influences their test performance. In addition, the application of SUSTAIN's principles provides insight into the question of how infant categorization abilities eventually approach adult competence.

Do people really represent the internal structure of categories in terms of clusters?

SUSTAIN has proven to be successful at accounting for a wide variety of findings in the categorization literature. However, in many cases, the success of the model has been demonstrated primarily by the quality of its fit to human data in a categorization task (Love *et al.*, 2004). This leaves open the question of whether humans actually represent the internal structure of categories in terms of intermediary clusters. One way to assess this is to explore the evidence for cluster-like representations in a secondary task that is given subsequent to category learning (but see also Wills *et al.*, 2006, Experiment 2). If cluster-like representations are created during the category learning task, these should have predictable influence on behaviour in the secondary task (similar to how rule-plus-exception categories modulate subsequent recognition memory).

To this end, Gureckis and Goldstone (2008) investigated the effect that learning categories that are internally organized in terms of sub-clusters has on a secondary perceptual discrimination task. It is well established that after category learning, perceptual discrimination between items that belong to the same category becomes more difficult while discrimination of items that come from different categories improves relative to pre-learning levels, an effect referred to as categorical perception (Goldstone, 1994; Harnad, 1987; Logan, Lively, & Pisoni, 1991). One reason why items that belong to the same category may be seen as more similar to one another while items from different categories are seen as more distinct may be that, after learning, category members share a new commonality by virtue of the learned category label, name, or other association that category non-members do not.

Gureckis and Goldstone (2008) hypothesized, consistent with SUSTAIN, that if participants represent categories as groups of similarity-based clusters, there should be evidence of changes in discrimination at the level of clusters as well as at the level of categories. In their experiment, subjects were first asked to discriminate between pairs of items that varied along two poorly defined and arbitrary dimensions (constructed using morphed faces, Goldstone & Steyvers, 2001; Steyvers, 1999, see Figure 10.4, left). Later, they learned to classify these stimuli into two groups via trial and error with corrective feedback. As shown in Figure 10.4 (left), successful categorization required attention to only one of the stimulus dimensions. However, the structure internal to each of the two categories was not uniform: within each category there were two sub-clusters or sub-prototypes of items (only the items in black were presented during learning). To the degree that learners are sensitive to both the demands of the categorization task *and* the distribution of exemplars within each category, one expects to find changes to the discriminability of items within each category consistent with the induced clustering of items (despite the fact that this clustering was irrelevant for success in the categorization task). More specifically, two items that belong to the same category but fall into different clusters within that category should

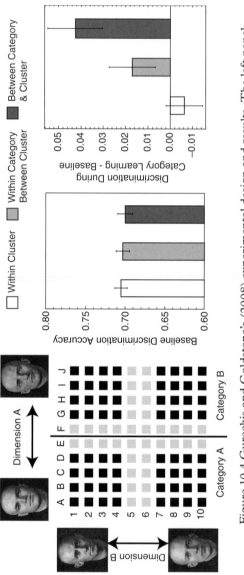

Figure 10.4 Gureckis and Goldstone's (2008) experimental design and results. The left panel shows the experimental design. Faces varied along two arbitrary morph dimensions. Grey stimuli were excluded from the experiment, thus stimuli were split into two response categories that themselves contained two clusters. Note that only one stimulus dimension was relevant to the category labels. The results on the right show that discrimination ability was similar for all stimulus pairs tested at first, but category learning led to changes in the discriminability of items consistent with a cluster-based learning mechanism.

be easier to discriminate, since even though they share the same overt label, they belong to different cluster-level representations. In contrast, items that belong to the same category and cluster should be less discriminable following learning.

As can be seen in Figure 10.4 (middle and right), prior to learning, discrimination for item pairs that belong to the same cluster, different clusters (but same category), and different categories was roughly equal. However, after learning, discrimination for items belonging to different categories (and clusters) was greatly improved while discrimination for items within the same cluster and category dropped or stayed the same. Interestingly, items that came from the same category but different clusters showed an improvement in discrimination despite the fact that these items shared the same category label. Simulations showed that this effect is not predicted by a number of popular category learning models, including backpropagation neural networks (Harnad, 1987) or ALCOVE (Kruschke, 1992). Instead, a version of SUSTAIN which was adapted to model perceptual discrimination provided a close account of the results. SUSTAIN created four clusters to solve the task, and the pattern of activity across the clusters and output units determined subsequent discrimination performance.

In this study, changes in perceptual discrimination act as a kind of 'flashlight' that illuminates the cognitive representations that learners adopt during learning. The results suggest that people do represent cluster-level information about a category even when that information is not critical for the primary task, consistent with similarity-based clustering mechanisms such as SUSTAIN.

Relationship to other models

As mentioned in the introduction, SUSTAIN is representative of a general class of adaptive clustering models. However, in an even broader sense SUSTAIN and many other models agree that human categorization is ultimately about developing internal representations of the structure of the environment that exploit regularities between experiences. This results in more efficient representations that compactly describe a domain. In the following section we consider the relationship between SUSTAIN and other modelling approaches, some of which are described in the present volume.

Other clustering models

The adaptive clustering principle upon which SUSTAIN is based has a rich history in models of concept acquisition and pattern recognition.

For example, like SUSTAIN, adaptive resonance theory (ART) attempts to learn, via unsupervised learning, a compact description of the training environment via a connectionist learning algorithm (Carpenter & Grossberg, 1988; Grossberg, 1976, 1987). In ART, cluster-like representations arise as dynamical attractors driven by both top-down and bottom-up activation patterns and competitive learning. New representations evolve in response to unfamiliar or novel patterns via a so-called 'orienting' subsystem (again like SUSTAIN's unsupervised cluster recruitment rule). However, while ART has been successfully applied to a broad range of psychological and neuroscientific data, it has not addressed the same range of categorization phenomena that SUSTAIN has. For example, while various versions of the framework have been proposed to solve particular learning problems (e.g., incorporating supervised feedback), it is unclear how the model would apply to standard categorization tasks like the Shepard, Hovland, and Jenkins (1961) categories, since the standard model does not incorporate notions of dimensional attention. Nevertheless, the ART and its descendants laid the basis for work on adaptive clustering and identified key principles which have been incorporated into later models of concept acquisition.

Anderson's (1991) rational model of categorization (RMC) holds that the goal of categorization is to be able to predict and infer unseen or unknown features of objects (see also Sanborn *et al.*, 2006, and Chapter 8 of this volume for extensions to this approach). This is accomplished in the model by representing items in terms of clusters which capture certain probabilistic relationships between features. Predictions or inferences for unknown features (including the category label of a to-be-categorized item) are found by weighting the probability of the target item having a given feature across all possible clusters. Category induction is accomplished using iterative Bayesian methods. Like SUSTAIN, the RMC includes a parameter that controls how likely it is to generate new clusters to accommodate particular items. When this parameter is high the model prefers a small number of clusters to describe a domain, while when the parameter is lower the probability of spawning new clusters increases. Although cluster recruitment in the two models is driven by different mechanisms, in practice they make similar predictions about what observations will result in new clusters. A more substantial difference lies in how the models use clusters to make inferences. The RMC makes classification decisions by optimally integrating over all possible clusters. In contrast, SUSTAIN's predictions depend entirely on the winning cluster (Equation 6). Some recent work suggests that the latter strategy may be more in line with human behaviour in category induction tasks (Murphy & Ross, 1994; Verde, Murphy, & Ross, 2005).

One way to view clustering models is in terms of compression: a clustering scheme is more compact than representing each item individually. A number of recent modelling accounts have attempted to formally evaluate this idea. For example, Pothos and Chater's simplicity model searches through possible clusterings of stimuli looking for those that provide the most compact representation of the similarity relationships between the items according to the minimum description length (MDL) principle (Chater, 1999; Pothos & Chater, 2002). Categories that have more compact descriptions are predicted to be easier to learn via supervised learning and are more likely to be spontaneously generated in unsupervised sorting tasks (Pothos & Bailey, 2009). A similar bias toward simplicity is also reflected in SUSTAIN's incremental growth process. Indeed, recent work has suggested a strong degree of convergence between these approaches for the variety of unsupervised learning tasks (Pothos et al., 2008). Similarly, the varying-abstractions model (VAM) attempts to search the space of possible clusterings to find those that best describe a participant's generalization and categorization responses (Vanpaemel et al., 2005). The simplicity model and VAM do not model the trial-by-trial acquisition of learning data, but they do explain why particular clustering solutions might be preferred over others in a normative or statistical sense.

Rule-based models

A separately important class of models assumes that categories are represented in terms of rule-based processes. Perhaps the most well-known example of this type of model is RULEX (Nosofsky et al., 1994). This model's category representations take the form of a set of if-then rules of varying complexity along with a partial exemplar store which can be deployed for rule-violating items. Like SUSTAIN, RULEX adopts a principle of incremental complexity, first considering simple uni-dimensional rules and only expanding to more complex rules when simpler explanations fail. Interestingly, the emergent properties from SUSTAIN's clustering solutions and selective attention processes allow it to mimic many of the properties of a system like RULEX. However, as discussed above, there are subtle predictions concerning the frequency with which a rule is instantiated that can differentiate these accounts (Sakamoto & Love, 2004). One salient place where incremental learning algorithms like SUSTAIN differ from rule-based accounts is on the degree to which learning will occur quickly and suddenly in rule-governed categories. It has been long noted that when learning many types of rule-based categories, individual learning curves exhibit a discontinuity where at some point participants fail to make any other errors (Rehder & Hoffman, 2005). This is consistent with the idea that participants test hypotheses until they find the rule that best explains the data (Bower & Trabasso, 1964), something akin to the search process in RULEX. More recently, new proposals have been put forward about the nature of rule-based categorization including rational approaches (Goodman *et al.*, 2009) and hybrid approaches that, like RULEX, incorporate more than one representational system with a more sophisticated gating mechanism (Erickson & Kruschke, 1998).

Exemplar models

Perhaps the most well studied class of category learning models are exemplar models. According to these accounts, categories are represented in terms of a set of separate memory traces for studied items. Classification decisions in these models are based on the relative summed similarity between the current item to every previous exemplar (Medin & Schaffer, 1978; Nosofsky, 1986). Overall, SUSTAIN, and adaptive clustering models in general, may be viewed as more general implementations of exemplar models. Exemplar models generate abstraction by pooling information across multiple experiences in memory, primarily at the time of retrieval. In contrast, clustering models assume that information is lost during encoding (Love & Gureckis, 2007). Importantly, SUSTAIN reduces to an exemplar model when one cluster is recruited for each training example. Thus, SUSTAIN can interpolate between the extremes of exemplar-based representations and prototype-based representations. A key insight is that clustering models offer a more concrete proposal about what an exemplar actually is (for instance, is every view of the same object a new exemplar?). SUSTAIN suggests that individuals should collapse across some representations rather than storing every experience and that this tendency should vary based on the demands of the task and the learner's goals.

The exemplar model most comparable with SUSTAIN is ALCOVE (Kruschke, 1992). ALCOVE blends connectionist learning rules with an exemplar category representation (i.e., the hidden units are exemplars). Like SUSTAIN, ALCOVE has a selective attention mechanism that orients it toward the most predictive stimulus dimensions. However, ALCOVE's attentional learning system is somewhat more sophisticated since it is based on gradient descent on the overall prediction error. SUSTAIN's attentional learning consists only in making clusters more discriminable. This may allow ALCOVE to account for particular attentional learning effects that SUSTAIN might not explain (such as blocking or highlighting). However, ALCOVE provides no account of how attention is allocated in unsupervised learning contexts, while SUSTAIN does. For example, SUSTAIN naturally explains the uni-dimensional bias often observed in unsupervised learning tasks as an emergent consequence of its attentional learning system (Ashby, Queller, & Berretty, 1999; Gureckis & Love, 2002; Pothos & Close, 2008).

Future challenges and directions

Although adaptive clustering models have been successful in accounting for many of the issues that arise in category learning, a number of topics remain to be addressed. In this section, we discuss possible future directions for research.

Adaptive reorganization of knowledge structures as learning proceeds

Consider a child learning to distinguish between birds and mammals. The clustering models we have described might solve this problem by forming two clusters based on whether animals had wings or four legs. This simple clustering scheme fails to accurately capture bats (which have wings but are mammals). According to a model like SUSTAIN, bats might be stored on their own as an exception cluster. Although this representation accurately captures the data, a more parsimonious explanation would involve rearranging the two clusters, re-centring the mammalian cluster around animals with fur, and re-centring the bird cluster around feathered animals. Thus, in some cases, new information warrants increased complexity (such as storing a new exception), but other times requires the reorganization of existing solutions toward a simpler, more parsimonious description of the category. Similarly, novice learners may have little sense of the features that are relevant for categorization, but after training may need to augment existing knowledge structures with additional dimensions (Blair & Homa, 2005). Such forms of knowledge reorganization are a critical aspect of human concepts and ones that could be easily addressed by adaptive clustering models. However, the majority of trial-by-trial clustering models to date (including SUSTAIN) assume that representational complexity can only grow as learning proceeds.

Recent models such as Sanborn *et al.*'s (2006) 'More rational' model (MRM) (Chapter 8) may offer one solution to this problem. The MRM uses a particle filter algorithm to track multiple hypothetical clustering solutions to a particular classification problem (Andrieu *et al.*, 2003; Daw & Courville, 2007; Doucet, Godsill, & Andrieu, 2000). As the number of particles approaches infinity, the set of clustering schemes in the particles converges on the full posterior distribution. If late learning reveals that solutions that seemed likely in early learning were sub-optimal, the model can reweigh the likelihood of particles that better predict the data (even adapting new solutions in dynamically evolving environments, Brown & Steyvers, 2009). Although avoiding over-complex or garden-path solutions is preferable, humans may still behave sub-optimally in some situations. For example, there is evidence that particular stimulus orderings can positively or negatively impact learning (Elio & Anderson, 1984; Mathy & Feldman, 2009; Medin & Bettger, 1994; Sakamoto, Jones, & Love, 2008). Thus, the best model for explaining human performance may prove to be a compromise between flexible reorganization, and early entrenchment of prior solutions. One interesting aspect of the MRM is that limiting the number of particles may increase the susceptibility of the model to entrenched ordering effects. Assuming that the number of particles reflects some type of memory capacity, the model may provide a psychological account of when knowledge reorganization is more or less likely to occur. Alternative solutions include mechanisms for merging clusters, and reorienting entire systems of clusters in the face of new data.

From categories to action

While categorization processes are clearly ubiquitous, the ultimate goal of categorization is to improve the ability of individuals to interact with their environment and to *use* their category knowledge (Markman & Ross, 2003). However, categorization is often studied in isolation of other areas of cognitive processing. One place where categorization plays a central role is in learning from interaction with the environment (i.e., reinforcement learning). In recent years there has been a growing interest in the neural and cognitive basis of learning from reinforcement (Daw & Touretzky, 2002; Fu & Anderson, 2006; Montague *et al.*, 1995; Schultz, Dayan, & Montague, 1997). Much of this interest has been based on the fortuitous congruence between the neural (Schultz *et al.*, 1997) and computational-level (Sutton & Barto, 1998) descriptions of reward-related areas in the brain. These findings have inspired an explosion of research looking at human behaviour in sequential decision tasks and how this relates to the neural systems supporting learning and deciding. A critical component of almost all existing RL algorithms is the notion of a *state* (owing to the close relationship between these algorithms and the mathematics of Markov decision processes). A state generally denotes a context in a learning environment where a particular set of actions are available, and are associated with a particular set of consequences. In dynamic or sequentially structured tasks, users must typically use their knowledge of the states of the world and the outcomes of their actions to achieve their goals. In many cases in such tasks, the state a user is in might be ambiguous: for example, a robot in a hallway might be uncertain whether it is oriented to the East or to the West, or which hallway it is in. In such a case, the problem of determining its state may be thought of as a categorization question, where states are categories (Gureckis & Love, 2009; Redish *et al.*, 2007). Learning thus involves not only learning which actions lead to the most reward, but also how to represent the environment to enable effective decision making. Recently, McDonnell and Gureckis (2009) found evidence that people use cluster-like representations to guide learning and decision making in probabilistic bandit tasks (see also, Gureckis & Love, 2009). Transitioning from traditional category learning tasks to more complex and dynamic learning tasks (such as those studied in computational reinforcement learning) helps to expose many of the features that make adaptive clustering models ideal models of human learning (namely the ability to search flexibly for efficient, generalizable representations of the environment).

Verbal decoding and recoding of clustering solutions

One important feature of human categorization is that information acquired can be verbalized and communicated to others. This raises the question of how cluster-based concept representation might be used to generate verbal descriptions of a learned category. In SUSTAIN, it is often possible for the experimenter to intuit the approximate rule the model acquired by examining the final clustering solution and pattern of attention. However, the question of how individuals bootstrap verbal descriptions (and how these verbal descriptions might influence clustering solutions) is poorly understood. For example, models such as COVIS (Ashby *et al.*, 1998) which posit a separate verbalizable rule-learning system fail to elaborate how people would develop verbal descriptions for more complex categories that contain substructures and exceptions. Of course, there is considerable empirical evidence that verbalizability is an important factor in category learning (Ahn & Medin, 1992; Alfonso-Reese, 1996) and much of the early work on categorization focused on logically described categories (Bruner *et al.*, 1956). Thus, an important area of future research with adaptive clustering models will be to understand how they interface to allow efficient verbal descriptions of the structure of a category and how this process influences learning. Fortunately, research in machine learning may offer insight into the computational mechanisms that enable this behaviour (Abidi, Hoe, & Goh, 2001; Michalski & Stepp, 1983) and newer approaches to rule learning offer innovative solutions (Goodman *et al.*, 2009).

REFERENCES

Abidi, S., Hoe, K., & Goh, A. (2001). Analyzing data clusters: a rough sets approach to extract cluster-defining symbolic rules. In *Advances in Intelligent Data Analysis* (pp. 248–257). Berlin: Springer-Verlag.

Ahn, W. K., & Medin, D. L. (1992). A two-stage model of category construction. *Cognitive Science*, **16**, 81–121.

Alfonso-Reese, L. (1996). *Dynamics of category learning.* Unpublished doctoral dissertation, University of Santa Barbara, Santa Barbara, CA.

Anderson, J. R. (1991). The adaptive nature of human categorization. *Psychological Review*, **98** (3), 409–429.

Andrieu, C., De Freitas, N., Doucet, A., & Jordan, M. (2003). An introduction to mcmc for machine learning. *Machine Learning*, **50**, 5–43.

Ashby, F., Alfonso-Reese, L., Turken, A., & Waldron, E. (1998). A neuropsychological theory of multiple system in category learning. *Psychological Review*, **105** (5), 442–481.

Ashby, F., Queller, S., & Berretty, P. (1999). On the dominance of unidimensional rules in unsupervised categorization. *Perception & Psychophysics*, **61**, 1178–1199.

Blair, M., & Homa, D. L. (2005). Integrating novel dimensions to eliminate category exceptions: when more is less. *Journal of Experimental Psychology: Learning, Memory, and Cognition*, **31**, 258–271.

Bower, G., & Trabasso, T. (1964). Presolution reversal and dimensional shifts in concept identification. *Journal of Experimental Psychology*, **67**, 398–399.

Brown, S., & Steyvers, M. (2009). Detecting and predicting changes. *Cognitive Psychology*, **58**, 49–67.

Bruner, J., Goodnow, J., & Austin, G. (1956). *A Study of Thinking.* New York: Wiley.

Carpenter, G. A., & Grossberg, S. (1988). The art of adaptive pattern recognition by a self-organizing neural network. *Computer*, **21** (3), 77–88.

Chater, N. (1999). The search for simplicity: a fundmental cognitive principle? *The Quarterly Journal of Experimental Psychology*, **52A** (2), 273–302.

Daw, N., & Courville, A. (2007). The pigeon as particle filter. In J. Platt, D. Koller, T. Singer, & S. Roweis (eds.), *Advances in Neural Information Processing Systems* (Vol. 20, pp. 369–376). Cambridge, MA: MIT Press.

Daw, N., & Touretzky, D. (2002). Long-term reward prediction in td models of the dopamine system. *Neural Computation*, **14**, 603–616.

Doucet, A., Godsill, S., & Andrieu, C. (2000). On sequential monte carlo sampling methods for bayesian filtering. *Statistics and Computing*, **10** (3), 197–208.

Elio, R., & Anderson, J. (1984). The effects of information order and learning mode on schema abstraction. *Memory & Cognition*, **12** (1), 20–30.

Erickson, M., & Kruschke, J. (1998). Rules and exemplars in category learning. *Journal of Experimental Psychology: General*, **127** (2), 107–140.

Fu, W., & Anderson, J. (2006). From recurrent choice to skill learning: a reinforcement-learning model. *Journal of Experimental Psychology: General*, **135** (2), 184–206.

Gluck, M., & Myers, C. (1993). Hippocampal mediation of stimulus representation: a computational theory. *Hippocampus*, **3** (4), 491–516.

Goldstone, R. (1994). Influence of categorization on perceptual discrimination. *Journal of Experimental Psychology: General*, **123** (2), 178–200.

Goldstone, R., & Steyvers, M. (2001). The sensitization and differentiation of dimensions during category learning. *Journal of Experimental Psychology: General*, **1**, 116–139.

Goodman, N., Tenenbaum, J., Feldman, J., & Griffiths, T. L. (2009). A rational analysis of rule-based concept learning. *Cognitive Science*, **32** (1), 108–154.

Grossberg, S. (1976). Adaptive pattern classification and universal recoding. II: feedback, expectation, olfaction, and illusions. *Biological Cybernetics*, **23**, 187–202.

(1987). Competitive learning: from interactive activation to adaptive resonance. *Cognitive Science*, **11**, 23–63.

Gureckis, T. M., & Goldstone, R. L. (2008). The effect of the internal structure of categories on perception. In B. C. Love, K. McRae, & V. M. Sloutsky (eds.), *Proceedings of the 30th Annual Conference of the Cognitive Science Society* (p. 843). Austin, TX: Cognitive Science Society.

Gureckis, T., & Love, B. (2002). Who says models can only do what you tell them? Unsupervised category learning data, fits, and predictions. In *Proceedings of the 24th Annual Conference of the Cognitive Science Society* (pp. 399–404). Hillsdale, NJ: Lawrence Erlbaum Associates.

(2003). Towards a unified account of supervised and unsupervised learning. *Journal of Experimental and Theoretical Artificial Intelligence*, **15**, 1–24.

(2004). Common mechanisms in infant and adult category learning. *Infancy*, **5** (2), 173–198.

Gureckis, T., & Love, B. C. (2009). Short term gains, long term pains: how cues about state aid learning in dynamic environments. *Cognition*, **113**, 293–313.

Harnad, S. (ed.) (1987). *Categorical Perception: The Groundwork of Cognition*. New York: Cambridge University Press.

Kohonen, T. (1982). Self-organized formation of topologically correct feature maps. *Biological Cybernetics*, **43**, 59–69.

Kruschke, J. (1992). ALCOVE: an exemplar-based connectionist model of category learning. *Psychological Review*, **99** (1), 22–44.

Logan, J., Lively, S., & Pisoni, D. (1991). Training Japanese listeners to identify English /r/ and /l/: a first report. *Journal of the Acoustical Society of America*, **89**, 874–886.

Love, B. (2005). Environment and goals jointly direct category acquisition. *Current Directions in Psychological Science*, **14** (4), 195–199.

Love, B., & Gureckis, T. (2005). Modeling learning under the influence of culture. In W. Ahn, R. Goldstone, B. Love, A. Markman, & P. Wolff (eds.), *Categorization Inside and Outside the Laboratory: Essays in Honor of Douglas L. Medin* (pp. 229–248). Washington, DC: APA Books.

(2007). Models in search of the brain. *Cognitive, Affective, & Behavioral Neuroscience*, **7** (2), 90–108.

Love, B., & Jones, M. (2006). The emergence of multiple learning systems. In *Proceedings of the 28th Annual Meeting of the Cognitive Science Society*. Mahwah, NJ: Erlbaum.

Love, B., Medin, D., & Gureckis, T. (2004). SUSTAIN: a network model of category learning. *Psychological Review*, **111** (2), 309–332.

Luce, R. D. (1959). *Individual Choice Behavior: A Theoretical Analysis*. Westport, CT: Greenwood Press.

Markman, A., & Ross, B. (2003). Category use and category learning. *Psychological Bulletin*, **4**, 592–613.

Mathy, F., & Feldman, J. (2009). A rule-based presentation order facilitates category learning. *Psychonomic Bulletin & Review*, **16**, 1050–1057.

McDonnell, J., & Gureckis, T. (2009). How perceptual categories influence trial and error learning in humans. In *Multidisciplinary Symposium on Reinforcement Learning*. Montreal, Canada.

Medin, D. L., & Bettger, J. (1994). Presentation order and recognition of categorically related examples. *Psychonomic Bulletin & Review*, **1**, 250–254.

Medin, D., & Schaffer, M. (1978). Context theory of classification learning. *Psychological Review*, **85** (3), 207–238.

Michalski, R., & Stepp, R. (1983). Learning from observation: conceptual clustering. In R. Michalski, J. Carbonell, & T. Mitchell (eds.), *Machine Learning: an Artificial Intelligence Approach* (Vol. I, pp. 331–363). Los Altos, CA: Morgan-Kaufmann.

Montague, P., Dayan, P., Person, C., & Sejnowski, T. (1995). Bee foraging in uncertain environments using predictive hebbian learning. *Nature*, **377** (6551), 725–728.

Murphy, G., & Ross, B. (1994). Predictions from uncertain categorizations. *Cognitive Psychology*, **27**, 148–193.

Nosofsky, R. M. (1984). Choice, similarity, and the context theory of classification. *Journal of Experimental Psychology: Learning, Memory, and Cognition*, **10** (1), 104–114.

(1986). Attention, similarity, and the identification-categorization relationship. *Journal of Experimental Psychology: General*, **115** (1), 39–57.

Nosofsky, R. M., Palmeri, T. J., & McKinley, S. C. (1994). Rule-plus-exception model of classification learning. *Psychological Review*, **101** (1), 53–79.

Palmeri, T. J., & Nosofsky, R. M. (1995). Recognition memory for exceptions to the category rule. *Journal of Experimental Psychology: Learning, Memory, and Cognition*, **21** (3), 548–568.

Pothos, E., & Bailey, T. (2009). Predicting category intuitiveness with the rational model, the simplicity model, and the generalized context model. *Journal of Experimental Psychology: Learning, Memory, and Cognition*, **35** (4), 1062–1080.

Pothos, E., & Chater, N. (2002). A simplicity principle in unsupervised human categorization. *Cognitive Science*, **26**, 303–343.

Pothos, E., & Close, J. (2008). One or two dimensions in spontaneous classification: a simplicity approach. *Cognition*, **107**, 581–602.

Pothos, E., Perlman, A., Edwards, D., Gureckis, T., Hines, P., & Chater, N. (2008). Modeling category intuitiveness. In B. Love, K. McRae, & V. Sloutsky (eds.), *Proceedings of the 30th Annual Conference of the Cognitive Science Society*. Austin, TX: Cognitive Science Society.

Redish, A., Jensen, S., Johnson, A., & Kurth-Nelson, Z. (2007). Reconciling reinforcement learning models with behavioral extinction and renewal: implications for addition, relapse, and problem gambling. *Psychological Review*, **114** (3), 784–805.

Rehder, B., & Hoffman, A. (2005). Eyetracking and selective attention in category learning. *Cognitive Psychology*, **51**, 1–41.

Rosch, E., & Mervis, C. (1975). Family resemblances: studies in the internal structure of categories. *Cognitive Psychology*, 7, 573–605.

Sakamoto, Y., Jones, M., & Love, B. (2008). Putting the psychology back into psychological models: mechanistic vs. rational approaches. *Memory & Cognition*, **36**, 1057–1065.

Sakamoto, Y., & Love, B. C. (2004). Schematic influences on category learning and recognition memory. *Journal of Experimental Psychology: General*, **133** (4), 534–553.

Sanborn, A., Griffiths, T., & Navarro, D. (2006). A more rational model of categorization. In R. Sun & N. Miyake (eds.), *Proceedings of the 28th Annual Meeting of the Cognitive Science Society*. Mahwah, NJ: Erlbaum.

Schultz, W., Dayan, P., & Montague, P. R. (1997). A neural substrate of prediction and reward. *Science*, **275**, 1593–1598.

Shepard, R., Hovland, C., & Jenkins, H. (1961). Learning and memorization of classifications. *Psychological Monographs*, **75** (13), Whole No. 517.

Smith, J., & Minda, J. (2000). Thirty categorization results in search of a model. *Journal of Experimental Psychology: Learning, Memory, and Cognition*, **26** (1), 3–27.

Steyvers, M. (1999). Morphing techniques for generating and manipulating face images. *Behavior Research Methods, Instruments, & Computers*, **31**, 359–369.

Sutton, R., & Barto, A. (1998). *Reinforcement Learning: An Introduction*. Cambridge, MA: MIT Press.

Vanpaemel, W., Storms, G., & Ons, B. (2005). A varying abstraction model for categorization. In *Proceedings of the 27th Annual Conference of the Cognitive Science Society*. Mahwah, NJ: Erlbaum.

Verde, M., Murphy, G., & Ross, B. (2005). Influence of multiple categories on the prediction of unknown properties. *Memory & Cognition*, **33** (3), 479–487.

Widrow, B., & Hoff, M. (1960). Adaptive switching circuits. *Institute of Radio Engineers, Western Electronic Show and Convention Record*, **4**, 96–104.

Wills, A. J., Noury, M., Moberly, N. J., & Newport, M. (2006). Formation of category representations. *Memory & Cognition*, **34**, 17–27.

Yamauchi, T., Love, B., & Markman, A. (2002). Learning nonlinearly separable categories by inference and classification. *Journal of Experimental Psychology: Learning, Memory, and Cognition*, **3**, 585–593.

Younger, B. (1985). The segregation of items into categories by ten-month-old infants. *Child Development*, **56** (6), 1574–1583.

Younger, B., & Cohen, L. (1986). Developmental change in infants' perception of correlations among attributes. *Child Development*, **57** (3), 803–815.

11 COBWEB models of categorization and probabilistic concept formation

Wayne Iba and Pat Langley

Description of the model

In this chapter, we describe a family of integrated categorization and category learning models that process and organize past experience to facilitate responses to future experience. The COBWEB system (Fisher, 1987) and its descendants CLASSIT (Gennari, 1990), OXBOW (Iba, 1991), LABYRINTH (Thompson & Langley, 1991), DÆDALUS (Langley & Allen, 1993), and TWILIX (Martin & Billman, 1994) comprise a family of models that share a genealogy, a search strategy, and a heuristic to guide that search. We will often refer to this entire family as COBWEB when the intended meaning is clear from the context.

These systems grew out of machine learning and cognitive science research that explored methods for acquiring concepts in an unsupervised context. In that setting, a teacher does not provide explicit category information for instances as the learner encounters them; instead, the learner must decide how to group or categorize a collection of instances. In contrast to most clustering methods, instances are encountered *incrementally*; the learner must make appropriate adjustments in response to each one as it comes. The COBWEB family of models view categorization as a conceptualization process or as the formation of ontologies.[1] That is, these models provide answers to the question, 'How does one form conceptual representations of similar experiences and how might those representations be organized?' However, these models also address the *use* of the acquired concepts to handle future situations. The framework embodies a collection of assumptions that together provide constraints on the design and implementation of computational systems for ontology formation and use. Such implemented models make it possible for agents to efficiently process new experiences and respond in an effective manner (for some definition of effectiveness).

---

[1] We use ontology in its narrow philosophical sense and do not intend the connotations associated with common knowledge frameworks and agent interchange languages.

Assumptions

The COBWEB models we describe here have emerged within the context of several assumptions. These assumptions may be grouped as philosophical, psychological and computational.

Philosophically, a conceptualization or ontology provides a means for agents to make sense of their experiences. We assume that conceptualizations conforming to the actual world will provide performance advantages over alternative conceptualizations. This emphasis on pragmatic benefits suggests that the contents or substance of concepts, as well as their organization and relationships, are important issues for these methods. Note that, although a particular conceptualization represents certain ontological commitments on the agent's part (Gruber, 1995), the systems need not be concerned with the metaphysical situation as long as the adopted ontology provides pragmatic value when responding to novel stimuli.

These models also grew out of several psychological assumptions. Following a grand tradition in artificial intelligence, we treat human cognition as an inspiration for the design of computational processes that exhibit intelligence. For example, if we believe that humans employ partial matching in categorization, then we would be wise to include a similar mechanism in our computational models. Likewise, cognitive limitations observed in humans should provide constraints on implementations in computer systems. If humans learn incrementally (subject to their ability to reprocess previous stimuli), these models should do the same. Although alternative methods not subject to such constraints may perform in some respects more effectively than methods that are subject to them, we know that, at a minimum, the constraints found in humans do not preclude intelligent behaviour or, in this case, the formation and use of conceptualizations. As stated by Fisher and Pazzani (1991, p. 26), 'principles which dictate preferred concepts in humans are good heuristics for machine concept formation.'

Several computational assumptions have influenced the design and development of COBWEB models. First, we recognize that nearly all of the concepts that humans form exhibit an imprecision that reveals itself, for example, when trying to pin down the meaning of words. This imprecision makes exact reasoning and communication a challenging task, but this imprecision also allows concepts considerable flexibility in their application to novel situations. So from our existence proof in humans we conclude that imprecise reasoning is sufficient for intelligence. From the way humans powerfully use the flexibility of such imprecision, we assume that such reasoning might prove to be necessary for intelligence.

Computationally, partial matching enables flexible reasoning about the membership of given objects with respect to alternative categories. Probability theory provides support for some types of partial matching, as well as an account for some of the imprecision in our language. Thus, COBWEB models share a commitment to probabilistic representation of concepts.

Second, we note that hierarchies are efficient data structures for storing and retrieving information and that humans frequently think about concepts in terms of 'is-a' or 'a kind of' hierarchies. In order to access one of n nodes organized in an appropriately structured hierarchy, we need only incur $\log_b(n)$ comparisons for uniform branching factor b. Even if it proves to be the case that humans do not organize concepts within hierarchies but only introspect as if they did, the computational benefit remains. So COBWEB models also assume that the probabilistic concepts they form are organized into some form of hierarchical structure. Furthermore, we assume that such hierarchies have the property that, when branches relate a parent to various children, the parent generalizes the more specific child concepts.

Finally we remember that conceptualizations provide value only in so far as they facilitate the processing of new experiences in an effective manner. It is only within the context of some performance task that a concept hierarchy proves its value. In one form or another, COBWEB models all rely on *flexible prediction* as their performance task (Fisher, 1987). Generally, we may think of flexible prediction as a measure of the average predictive power derived from a conceptualization. For a given object, flexible prediction measures the average predictive accuracy on unseen attributes. When evaluating learned concept hierarchies, we take a test instance and withhold each attribute, comparing the model's prediction of the missing attribute to the withheld value.[2] The average accuracy on these individual predictions provides the measure of flexible prediction. These models implicitly seek to maximize this average predictive ability.

Details of the model

We are now ready to describe the common elements of this family of methods and point the reader to other sources that explain significant variations. The model's core consists of three elements: the internal representation of concepts, search operators for exploring the space of

---

[2] In the limit, we withhold every possible non-empty proper subset of attributes and ask the model to predict all missing ones.

conceptualizations, and the heuristic evaluation function for guiding the search. These three elements are employed in a uniform manner for both performance and learning. COBWEB uses the same process for forming conceptualizations as it does for categorization or flexible prediction. The difference between learning and performance is the object of interest – the new conceptualization as a whole in the first case, and the values of a specific concept in which a test instance is classified in the second.

Representing conceptualizations Concepts, organized within hierarchies, serve as the basis for categorization in COBWEB models. A given concept subsumes or summarizes a number of child concepts that are each more specific than it. For example, the concept 'bird' may have subconcepts 'robin', 'goldfinch', and 'turkey'. Although some COBWEB models maintain a strict tree hierarchy and others allow a directed graph structure,[3] each concept is a child of a more general concept and in turn has some number of more specific child concepts below it. The exceptions are the root of the concept hierarchy, which has no parent, and leaves, which are maximally specific concepts corresponding to single instances or collections of indistinguishable instances.

These models represent individual concepts probabilistically. Each node in a conceptualization summarizes the previously observed objects deemed to have been members of that particular category. The system summarizes these instances by estimating the probability distributions for each attribute under an assumption of conditional independence. The respective values observed for a given attribute form the estimate of the probability distribution for that attribute. If the attribute is numeric instead of symbolic, one approach is to model it as a mean and standard deviation under the assumption that its range of values satisfies a normal distribution. As will be seen, the model also needs to know the prior probability of a category; it stores a count of the number of objects classified at each category and estimates its base rate as this count divided by the total number of objects in its parent.[4]

All COBWEB models represent the attributes of concepts in a probabilistic fashion along these lines. However, two of the methods, LABYRINTH and OXBOW, additionally model the components that comprise structured stimuli and treat these components as some form of attributes along with the regular attributes. For example, OXBOW forms concepts

---

[3] For example, TWILIX allows a given concept to participate in multiple contexts, effectively giving it multiple parent concepts (Martin & Billman, 1994).

[4] Technically, this is the conditional probability that an instance belongs in a particular class given that it belongs in the parent class.

of movement skills and includes probabilities on components of the skill, treating a component as a kind of attribute. Alternatively, LABYRINTH might represent chairs as having a seat component and one or more legs that support the seat. These particular models point to the variety of representations that are possible within COBWEB's framework of probabilistic hierarchies.

Searching for conceptualizations   The manner in which these models form hierarchies of probabilistic concepts may be viewed as a search through the space of such hierarchies. Specifically, COBWEB conducts this search in an incremental hill-climbing manner, locally maximizing the quality of the hierarchy as described below. Steps between states involve either modifications to the particular concepts, modifications to their hierarchical organization, or a combination of both. Updates to concepts reflect changes to probability estimates, and revisions to the hierarchy itself reflect the addition, merging, or splitting of concepts. Drawing inspiration from the incremental character of human concept learning, COBWEB models consider local revisions to the current concept hierarchy based on single instances.

For a given training stimulus, i, and a node into which the stimulus has been categorized (initially the root), COBWEB evaluates several alternatives regarding the concepts c_k that are the immediate children of the given node. First, the system considers adding the new instance, i, to the child concept, c_k, into which it fits best according to the search heuristic described below. Second, if the new instance is sufficiently unlike all of the existing children, the system creates a new singleton concept with the instance and adds the new concept as a sibling of the existing child concepts.

Because order effects can sometimes cause COBWEB to mistakenly add new singleton concepts or classify new instances as existing concepts, the model employs two structural revision operators that simulate a form of backtracking. Thus, as a third alternative, the system considers merging the two best-fitting child concepts and adding the new instance to this merged concept. Finally, it considers splitting the best child concept, promoting its children to the current set of children, and adding the new instance to the best over the resulting set of child concepts. These two structural revision operators do not reprocess previously encountered examples but instead depend on probabilistic summaries stored at the current level of the hierarchy. Given the four alternative conceptualizations arising from these search operators, the system selects among them according to its evaluation function, as discussed shortly.

Recursively, the system repeats this comparison between competing classifications until it creates a leaf node with the new instance (second alternative above). Thus, a new instance triggers a sequence of updates to probabilistic representations of concepts, possibly interspersed with revisions of the local hierarchical structure, finally culminating in the addition of a new singleton concept.

Guiding the search for conceptualizations   The manipulations described above occur under the guidance of a heuristic evaluation function that measures the quality of the children of a given concept in the hierarchy. Gluck and Corter (1985) propose *category utility* as a numeric measure of how good or useful a particular partition is with respect to the parent concept. Fisher (1987) generalized Gluck and Corter's formula to multiple categories as:

$$\mathrm{CU}(C) = \frac{1}{K}\left[\sum_{k=1}^{K} P(C_k \mid C) \sum_i \sum_i P\big(A_i = V_{ij} \mid C_k\big)^2 - \sum_i \sum_j P\big(A_i = V_i \mid C\big)^2 \right] \qquad (1)$$

where K is the number of classes at the current level of the hierarchy, $P(C_k \mid C)$ is the base-rate probability that an instance belongs to the child class given it belongs to the parent class C, $P(A_i = V_{ij} \mid C_k)$ is the probability that attribute i will have value j given that we know the instance belongs to category C_k, which is summed first over the possible values of attribute i, and then over all attributes i. Similarly, $P(A_i = V_i \mid C)$ is the same summed quantity when we only know that the instance belongs to the parent class. This formula applies to nominally valued attributes; for continuous attributes, the corresponding generalization (Gennari, 1990) is defined as:

$$\mathrm{CU}(C) = \frac{1}{K}\left[\sum_{k=1}^{K} P(C_k \mid C) \sum_i \frac{1}{\sigma_{ik}} - \sum_i \frac{1}{\sigma_{ip}} \right] \qquad (2)$$

where σ_{ik} is the standard deviation of attribute i in child class C_k and σ_{ip} is the standard deviation of the attribute in the parent class C. Using this metric, COBWEB evaluates the quality of alternative revisions to this part of the hierarchy and selects the best alternative. Unless a new singleton class is created, the process is repeated with the selected node as the nominal root and its children as the partition over the objects that have previously been classified here.

Again, note that COBWEB models tightly couple performance and learning. The process of classifying an instance updates the probability distribution of the class where the instance ultimately comes to rest, as well as all the distributions of concepts along the path back to the root concept. Additionally, the process of classifying the instance may trigger local revisions to the hierarchy along that path. Thus, we might think of classification (performance) taking place by incorporating (learning) the instance to be predicted, and learning taking place by classifying a newly observed instance (at each step of the process, alternative classifications are considered and the best forms the basis for updates).

Motivation

Most generally, a simple recognition that most human learning takes place in non-teaching environments underlines the need to understand unsupervised category learning. By the time children master several hundred words, they have learned a vast quantity of information about the way their world works. The knowledge they accumulate spans objects they have experienced through one or more (often all) of the senses, motor skills they have refined for moving through and manipulating their environment, and basic reasoning skills for accomplishing their goals (or more often getting others to fulfil them). Infants and toddlers acquire most of this knowledge through what corresponds to the unsupervised learning process described above. Thus, we want to explore methods by which such accumulation and organization of knowledge can take place. By actually implementing such methods, we verify their practicability and utility. The model and assumptions we have described above grow out of prior inclinations or sensibilities that situate and motivate our model-building activities.

Philosophical sensibilities

The conceptualization process fundamentally entails the formation of a world model. Philosophically, we assume the value of such conceptualizations lies solely in their predictive advantage. For two alternative conceptualizations of prior experience, an intelligent agent should prefer the one that makes relevant predictions more accurately. Thus, the ontological commitments implicit in a conceptualization refer to the utility of the model rather than to the way the world 'actually is'.

Note that reference to utility carries with it a notion of value. Clearly, the ability to predict some features is more valuable than others. For example, seeing a four-legged animal, we have much higher utility from accurately predicting the animal's likelihood of attacking and harming us than in accurately predicting its body temperature. Most of the Cobweb models treat all attributes as having equal utility. However,

Martin and Billman (1994) have explored relaxing this assumption by maintaining weights that they associates with features as a representation of their respective values.

Psychological sensibilities

Human behaviour and cognition provide an unending source of phenomena to understand and explain, but conceptualization is particularly important. A long tradition of artificial intelligence work has sought insights from psychology to fuel the implementation of computational models and research in the COBWEB family is a clear instance of this tradition.

We assume that insights from human concept formation will tend to provide useful implementation constraints. Humans, as examples of intelligent agents, motivate and justify this assumption. Note that humans process experiences incrementally, have a limited capacity to remember and reprocess these experiences, and reason imperfectly about them. If we consistently and faithfully designed with respect to the patterns and constraints observed in humans, then our models should exhibit important aspects of intelligent behaviour. However, we also assume that intelligence is not a uniquely human characteristic. Thus, we view human cognition as providing soft constraints that may be ignored as needed.

Computational sensibilities

In addition to the sensibilities identified above, we also expect that if COBWEB captures characteristics of human intelligence, then it can also function as a practical tool. That is, we want it to process data and provide results in a reasonable amount of time. Our choice of modelling concepts with probabilities provides an example of tensions between sensibilities. Probability theory nicely models certain aspects of intelligence. Dretske (1999) has argued that probability and information theory provides a formal basis for understanding knowledge. However, we know that humans do not reason according to Bayes-optimal principles. Thus, our models employ a probabilistic representation without a commitment to such reasoning. Given our primary interest in forming reliable models that allow agents to operate effectively, probabilistic representations provide a natural, efficient and well-grounded foundation.

In the case of our choice to organize concepts in hierarchies, our psychological and computational sensibilities work in harmony. In computer science applications, the tree serves as a common and well-used data structure. Although other structures have superior characteristics along particular dimensions, the tree excels in its combination of

Table 11.1 *Generic algorithm for the family of* COBWEB *models*

```
// for parent concept p and new instance i
classify(p, i)
  if p is a leaf and has no children,
    create copy of p as new-p;
    create singleton node from i as new-i;
    update p's probabilities based on i;
    add new-p and new-i as children of p;
  else with each child c_k of p
    select best of these four according to CategoryUtility(p)
      1. add i to each child c_k of p;
        rank order their resulting partitions;
      2. add i as new singleton child of p;
      3. merge the best and second-best children from 1;
        add i to merged result;
      4. promote children of best child to be children of p;
        add instance to best of children;
    unless 2 is selected, continue with classify(c_k, I)
      where c_k is the child that gets i.
```

flexibility and efficiency. For example, a hash map provides faster access to stored items, but it would not store two related concepts near each other. On the other hand, a tree organizes concepts so that similar concepts are close and provides efficient access to them. Furthermore, this structure increases the expressivity of the simple conditional probability scheme described above by embedding implicit conditional assumptions based on a concept's chain of parents.

Implementing COBWEB

Having described the motivations and the general outlines for the model, we can provide the details necessary for a rational reconstruction. To implement a COBWEB model, one must define: (1) the data structures for representing probabilistic concept hierarchies, (2) a function for updating the estimate of the probability distribution in response to a new instance, (3) the category utility function for deciding among the alternatives that are generated by (4) the four search operators that revise the hierarchy. Table 11.1 presents the schematic algorithm for the family of models we have discussed.

Representing and updating probabilistic concepts

Hierarchies consist of concept nodes, which in turn consist of prior probabilities for the concept itself, symbolic names, attributes and their values, conditional probability distributions over these attributes and values, and a collection of concept nodes representing the more specific concept nodes that are children of the given concept. Because COBWEB works incrementally, processing one instance at a time, it updates its probability distributions without reprocessing previous instances. The model represents base-rate probabilities by storing the counts of instances classified at each concept; the ratio of the count at the child to the count of the parent represents the base-rate probability of the child concept.

The treatment of probability distributions over attributes depends on whether the attribute is nominally or continuously valued. To maintain the probability distribution of a nominal attribute, one need only tabulate a total count for the attribute and counts for each observed value for that attribute. The ratio of a particular value's count to the number of times that attribute was observed provides the conditional probability of the attribute having that value given that the instance is a member of the class. We can have the model process continuous attributes either by employing some discretization method and treating values as nominal or by estimating the density as a normal distribution. When choosing the latter, the model maintains two running sums – one for the values of the attribute and the other for the sum of the squared values. With these two sums it can incrementally compute the standard deviation by expanding the expression from the traditional definition.

Revising the concept hierarchy

Table 11.1 identifies four alternative updates that a COBWEB model must generate and evaluate. The first two – adding the new instance to the best child and creating a new singleton concept – present no significant implementation issues. The operation described above for updating probabilistic concepts takes care of the first and a simple addition of a new concept node to the collection of child concepts handles the second. However, experience suggests that the merge and split operators require considerable development and debugging time.

The merge operator inputs two existing concepts and creates a new concept. The system determines the instance count for the new concept by adding the counts of the two concepts to be merged; similarly, the system computes the attribute models in the merged concept by adding the counts from corresponding attributes when nominally valued and by adding sums and sum of squares when continuously valued. The new merged concept contains a collection of child concepts created by combining the children of the two concepts being merged.

When splitting a concept, the system removes the concept to be split from the collection in which it occurs, then adds to that collection each child of the split node. Because these children comprise the summary information found in the deleted node, no counts or models need to be updated. We assume that, when computing category utility, the correct size of the collection is used as the discount factor, $1/K$, in Equation 1.

Other details

For both splitting and merging, the implementer should take care that, when creating the alternative local revisions to the concept hierarchy, she either maintains an original copy or provides reversibility of all operators. Creating copies of the hierarchy for each candidate might at first seem to be a memory-intensive operation. However, with the exception of the split operator, the revisions only impact the immediate context – the parent and its children. Thus, we need not copy more specific layers of the existing hierarchy as long as we handle the split operator properly.

Another detail arises in situations where one decides to estimate the probability distribution of a numeric attribute using a mean and standard deviation. For such cases, one must allow for singleton concepts where the standard deviation on attribute values will be zero and consequently the category utility will be undefined. A response employed by several COBWEB models introduces an acuity parameter, which represents the minimum variance for an attribute. This parameter bears similarity to the psychological notion of a *just noticeable difference*, the quantity by which two attribute values must differ in order to be distinguishable.

On a related note, the implementer may choose to include a cutoff parameter that serves as an alternative termination to the recursive algorithm presented in Table 11.1. Either for efficiency reasons (space or time) or because of cognitive limitations in humans, the classification process may reach a point where further subdivision into more specific concepts provides no additional predictive benefit. One natural approach to implementing the cutoff depends on the gain in information between the parent and the partition of children; when the gain falls below some predetermined cutoff value the system stops making sub-classes.

An example of COBWEB's operation

A simple example may clarify the operation of COBWEB models. Suppose our system is learning about musical instruments for the first time. In this scenario, assume the system has encountered four instruments:

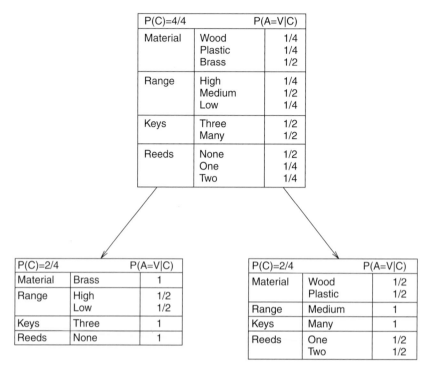

Figure 11.1 A possible concept hierarchy that captures probabilistic knowledge of musical instruments in two categories – brass and woodwind.

an oboe, a clarinet, a trumpet, and a tuba. Instruments are described by four attributes: the primary material of which they are constructed (wood, brass or plastic),[5] their musical range (low, medium or high), the number of keys for forming different pitches (three, four or many), and the number of reeds (none, one, two or many). The trumpet and the tuba are made of brass, have three keys, no reeds, and have a high and low musical range, respectively. The oboe and the clarinet both have many keys and a medium range, but the oboe is made of wood and has two reeds while the clarinet is made of plastic and has only one reed. Let us suppose that, based on these four musical instruments, the system has formed the concept hierarchy as shown in Figure 11.1, where the hierarchy consists of two classes corresponding to our traditional notions of brass and woodwind instruments.

[5] Here we use 'plastic' to stand for composite products that are occasionally used in the construction of less expensive woodwind instruments.

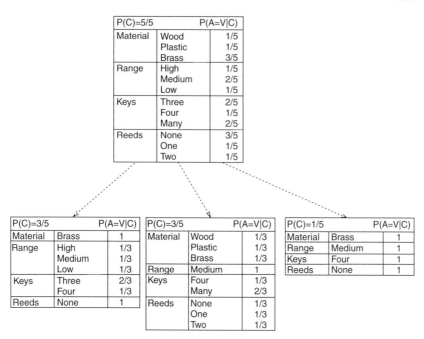

P(C)=5/5		P(A=V|C)
Material	Wood	1/5
	Plastic	1/5
	Brass	3/5
Range	High	1/5
	Medium	2/5
	Low	1/5
Keys	Three	2/5
	Four	1/5
	Many	2/5
Reeds	None	3/5
	One	1/5
	Two	1/5

P(C)=3/5		P(A=V|C)
Material	Brass	1
Range	High	1/3
	Medium	1/3
	Low	1/3
Keys	Three	2/3
	Four	1/3
Reeds	None	1

P(C)=3/5		P(A=V|C)
Material	Wood	1/3
	Plastic	1/3
	Brass	1/3
Range	Medium	1
Keys	Four	1/3
	Many	2/3
Reeds	None	1/3
	One	1/3
	Two	1/3

P(C)=1/5		P(A=V|C)
Material	Brass	1
Range	Medium	1
Keys	Four	1
Reeds	None	1

Figure 11.2 A rendering of multiple alternative updates to the concept hierarchy as a result of encountering a French horn. The root concept has been updated and one of the three alternatives (or merge or split) would be selected as the basis for a new partition consisting of the modified class and the original classes.

At this point, assume we show the system a particular French horn, which has the standard three valves plus a fourth rotary valve. COBWEB incorporates the new instrument (brass, medium, four, none) into the root of its conceptualization in a straightforward manner, updating the counts on attribute values. Next, the model decides between the various alternative operators described earlier. First, it considers adding it to the left-hand class corresponding to brass instruments. As a result, the prior probability on the class node becomes 3/5. COBWEB also updates the conditional probabilities for each attribute-value given the brass class. In the case of the material and reeds attributes, these probabilities do not change, as the French horn has the same values. However, it differs from the other brass instruments encountered in that the French horn's musical range attribute value is medium and it has four keys instead of three. We show the new probabilities for the category in the lower-left concept in Figure 11.2. Note this figure does not show an actual hierarchy but rather the alternative revisions to the respective classes that would result from incorporating the new instrument and the possible third class created from the single French horn. That is, the three child classes in Figure 11.2 represent the mutually exclusive updates for finding the best child and creating a new singleton (steps 1 and 2 in the algorithm given in Table 11.1). The system evaluates the partition that results from the respective updates together with the other original classes, having updated only their prior probabilities.

With the alternative updates in hand, COBWEB must determine which alternative to prefer according to the category utility metric. The computation[6] from Equation 1 reveals that the partition resulting from the addition of the French horn to the brass class has a score of 44/30; the new prior for the class, 3/5, times the sum of squared conditional probabilities 26/9, plus the score for the existing woodwind class (with updated prior) 2/5 times 3, all discounted by 1/2 for the number of classes in the partition. Similarly, the score for adding the new instance to the woodwind instruments is the score from the original brass class with the prior update (2/5 times 7/2) plus the updated woodwinds class shown in the middle-bottom of Figure 11.2 (3/5 times 20/9) for a total score of 41/30, after applying the discount of 1/2. Finally, the option for creating a third class consisting of just the French horn has an overall score of only 34/30. In the last case, note that although the singleton class has high conditional probabilities, the low base-rate for the new class 1/5 and the larger discount penalty for the extra class (1/3 instead of 1/2) lower this alternative's partition score substantially.

Because there are only two classes in the initial concept hierarchy, COBWEB would not consider merging them as described earlier. Given that the brass class is the best option, the system would finally consider promoting its two children, the singleton trumpet and tuba that it started with, and then check again to determine into which class it would be best to add the French horn. The overall score of this split option is 32/30, also a relatively low result. Consequently, the French horn would be placed with the other brass instruments (as we intuitively expected all along) and continue the process recursively.

This example portrays the concept formation process at an early stage of learning. As more examples are observed over time, the hierarchy becomes wider and deeper. Concepts near the top of the hierarchy summarize a large number and a wide variety of instruments observed

---

[6] We have omitted subtracting the parent's value of 42/25 because this same amount is subtracted from each option. The parent's value plays a significant role only when implementing a cutoff mechanism.

by the system; concepts near the leaves of the tree summarize a small number of very similar instruments. In the musical instruments domain, we could expect COBWEB to form two top-level concepts for brass and woodwinds, with the woodwinds concept having three children, for single-reed instruments like the clarinet and various types of saxophones, double-reed instruments such as the oboe, and non-reed woodwinds like the flute.

This simple example should convey the core method employed by this family of concept learning systems. However, several issues bear mentioning. First, some attribute information may be missing from instances. That is, the system may not initially perceive all of the features that describe observed objects. For example, many people would not take notice of the presence or absence of a spit-valve on brass instruments. But when the system starts noticing such a feature, COBWEB updates counts on the individual attributes and modifies the category utility function accordingly. Second, instead of simple attribute-value representations, objects may consist of components and these components may be structurally related. In general, this structural information cannot be compressed into an attribute-value format. In such cases, we must extend the representation and evaluation function employed by the model. Also, the control structure must be augmented in some way to confront the partial matching problem. Iba's (1991) OXBOW addressed both of these issues by forming classes of observed and practised motor skills. Likewise, Thompson and Langley's (1991) LABYRINTH system extended COBWEB to learn concepts that describe complex objects and relations among their parts. Finally, one may relax the constraint that a concept hierarchy must be a tree and instead allow a directed acyclic graph. In this context, parent concepts still summarize their children but a given child may be summarized by multiple parents. Martin and Billman (1994) employed this strategy in their TWILIX system, thereby allowing it to learn concepts that participate in multiple partitions. For example, the concept for 'bugle' might appear as a child of the 'brass' concept, and also as a child of a 'signal mechanism' class.

Relation to other models

Now that we have reviewed the COBWEB class of models, let us consider their similarities and differences from other approaches presented in this volume and elsewhere. We can view these relations along several dimensions: the representation and organization of categories, how categorizations are formed and used, and motivational commitments.

Representing and organizing categories

Most models for representing categories rely on either exemplars, proto-types, or some hybrid of them. We can view COBWEB as a hybrid, as it forms a hierarchy with concepts at higher levels that resemble proto-types and leaves of the hierarchy that serve as exemplars. The SUSTAIN model (Chapter 10) provides a similar hybrid. Like COBWEB, it starts with exemplars and lets them evolve into prototypes. Exemplars in SUSTAIN become more abstract in a context-sensitive manner guided by stimuli; this lets prototypes and exemplars co-exist and compete at the same level, potentially leading to interesting interactions. In prin-ciple, COBWEB could have both exemplars and prototypes in the same collection of concepts, but typically they are stratified by depth in the hierarchy. SUSTAIN represents categories in a connectionist framework but does not provide a hierarchy for them.

COBWEB'S probabilistic representation of concepts also bears similar-ities to Griffiths *et al.*'s (Chapter 8) mixture models for density estima-tion. In COBWEB, each concept provides an estimate of the probability distribution over the instances classified by it. Both systems support a unification of the prototype and exemplar models, COBWEB assigns instances to multiple categories along the classification path spanning multiple levels of the hierarchy, whereas the mixture models assign instances to multiple categories at the same level. The approaches also differ in their performance methods, with COBWEB using the category utility function grounded in information theory and the nonparametric models described by Griffiths *et al.* employing Bayesian methods.

COBWEB organizes its categories in a hierarchy of increasingly specific clusters. Most of the models presented in this volume do not address the organization of categories – hierarchical or otherwise. Pothos, Chater, and Hines (Chapter 9) describe the simplicity model, whose agglomera-tive method could be extended to hierarchies in a natural and straight-forward manner. Griffiths *et al.* describe a hierarchical model in which clusters may participate in multiple categories, although this hierarchy has little resemblance to the multi-level concept hierarchy produced by COBWEB. Anderson and Matessa (1991) present a hierarchical ver-sion of their model that bears similarities to the COBWEB framework. Feigenbaum's (1961) EPAM system also forms hierarchical structures, although concepts appear at the leaves and internal nodes influence classification of novel stimuli.

Historically, Fisher's (1987) COBWEB grew out of ideas found in earl-ier systems such as UNIMEM (Lebowitz, 1982), CYRUS (Kolodner, 1983), and EPAM. To our knowledge, COBWEB was the first model of categorization and category learning to employ probabilistic representations for incrementally learning concepts organized within a general-to-specific Is-A hierarchy. The synthesis represented by Cobweb and its direct descendants stimulated a number of exciting approaches that have fruitfully branched in other directions (e.g., Anderson & Matessa, 1991; Cheesman *et al.*, 1988; Griffiths *et al.*, Chapter 8).

Using and learning categories

Many models of categorization utilize measures of similarity between stimuli to guide their classification and, where applicable, their formation of conceptualizations. These similarity measures are often based on distance metrics. In contrast, Cobweb uses probability estimates stored in concepts at each level of its hierarchy to categorize a new example and updates the estimates for the concept to which it is assigned. The use of category utility in this estimation serves as a unifying feature of the Cobweb family of methods.

Like most of the models in this volume, Cobweb forms its conceptualization in an incremental fashion. Such methods must contend with order effects resulting from non-representative sequences of stimuli. In fact, order effects in humans are such a fundamental assumption that experimental regimes always attempt to control for them. Pure exemplar models (e.g., Nosofsky's GCM, Chapter 2) may be sensitive to a peculiar initial sample of stimuli, but in the long run order effects should not impact such methods. Likewise, prototype models (e.g., Minda & Smith, Chapter 3) would not notice order effects in the long run if applied in a supervised learning context. However, hybrid or prototype models that incrementally *form* categories (e.g., Ashby *et al.*'s COVIS, Chapter 4, and McDonnell and Gureckis's SUSTAIN, Chapter 10) will be susceptible to such effects. SUSTAIN provides mechanisms for adding clusters but apparently does not have an operator for backtracking from an ill-advised cluster. Presumably the impact of such choices can be eliminated over time by adjustment of weights.

An earlier relative of Cobweb, McKusick and Langley's (1991) Arachne, attempts to eliminate order effects by adopting an alternative search heuristic. Instead of using category utility to guide the search for a hierarchy of probabilistic concepts, it uses structural properties of the hierarchy to guide the addition of new categories or the revision of existing concepts via merging and splitting. In general, the resulting structural revisions are more extensive than Cobweb's. Empirical results demonstrated that Arachne was less sensitive to noise in the domain and more adept at utilizing background knowledge. Which method provides a more realistic model of order effects in human learning remains a topic for future research.

Guiding motivations

The models presented in this volume span a range of commitments in both their details and their motivations. Some present a rational model for categorization irrespective of its value as a model of human category learning or performance (e.g., Griffiths *et al.*, Chapter 8). Many others focus on explaining specific phenomena from constrained recognition and choice selection tasks (e.g., Ashby *et al.*'s COVIS, Chapter 4). Models in the COBWEB family fall between, addressing problems that we might expect an agent to encounter when trying to make sense of, navigate, and manipulate its environment, while also attempting to explain high-level psychological phenomena. For example, COBWEB provides an account of the basic level (see also Pothos *et al.*'s simplicity model, Chapter 9), typicality effects, and the power law of learning. Taken together, the similarities and differences between COBWEB and other models underline areas of active research and areas where further work will be helpful.

Directions for future research

COBWEB models of categorization and category learning account for a wide range of psychological phenomena, including basic and typicality effects, fan effects, and the power-law of learning (Fisher & Langley, 1990; Iba, 1991). We have successfully applied these models in several domains. Thus, several directions of research hold promise for fruitful investigations and insightful results. Broadly, these involve two lines of work – improving the model itself and applying the model.

It is widely established that as concepts become well established they become more resistant to change. This raises the issue of how COBWEB reorganizes its concept hierarchy over time. Should the hierarchy become less plastic with increasing experience? Certainly, in clusters of concepts near the root of the hierarchy, new examples will be unlikely to become a new singleton concept. At the leaves, the structure will be more fluid regardless of how much experience is captured in the hierarchy as a whole. Because new examples trigger merging and splitting, and because the influence of a single instance near the top of the hierarchy will be minimal later in training, such reorganizations should take place more frequently near the leaves. Future work should evaluate and characterize the reorganizations according to level and timing.

It is also well established that the order in which a learner observes stimuli significantly impacts what is learned. Another line of exploration would look at order effects. Clearly, humans are influenced by the order of training stimuli and we should try to characterize the nature of those effects (Clapper & Bower, 2002; Langley, 1995). We can use COBWEB to articulate hypotheses regarding the order effects that we would expect to find in humans. Given a specific task with, say, three categories of stimuli, we could present examples for two of the categories and vary the onset for introducing instances from the third category. This evaluation would aim to characterize the influence of novel but meaningful stimuli as a function of their position in the training sequence.

As an implemented system, some components exist not as commitments of the model but to make things work; if such components cannot be integrated with the model they should be pruned. An example of this appears in MÆANDER, which Iba (1991) developed to acquire and improve motor skills through observation and practice. The approach employed inner concept hierarchies within each motor skill concept; these private hierarchies captured the temporal structure of a given motor program. This approach should be generalized so that a single hierarchy organizes both complete motor skills as well as their temporal components.

In addition to investigating model features, COBWEB systems can be applied to various problems of practical value. For example, MÆANDER has been employed to analyse telemetry from the NASA space shuttle (Iba, 1993) and to the early detection of faults in industrial pumps. Also, many extensions to the basic COBWEB system were designed to support abilities required by intelligent agents operating in physical environments, including categorization and learning with continuous attributes (Gennari, Langley, & Fisher, 1989), structured objects (Thompson & Langley, 1991), motor skills (Iba, 1991), and plan knowledge (Langley & Allen, 1993). We believe the application of models to real-world problems has the benefit of refining their explicit and implicit assumptions. The successful applications of COBWEB models to such tasks and the richness of their accounts of psychological phenomena, demonstrate the potential of the theoretical framework.

REFERENCES

Anderson, J. R., & Matessa, M. (1991). An incremental Bayesian algorithm for categorization. In D. H. Fisher, M. J. Pazzani, & P. Langley (eds.), *Concept Formation: Knowledge and Experience in Unsupervised Learning*. San Mateo, CA: Morgan Kaufmann.

Cheeseman, P., Kelly, J., Self, M., Stutz, J., Taylor, W., & Freeman, D. (1988). AUTOCLASS: A Bayesian classification system. In *Proceedings of the Fifth International Conference on Machine Learning* (pp. 54–64). Ann Arbor, MI: Morgan Kaufmann.

Clapper, J. P., & Bower, G. H. (2002). Adaptive categorization in unsupervised learning. *Journal of Experimental Psychology: Learning, Memory, and Cognition*, **28** (5), 908–923.

Dretske, F. (1999). *Knowledge and the Flow of Information*. Palo Alto, CA: CSLI Press.

Feigenbaum, E. (1961). The simulation of verbal learning behavior. In *Proceedings of the Western Joint Computer Conference* (pp. 121–132). Reprinted in J. W. Shavlik & T. G. Dietterich (eds.) (1990). *Readings in Machine Learning*. San Mateo, CA: Morgan Kaufmann.

Fisher, D. H. (1987). Knowledge acquisition via incremental conceptual clustering. *Machine Learning*, **2**, 139–172.

Fisher, D. H., & Langley, P. (1990). The structure and formation of natural categories. In G. H. Bower (ed.), *The Psychology of Learning and Motivation: Advances in Research and Theory* (Vol. 26). Cambridge, MA: Academic Press.

Fisher, D. H., & Pazzani, M. J. (1991). Computational models of concept learning. In D. H. Fisher, M. J. Pazzani, & P. Langley (eds.), *Concept Formation: Knowledge and Experience in Unsupervised Learning*. San Mateo, CA: Morgan Kaufmann.

Gennari, J. H. (1990). *An experimental study of concept formation*. Doctoral dissertation, Department of Information & Computer Science, University of California, Irvine, CA.

Gennari, J. H., Langley, P., & Fisher, D. H. (1989). Models of incremental concept formation. *Artificial Intelligence*, **40**, 11–61.

Gluck, M., & Corter, J. (1985). Information, uncertainty and the utility of categories. In *Proceedings of the Seventh Annual Conference of the Cognitive Science Society* (pp. 283–287). Irvine, CA: Lawrence Erlbaum.

Gruber, T. R. (1995). Toward principles for the design of ontologies used for knowledge sharing. *International Journal of Human-Computer Studies*, **43**, 907–928. Available on-line.

Iba, W. (1991). *Acquisition and improvement of human motor skills: learning through observation and practice*. Doctoral dissertation, Department of Information & Computer Science, University of California, Irvine, CA.

(1993). Concept formation in temporally structured domains. In *NASA Workshop on the Automation of Time Series, Signatures, and Trend Analysis*. Moffett Field: NASA Ames Research Center.

Iba, W., & Langley, P. (2001). Unsupervised learning of probabilistic concept hierarchies. In G. Paliouras, V. Karkaletsis, & C. D. Spyropoulos (eds.), *Machine Learning and its Applications*. Berlin: Springer.

Kolodner, J. L. (1983). Reconstructive memory: a computer model. *Cognitive Science*, 7, 281–328.

Langley, P. (1995). Order effects in incremental learning. In P. Reimann & H. Spada (eds.), *Learning in Humans and Machines: Towards an Interdisciplinary Learning Science*. Oxford: Elsevier.

Langley, P., & Allen, J. A. (1993). A unified framework for planning and learning. In S. Minton (ed.), *Machine Learning Methods for Planning and Scheduling*. San Mateo, CA: Morgan Kaufmann.

Lebowitz, M. (1982). Correcting erroneous generalizations. *Cognition and Brain Theory*, **5**, 367–381.

Martin, J. D., & Billman, D. O. (1994). Acquiring and combining overlapping concepts. *Machine Learning*, **16**, 121–155.

McKusick, K. B., & Langley, P. (1991). Constraints on tree structure in concept formation. In *Proceedings of the Twelfth International Joint Conference on Artificial Intelligence* (pp. 810–816). Sydney: Morgan Kaufmann.

Thompson, K., & Langley, P. (1991). Concept formation in structured domains. In D. H. Fisher, M. J. Pazzani, & P. Langley (eds.), *Concept Formation: Knowledge and Experience in Unsupervised Learning*. San Mateo, CA: Morgan Kaufmann.

12 The knowledge and resonance (KRES) model of category learning

Harlan D. Harris and Bob Rehder

As this volume reflects, the dozens of models proposed to account for supervised category learning and classification over the last several decades differ from one another in multiple ways. One dimension of variation concerns activation dynamics. Under many sorts of theories, a stimulus is perceived, is compared to category representations, and is then (perhaps probabilistically) assigned to a category (Gluck & Bower, 1988; Kruschke, 1992; Love, Medin, & Gureckis, 2004; Medin & Schaffer, 1978). Much of the research in this framework explores the nature of the similarity processes that are used to compare stimuli to category representations.

Other lines of research have hinted that this sort of unidirectional flow of information from stimulus to category label may be inadequate to explain a number of phenomena. For example, Wisniewski and Medin (1994) found evidence for reinterpretation of ambiguous visual features based on prior conceptual knowledge. Thus, an alternative class of models views categorization as a constraint-satisfaction process, where representations of the stimulus and category representations interact to form an internally consistent representation (Goldstone & Medin, 1994; Rehder & Murphy, 2003). An assumption of interactivity is consistent with the many psychological systems that incorporate complex perceptual constraints at the earliest stages of processing (e.g., Balcetis & Dale, 2007; Friston, 2003; Spratling & Johnson, 2006; Tanenhaus *et al.*, 1995).

A second dimension of variation concerns the nature of category representations. One common assumption is that categories can be represented as a prototype, a single representation that encodes the central tendency of the category (Gluck & Bower, 1988; Hampton, 1979, 1995; Smith & Minda, 1998). Conversely, a wealth of research shows that

This work was supported by NIH grants F32MH076452 to Harlan D. Harris, and MH041704 to Gregory L. Murphy. Thanks to Gregory Murphy, Todd Gureckis, Aaron Hoffman, Dylan Simon and many others for very helpful suggestions on this line of research.

people can learn categories defined by configural information, that is, information about combinations of features that is not represented in a prototype (Kruschke, 1992; Medin & Schaffer, 1978; Nosofsky, 1986).

A third dimension of variation concerns whether a model assumes that category learning is purely a 'bottom up' process (is based solely on the category exemplars that one directly observes) or whether the learning of new categories can be influenced by existing semantic knowledge (Choi, McDaniel, & Busemeyer, 1993). A substantial line of research has explored the ways that prior concepts and prior beliefs affect new conceptual learning (see Heit & Bott, 2000; Murphy, 2002, for reviews).

In this chapter we present an analysis of the knowledge resonance (KRES) model originally proposed by Rehder and Murphy (2003). KRES is an interactive model with prototype representations and the ability to represent prior knowledge that has been shown to account for many of the effects of prior semantic knowledge on category learning. However, as we will show, there is considerable uncertainty regarding which properties of KRES are responsible for its behaviour. Thus, our approach is to 'deconstruct' KRES by testing a series of alternative models that contain only subsets of its key mechanisms. In this endeavour, we use as a reference point the well-known ALCOVE model (Kruschke, 1992) which is diametrically opposed to KRES on the three dimensions we have identified: it is feedforward rather than interactive, represents exemplars rather than prototypes, and does not represent prior knowledge. Thus, to analyse KRES, we 'fill out' the three-dimensional matrix of possible models by making versions of KRES that are more like ALCOVE and versions of ALCOVE (which we dub KOVE for Knowledge+ALCOVE) that are more like KRES. Analysis of these models will identify which aspects of KRES are responsible for which aspects of its behaviour.

Design dimensions and comparison to other models

Dimension 1: activation dynamics

The processing assumptions of ALCOVE (and our KOVE descendants) are well known so we summarize them briefly here (see Chapter 6 for a review of ALCOVE). ALCOVE is a feedforward model in which input representations activate similar exemplar representations which then activate category nodes (based on learnable exemplar-category weights), which then are transformed into response probabilities. ALCOVE has per-dimension attention weights and a learning rule that uses backpropagation to update both exemplar-category weights and the attention weights.

KRES is a very different sort of model. (See the Appendix for a mathematical description.) All nodes in a KRES model have continuous activation values, computed by a non-linear (sigmoidal) activation function of their inputs. Nodes are connected by bidirectional weights such that the network acts like a dynamic attractor network (Hopfield, 1982, 1984). That is, input to the network consists of activation being supplied to a set of input nodes whose activation then causes additional activation to flow throughout the network. Over time, the network will settle into a state as consistent as possible with the weighted connections (Smolensky, 1986). The activations of nodes connected by large positive weights will tend to be similar whereas those connected by near-zero weights will tend to be uncorrelated. The relative activation of the category nodes determines the model's response probabilities.

Figure 12.1 below illustrates a simple KRES model with five input dimensions, each with two features, learnable connections to two output nodes, and fixed inhibitory and (when knowledge is applicable) excitatory links among nodes. Several points are worth noting. First, all nodes have identical activation and response properties and differ only on their connections and their biases. Second, the connections specify constraints in the network. A stimulus dimension consisting of multiple mutually exclusive nodes (e.g., *large* versus *small*) can be instantiated with fixed inhibitory weights. Prior semantic knowledge relating two nodes can be rendered as a fixed excitatory weight. Third, top-down feedback will change the representation of the stimulus from what was provided externally. Consider a network with positive weights between each of two input feature nodes (F1 and F2) and a category node. If F1 receives activation representing perception of that feature, activation first flows up to increase activation of the category node but then flows back down. As a result, the initially quiescent F2 begins to activate. That is, the stimulus's representation is 'filled in' by the constraint satisfaction processes. The activation of the category node is then further increased, and so on. The non-linear activation function prevents runaway activation in the network, ensuring that it converges to a steady state.

Learning in the KRES network proceeds via contrastive Hebbian learning (CHL, O'Reilly, 1996) which makes use of the same activation dynamics. Briefly, in CHL the network first settles in response to the input, the desired output is added as external input and the network resettles, and then the connection weights are changed so that the network will respond with the desired output in the future.

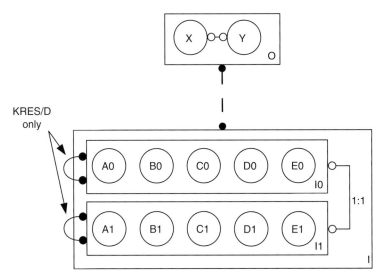

Figure 12.1 An example of a KRES network. There are five
dimensions (A–E), each with two features (0, 1), and two output
categories (X, Y). Connections depicted with solid lines are fixed
weights; dashed lines denote CHL-learnable weights; solid circles
denote fixed excitatory; open circles denote fixed inhibitory.
Connections to a bank of nodes (a box) are between all pairs of units
within the bank, unless the connections are labelled 1:1, in which
case they are one-to-one, as with the inhibitory connections between
each pair of features in an input dimension. When knowledge is
applicable, a version of KRES referred to as KRES/D includes lateral
excitatory connections at the input layer that distort the input. The
network in this figure will be used to simulate the 5-D conditions of
the Hoffman *et al.* (2008) task discussed later in the chapter.

Dimension 2: forms of prior knowledge

KRES can incorporate two types of prior knowledge, prior concept
nodes and lateral connections (Rehder & Murphy, 2003). These two
types of prior knowledge are implementations of what Heit (1994)
called *integration* and *distortion* theories. In integration models, new concepts are built up out of existing concepts combined with new feature-
category associations. An iPhone is like a cell phone but with additional
features. In distortion models, knowledge changes the representations
of stimuli such that the learned concept is different than it would be
without knowledge. This type of knowledge, implemented in KRES by
excitatory or inhibitory connections among features, might be used to
represent semantic associations such as causal relations (sunlight causes

sunburn), part-whole relationships (tables have legs), and so forth (Rehder & Murphy, 2003). (Heit also suggests a third type of knowledge process, *weighting* models, which we will not discuss.)

In KRES's implementation of the first form of knowledge, prior concept nodes are activated to the extent that the input is similar to the prior concept (Heit & Bott, 2000). Connections between these nodes and the nodes representing the category units are initially zero, but can be learned. This form of knowledge says that when the category to be learned is similar to an existing category, the existing knowledge can augment, or substitute for, learning associations between stimulus associations and the new categories. KOVE extends ALCOVE by representing prior concept nodes in a similar way (see below).

The second form of knowledge, distortion, involves existing semantic knowledge of relations (e.g., causal relations) rather than concepts. In KRES, these relations are represented as excitatory connections, such that if one feature is present, related features receive additional activation. In KOVE, there is a distortion matrix that changes the input vector by allowing some input features to affect others. Unlike with KRES, this process involves only the input representation and so is insulated from higher layers of the model. In both models, these associations are hand coded by the modeller.

Dimension 3: representing exemplars

The next design decision has to do with the implementation of exemplars. KOVE inherits its assumptions about exemplar representation from ALCOVE (Kruschke, 1992), but the original version of KRES shared with prototype models the ability to represent only linearly separable concepts. People, however, are able to learn at least some non-linearly separable concepts (Medin & Schwanenflugel, 1981), so some sort of more complex representation is necessary. Therefore, we have added optional exemplar nodes to KRES (Harris & Rehder, 2006). Just as with prior concept nodes (see Figure 12.4 below) exemplar nodes have fixed connections to inputs and learnable connections to category nodes.

There are several issues involved in implementing exemplars in a model of categorization. One is whether exemplars are added to the network when they are first presented to the network or whether they are present from the beginning of training. ALCOVE was originally designed to include many exemplar nodes from the very beginning of training, a 'covering map' of the possible stimulus space (Kruschke, 1992). Most ALCOVE models initialize the exemplar layer with the set of exemplars that will eventually be presented to the model. This is unrealistic, but typically has only minimal consequences. With KRES, the interactive properties of the network may yield a stronger effect on learning, as exemplars can constrain input node activations in substantial ways. Therefore, we implemented KRES and KOVE such that exemplar nodes are added only when first observed.

The second issue is what the stored exemplar actually represents. In ALCOVE, the exemplar represents precisely what was seen in the input layer, the *veridical* representation. Later presentations of an item perfectly match this exemplar. With KRES and KOVE, however, the ultimate activations of input nodes may differ from a stored veridical exemplar due to effects of knowledge and/or feedback. Distortion due to knowledge in a KOVE model is deterministic, so distorted exemplars could be used. With KRES, however, distortion and feedback results in very different input node activations over the course of learning. Because extension of KRES to use non-veridical exemplars would be a complicated undertaking, we elected to use the simplest option, veridical exemplars, in both the KRES and KOVE models. In the future, we think that examination of what is stored during each learning trial is an important goal, and exemplar representations distorted by the constraints imposed by prior knowledge may be components of comprehensive models. We appreciate the SUSTAIN model's insight into clustering of similar exemplars (Love *et al.*, 2004), and are intrigued by models that incorporate realistic memory processes such as forgetting (e.g., Sikström, 2002). However, for our purposes, where the role of prior knowledge is the focus of the models, this limitation does not seriously impair the models' applicability.

Additional issues: direct feature/category connections and attention

As mentioned, KRES was originally designed as a prototype model, with direct connections between stimulus features and category labels. The addition of exemplar nodes to KRES does not preclude the model from having these direct connections, if the modeller desires, and indeed in earlier work we considered the parallel use of both direct connection (prototype) learning and exemplar learning (Harris & Rehder, 2006). Thus, we similarly grant KOVE the ability to learn direct feature/category connections. As when direct connections are present, exemplar/category connections need not be, both KRES and KOVE can include any combination of direct connections, exemplar nodes, and prior concept nodes in a given model. This allows KOVE to emulate the performance of the Baywatch model, which includes direct connections and prior concept nodes but no exemplar nodes (Heit & Bott, 2000).

Finally, we note that KRES does not have a dimensional-attention learning component (as CHL has not been extended to incorporate this feature), and so cannot account for data showing people's learned inattention to non-predictive or redundant stimuli. Accordingly, KOVE's attentional learning mechanisms were turned off in the ensuing simulations.

Implementations and algorithms

We have developed KRES and KOVE models in Matlab that can be downloaded from http://code.google.com/p/kres. The models are implemented as libraries (APIs) with functions that can be called from Matlab scripts written by a researcher. Although graphical user interfaces (GUIs) can make running simple models easy, they can also make running complex models difficult or impossible. We have forgone the implementation of a GUI and instead focused on a maximally flexible API. To simulate training of a model, a researcher creates configuration and stimuli files, then writes a Matlab script with loops representing trials, blocks, and replications. The models provide some information about their performance directly, and we have developed flexible logging libraries that can save weights, activations, and other information into text files for further analysis. The scripts used to perform the simulations reported below are included in the downloadable package, along with supporting Perl scripts for analysis of log files and R scripts for generation of visualizations.

KRES

To create a KRES model, the researcher describes the graph structure of the model (as shown in Figures 12.1 and 12.4 below) using a Matlab data structure. That data structure lists each of the nodes (input, category, prior knowledge, exemplar), along with the various sorts of connections (fixed, learnable, exemplar) among nodes or sets of nodes. For the purposes of distinguishing among models, we append the letter E to KRES models with exemplar nodes, and I or D to KRES models that implement integration (with prior concept nodes) or distortion (with lateral knowledge connections) functionality. Inclusion of prior knowledge is as simple (and as flexible) as specifying the appropriate nodes and connections in the network specification. The Appendix describes the constraint satisfaction and CHL algorithms that underlie KRES (Rehder & Murphy, 2003). There are two changes from the previously published algorithms. One is the addition of an α parameter, which changes the slope of the activation function of the model nodes: $act_i = 1/(1 + \exp(-\text{input} \star \alpha)$. In earlier simulations α was fixed at 1.0. Larger values of α force the activations of nodes to be pushed towards 0 or 1. Psychologically, this parameter may relate to the c and γ parameters of the extended GCM, which determine exemplar sensitivity and response determinism. The other change is the addition of exemplar nodes, as described above. There is one new KRES parameter for exemplar nodes – the weighting of the afferent connections from the input nodes. With models with other types of connectivity (prior concept nodes, direct connections), adjusting this parameter can increase or decrease the relative importance of the exemplar nodes.

KOVE

KOVE is primarily a set of extensions to ALCOVE, so we only briefly mention two new parameters here. In KOVE/I, ALCOVE with prior concept nodes, the B parameter scales activation relative to standard exemplar nodes. If $B = 10$, then the prior concept node or nodes will affect category responses 10 times as much as an equivalent exemplar node, biasing the final learned weights to rely more on the prior concept and less on empirical learning. For KOVE/D, ALCOVE with distortion of input representations, we typically use a w_D parameter ranging from 0 to 1 to define the off-diagonal values in the distortion matrix and indicate how much representations are pulled towards the knowledge prototype. For more information, interested readers are referred to the sample simulations available on the web site.

Sample result 1: resonance and categorizing partial items

To illustrate the role of top-down feedback in categorization processes, and how that feedback in turn interacts with prior knowledge, we report simulations of Hoffman, Harris, and Murphy's (2008) studies of categorization of whole items and single features with and without prior knowledge. (This section partially recapitulates results from that paper.)

Hoffman *et al.* (2008) trained subjects on category structures with either 5 or 10 dimensions, where the features of those dimensions either all were or all were not associated with prior knowledge. Part of their results, the effect of dimensionality on learning, is not of particular interest here (see also Hoffman & Murphy, 2006). We focus on the results from a test phase, in which subjects were presented with both trained whole items (WI), with all dimensions present, as well as novel single feature (SF) items, with only a feature from one dimension present. When prior knowledge was absent, Hoffman *et al.* found that the accuracy on the SF tests was quite high, often nearly as high as the accuracy on the WI tests. For example, with 5 dimensions, subjects were 83% accurate on SF tests and 91% accurate on WI tests. And when features were linked by prior knowledge (the stimuli were descriptions of vehicles, with jungle-like or arctic-like properties in the knowledge condition), subjects responded as if they had learned nearly all of the features.

Hoffman *et al.* (2008) compared the KRES model to other category learning models and found a substantially better fit with KRES. Here, we extend that analysis with a detailed exploration of the top-down feedback processes of KRES, showing how missing information is filled in, and a brief exploration of distortion processes in the KOVE model, illustrating the effects of knowledge.

KRES, learning and feedback

What happens in a KRES model as it learns new categories? How does feedback affect the responses and the learning process? To address these questions, in this section we present data illustrating the connection weights and unit activations of KRES as it learns. We note, but do not focus on, the ability of KRES to represent and learn with prior knowledge.

Figure 12.1 shows the architecture of the KRES/D model we tested. Hoffman *et al.* (2008) used a coarse iterative grid search approach to find a set of parameters[1] that fit the empirical data relatively well. Training of the model paralleled that of the human experimental participants. The model was presented with each item once in each block of trials, in random order, and there were four blocks of training. With $\lambda = 0.25$, $\alpha = 0.75$, inhibitory fixed weights of -2.5, and excitatory fixed weights of 0.5 (used only with knowledge), and with biases of -1 on the output nodes only, KRES/D learned about as well as human subjects in the various conditions (Table 12.1). Without knowledge, the model has high accuracy on the trained items, and fairly high accuracy on the SF tests. The model also showed the observed interaction with prior knowledge, with near-perfect accuracy on both WI and SF tests.

Figure 12.2 shows the improvement in accuracy, the changes in weights, and the changes in input node activations over the course of training, for a KRES model learning the 5-D structure without knowledge. This

---

[1] Hoffman *et al.* (2008) set initial feature-category weights randomly from a U(–1, +1) distribution. Here, to minimize potential issues with uneven weights (see Harris, in preparation), we set initial weights randomly from a U(–0.2, +0.2) distribution. The model's accuracy results do not substantially differ from the previously published numbers.

Table 12.1 *KRES/D and KOVE/D fits to Hoffman et al.'s (2008)*
accuracy data

	Measure	Unrelated		Knowledge	
		5-D	10-D	5-D	10-D
HHM08	WI	0.91	0.94	0.95	0.95
	SF	0.83	0.72	0.91	0.96
	E(SF)	0.65	0.59	0.69	0.62
KRES/D	WI	0.93	0.95	0.96	0.98
	SF	0.86	0.82	0.95	0.97
KOVE/D	WI	0.91		0.93	
	SF	0.69		0.78	

Model parameters are given in the text. E(SF) indicates expected SF accuracy given observed WI accuracy, for a model that combines equally weighted cues optimally. KOVE/D was only fit to the 5-D condition.

visualization illustrates several important aspects of the dynamics of KRES. The weights between each of the banks of input nodes and the two output nodes change gradually, with positive associations changing more dramatically than negative associations. This is because the resting activations of the nodes are not at 0.5, because of the inhibitory connections between pairs of input nodes (e.g., A1 and A0, see Figure 12.1). The next observation is that the activations of the input nodes (after the network 'settles' on each trial) change over the course of training due to changes in the weights with the category labels. For example, given the input 10000, the A1 node's activation is pushed by top-down feedback from the category node from its initial value of 0.68 to 0.55. KRES is a constraint-satisfaction categorization model, and when inputs to the model do not agree with everything else the model knows (in this case, that B0 through E0 all predict category X, not Y as predicted by the initially high activation of A1), the constraints change the inputs to make more 'sense'.

Next, we considered how this KRES model performed on the three types of test items: prototypes, WIs, and SFs. Figure 12.3 shows the activation of the 10 input nodes on the prototype, WI, and SF test items. (Corresponding response accuracies were 0.95, 0.91, and 0.86, respectively.) When the network was provided with the prototype input (11111), the initial activation of 1 input nodes was 0.68, but final activation was substantially increased by top-down feedback. When one of the dimensions had a cross-over feature (e.g., 11110), the activation of that feature, in this case E0, decreased from 0.68 to 0.57, reflecting

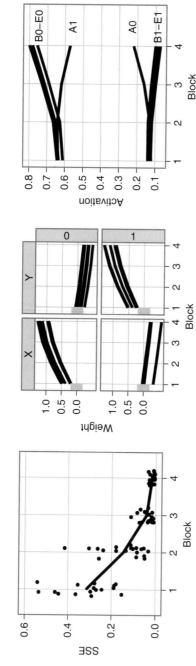

Figure 12.2 Performance of a KRES model on Hoffman *et al.*'s (2008) task, 5 dimensions, no knowledge. Left: sum squared error over the course of learning, relative to the training targets. Points (jittered horizontally) are individual items; the line is the mean. Centre: weights from input units A0–E0 (0) and A1–E1 (1) to output units (X and Y), over the course of training. Weights were initialized to random near-zero values, range shown as grey bars. Right: final activation (following settling) of input nodes, given input 10000 (A1, B0–E0), over the course of training.

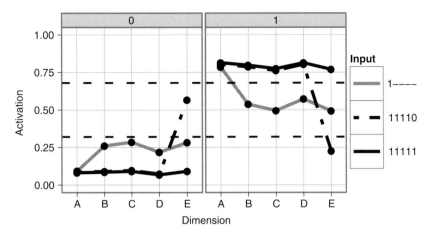

Figure 12.3 Testing performance of a KRES model on Hoffman
et al.'s (2008) task, 5 dimensions, no knowledge. Post-settling
activation of the input nodes is shown for examples of the three
different item types. The panels show the 1 nodes (A1, B1, etc.)
and 0 nodes (A0, B0, etc.). The dashed horizontal lines show the
activation of nodes given an input (feature present, upper horizontal
line; feature absent, lower horizontal line), but with input-output
weights equal to 0 (i.e., with no top-down feedback).

constraint-satisfaction processes. Most importantly, when the model
sees an SF item (e.g., 1—), activation of the unobserved nodes is entirely
driven by feedback and constraint satisfaction. Feedback pushes the
nodes consistent with the A1 node (B1–E1) to have higher activation,
and the nodes consistent with the A0 node (B0–E0) to have lower activation. This in turn affects output node activation, which explains why
the response probability for SF items is as high as 0.86, despite having
only 1/5th of the featural information available in WI items.

This analysis illustrates that KRES learns a family resemblance concept by gradual changes in weights, and that when tested on only a
single dimension at a time, its constraint-satisfaction processes result
in response probabilities similar to those observed. KRES/D can also
simulate the changes observed when the features are associated with
prior knowledge. Lateral excitatory connections directly feed activation from input nodes activated by the SF input to the nodes without
input, increasing the model's predicted response accuracy for those
items (Table 12.1). Instead of analysing knowledge effects in KRES,
we instead press on and briefly discuss the analogous processes in a
KOVE simulation.

KOVE, knowledge and distortion

We constructed a KOVE/PD model analogous to the KRES model described above. Like KRES/D, this model learned a prototype representation of the categories, and used a distortion matrix at the input layer to implement the effects of knowledge. We hand selected parameters that gave reasonable overall accuracy (see Table 12.1): $\lambda = 0.05$, $c = 1.0$, $\varphi = 1.25$. The distortion matrix had 1s on the diagonal and 0.3 on the off-diagonal values when knowledge was applicable. The result of this distortion on the input representation is that the cross-over feature in a stimulus such as 01111 is no longer a cross-over, it merely has a lower activation than the other features of the input (at least for these parameter values). This distortion, in turn, reduces the magnitude of the error made by the model for a particular weight level, reducing the size of weight changes. Although KOVE/PD made fewer errors during learning with knowledge, the asymptotic weights were somewhat smaller (0.26 versus 0.41). In other words, distortion knowledge allowed the model to learn less while attaining a similar level of accuracy.

Table 12.1 shows the test accuracy of the trained KOVE/PD model. Knowledge sped learning, and especially did so for the SF stimuli. Distortion more strongly affected missing features, with activation near the centre of the sigmoidal activation, than features whose activation is near the maximum or minimum. On the other hand, KOVE/PD cannot account for the relatively high observed SF accuracy, while KRES/D with its top-down feedback processes can.

Discussion

These analyses show not only that KRES/D provides a reasonable account of the Hoffman *et al.* (2008) dataset but also provide insight into why it does so. We think it is notable that the resonance processes of KRES were not necessary to account for the effects of knowledge in this experiment. Instead, what is necessary is to distort the inputs in the direction of prior knowledge, and the alternative distortion process of KOVE/PD shows that constraint satisfaction is not the only way to achieve this. Of course, other sorts of knowledge effects may not be amenable to the distortion process of KOVE/D (the top-down feature interpretation results of Wisniewski & Medin, 1994, come to mind), but the results point the way to alternative implementations of knowledge effects within the class of feedforward network architectures.

Nevertheless, we found that the resonance processes of KRES did account for an important aspect of the results, namely, the unexpectedly high performance on the single feature test items. We think this result opens the door to an important new area of investigation, namely, how the evidence provided by objects with unobserved features (which includes most objects we observe in the real world) is integrated into a category decision. As is the case with knowledge-based distortion processes, it may be that there are processes other than resonance that can account for the high single feature performance, but until those processes are elucidated, the resonance processes implemented by the KRES class of models remain an important point in their favour.

Sample result 2: exemplars and different types of prior knowledge

Next, to demonstrate the ability of these models to account for effects requiring both exemplar representations and prior knowledge, we report an exploration of the Wattenmaker *et al.* (1986) study of learning categories with and without relevant prior knowledge. In their Experiments 1 and 2, Wattenmaker *et al.* trained participants to learn one of two category structures, instantiated by one of two sets of features. One structure (see Table 12.2) consisted of two categories, each with four binary features, that could be distinguished by use of a summing strategy. This linearly separable (LS) structure could be learned by identifying the features prototypically associated with the two categories, and responding A if three or more features were of the A category, or B if two or more features were of the B category. The other structure consisted of two categories that could not be distinguished with such a strategy. This non-linearly separable (NLS) structure could only be learned by some sort of memorization of at least a subset of the items.

In the *knowledge* condition, subjects could associate all of the '1' features together and all of the '0' features together based on their prior knowledge (e.g., of properties of tools). In the *unrelated* condition, features were uncorrelated with any existing concept. As their two experiments used identical category structures and the same procedure and manipulation, we averaged the results, weighted by the number of subjects in each experiment, to get more stable data to be compared with the models.

Wattenmaker *et al.* (1986) found that, in the unrelated conditions, subjects made about the same number of errors during learning, whether the category was LS or NLS. With knowledge, however, learners made substantially fewer errors (than without knowledge) when learning the LS category structure, but only slightly fewer errors when learning the NLS structures. This is not too surprising, as knowledge could help learners

Table 12.2 *Wattenmaker* et al.'s *(1986) category structure*

Linearly separable		Non-linearly separable	
Stimulus	Item	Stimulus	Item
1110	A1	1000	A1
1011	A2	1010	A2
1101	A3	1111	A3
0111	A4	0111	A4
1100	B1	0001	B1
0001	B2	0100	B2
0110	B3	1011	B3
1010	B4	0000	B4

identify the prototypes that underlie the LS structure, but the prototypes could be misleading when learning the NLS structure. To help ground the issues and focus theories, we constructed models using various sorts of prior knowledge and simulated them on this task.

KRES, parameter space analysis

To illustrate the ability of KRES to account for the Wattenmaker *et al.* (1986) data, and to show how the models can be used to infer how prior knowledge may be represented, we constructed KRES/EI and KRES/ED models and explored their performance on the task. Figure 12.4 illustrates the architecture of these models, including the KRES/E model that simulates learning with no prior knowledge.

The KRES models have five free parameters. To explore the qualitative performance of the model, we surveyed this parameter space by picking 1000 quasi-random parameter vectors and running the models with each set of parameters. The learning rate was chosen from the interval (0.01, 3.01), the exemplar strength was chosen from the interval (0.1, 2.1), α was chosen from the interval (0.25, 4.25), the inhibitory weight strength was chosen from the interval (−5.1, −0.1), and the excitatory weight strength (for the prior knowledge connections in KRES/EI and KRES/ED) was chosen from the interval (0.1, 3.1). Additionally, the prior knowledge and output nodes were given a fixed bias of −1, and the exemplar nodes were given a negative bias that fixed their activation at 1/8 when there was no input to the model.

For each model and parameter vector, the network was trained on the two category structures (LS and NLS) and the number of training errors was tabulated. As the models are somewhat stochastic (due

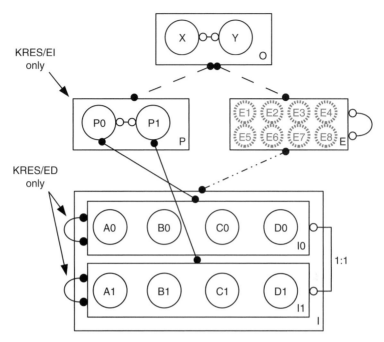

Figure 12.4 KRES networks used to simulate Wattenmaker *et al.*'s (1986) task. Connections depicted with solid lines are fixed weights; dash-dotted lines denote set-once exemplar weights; dashed lines denote CHL-learnable weights. KRES/EI includes the prior knowledge nodes and associated connections; KRES/ED includes the lateral excitatory connections at the input layer; KRES/E, without knowledge, includes neither component.

to random initial weights and random item orders in each block), no formal parameter fitting was done. Instead, following recent trends in the analysis of complex models (Pitt *et al.*, 2006) we examined the *qualitative* performance of KRES over a wide range of parameters. The training error counts on each model run (LS and NLS structures, with and without knowledge) was converted into an ordinal code representing the rank order of those counts. For example, the (averaged) empirical data were 53.9, 29.4, 49.6, and 40.6 errors, for the LS/U, LS/K, NLS/U, and NLS/K conditions, respectively. The LS/U condition was most difficult, followed by the NLS/U condition, etc. Error counts that were within 10% of the magnitude of each other were considered ties, so the empirical rank code was 3132. If the NLS/U error count had been slightly lower, the empirical pattern would have been 4132 instead.

Across the 1000 simulations, the KRES/EI model fit the empirical 3132 pattern 11.3% of the time (the most commonly observed pattern), and the similar 4132 pattern 1.1% of the time. The 1111 pattern, which often happened with no significant learning at all, was obtained 10.7% of the time (the second most commonly observed pattern). The next most common pattern, 2113, was observed 5.2% of the time. KRES/EI accounted for the observed pattern (a larger knowledge benefit for the LS structure than the NLS structure) over a substantial part of its parameter space. The observed pattern is the plurality prediction of KRES/EI.[2] By comparison, KRES/ED never accounted for the observed and nearly observed 3132 and 4132 patterns at all over 1000 parameter samples. The 1111 pattern was most frequent, observed 24.5% of the time, followed by the 2211 pattern, indicating little effect of knowledge, 9.1% of the time, and the 1213 and 2313 patterns, indicating negative effects of knowledge, 8.6% and 6.7% of the time. Although KRES/ED might potentially be able to account for the qualitative pattern under some specific parameter settings, it does not seem to be inherent to its architecture. KRES/EI is therefore the preferred of the two models.

It can also be useful to examine error rates of individual items. Wattenmaker *et al.* (1986) did not report standard errors on their per-item data, but did report some overall ANOVAs that give the impression that differences in errors of up to 3.0 were unlikely to be statistically significant. Figure 12.5 shows the averaged per-item error rates of Wattenmaker *et al.*'s Experiments 1 and 2, along with the per-item error rates of a reasonably well-fitting KRES/EI model, generated as part of the parameter space analysis above. That model, with learning rate 0.03, exemplar strength 0.98, $\alpha = 2.37$, inhibitory weights –2.38, and excitatory weights 2.72, had overall error counts of 52.8, 24.8, 48.7, and 37.1, which is quite close to the empirical values. Several patterns are apparent. First, the relative difficulties of the four tasks are visible. For the LS category structure, there is a large and consistent reduction in training errors with knowledge. For the NLS category structure, there is a smaller, inconsistent reduction in training errors. Second, the cross-over items (A1 and B3) are not helped or are slightly impaired by knowledge,

---

[2] Readers may wonder whether finding the empirical pattern in only 11.3% of the parameter space is a good result. In fact it is; Pitt *et al.* (2006) studied the Shepard *et al.* (1961) task with a similar method and found the empirical pattern only 0.52% of the time, versus a pattern indicating no learning 39% of the time. 'Despite [the empirical pattern's] smallish size, the volume analysis as a whole shows that [it] is in fact 'central' to the model, in the sense that the dominant alternative patterns are quite similar to the empirical one' (Pitt *et al.*, 2006, p. 66). The absolute proportion of the parameter space is less important than the tendency of the model to exhibit qualitatively reasonable patterns, supporting an architecture-driven rather than parameter-driven account of the data.

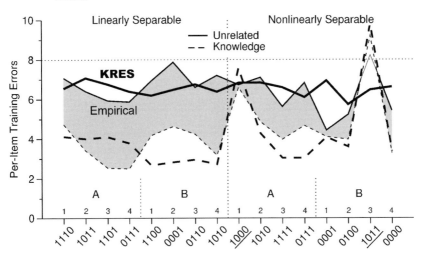

Figure 12.5 Per-item error counts for the Wattenmaker *et al.* (1986) Experiments 1 and 2 (black lines, shading) along with the counts for a KRES/EI model (grey lines, no shading). The grey area shows the improvement in error counts due to prior knowledge. The vertical lines separate the A and B categories and the two category structures. The horizontal line indicates chance performance. Underlined items (A1, B3) are the cross-over items in the NLS category structures.

both empirically and in the KRES model. Third, with the exception of those two items, the correlation between the model fits and the data is not very high. This might seem to be a concern, but most of these variations among per-item error counts appear to be noise. The empirical correlations between the per-item results of Experiments 1 and 2 from Wattenmaker *et al.* (1986) are illustrative. Without prior knowledge (solid black line), the correlation between the two experiments was fairly low ($r^2 = 0.26$). With prior knowledge (dashed black line), when the two cross-over items are removed, the correlation is even lower ($r^2 = 0.13$). Overall, KRES/EI does a good job of accounting for the overall effects of the category structures and the specific effects of prior knowledge. The new exemplar nodes in particular allow the model to account for the interaction between knowledge and individual item learnability.

KOVE, types of knowledge

Another common analysis is to examine the effects of systematically changing a single parameter of a model. Here, we modulate the strength

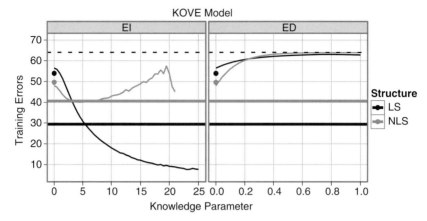

Figure 12.6 Effect of knowledge parameter variation on KOVE models simulating the Wattenmaker *et al.* (1986) experiments. Dots to the left of each graph indicate empirical error counts with unrelated features. Wide horizontal bars indicate empirical error counts with knowledge-related features. The thin dashed line at 64 errors indicates chance performance. Note that the performance of KOVE/EI on the NLS structure becomes erratic when the weight exceeds about 20.

of the two sorts of prior knowledge on a KOVE/E (ALCOVE) model, applied to the Wattenmaker *et al.* (1986) task. The simulations speak to the different ways that the architecturally different knowledge implementations affect the learning processes of the models.

The KOVE/E model approximately fits the unrelated task learning counts with the following parameters: $\lambda = 0.026$, $c = 0.55$, and $\varphi = 1.6$. For KOVE/EI, the knowledge parameter (B) was varied from 0 (no knowledge) to 25 (prior knowledge nodes are equivalent to 25 exemplar nodes). For KOVE/ED, the knowledge parameter (w_D) was varied from 0 (no distortion) to 1.0 (the input representation is fully distorted to the nearest prior concept).

The results are shown in Figure 12.6. For KOVE/ED (right panel), distortion pulled the input activation away from the veridical exemplar representations, reducing overall learning. In the LS case, distortion can result in other exemplars of the same category having somewhat increased activation, mitigating this effect. In the NLS case, however, distortion can often increase the activation of exemplars from the opposite category, further reducing response probabilities and learning. This pattern is evident in the faster degradation of performance in the NLS condition as compared to the LS condition as parameter B increases.

(We also simulated a KOVE/ED model using distorted rather than veridical exemplars, and likewise found that the model incorrectly predicts
a deterioration of NLS learning due to knowledge.)

KOVE/EI (left panel) shows the correct qualitative effect, with a modest facilitatory effect of knowledge on the NLS category structure, but
a strong facilitatory effect of knowledge on the LS structure. With the
knowledge parameter around 5.5 (i.e., knowledge is 5.5 times stronger
than one exemplar), the NLS structure is learned with about 7.6 fewer
errors, while the LS structure is learned with about 27 fewer errors.

Discussion

Our model-based analyses suggest that the integration account is appropriate for the type of knowledge invoked in Wattenmaker *et al.* (1986).
Moreover, that the same conclusion is reached for different classes of
models (recurrent KRES and feedforward KOVE) enhances confidence
that this finding is not due to any idiosyncratic characteristic of either
model. These models succeed because the prior knowledge nodes can
be directly associated with the category nodes, which aids the consistent
items in the LS category structure. With the NLS category structure,
although some items strongly activate the prior knowledge nodes and
are thus learned quickly, the cross-over items highly activate the incorrect prior knowledge nodes, requiring extensive exemplar learning to
counteract them. Moderate contributions from prior knowledge facilitate overall learning, but excessive contributions from prior knowledge
prevent exemplar learning from being successful. Unlike the distortion
accounts, the integration account implemented by KRES/EI and KOVE/
EI allows knowledge to be overridden by exemplar learning if the knowledge is not fully consistent with the stimuli.

Future plans

We conclude with some thoughts on future enhancements to these models, and some suggestions for research programmes that could be supported by them. First, the relationship between prior knowledge and
attentional processes is not well understood. It seems likely that, at least
under some circumstances, knowledge focuses attention towards knowl-
edge-relevant dimensions and away from knowledge-irrelevant features.
None of the variants of the KRES and KOVE models currently implemented can simulate this process. Empirically, eyetracking data have suggested that knowledge can indeed modulate selective attention, at least
for some learners (Kim & Rehder, in press).

Second, although we have made much of the abilities of KRES and KOVE to simulate different sorts of knowledge processes, we have yet to show which sorts of knowledge processes are actually at work as people learn new knowledge-related categories. Heit (1994) concluded that integration models can best account for data from experiments where people made probability judgements after observing knowledge-related categories. In our work, we have also seen superior fits from the integration model. So far, we have been unsuccessful at finding category learning tasks or types of knowledge where distortion (or weighting) procedures are required to successfully fit the data. However, existing experimental procedures may be too coarse to adequately distinguish among models using different types of knowledge, and we await future data from sensitive measures such as eyetracking that could potentially account for trial-by-trial attention and decision measures.

Lastly, the models presented here both simulate one specific laboratory task – supervised classification of individually presented items. Much category learning in the real world uses other procedures, such as inference (Yamauchi & Markman, 1998), where learners predict the values of various unobserved features given the category and perhaps other features, and unsupervised clustering (Medin, Wattenmaker, & Hampson, 1987), where learners form categories based only on inter-item similarities and differences. KRES could easily be used to simulate learning with inference; its learning algorithm is agnostic to which features are presented at input and which features are used as training signals. The effects of prior knowledge on inference tasks have only recently been studied (Erickson, Chin-Parker, & Ross, 2005; Rehder & Ross, 2001). Finally, there is a clear need for broader models of unsupervised category learning (clustering), especially when such learning is influenced by prior knowledge (Spalding & Murphy, 1996). Existing models (e.g., Anderson, 1991; Love et al., 2004; Pothos & Chater, 2002; see also Chapters 8, 9, 10) are relatively limited in their scope, and new models could focus research and theory development, just as models have done with supervised learning.

REFERENCES

Anderson, J. R. (1991). Is human cognition adaptive? *Behavioral and Brain Sciences*, **14**, 471–517.
Balcetis, E., & Dale, R. (2007). Conceptual set as a top-down constraint on visual object identification. *Perception*, **36**, 581–595.
Choi, S., McDaniel, M. A., & Busemeyer, J. R. (1993). Incorporating prior biases in network models of conceptual rule learning. *Memory & Cognition*, **21**, 413–423.

Erickson, J. E., Chin-Parker, S., & Ross, B. H. (2005). Inference and classi-fication learning of abstract coherent categories. *Journal of Experimental Psychology: Learning, Memory, and Cognition*, 31, 86–99.

Friston, K. (2003). Learning and inference in the brain. *Neural Networks*, 16, 1325–1352.

Gluck, M. A., & Bower, G. H. (1988). From conditioning to category learn-ing: an adaptive network model. *Journal of Experimental Psychology: General*, 117, 227–247.

Goldstone, R. L., & Medin, D. L. (1994). Similarity, interactive activation, and mapping: an overview. In K. Holyoak & J. Barnden (eds.), *Advances in Connectionist and Neural Computation Theory, Vol. 2: Analogical Connections* (pp. 321–362). New York: Ablex.

Hampton, J. A. (1979). Polymorphous concepts in semantic memory. *Journal of Verbal Learning and Verbal Behavior*, 18, 441–461.

(1995). Testing the prototype theory of concepts. *Journal of Memory and Language*, 34, 686–708.

Harris, H. D. (in preparation). Uneven weights in category learning revealed by tests of partial items.

Harris, H. D., & Rehder, B. (2006). Modeling category learning with exem-plars and prior knowledge. In R. Sun (ed.), *Proceedings of the 28th Annual Conference of the Cognitive Science Society* (pp. 1440–1445). Mahwah, NJ: Lawrence Erlbaum Associates.

Heit, E. (1994). Models of the effects of prior knowledge on category learning. *Journal of Experimental Psychology: Learning, Memory, and Cognition*, 20, 1264–1282.

Heit, E., & Bott, L. (2000). Knowledge selection in category learning. In D. Medin (ed.), *Psychology of Learning and Motivation* (Vol. 39, pp. 163–199). San Diego, CA: Academic Press.

Hoffman, A. B., Harris, H. D., & Murphy, G. L. (2008). Prior knowledge enhances the category dimensionality effect. *Memory & Cognition*, 36, 256–270.

Hoffman, A. B., & Murphy, G. L. (2006). Category dimensionality and feature knowledge: when more features are learned as easily as fewer. *Journal of Experimental Psychology: Learning, Memory, and Cognition*, 32, 301–315.

Hopfield, J. J. (1982). Neural networks and physical systems with emergent collective computational abilities. *Proceedings of the National Academy of Sciences*, 81, 3088–3092.

(1984). Neurons with graded responses have collective computational prop-erties like those of two-state neurons. *Proceedings of the National Academy of Sciences*, 81, 3088–3092.

Kim, S., & Rehder, B. (in press). How prior knowledge affects selective attention during category learning: an eyetracking study. *Memory and Cognition*.

Kruschke, J. K. (1992). ALCOVE: an exemplar-based connectionist model of category learning. *Psychological Review*, 99, 22–44.

Love, B. C., Medin, D. L., & Gureckis, T. M. (2004). SUSTAIN: a network model of category learning. *Psychological Review*, 111, 309–332.

Medin, D. L., & Schaffer, M. M. (1978). Context theory of classification learning. *Psychological Review*, **85**, 207–238.

Medin, D. L., & Schwanenflugel, P. J. (1981). Linear separability in classification learning. *Journal of Experimental Psychology: Human Learning and Memory*, 7, 355–368.

Medin, D. L., Wattenmaker, W. D., & Hampson, S. E. (1987). Family resemblance, conceptual cohesiveness, and category construction. *Cognitive Psychology*, **19**, 242–279.

Murphy, G. L. (2002). *The Big Book of Concepts*. Cambridge, MA: MIT Press.

Nosofsky, R. M. (1986). Attention, similarity, and the identification-categorization relationship. *Journal of Experimental Psychology: General*, **115**, 39–57.

O'Reilly, R. C. (1996). Biologically plausible error-driven learning using local activation differences: the generalized recirculation algorithm. *Neural Computation*, **8**, 895–938.

Pitt, M. A., Kim, W., Navarro, D. J., & Myung, J. I. (2006). Global model analysis by parameter space partitioning. *Psychological Review*, **113**, 57–83.

Pothos, E. M., & Chater, N. (2002). A simplicity principle in unsupervised human categorization. *Cognitive Science*, **26**, 303–343.

Rehder, B., & Murphy, G. L. (2003). A knowledge-resonance (KRES) model of category learning. *Psychonomic Bulletin & Review*, **10**, 759–784.

Rehder, B., & Ross, B. H. (2001). Abstract coherent categories. *Journal of Experimental Psychology: Learning, Memory, and Cognition*, **27**, 1261–1275.

Shepard, R. N., Hovland, C. I., & Jenkins, H. M. (1961). Learning and memorization of classifications. *Psychological Monographs: General and Applied*, **75**.

Sikström, S. (2002). Forgetting curves: implications for connectionist models. *Cognitive Psychology*, **45**, 95–152.

Smith, J. D., & Minda, J. P. (1998). Prototypes in the mist: the early epochs of category learning. *Journal of Experimental Psychology: Learning, Memory, and Cognition*, **23**, 1411–1436.

Smolensky, P. (1986). Information processing in dynamical systems: foundations of harmony theory. In D. E. Rumelhart, J. L. McClelland, & the PDP Research Group (eds.), *Parallel Distributed Processing: Explorations in the Microstructure of Cognition* (Vol. 1, pp. 194–281). Cambridge, MA: MIT Press.

Spalding, T. L., & Murphy, G. L. (1996). Effects of background knowledge on category construction. *Journal of Experimental Psychology: Learning, Memory, and Cognition*, **22**, 525–538.

Spratling, M. W., & Johnson, M. H. (2006). A feedback model of perceptual learning and categorization. *Visual Cognition*, **13**, 129–165.

Tanenhaus, M. K., Spivey-Knowlton, M. J., Eberhard, K. M., & Sedivy, J. C. (1995). Integration of visual and linguistic information in spoken language comprehension. *Science*, **268**, 1632–1634.

Wattenmaker, W. D., Dewey, G. I., Murphy, T. D., & Medin, D. L. (1986). Linear separability and concept learning: context, relational properties, and concept naturalness. *Cognitive Psychology*, **18**, 158–194.

Wisniewski, E. J., & Medin, D. L. (1994). On the interaction of theory and data in concept learning. *Cognitive Science*, **18**, 221–281.

Yamauchi, T., & Markman, A. B. (1998). Category learning by inference and classification. *Journal of Memory and Language*, **39**, 124–148.

Appendix: KRES equations

The following equations and pseudocode describe the behaviour of a KRES model, including extensions described here not present in the original Rehder and Murphy (2003) formulation.

A KRES model is described by a symmetrical $n \times n$ weight matrix, **W**, which describes the weights between each pair of n units. All units have the same underlying dynamics. For any given trial, vectors **I** and **O** indicate the external input to each unit and the desired activation of each unit (for training or testing purposes). Input and output units are defined by the set of non-zero elements in **I** and **O**, respectively.

On a given trial, the following algorithm is performed to find the activation of each unit, **A**, given **W**, **I**, and a per-unit bias **B**:

$$I^{\text{ner}} \leftarrow 0; I^{\text{adj}} \leftarrow 0 \tag{1}$$

$$I^{\text{total}} \leftarrow i^{\text{net}} + I + B \tag{2}$$

$$I^{\text{adj}} \leftarrow I^{\text{adj}} + \frac{I^{\text{total}} - I^{\text{adj}}}{g} \tag{3}$$

$$A \leftarrow \frac{1}{1 + e^{-\alpha I^{\text{adj}}}} \tag{4}$$

$$I^{\text{net}} \leftarrow AW \tag{5}$$

$$H \leftarrow \Sigma\, A I^{\text{net}} \tag{6}$$

H is the harmony of the network, representing how consistent the activations of the unit are to the weights in the network. Equations 2 through 6 are repeated until the network converges, $\dot{H} \approx 0$. Equation 3 implements a smoothing function over $\mathbf{I}^{\text{total}}$, with g typically fixed at 4.0. Equation 4 is a sigmoidal squashing function, with an α parameter that is often around 1.0.

Once the network has converged, the activation of the output unit, $\mathbf{A}^O = \mathbf{A}[O \neq 0]$, is transformed by a choice rule to give a vector of (typically two) response probabilities, $A^O / \Sigma A^O$.

To train the network, the above procedure is run twice. During the first convergence, the input is **I**; during the second, the input is **I** + **O**.

The activation of the first phase is called **A⁻** and of the second is called **A⁺**. Then, the weights are updated according to the contrastive Hebbian learning rule:

$$\Delta W \leftarrow \lambda \#_{CHL}\left(A^{+T}A^{+} - A^{-T}A^{-} \right) \tag{7}$$

$\#_{CHL}$ is a masking matrix the same size as **W**, with 1s indicating weights that can be updated by the CHL rule, and 0s elsewhere. λ is the CHL learning rate. The remainder of the rule computes how much each weight in the network should change to make activation given **I** more closely resemble the activation given **I** + **O**.

A complication has to do with exemplar units in KRES/E. The units themselves have the same dynamics as other units, but the weights are somewhat different. The modeller creates a pool of units that can be recruited to form new exemplar units as needed. An exemplar unit is recruited whenever a new exemplar is seen (i.e., no existing units do not have their maximum activation) and when unassigned units are available. These units have two types of connections to other units, specified by the modeller. One type (afferent) has fixed weights of 0 until the exemplar unit is recruited, at which point it gets fixed weights equal to $\lambda_{E}I$ where λ_{E} is an exemplar strength parameter that affects activation dynamics of those units. The other type of connection (efferent) has fixed weights of 0 until the exemplar unit is recruited, at which point its weights become initialized and trainable by CHL.

13   The contribution (and drawbacks) of models to the study of concepts

Gregory L. Murphy

A book that focuses on computational models carries with it the presupposition that modelling is an important and useful activity. And so it is. But why? What does modelling add that other kinds of theorizing or empirical work do not? And what can go wrong in modelling? In this chapter, I will take a step back to address these questions. I cannot hope to teach much to experienced researchers in this field, but I think that for students, newcomers, and sceptics, it is useful to consider what modelling adds and how it can sometimes detract from the enterprise of doing cognitive psychology. On the whole, I think that the contribution of computational models has been positive to our understanding of concepts. But at the same time, I think that some of the persisting shortcomings in the field of concepts are in part due to an emphasis on modelling or to the way researchers use models as a tool to enhance our understanding of concepts.

We can learn about concepts by doing category-learning experiments, by making cross-cultural comparisons, by carrying out observational studies, and by studying the properties of natural categories, among other techniques. Each of these will tell us some things but cannot tell us other things. So it is with building models of concepts. A chapter such as this one might focus more on problems than on benefits, but it should be understood that there are pitfalls and limitations in every method. The trick is to know what the pitfalls are and to do one's best to avoid them, whichever method one uses.

Why model?

Why even make a model? It's a big pain and a time sink. Clearly, it would be much more convenient to just sketch a flowchart or jot down your

Thanks to Todd Gureckis, Harlan Harris, Bob Rehder, and the editors for very useful comments on a draft of this chapter. However, none of the views herein should be attributed to them.

ideas of how the mind works. People have done that for years. What is the advantage of going to all the trouble to program a model?

When I was a student, this question was something of a sore point in the field. Many people divided themselves into two camps – those who thought that only computational models could qualify as doing scientific psychology versus those who thought that traditional 'verbal' models could still be helpful (including a few who believed that computational models were a waste of time). People don't seem to split on this issue quite so deeply any more. Of course, some researchers have focused most of their efforts on models and some have spent no time on them, but, like other previously hot controversies in the field, we now have more of a let-a-thousand-flowers-bloom attitude. Modelling can clearly offer an important perspective that other approaches cannot, but it is not the only way to come to knowledge of the mind's workings. It is one of a number of approaches that people can use, including constructing verbal or higher-level theories, neuropsychological theories, developmental analyses, and so on.

That leads us back to the question of what modelling offers that other kinds of theorizing do not. The main answer that has been given is that a computational model requires the researcher to be explicit about the theory in a way that a verbal theory does not. If I say that categorization is done 'by similarity', then I get a lot of free wiggle room from the fact that the word *similarity* has a number of different senses and that it shifts its meaning somewhat depending on what it is applied to. I am relying on the reader's intuitive sense of what *similarity* means rather than spelling it out. Therefore, I have incorporated the reader's intuition into my theory without properly accounting for it. If I have to make a similarity computation in a model, however, I immediately discover that my computer, even though it is a Mac, does not have an intuition about what similarity is. I have to tell it every detail of how the items are represented, how they are to be compared, how a similarity score arises from that computation, and how that score is used in classification or other processes. Now my theory must be much more explicit and detailed.

Related to this, as I try to program my model, I will be confronted with the fact that similarity is a lot more complicated than I had thought. Schank and Abelson (1977) emphasized this aspect of modelling in their early models of narrative comprehension. They discovered that the amount of knowledge and processing necessary to understand simple, three-line stories was unbelievable. This fact was not obvious before they began their work, because theorists filled gaps in their verbal theories with their own knowledge and processing. Researchers did not realize just how much inferencing was necessary to connect sentences in a discourse until they tried to get their programs to connect them. Hours later, as they entered more and more knowledge into their databases and had to do more and more work to get the model to process this knowledge correctly, they began to realize all the thought that *they* had unconsciously done in order to make sense of their simple story. Similarly, as categorization models had to specify what they meant by similarity, they had to deal with problems related to different kinds of stimuli that seem to evoke different forms of similarity, issues of featural versus relational similarity, problems of content influencing how similarity is perceived, and so on. Creating the program would bring me face to face with the details that I didn't have to think about when I just said, 'People judge the item's similarity to the category representation.'

Another early modeller in cognitive psychology, John Anderson (1976, pp. 17–18) emphasized that it is often difficult to derive predictions from verbal theories. This is in part due to the aforementioned vagueness in such theories, which often leads to bitter disputes as to what exactly the theory predicts. If you test my theory by showing that people pay attention to associations between stimuli, therefore arguing that my similarity theory is wrong, I will reply by arguing that associations are part of similarity and that you are interpreting my theory overly specifically in order to disconfirm it. Then follows an undignified dispute in which we propose duelling definitions of what *similarity* means and of what *I* meant when I said it. Such disputes are seldom edifying. According to Anderson and others, models can avoid this problem because they mechanically produce an answer without the investigator providing an interpretation or excuse. Therefore, anyone can trace the model's predictions, so long as they have a copy of the program.

A related point that Anderson makes is that one can run the model and see just what it does, which may not be obvious. It is a common comment by people who make models that they are surprised at what the model does – and not always pleasantly surprised. As a model becomes more complex, one is no longer just verifying that it behaves as planned, one is discovering how all its parts interact to produce emergent behaviour that couldn't be predicted by understanding each component on its own. Given that the mind is surely composed of many different components that interact in complex ways, modelling may be necessary to understand how multiple components work together to produce actual behaviour. With a very complex verbal model, no one can be sure just how its components interact, so its predictions are uncertain.

Why not model?

With all these benefits, one might well ask why *every* theory isn't represented through a computational model. Why would anyone stick with these verbal theories, which are vague, don't make clear predictions, or are too complex to figure out how they actually work? I think that there are two general answers, which are worth explicitly putting forth even if they are fairly obvious.

First, in some cases, one simply doesn't have enough information to make the model. When first investigating a topic, you might not have a theory at all. You might simply be making up explanations as results come in, changing your notion of what is going on with each successive experiment. Science is not only about making detailed theories but is also about making discoveries and empirical generalizations. When you are making those discoveries, what you need is an accurate description of what is going on. That must precede theoretical development.

The problem with making a model prematurely is that it can lock you in to a certain explanation before you have enough data to know just what you should be modelling. Making a model leads you to do experiments that test the model, or at least that are inspired by it, as I'll discuss below. Therefore, if you make the model before you have fully explored the empirical effects, it can have the effect of stifling discovery. Of course, in other cases, experimental paradigms have been employed for years, and one is right to expect very explicit theories of people's behaviour in such tasks.

The second reason for not making a model is when you are focusing on one tiny sliver of cognition, but the task requires a whole bunch more cognition. A model of the entire task would require you to specify dozens of things that you are not particularly interested in (from the present perspective) and that you are not necessarily making claims about. But you would have to specify those things if the model is to work. Of course, specifying them is necessary if you want to have a complete theory, but when researchers are doing empirical investigation into a specific topic, it is inefficient and not very useful to spend one's time making a model of all those processes, when they are just investigating one of them.

When modelling goes awry

Modelling also brings with it a set of pitfalls. Some pitfalls cannot be completely avoided, but once one is aware of them, the damage can be limited. I describe below some of the pitfalls that I have observed in model usage in the domain of concepts. Because this section focuses on negative aspects, I avoid discussing specific examples as much as possible, because I don't want to give the impression that I am picking on one or another model or research team. And let me restate that every research method has problems, some of which can be avoided and some of which cannot. So, this description of modelling problems does not imply that modelling is not extremely helpful. Research programmes that avoid the following problems will make their models most useful to the field. Those that fall into the problems will not be as helpful.

Falling in love

It is important not to fall in love with your model. After the hours of developing it, programming it, doing experiments based on it, and fitting huge data sets, it's natural to identify with your model. But let's be clear: every computational model of concepts is wrong. Indeed, every theory in psychology is wrong. All the theories are incomplete, none of them explains all currently known data (much less all future data), and all are oversimplified. The mind is incredibly complex, and all our theories are orders of magnitude simpler. This is true of verbal theories just as much as with computational models, perhaps even more so. However, I suspect that researchers are more likely to fall in love with their computational models, after all the time they have spent together, than they are to fall in love with their verbal theories.

The problem of love is that one becomes blind to the model's limitations and failures. One of the main purposes of a psychological theory is to provide a target for other researchers to respond to. Your theory seems right to them, except that it cannot possibly explain concepts of type X, say, social concepts. This then leads them to do experiments on the difference between social and object concepts, and show that your model does ok on the first but terribly on the second. This is the way that knowledge is increased in the field. However, the researcher in love with his or her model cannot accept this mode of discovery and must instead respond bitterly that the social concepts are not really concepts, that the model does so explain them (with a few perfectly understandable adjustments – see below), and that the criticisms of the model are simply unfair. But perhaps the issue should not really be whether someone is being fair or unfair to your model, but rather whether your model is spurring interesting research and exploration. Sometimes a model that is wrong is much more useful than one that is right. A model's limitations can often tell us much about what people are doing, and so constantly denying that the model has these limitations can have a paradoxical effect of limiting the discoveries that your model could lead you to.

Let me consider a more positive example of a model that has greatly benefited the field in large part by stimulating research into its limitations, namely the Osherson *et al.* (1990) mathematical model of category-based induction. This model was an extremely impressive accomplishment in explaining how people make generalizations from one or more categories to another one (e.g., if robins and penguins have sesamoid bones, how likely is it that eagles have sesamoid bones?), focusing on similarity relations among the categories as the inductive engine. It led to empirical discoveries of various phenomena of induction and was shown to account for most of them. It was also extremely well specified. The model was so impressive that many of the best minds in the field took up the task of trying to figure out how it was wrong. This led to a number of important discoveries, such as the fact that a single similarity metric was insufficient to account for induction (e.g., Heit & Rubenstein, 1994; Ross & Murphy, 1999) or that people spontaneously use causal reasoning in making inductions when possible (Proffitt, Coley, & Medin, 2000; Rehder, 2009). Others sought simpler or arguably more plausible processes to accomplish the same things as this model (Sloman, 1993). It led to much empirical investigation in comparing different populations (e.g., children, non-literate dwellers in the rain forest) in the phenomena it predicted.

The Osherson *et al.* model is wrong. It actually works very well within a limited domain, and this success set it up as a target for comparison for other research in different domains. Without its careful framing and success in its original domain, I am convinced that the later researchers would not have done many of the experiments that they did to show that it could not handle different materials or kinds of induction. Therefore, that model served two purposes. It provided a successful account of induction of some kinds of materials in some domains, and it spurred discoveries in different domains that it could not itself account for. To my mind, these two results are equally important contributions the model made, even though its authors no doubt would have preferred to be spared the second one.

Some modellers, however, stand in the way of the second form of progress. Showing the limitations of their model does not seem to be progress to them, but rather is unfair and wrong. This manifests itself in a number of ways, as discussed in the next sections.

Model limitations lead to research limitations

A model cannot do everything. Researchers who are interested in one aspect of concepts and conceptual behaviour focus on that particular aspect and often short-change, perhaps unconsciously, other aspects that other researchers work on. Models of category learning do not necessarily provide a basis for category-based induction; models of classification do not necessarily learn very well. Models of the typical two-category learning experiment do not provide representations that can be grouped hierarchically as natural concepts often are. Such limitations are to be expected.

The problem for the researcher and eventually the field is when these models restrict the topics that are investigated (Murphy, 2005). If you have a wonderful model of category learning in the two-category context, and this leads you to do nothing but that kind of learning experiment for 10 years, I think that you have overly limited your research interests. People learn more than two categories; they learn different kinds of categories; they do things with the categories after they learn them; they draw generalizations from categories; they use categories to reason. No one has to study all these things, but a continuing problem in the field is that people who study one kind of task or issue generally devise their theory of concepts to explain just that task or issue. Sometimes it is apparent that it cannot possibly explain some other well-known phenomenon. Sometimes it isn't apparent whether that theory is or isn't extendable to a different issue, because its proponents have never attempted to extend it. It's possible that one's model can be simply extended to do a different task. But it may also be possible that one has to start from scratch. That is a very useful fact, which tells us something about how the mind is organized. That is, the success of a model in one domain but failure in another suggests that different principles (or representations, processes, *something*) are operating in those different domains.

The worst failing in this regard is when researchers go so far as to deny, scoff at, or diminish the importance of the problems that their model doesn't address. I have had the experience of a modeller telling me that my work on knowledge-based category learning 'is not what I call concepts', thereby indicating that his model (and theory and experiments) did not have to address my results. Now, I believe it is very questionable that this person's categories were more like normal human concepts than the categories I was studying, but what I found most disturbing about this interchange was how the person felt perfectly at ease in rejecting whole scientific questions and topics in psychology because they did not qualify as what he called concepts. Of course, researchers may choose to look at different problems due to differences in taste and background, but I strongly suspect in this case that the cause was to a large degree that the person's model had no apparent way of being extended to deal with the phenomena I was interested in. Once you have a 'model of concepts', things that are distant from your model must *ipso facto* not be concepts.

This problem is by no means unique to those who use models, nor to psychologists. As *The Economist* (2009) remarked, when discussing the failure of macroeconomic models to predict the financial collapse of

2008, 'Economists can become seduced by their models, fooling themselves that what the model leaves out does not matter,' arguing that the things that most economic models omitted (details of market transactions) were what in fact caused the economic meltdown. I think that models can exaggerate this problem, because they are so good at doing what they do that what they cannot do seems somehow less important and interesting.

Model tinkering

As imperfect theories, models go through the usual process of development and improvement. Scientific theories are not static objects that either work perfectly or else are discarded. If at first they don't succeed, their developers try and try again to fix them by changing what seems wrong and keeping the essential components of the theory. The same holds for computational models. Usually they begin fairly simple and are expanded to include more situations and to explain more phenomena. The trick, though, is for researchers to identify when they are going through a normal expansion and development, and when they are simply fixing the model in an ad hoc way. Deciding when to give up on one's theory is one of the most difficult decisions scientists make.

For example, consider my model of concepts, the FPC (Free Parameter model of Concepts). It has a basic form of stimulus representation, a similarity metric to compare stimuli to the concept representation, and a decision rule that determines how an item is classified. Each of these components has a number of parts, along with some parameters that can vary depending on the stimuli or conditions. I introduced this model in a paper where I analysed some classic data in the categorization field and showed that it did better than the original model applied to those data. Great!

Unfortunately for me, other researchers have not been so kind. Person A tested new stimuli and found that my model didn't do so well. Person B tested a different category structure and said that my model stunk. Person C tested classification after a delay and then laughed in my face. After a brief period of despair, I got back to work and responded to these challenges in the following way. First, I pointed out that stimuli can be represented analytically or holistically – or both! – and so I added this new form of representation to the model (along with a parameter to choose the correct form) and found that I then accounted for Person A's data. Then I pointed out that my similarity rule was only one of a number of possible rules, and when the rule is generalized (along with a parameter that specifies the specific rule in any experiment), I could now account for Person B's data. Finally, I expanded the decision rule, under the assumption that delayed decisions are not the same as immediate decisions, and I found that when I generalized the model, it could now account for Researcher C's data. Problem solved!

Or is it? I seem to have the view that so long as my model can be adapted to account for new data, the model is 'successful'. Even though my model didn't actually predict any of these effects, and even though the changes made to it may not be carried forward to new versions of the model (because I am still using the same old stimuli and test delay I started out with, so why bother?), I still consider my model a contender.

I find this way of using models problematic. Rather than giving support for the model and the theory underlying it, it seems to me to give support for my own cleverness or industry in responding to these failures. If I am going to tinker with the model every time a new result comes in, it is unclear what the model *is*, and so it loses the advantage of making clear predictions and being falsifiable, which was our original motivation for constructing a model. I think that models tell us as much in the ways that they are wrong as they do about the ways that they are right. When people followed up the Osherson *et al.* (1990) induction model, it became clear that simple similarity could not account for induction of different kinds of properties. The contrast between that model's clear predictions and content effects made it possible to draw a strong conclusion. If the authors had added a parameter that allowed different forms of similarity or causal relations to be used, what would have been learned from this?

Again, modifying a model is normal, and some amount of tinkering is necessary and useful. The trick is to realize when it is a normal process of theory expansion and when it is simply stubbornness. Perhaps it is reasonable for me to extend my model to account for new kinds of stimuli other than the ones I originally considered. But perhaps the changes I made to handle the effect of test delay are not reasonable. How can one tell whether the extension is a normal, useful one and not an ad hoc attempt to save face? I think that part of the answer is whether one tests the model components as psychological hypotheses, discussed next. Another, less quantifiable factor is whether changes to the model are natural outgrowths of the underlying theory and model structure. If the model is changed radically, and if whatever was unique about it is now gone, then the charge of tinkering seems justified.

Model testing

The predominant way of testing models is in terms of global measures of fit. When I made the FPC model, I tested it on classic data, and maybe even ran some new experiments. The model accounted for 92% of the variance, say. That sounds pretty good. But when I made the changes to the model, did I do any research to prove that these changes truly explain the discrepant results? For example, when I changed the stimulus representation, I was essentially claiming that the effect found by Person A was due to a difference in perceptual representation, and not the other components of the model (because I changed the model's perceptual input). And when I changed the decision rule to explain the results of delayed testing, I was thereby claiming that what changes with delay is the decision rule. Too often model testing ends with making a change in the model and then showing that it now fits the results – with the change, the FPC can now account for 93% of the variance in Person A's data. What is needed to make this argument truly convincing is further experimentation to find evidence *for the psychological claims made by the model.*

It is possible to experimentally test whether the different stimuli used by Person A do have a different perceptual representation. It is possible to test whether delay influences decision processes, as opposed to stimulus or concept representation, say. The fact that the model does well with this change does not by itself show that the results come about for the reason the model says. Does delayed testing really change the way people make decisions? Why should delay have such an effect? Wouldn't it be more likely to change the concept representation in some way, through the normal process of memory decay or interference?

Indeed, the same question can be asked about my original model and its parameters. It surely speaks in favour of my model that it can handle a range of different data well, because its parameters can change the model behaviour in different conditions. But does the model's explanation truly account for the differences in people's performance? The way to construct such a test is (1) to analyse how the model accounts for a given effect, such as differences in stimulus format or delay of testing – perhaps as reflected in different parameter values used to account for different conditions; and then (2) to design an experiment that examines whether the effect is due to whatever the model says it is. For example, if my model explains different results by differing similarity computations, can I derive independent evidence that subjects' perception of similarity differs in this way? Of course, designing such experiments is not trivial, but it is just the usual difficulty of doing cognitive psychology. Creating a model cannot reduce the necessity of such jobs – it can only help us decide what experiments are the most useful.

Your model is your theory of concepts (or classification or whatever), and you are claiming that the parts in your model correspond to parts in the human conceptual system, and that the way your model works is similar to the way those components work in people. Simply finding that the conglomeration of components together can account for a set of results is only a first step. Better is to show that your components map onto components in the mind.

This is necessary because a given effect can often be accounted for by a number of the model's components. For example, suppose someone (that idiot Person C!) finds that categorization results are different when tested after a delay (e.g., as in Posner & Keele, 1970), and my model doesn't fit those results well. I could possibly fit the results by changing the input stimulus representation (e.g., making it fuzzier), by changing the category representation (e.g., decay), by changing the similarity computation (e.g., 'spread'), or by changing the decision rule (e.g., making it more probabilistic) with delay. Possibly *any one* of these changes could improve my model's fit. After I've tried one of them, and it works, how do I know that that is the right one? A worse problem is when the model already has a parameter in one of those components that can explain the result. For example, if I already had a parameter that made the similarity computation strict or fuzzy, then I could account for the effect of delay without making any further changes in the model. Without a delay, similarity would be fairly strict (i.e., only close similarity would count), and with a delay, similarity would be fuzzy, by the usual techniques of parameter fitting. Such a parameter could explain Posner and Keele's results.

However, although I certainly love the FPC, I have to tell you frankly that I don't think that testing delay actually changes the way people determine similarity. I think it causes decay in the memory for the concept (exemplars, prototype, or whatever). So, even though my model accounted for the effect of this variable without having to make any changes (because of the free parameter), the model is wrong. The reason it gets the effect is not the reason that people show the effect.

I think that this sort of situation is the most difficult one for any modeller to deal with. You face an almost ethical dilemma when your model seems to work, but you suspect that it is working for the wrong reason. Are you going to criticize and undermine your own model? That is clearly a difficult situation to be in, especially when there are others in the field who are more than happy to criticize it for you. However, when I have observed researchers who show that their model's explanation is not exactly right, I have never thought 'What a dumb model!' but instead have always thought that we are really learning something, something that might not have been learned without this testing of the model's explanation.

What is especially useful is an analysis of different parameter settings of a model, and whether they are likely psychological explanations of the effects being modelled. Doing this testing would no doubt show shortcomings of some of a model's explanations (as doing testing often finds shortcomings of any theory), but that is just how progress is made. Although the model might have to be revised or rejected, it was essential to making these discoveries of how people work, and that is just what models are there for – to lead us to a deeper understanding of psychological processes.

Model as a comprehension engine

Related to this last point, I would like to end with more positive recommendations on modelling. My own experience in using models is very limited, perhaps leading readers to question why I should be making these recommendations. However, I am an active consumer of models of concepts, and I have a view of what makes a model useful from the perspective of theoretical advancement of the field. Of course, others might differ with my recommendations.

Suppose one has a model that has done fairly well in explaining a range of data. If we assume that the model is approximately correct within this range, we can get a better understanding of what people do, and why, by using the model as an analytical tool. So, how much of the model's success is determined by its assumptions about input representation? You can find out by messing around with the input, trying out different formats or including different information, to see how this changes the results. How critical is the learning rule? If you used a different learning rule, would this make any difference? What effects are dependent on it? Some researchers provide such analyses, but some seem happy with simply presenting one version of the entire model (or perhaps the editors of their journals don't allow room for such analytical testing).

By systematically testing different aspects of the model in this way, one can better understand just why it does what it does. But this is important for another reason. Recall my statement that all models are wrong. One of the ways they are wrong is that different people do different kinds of things: children don't behave the same as adults; brain damage changes the way we process information; experts are often different from novices. People also do different things in different situations. The analysis of the model can give us ideas about how to extend the model to different populations and situations. Perhaps your learning rule is excellent for the typical classification learning paradigm, but it doesn't work very well when people learn categories while using the items for a different task (Ross, 1996). If you've done an analysis of your learning rule, you can then use this to suggest why people are different in these two situations. For example, error-driven learning might be involved in classification learning, just as your model said, but different empirical results in a different learning paradigm suggest that error-driven learning may not be operating there. In fact, if you change your learning rule, you get results that are much better for the category-use learning condition. The analysis you did prior to the new data helped explicate the difference between these two conditions and led you to think about how people in this new condition might differ from what your model normally does. Rather than objecting to the use of a non-standard learning procedure (and defending your original model), you used the model to explicate what happens in that procedure compared to the one your model accounts for.

In this way, I think that researchers can get away from the idea of trying to prove that their model is 'correct' or, less ambitiously, the best current model. Instead, the role of the model is to provide a way of analysing people's behaviour, by providing a basic framework that supports systematic testing. Following Anderson's (1976) point that models are useful for making specific predictions, we can treat the model as a set of hypothetical models: the model without the fancy stimulus encoding, the model with a different learning rule, the model with a different similarity computation, and so on. These alterations create a space of possible models. When we find that the model has to change in such-and-such a way to account for some variable, we have a hypothesis readily available to explain it (e.g., the decision rule must change). If we find that human data never enter one part of a model's parameter space, this implies that this version of the model isn't psychologically real (e.g., holistic stimuli plus fuzzy similarity with highly deterministic responses), and that may be revealing of broader principles of the mind. If we find data that cannot be accounted for by any permutation of the model, that may tell us that some basic assumption the model has is wrong, under those testing conditions.

This suggestion helps to answer the question of when one is normally expanding a model or just tinkering with it to make it work. The critical difference is in how one treats the testing and model alterations. If my conclusion were simply, 'The new, expanded FPC accounts for all the data', then I think that little has been learned. Furthermore, if all the changes to the model are made post hoc, to explain discrepant results, the enterprise is suspect – I'm just tinkering. On the other hand, if my goal is to discover how people differ in different conditions, and exploring the model helps me learn about this, then I won't be so focused on defending my model per se (which now exists in various forms, depending on the conditions) and will instead be using it as a tool rather than an end in itself. Because I'm testing the model against people in different conditions, it's going to lead to psychological insight above and beyond 'the model works well'.

In my view, using models as analytical tools in this way could be one of their most useful functions for the theorist. Doing this requires giving up one's infatuation with the version of the model that has been successful in explaining some subset of results and also recognizing that the model may simply be wrong in explaining important and interesting phenomena. Realizing that your model is wrong – for some population or task – is making progress in understanding the whole range of conceptual behaviour. In giving up our love affairs with our own models, we may gain a more useful tool for understanding the mind.

REFERENCES

Anderson, J. R. (1976). *Language, Memory, and Thought.* Hillsdale, NJ: Erlbaum.

The Economist (July 18, 2009). The other-worldly philosophers. *The Economist,* **392** (8640), 65–67.

Heit, E., & Rubinstein, J. (1994). Similarity and property effects in inductive reasoning. *Journal of Experimental Psychology: Learning, Memory, and Cognition,* **20**, 411–422.

Murphy, G. L. (2005). The study of concepts inside and outside the lab: Medin vs. Medin. In W. Ahn, R. L. Goldstone, B. C. Love, A. B. Markman, & P. Wolff (eds.), *Categorization Inside and Outside the Lab: Essays in Honor of Douglas Medin* (pp. 179–195). Washington, DC: APA.

Osherson, D. N., Smith, E. E., Wilkie, O., López, A., & Shafir, E. (1990). Category-based induction. *Psychological Review,* **97**, 185–200.

Posner, M. I., & Keele, S. W. (1970). Retention of abstract ideas. *Journal of Experimental Psychology,* **83**, 304–308.

Proffitt, J. B., Coley, J. D., & Medin, D. L. (2000). Expertise and category-based induction. *Journal of Experimental Psychology: Learning, Memory, and Cognition,* **26**, 811–828.

Rehder, B. (2009). Causal-based property generalization. *Cognitive Science,* **33**, 301–344.

Ross, B. H. (1996). Category representations and the effects of interacting with instances. *Journal of Experimental Psychology: Learning, Memory, and Cognition,* **22**, 1249–1265.

Ross, B. H., & Murphy, G. L. (1999). Food for thought: cross-classification and category organization in a complex real-world domain. *Cognitive Psychology,* **38**, 495–553.

Schank, R. C., & Abelson, R. P. (1977). *Scripts, Plans, Goals and Understanding.* Hillsdale, NJ: Erlbaum.

Sloman, S. A. (1993). Feature-based induction. *Cognitive Psychology,* **25**, 231–280.

14 Formal models of categorization: insights from cognitive neuroscience

Lukas Strnad, Stefano Anzellotti and Alfonso Caramazza

Introduction

Category-specificity is a salient phenomenon in cognitive neuroscience. It has been reported in a wide variety of contexts and experimental paradigms. Much of the theoretically significant observations come from studies of patients with category-specific deficits and from imaging studies. Here, we will discuss how imaging and patient studies of category-specific phenomena can point to potential limitations of formal models of categorization, and inform their future development. We will point out that these models treat categorization in a domain-general manner. That is, categorization of all objects, irrespective of their domain, proceeds according to an identical mechanism. If the models are to encompass categorization of entities from the elementary categories that appear in neuropsychological studies, for example animals, tools, or conspecifics, without abandoning their domain-generality, a question arises as to how domain-specific phenomena can arise in conjunction with a completely domain-general mechanism of categorization. We will argue that an answer to this question is closely related to the theories of organization of conceptual knowledge that originally arose in the context of neuropsychology. These theories, in our opinion, constrain the possible accounts reconciling the domain-generality of formal models with the domain-specific phenomena known from neuropsychology.

The term 'categorization' denotes a set of cognitive mechanisms that involve different memory systems (Smith & Grossman, 2008) and vary as a function of the tasks performed and the strategy employed (Ashby & O'Brien, 2005). Given this diversity, it is not obvious whether the neuroscientific evidence that we discuss on the one hand, and the behavioural data that formal models aim to explain on the other hand, do, in fact, relate to the same mechanism. However, it is possible to remain agnostic on this issue and consider whether formal models of categorization, with their current assumptions, can be part of a broad framework for explaining the neuroscientific data.

A synopsis of the neuropsychological and imaging evidence

Patient studies

Some of the most striking clues about the organization of conceptual knowledge in the brain come from the studies of brain-damaged patients with category-specific semantic deficits. These patients exhibit selective sparing or impairment of different semantic categories that cuts across different types of knowledge and different modalities. There is a large body of evidence suggesting that such impairments can be truly semantic in nature, rather than on the level of pre-semantic perceptual processing of the relevant test stimuli, or production of the output in the relevant experimental tasks (for a review, see Capitani *et al.*, 2003). Although the category-specific deficits are often associated with impaired performance on all semantic categories, patients can sometimes perform as well as matched control subjects on the spared categories (e.g. patient EW from Caramazza & Shelton, 1998). Furthermore, the impairment is usually permanent, with only a few cases of partial recovery of the afflicted categories reported in the literature (e.g. Laiacona, Barbarotto, & Capitani, 2005). Since these deficits shed light on how concepts belonging to different semantic categories are represented in the brain, they can prove to be a pertinent source of evidence to inform formal models of categorization.

A crucial point about category-specific deficits concerns their granularity. There are roughly four categories whose impairment has been reliably reported. These include animate biological objects, i.e. animals, (see Blundo, Ricci, & Miller, 2006; Caramazza & Shelton, 1998), inanimate biological objects like fruits, vegetables, and plant life (Hart, Berndt, & Caramazza, 1985; Samson & Pillon, 2003; discussion of EA in Capitani *et al.*, 2003), artifacts (Hillis & Caramazza, 1991; Laiacona & Capitani, 2001), knowledge of facts about familiar persons (Miceli *et al.*, 2000). There is a considerable controversy as to whether these four broad semantic categories can be fractionated further in brain-damaged subjects. For example, in the presence of a selective impairment of biological objects, knowledge of body parts is often spared, but its deficits are, in turn, frequently associated with impairment of the category of artifacts (see the discussion in Capitani *et al.*, 2003). However, sparing of body parts can also occur in conjunction with a selective impairment of artifacts (Shelton, Fouch, & Caramazza, 1998). Therefore, the status of body parts as a distinct category, or its association with one of the broader categories remain unclear (but see Urgesi, Berlucchi, & Aglioti, 2004).

An important aspect of these category-specific deficits is the fact that they are not associated with any particular type of knowledge. Patients have often been separately tested on the perceptual knowledge and on the functional/associative knowledge of the relevant categories. The two kinds of knowledge generally tend to be impaired to the same degree (Capitani et al., 2003), but it is possible at least for functional/associative knowledge to be spared independently of perceptual knowledge (Papagno, Capasso, & Miceli, 2009; Sartori, Job, & Coltheart, 1993). It should be further noted that while knowledge based on some particular type of perceptual information might be damaged for one category, knowledge of another category based on very similar perceptual information can be spared. For instance, patient EW from Caramazza and Shelton (1998) could not recognize animals by the sounds they made, but could recognize objects from other categories by sound.

All of the reports cited above involve patients who sustained brain damage at an adult age. However, there have also been rare but important developmental cases of category-specific deficits. For instance, Farah and Rabinowitz (2003) discuss the case of patient Adam, who sustained brain damage at 1 day of age, and never acquired normal knowledge of animals, even though he learned all other categories normally.

Imaging studies

In agreement with the neuropsychological findings, brain imaging studies have identified networks of brain regions preferentially activated by the categories of objects that have been observed to dissociate in neurological cases.

Puce and colleagues, using functional magnetic resonance imaging (fMRI), found a region in the brain where the blood oxygenation level dependent (BOLD) signal in response to faces was stronger than that in response to letter strings and textures (Puce et al., 1996). In line with this result, Kanwisher, McDermott, and Chun (1997) reported a region, which has been labelled the fusiform face area, showing greater BOLD responses for faces than for a variety of other stimulus types.

Other studies have identified regions showing differential activity for animals versus manmade objects (Chao, Haxby, & Martin, 1999; Chao, Martin, & Haxby, 1999; Martin & Chao, 2001; Martin et al., 1996; Mummery et al., 1998), faces versus places (Epstein & Kanwisher, 1998), and 'biological' motion versus 'mechanical' motion (Martin & Weisberg, 2003). A region in the lateral occipital complex was reported to be differentially active for body parts (Downing et al., 2001) and repetitive transcranial magnetic stimulation (rTMS) of that region was shown to lead to deficits specific for body parts (Urgesi *et al.*, 2004). These reports have contributed to a more precise localization of the brain areas involved in processing objects belonging to different categories, and have revealed the complexity of the neural systems involved in object recognition.

A much debated issue concerns whether the regions that show greater activation for a category of objects are 'category-specific', in the sense that they are modules optimized for processing a particular category of objects. In contrast with the 'category-specific' proposal, some researchers hold that object knowledge is represented by widely distributed representations. In an fMRI experiment by Haxby and colleagues (2001), participants saw pictures of objects belonging to different categories. Analysing the data with pattern recognition techniques, the authors showed that it is possible to determine with good accuracy the category to which an object that a participant is viewing belongs. This result held even when the voxels that showed greater activation for that semantic category were excluded from the analysis (Haxby *et al.*, 2001). Haxby and colleagues concluded that object knowledge is widely distributed. However, their results are consistent with the view that different brain regions are differentially important for the discrimination of individual objects belonging to specific categories (Spiridon & Kanwisher, 2002).

Most of the fMRI studies on the organization of object knowledge investigated brain activity in sighted participants during picture viewing. Some recent studies investigated representations of objects, nouns and verbs in blind participants (Bedny *et al.*, 2008; Pietrini *et al.*, 2004). Mahon and Caramazza (2009) have shown that analogous category effects can be observed in both sighted and congenitally blind individuals performing size judgments in response to object names. The organization by category in individuals who never had visual experience might arise from experience in other modalities (e.g. touch). Another possibility is that the organization by category is the result of innate biological constraints. The case of patient Adam discussed above supports this hypothesis.

Relating the neuropsychological evidence to theoretical models of categorization

In relation to the neuropsychological evidence, the most relevant property of formal models of categorization is their domain-generality. All of the models considered here (Griffiths *et al.*, 2007, see Chapter 8; Johansen & Kruschke, 2005; Kruschke, 2008, see Chapter 6; Love, Medin, & Gureckis, 2004, see Chapter 10; McLaren & Mackintosh, 2002, see Chapter 7; Minda & Smith, 2002, see Chapter 3; Nosofsky & Zaki,

2002, see Chapter 2; Rehder & Kim, 2006, see Chapter 12; Rehder & Murphy, 2003; Rogers & McClelland, 2008, see Chapter 5; Zaki *et al.*, 2003) are conceived broadly enough to handle classification of any object that is defined in terms of a set of features. A feature can, in turn, be any property associated with the object – perceptual, relational, causal, or other. Importantly, the models place no a priori constraints on what these features may be, or on the size of the set of features constituting an object. Consequently, insofar as objects can be described as sets of features, the models are in principle capable of performing categorization on any object, including those from categories like animals or tools. Furthermore, all of the models define a single mechanism that is used for categorization of all objects, regardless of their particular features, or a broad class of categories they belong to. This is what we refer to as the domain-generality of the models.

If the formal models aim to encompass categorization of objects from categories highlighted by the neuropsychological evidence, while maintaining their assumption of domain-generality, they carry the burden of explaining how category-specific phenomena can arise in the context of a domain-general categorization mechanism. As we have noted earlier, category-specific deficits concern most aspects of semantic knowledge of the affected category. These include the ability to perform basic-level categorization of items belonging to the category in question. The ability to perform categorization on a more general level, for example. deciding whether an object is a tool or an animal, is typically preserved (see for instance Basso & Capitani, 1988). Similarly, damage to regions showing category-selectivity tends to be accompanied by an impairment of the relevant category (Damasio *et al.*, 2004). It therefore seems that categorization of everyday objects like tools or animals depends on mechanisms whose organization exhibits category-specific patterns. This begs for an explanation of how these mechanisms can underpin a domain-general categorization system proposed by the formal models.

An answer to this question is, in our opinion, closely related to the competing theories of the organization of conceptual knowledge debated in neuropsychology (for a more detailed review, see Mahon & Caramazza, 2009). These theories were originally motivated by an effort to account for category-specific semantic deficits that emerged from patient studies. They are relevant in the present context, because many of them argue that category-specific patterns in patient and imaging studies arise as a result of domain-general principles that underpin the organization of conceptual knowledge in the brain. In this respect, they are akin to accounts that might attempt to tie the domain-general categorization mechanisms of the formal models with the available neuropsychological evidence.

Theories based on the correlated structure principle are perhaps the most natural fit for the formal models of categorization. According to the correlated structure principle, co-occurrence of properties of objects in the world is what drives the organization of knowledge of these objects (Caramazza *et al.*, 1990). Thus, different object features are differentially important for various categories, and this, in turn, determines the segregation of the representations of these categories in the brain. However, theories based on the correlated structure principle have faced a number of difficulties. For instance, there has been little consensus on the question of which features in particular are relevant for different categories. Furthermore, these theories have made inconsistent predictions about the nature of category-specific deficits. Tyler and Moss (2001) have proposed that animals tend to share more features than tools, and that the features shared by animals tend to be highly correlated with each other. They have argued that this should render animals more resistant to damage. On the other hand, Devlin *et al.* (1998) have made the opposite predictions on the basis of the same premise, arguing that high correlation of features should lead to a higher propensity for impairment. As is apparent from the double dissociations observed in the patient studies reviewed above, neither proposal finds empirical support (see also Garrard *et al.*, 1998; Zannino *et al.*, 2002, 2006).

Selection of concrete features that are prominent for different categories represents a further problem for this class of theories. Some attempts have been made to establish sets of features that are characteristic of different categories, for instance using feature listing tasks (Cree & McRae, 2003), or by constructing non-linear measures of distinctiveness of certain features for different categories (Sartori, Lombardi, & Mattiuzzi, 2005). However, none of these approaches have yielded satisfactory results (Mahon & Caramazza, 2009).

A different class of theories explaining category-specific phenomena with an appeal to domain-general principles are the sensory-functional theories. Their basic assumption is that different types of features are differentially important for various categories. An early sensory-functional theory, Warrington and Shallice (1984), argued that perceptual features are most important for categories like animals, plants, or foods, whereas categories like tools are prominently characterized by their functional properties. On this account, a category-specific semantic deficit would translate into an impairment of the knowledge of specific types of features which are critical for the given category. However, this prediction is at variance with the available data – cases have been reported in which a patient's knowledge of a category, say animals, is impaired without a corresponding impairment of processing of the relevant features, in this case visual features (for examples of such dissociations see Blundo *et al.*, 2006; Caramazza & Shelton, 1998; Laiacona & Capitani, 2001). The theory also implies the converse of the above, i.e. a category-specific impairment should follow if processing of the relevant features is impaired. Again, this is at variance with empirical data (Lambon Ralph *et al.*, 1998). Since the early sensory-functional theories, more fine-grained discriminations of feature types and the corresponding semantic categories have been proposed (for proposals along these lines see Cree & McRae, 2003; Vinson *et al.*, 2003). However, no consensus has been reached as to the relevant dimensions along which objects from different categories should be discriminated.

A third major approach has been proposed to account for category-specific neuropsychological phenomena – the domain-specific hypothesis (Caramazza & Shelton, 1998; Mahon & Caramazza, 2009). According to this hypothesis, certain categories with an evolutionarily relevant history like animals, conspecifics and possibly tools are represented in spatially separable optimized regions of the brain, and category-specific deficits arise when one or more of these regions are damaged. The hypothesis accounts well for the observed grain of the category-specific deficits, as all the deficits reviewed above concern categories that could arguably have been evolutionarily relevant. There is some controversy as to whether tools constitute such a category. However, even if they do not, the observed data would be consistent with the hypothesis, as the observed impairment for tools could in this case result from damage to the regions that are not optimized for a particular category. This would explain why tools could be impaired while, for instance, animals and conspecifics are spared. Yet, as the hypothesis argues that the representation of conceptual knowledge is organized along categorical lines, reconciling the category-specific phenomena from neuropsychology, and the domain-general categorization systems proposed by the formal models would call for a separate, independent explanation.

Most of the formal models of categorization assume that experience is the only factor to shape the structure of categorization processes. However, a recent fMRI study has shown that visual experience is not necessary for inducing category-dependent patterns of activation in the brain (Mahon & Caramazza, 2009). In fact, an analogous organization by semantic category was observed in the BOLD signal of sighted and congenitally blind subjects hearing words denoting living and non-living objects. The study by Mahon and colleagues does not exclude the possibility that experience coming through different sensory modalities (e.g. haptic) played a crucial role in shaping the observed patterns of activation. However, the study calls for a more careful consideration of the extent to which different types of experience can modify the structure of the processes involved in the categorization of everyday objects.

Furthermore, in the context of neuropsychology, the case of patient Adam (Farah & Rabinowitz, 2003), who developed a deficit specific for animals after damage sustained at the age of one day, produces converging evidence that the organization of object knowledge can be importantly shaped by innate constraints.

Putting the question of reconciling category-specificity and domain-generality aside for now, we would also like to point to some issues related to the notion of feature as it is deployed in the formal models of categorization. We have noted earlier that the formal models use it both ubiquitously and very loosely: they define objects as sets of features, and virtually any property that is associated with an object can play the role of a feature. No explicit constraints on what a feature can be are specified. Such generality makes the models prone to confounding the inputs and the outputs of the categorization mechanism they try to explain. The clearest examples of this can be found in models in which features are actually objects (e.g., head, legs; Minda & Smith, 2002). In this case, the mechanism that, for instance, allows one to judge that an object 'is a bird' because, among other reasons, it 'has wings', might plausibly be the same mechanism that allows one to determine that an object 'has wings'. Features themselves can thus be products of the categorization mechanism.

This may have several implications. One possibility is that categorization processes are constituted of different layers that first categorize 'features' and then objects. In this case, the models of categorization would not be models of categorization in toto, but of a particular step or subset of steps within the stream of the categorization processes, namely, those leading from pre-categorized features to the categorization of objects. Another possibility is that the very same mechanisms at the same level in the stream of processing lead to categorization of an object and of its parts. Then, for instance, we would be able to categorize something as a bird without having to categorize its wings as wings before. In either case, it is critical for the models to specify sets of particular features that could plausibly serve as inputs into their mechanism from other systems in the brain. One key lesson emerging from our discussion of the theories of organization of conceptual knowledge is that this is a notoriously hard thing to do even for broad categories of common objects like animals and tools. Indeed, as the problems of both the theories based on the correlated structure principle and the sensory-functional theories testify, no consensus has been reached on at least the broad outlines of what such features should be.

In this brief review, we have tried to draw a parallel between the formal models that propose a domain-general mechanism of categorization, and attempts to construct theories of organization of conceptual knowledge based on domain-general principles. We have argued that the formal models need to try to grapple with the category-specific neuropsychological phenomena, and the lessons learned in the course of the development of the theories of organization of conceptual knowledge may be of use to them. In particular, the experience with these theories makes it very clear that domain-general principles make it either very hard, or impossible, to account for category-specificity. The need to put flesh on the abstract notion of feature, which both the formal models and the domain-general theories freely operate with, tends to be one of the most prominent sources of problems. However, it is also important to acknowledge that our comparison between the formal models and theories of organization of conceptual knowledge has its limitations. The two endeavours were originally motivated by different empirical phenomena – the former by the human performance in category learning tasks, and the latter by the category-specific deficits in patients. As we have argued above, the two must concern some of the same mechanisms, at least in the case of very familiar categories like tools or animals. Still, the two only meet at a relatively restricted section of the vast array of phenomena in psychology grouped under the cap of categorization.

REFERENCES

Ashby, F., & O'Brien, J. (2005). Category learning and multiple memory systems. *Trends in Cognitive Science*, 9 (2), 83–89.

Basso, A., Capitani, E., & Laiacona, M. (1988). Progressive language impairment without dementia: a case with isolated category specific semantic deficit. *Journal of Neurology, Neurosurgery and Psychiatry*, 51, 1201–1207.

Bedny, M., Caramazza, A., Grossman, E., Pascual-Leone, A., & Saxe, R. (2008). Concepts are more than precepts: the case of action verbs. *Journal of Neuroscience*, 28, 11347–11353.

Blundo, C., Ricci, M., & Miller, L. (2006). Category-specific knowledge deficit for animals in a patient with herpes simplex encephalitis. *Cognitive Neuropsychology*, 23 (8), 1248–1268.

Capitani, E., Laiacona, M., Mahon, B., & Caramazza, A. (2003). What are the facts of semantic category-specific deficits? A critical review of the clinical evidence. *Cognitive Neuropsychology*, 20 (3–6), 213–261.

Caramazza, A., Hillis, A. E., Rapp, B. C., & Romani, C. (1990). The multiple semantics hypothesis: multiple confusions? *Cognitive Neuropsychology*, 7, 161–189.

Caramazza, A., & Shelton, J. (1998). Domain-specific knowledge systems in the brain the animate-inanimate distinction. *Journal of Cognitive Neuroscience*, 10 (1), 1–34.

Chao, L., Haxby, J. V., & Martin, A. (1999). Attribute-based neural substrates in posterior temporal cortex for perceiving and knowing about objects. *Nature Neuroscience*, **2**, 913–919.

Chao, L., Martin, A., & Haxby, J. V. (1999). Are face-responsive regions selective only for faces? *NeuroReport*, **10** (14), 2945–2950.

Cree, G., & McRae, K. (2003). Analyzing the factors underlying the structure and computation of the meaning of chipmunk, cherry, chisel, cheese, and cello (and many other such concrete nouns). *Journal of Experimental Psychology: General*, **132** (2), 163–201.

Damasio, H., Tranel, D., Grabowski, T. J., Adolphs, R., & Damasio, A. (2004). Neural systems behind word and concept retrieval. *Cognition*, **92**, 179–229.

Devlin, J., Gonnerman, L., Andersen, E., & Seidenberg, M. (1998). Category-specific semantic deficits in focal and widespread brain damage: a computational account. *Journal of Cognitive Neuroscience*, **10**, 77–94.

Downing, P., Jiang, Y., Shuman, M., & Kanwisher, N. (2001). A cortical area selective for visual processing of the human body. *Science*, **293** (5539), 2470–2473.

Epstein, R., & Kanwisher, N. (1998). A cortical representation of the local visual environment. *Nature*, **392** (6676), 598–601.

Farah, M., & Rabinowitz, C. (2003). Genetic and environmental influences on the organization of semantic memory in the brain: is 'living things' an innate category? *Cognitive Neuropsychology*, **20** (3–6), 401–408.

Garrard, P., Patterson, K., Watson, P. C., & Hodges, J. R. (1998). Category-specific semantic loss in dementia of Alzheimer's type: functional-anatomical correlations from cross-sectional analyses. *Brain*, **121**, 633–646.

Griffiths, T. L., Canini, K. R., Sanborn, A. N., & Navarro, D. J. (2007). Unifying rational models of categorization via the hierarchical Dirichlet process. *Proceedings of the Twenty-Ninth Annual Conference of the Cognitive Science Society*. New York: Lawrence Erlbaum.

Hart, J., Berndt, R., & Caramazza, A. (1985). Category-specific naming deficit following cerebral infarction. *Nature*, **316** (6027), 439–440.

Haxby, J., Gobbini, M., Furey, M., Ishai, A., Schouten, J., & Pietrini, P. (2001). Distributed and overlapping representations of faces and objects in ventral temporal cortex. *Science*, **293** (5539), 2425–2430.

Hillis, A., & Caramazza, A. (1991).Category-specific naming and comprehension impairment: a double dissociation. *Brain*, **114** (5), 2081–2094.

Johansen, M., & Kruschke, J. (2005). Category representation for classification and feature inference. *Journal of Experimental Psychology: Learning, Memory, and Cognition*, **31** (6), 1433–1458.

Kanwisher, N., McDermott, J., & Chun, M. (1997). The fusiform face area: a module in human extrastriate cortex specialized for face perception. *Journal of Neuroscience*, **17** (11), 4302–4311.

Kruschke, J. K. (2008). Models of categorization. In R. Sun (ed.), *The Cambridge Handbook of Computational Psychology* (pp. 267–301). New York: Cambridge University Press.

Laiacona, M., Allamano, N., Lorenzi, L., & Capitani, E. (2006). A case of impaired naming and knowledge of body parts: are limbs a separate subcategory? *Neurocase*, **12** (5), 307–316.

Laiacona, M., Barbarotto, R., & Capitani, E. (2005). Animals recover but plant life knowledge is still impaired 10 years after herpetic encephalitis: the long-term follow-up of a patient. *Cognitive Neuropsychology*, **22** (1), 78–94.

Laiacona, M., & Capitani, E. (2001). A case of prevailing deficit of nonliving categories or a case of prevailing sparing of living categories? *Cognitive Neuropsychology*, **18**, 39–70.

Lambon Ralph, M. A., Howard, D., Nightingale, G., & Ellis, A. W. (1998). Are living and nonliving category-specific deficits causally linked to impaired perceptual or associative knowledge? Evidence from a category-specific double dissociation. *Neurocase*, **4**, 311–338.

Love, B., Medin, D., & Gureckis, T. (2004). SUSTAIN: a network model of category learning. *Psychological Review*, **111** (2), 309–332.

Mahon, B., & Caramazza, A. (2009). Concepts and categories: a cognitive neuropsychological perspective. *Annual Review of Psychology*, **60**, 27–51.

Martin, A., & Chao, L. (2001). Semantic memory and the brain: structure and processes. *Current Opinion Neurobiology*, **11** (2), 194–201.

Martin, A., & Weisberg, J. (2003). Neural foundations for understanding social and mechanical concepts. *Cognitive Neuropsychology*, **20**, 575–587.

Martin, A., Wiggs, C., Ungerleider, L., & Haxby, J. (1996). Neural correlates of category-specific knowledge. *Nature*, **379** (6566), 649–652.

McLaren, I., & Mackintosh, N. (2002). Associative learning and elemental representation: II. Generalization and discrimination. *Animal Learning & Behavior*, **30** (3), 177–200.

Miceli, G., Capasso, R., Daniele, A., Esposito, T., Magarelli, M., & Tomaiuolo, F. (2000). Selective deficit for people's names following left temporal damage: an impairment of domain-specific conceptual knowledge. *Cognitive Neuropsychology*, **17** (6), 489–516.

Minda, J., & Smith, J. (2002). Comparing prototype-based and exemplar-based accounts of category learning and attentional allocation. *Journal of Experimental Psychology: Learning, Memory, and Cognition*, **28** (2), 275–292.

Mummery, C., Patterson, K., Hodges, J., & Price, C. (1998). Functional neuroanatomy of the semantic system: divisible by what? *Journal of Cognitive Neuroscience*, **10** (6), 766–777.

Nosofsky, R., & Zaki, S. (2002). Exemplar and prototype models revisited: response strategies, selective attention, and stimulus generalization. *Journal of Experimental Psychology: Learning, Memory, and Cognition*, **28** (5), 924–940.

Papagno, C., Capasso, R., & Miceli, G. (2009). Reversed concreteness effect for nouns in a subject with semantic dementia. *Neuropsychologia*, **47** (4), 1138–1148.

Pietrini, P., Furey, M. L., Ricciardi, E., Gobbini, M. I., Wu, W. H., Cohen, L., Guazzelli, M., & Haxby, J. V. (2004). Beyond sensory images: object-based representation in the human ventral pathway. *Proceedings of the National Academy of Sciences of the USA*, **101**, 5658–5663.

Puce, A., Allison, T., Asgari, M., Gore, J., & McCarthy, G. (1996). Differential sensitivity of human visual cortex to faces, letterstrings, and textures: a functional magnetic resonance imaging study. *Journal of Neuroscience*, **16** (16), 5205–5215.

Rehder, B., & Kim, S. (2006). How causal knowledge affects classification: a generative theory of categorization. *Journal of Experimental Psychology: Learning, Memory, and Cognition*, **32** (4), 659–683.

Rehder, B., & Murphy, G. (2003). A knowledge-resonance (KRES) model of category learning. *Psychonomic Bulletin & Review*, **10** (4), 759–784.

Rogers, T., & McClelland, J. (2008). Précis of semantic cognition: a parallel distributed processing approach. *Behavioral Brain Sciences*, **31** (6), 689–749.

Samson, D., & Pillon, A. (2003). A case of impaired knowledge for fruit and vegetables. *Cognitive Neuropsychology*, **20** (3–6), 373.

Sartori, G., Job, R., & Coltheart, M. (1993). The organization of object knowledge: evidence from neuropsychology. In D. E. Meyer & S. Kornblum (eds.), *Attention and Performance XIV (Silver Jubilee Volume): Synergies in Experimental Psychology, Artificial Intelligence, and Cognitive Neuroscience* (pp. 451–465). Cambridge, MA: MIT Press.

Sartori, G., Lombardi, L., & Mattiuzzi, L. (2005). Semantic relevance best predicts normal and abnormal name retrieval. *Neuropsychologia*, **43**, 754–770.

Shelton, J. R., Fouch, E., & Caramazza, A. (1998). The selective sparing of body part knowledge: a case study. *Neurocase*, Special issue: Category-specific deficits, **4**, 339–351.

Smith, E., & Grossman, M. (2008). Multiple systems of category learning. *Neuroscience and Biobehavioral Reviews*, **32** (2), 249–264.

Spiridon, M., & Kanwisher, N. (2002). How distributed is visual category information in human occipito-temporal cortex? An fMRI study. *Neuron*, **35** (6), 1157–1165.

Tyler, L., & Moss, H. (2001). Towards a distributed account of conceptual knowledge. *Trends in Cognitive Science*, **5** (6), 244–252.

Urgesi, C., Berlucchi, G., & Aglioti, S. (2004). Magnetic stimulation of extrastriate body area impairs visual processing of nonfacial body parts. *Current Biology*, **14** (23), 2130–2134.

Vinson, D. P., Vigliocco, G, Cappa, S., & Siri, S. (2003). The breakdown of semantic knowledge: insights from a statistical model of meaning representation. *Brian and Language*, **86**, 347–365.

Warrington, E., & Shallice, T. (1984). Category specific semantic impairments. *Brain*, **107** (3), 829–854.

Zaki, S., Nosofsky, R., Stanton, R., & Cohen, A. (2003). Prototype and exemplar accounts of category learning and attentional allocation: a reassessment. *Journal of Experimental Psychology: Learning, Memory, and Cognition*, **29**, (6), 1160–1173.

Zannino, G. D., Perri, R., Carlesimo, G. A., Pasqualetti, P., & Caltagirone, C. (2002). Category-specific impairment in patients with Alzheimer's disease as a function of disease severity: a cross-sectional investigation. *Neuropsychologia*, **40**, 2268–2279.

Zannino, G. D., Perri, R., Pasqualetti, P., Caltagirone, C., & Carlesimo, G. A. (2006). Analysis of the semantic representations of living and nonliving concepts: a normative study. *Cognitive Neuropsychology*, **23**, 515–540.

15 Comments on models and categorization theories: the razor's edge

Douglas Medin

If I may make a personal remark, one sign of old age is that people ask you to write commentaries on new(er) work. In the present case the invitation for me to write something may be linked to the publication of the Medin and Schaffer (1978) context theory of categorization model more than 30 years ago and/or the Smith and Medin (1981), *Categories and Concepts* book, almost as old. This ought to provide enough distance to view cumulative progress in this area of research and theory. Of course there was more than a little earlier work by Posner and Keele (1968), Reed (1973), and Smith, Shoben and Rips (1974) relevant to models and by Rosch, Mervis and others (e.g. Rosch, 1973, 1975; Rosch & Mervis, 1975; Rosch *et al.*, 1976) laying out basic levels and goodness of example or typicality effects that reverberated through the cognitive sciences. The basic levels work was so important that it now has the status of being presupposed in developmental studies on the interaction of language and conceptual development (e.g., Waxman, 1989, 2002; Waxman & Lidz, 2006).

One way of assessing progress in an area is to evaluate how it is doing with respect to narrowness and insularity versus breadth. Cutting edge research seems like something that is inherently good, but it may be useful to examine what is being cut and how that edge is related to broader configurations. If we take the state of categorization research in 1980 as a benchmark, one could provide the following list of limitations of theory and data on categories and concepts.

1. Although concepts serve multiple functions (categorization, inference, communication, etc.) virtually all attention was directed at the categorization function of concepts.
2. Although there was a body of work on natural language concepts and a body on artificially created concepts (e.g., Posner dot patterns) and similar empirical results, the two literatures had little, if anything, to say to each other.
3. Almost all the adult research was conducted with undergraduate students at major research universities.

4. Almost all of the adult research used tasks that could be completed within an hour and nearly always involved exactly two categories.
5. Virtually all of the empirical work was on supervised categorization.
6. The models of categorization focused primarily on predicting transfer performance to new stimuli given after a category training period.
7. The stimuli themselves tended to be visual figures having little meaning or relevance to research participants.
8. The representation of the stimuli was assumed to be fixed and subject only to attentional weighting (a convenient assumption in comparing different models of category learning). Furthermore, the constituent features or dimensions were assumed to be independent and relational properties were ignored (and researchers did a good job of selecting stimuli where this assumption was not obviously violated).
9. There was relatively little categorization research in the cognitive neurosciences (other than the Wisconsin Card Sort task) and virtually none of it employed categorization models.

Let's start with these earlier limitations and examine the current state of affairs, paying special attention to the chapters in this volume. Progress has been considerable and almost everyone is on the cutting edge (of something). In the next few paragraphs I review some of that progress and then turn to what I take to be serious residual challenges to the field.

1. Past: Although concepts serve multiple functions (categorization, inference, communication, etc.) virtually all attention was directed at the categorization function of concepts.
   Present: Here is an area of clear progress. Brian Ross, Art Markman and others have done a number of studies on the inference function of concepts and there is now enough literature to review (Markman & Ross, 2003) and models to predict results from such studies.
   Under the influence of Rips, Osherson, Smith and others there is also something of a literature on the use of categories in reasoning, also known by the term 'category-based induction' (e.g., see Feeney & Heit, 2007, for a review). Finally, there is some work on conceptual combination (again stimulated by Osherson and Smith) as well as some corresponding computational models. Conceptual combination tends to be neglected because it is so challenging even to predict how novel noun-noun combinations will be interpreted (Gagné & Shoben, 2002; Wisniewski, 1997).

Neither of these latter two lines of work is represented in this volume, perhaps a continuing sign that the natural language and artificial, perceptual stimuli literatures still are not on good speaking terms.

2. Past: Although there was a body of work on natural language concepts and a body on artificially created concepts (e.g. Posner dot patterns) and what appear to be similar empirical results, the two literatures had little, if anything, to say to each other.

   Present: One can point to some nice work by Gert Storms and his colleagues applying models of categorization to natural language stimuli (e.g., Storms, De Boeck, & Ruts, 2000), but aside from this exception the two literatures remain as segregated as North and South Korea.

3. Past: Almost all the adult research was conducted with undergraduate students at major research universities.

   Present: This remains largely true with the exception of work on category-based induction which has included a range of participant populations.

4. Past: Furthermore, almost all of the adult research used tasks that could be completed within an hour and nearly as many involved exactly two categories.

   Present: There is now a modest amount of work looking at expertise either by identifying real-world experts (e.g. Medin *et al.*, 1997) or by dint of training in the lab (e.g. Gauthier & Tarr, 1997; Goldstone, 1998). This research is directly relevant to limitation 8 and has not tended to be addressed by models of categorization (but see Chapter 10 by McDonnell and Gureckis).

5. Past: Virtually all of the empirical work was on supervised categorization.

   Present: Although the absolute amount of work on unsupervised categorization remains small, it has experienced a relatively large increase from its low base (see Chapters 9 and 10 by Pothos *et al.* and McDonnell and Gureckis). It now seems to be a realistic expectation that models of categorization should account for unsupervised categorization (a.k.a. free sorting).

6. Past: The models of categorization focused primarily on predicting transfer performance to new stimuli given after a category training period.

   Present: There is increasing attention directed to the learning side of category learning. This ranges from predicting the relative difficulty of learning different category partitionings (a tradition stemming from the classic Shepard, Hovland, & Jenkins 1961

monograph), to predicting overall learning curves, to predicting learning curves for different stimuli (e.g. see Chapter 8 by
Griffiths *et al.*).
7. Past: The stimuli themselves tended to be visual figures having little
meaning or relevance to research participants.
Present: This picture is largely unchanged. There are notable exceptions (see Chapter 12 by Harris and Rehder) by brave souls like
Greg Murphy (e.g. Murphy, 2004; Murphy & Allopenna, 1994)
aiming to account for the role of prior knowledge and meaningfulness on category learning. I'm still fond of the Wisniewski and
Medin (1994) paper showing that meaningful category labels
affect what is likely to count as a feature as well as category learning. Ed and I were dying to develop a computational model for
this sort of context and the progress represented in the Rehder
and Murphy (2003) KRES model (Chapter 12) suggests that it's
not impossible.
8. Past: The representation of the stimuli was assumed to be fixed and
subject only to attentional weighting (a convenient assumption in
comparing different models of category learning). Furthermore,
the constituent features or dimensions were assumed to be independent and relational properties were ignored (and researchers
did a good job of selecting stimuli where this assumption was not
obviously violated).
Present: See the comment on expertise and feature learning above.
Work on feature learning is important but inconvenient for modellers who prefer to model a steady-state, fixed representation. The
same may hold for ignoring relational properties, despite the fact
that relations are central to computational models of analogy and,
arguably, to models of similarity (Markman & Gentner, 2000;
Medin, Goldstone, & Gentner, 1993).
9. Past: There was relatively little categorization research in the cognitive neurosciences (other than the Wisconsin Card Sort task) and
virtually none of it employed categorization models.
Present: This may be a case where a rising tide boosts all ships. The
burgeoning of cognitive neuroscience has been associated with
serious and successful efforts to link brain processes with categorization processes (see Chapter 4 by Ashby *et al.*). As they note,
one of the large gains is that brain activity becomes an important dependent variable for constraining and testing models of
categorization.

Some researchers might quibble with this list of criteria and important issues. It's fairly obvious why models of categorization should care

about knowledge effects, feature inference and unsupervised categorization but perhaps it's more debatable as to how important it is to extend learning procedures to more realistic durations, employ a wider range of stimulus materials or sample a broader set of study populations. My first response to this issue is why would one not want to show that a model has explanatory power beyond the confines of a narrow set of stimuli, procedures and populations? Perhaps more telling than this in principle statement is the in practice fact that generalizations about categorization and inferencing derived from studies with undergraduates do not appear to carry well to other populations (e.g. Medin & Atran, 2004). Indeed, some researchers (Henrich et al., 2010) argue that undergraduates are 'the weirdest people in the world'.

In summary, I think the overall picture is at once mildly encouraging and seriously discouraging. The most positive developments are in cognitive neuroscience and forays into building theory and data on knowledge effects with meaningful materials, as well as bridging between natural language stimuli and the artificial.

A number of the chapters in this volume illustrate encouraging breadth in different ways. John Kruschke's chapter (Chapter 6) describes a programme of research on attention in learning that nicely bridges with work in associative learning, including research with non-human animals. Livesey and McLaren's treatment (Chapter 7) is more conservative but provides some useful model contrasts. Nosofsky's chapter (Chapter 2) shows the latest, greatest in developing and defending exemplar models of categorization and Minda and Smith's chapter (Chapter 3) does the same for prototype models of categorization. Iba and Langley's chapter (Chapter 11) reminds us that the machine learning area is also an important source of models. I couldn't help feeling some nostalgia because around 1990 there was a great deal of interaction between psychology and machine learning on categories and concepts, something that seems largely absent nowadays. Pothos et al. (Chapter 9) show another direction of breadth and generality by pushing the idea of simplicity. Griffiths et al. (Chapter 8) provide a vision of how models might address more complex stimuli and relational structures. These are all useful contributions.

But this picture is also seriously discouraging. I remember reading research on impression formation in the 1970s and 1980s where participants were given a list of traits or behaviours and then asked to make an overall judgment concerning the person being described. Papers in this considerable literature almost always cited Solomon Asch's (1952) book. At one point I finally got around to reading this classic work and I distinctly remember being shocked at how his book was full of ideas that could be explored and also at the fact that impression formation only constituted a tiny fraction of it. The work that followed seemed at best to be a pale imitation of Asch. The psychology of concepts and categories wasn't driven so much by a book as it was by findings on basic levels and typicality effects by people like Eleanor Rosch and Edward Smith. It may share with social cognition a sense that a lot more could and should be done. So while I congratulate these authors on some very interesting and cutting edge chapters, I also challenge them to pursue greater breadth in participants, paradigms and procedures and to aim for more integrative theories capable of bridging between perceptual stimuli and those carrying knowledge and meaning, between novices and various forms of expertise between categories on the one hand and concepts on the other. It's time to get off the razor's edge.

REFERENCES

Asch, S. (1952). *Social Psychology.* Englewood Cliffs, NJ: Prentice Hall.

Burnett, R., Medin, D., Ross, N., & Blok, S. (2005). Ideal is typical. *Canadian Journal of Experimental Psychology,* **59** (1), 5–10.

Feeney, A., & Heit, E. (eds.) (2007). *Inductive Reasoning.* New York: Cambridge University Press.

Gagné, C. L., & Shoben, E. J. (2002). Priming relations in ambiguous noun-noun combinations. *Memory & Cognition,* **30**, 637–646.

Gauthier, I., & Tarr, M. J. (1997). Becoming a 'Greeble' expert: exploring mechanisms for face recognition. *Vision Research,* **37**, 1673–1682.

Goldstone, R. L. (1998). Perceptual learning. *Annual Review of Psychology,* **49**, 585–612.

Henrich, J., Heine, S. J., & Norenzayan, A. (2010). The weirdest people in the world? *Behavior and Brain Sciences,* **33**, 61–83.

Markman, A. B., & Gentner, D. (2000). Structure-mapping in the comparison process. *American Journal of Psychology,* **113** (4), 501–538.

Medin, D. L., & Atran, S. (2004). The native mind: biological categorization and reasoning in development and across cultures. *Psychological Review,* **111**, 960–983.

Medin, D. L., Goldstone, R. L., & Gentner, D. (1993). Respects for similarity. *Psychological Review,* **100**, 254–278.

Medin, D. L., Lynch, E. B., Coley, J. D., & Atran, S. (1997). Categorization and reasoning among tree experts: do all roads lead to Rome? *Cognitive Psychology,* **32**, 49–96.

Medin, D. L., & Schaffer M. M. (1978). A context theory of classification learning. *Psychological Review,* **85**, 207–238.

Murphy, G. L. (2004). *The Big Book of Concepts.* Cambridge, MA: MIT Press.

Murphy, G. L., & Allopenna, P. D. (1994). The locus of knowledge effects in concept learning. *Journal of Experimental Psychology: Learning, Memory, and Cognition,* **20**, 904–919.

Posner, M. I., & Keele, S. W. (1968). On the genesis of abstract ideas. *Journal of Experimental Psychology,* **77** (3), 353–363.

Reed, S. K. (1973). *Psychological Processes in Pattern Recognition*. New York: Academic Press.

Rehder, B., & Murphy, G. L. (2003). A knowledge-resonance (KRES) model of category learning. *Psychonomic Bulletin & Review*, 10, 759–784.

Rosch, E. (1973). Natural categories. *Cognitive Psychology*, 4, 328–350.

—— (1975). Cognitive representations of semantic categories. *Journal of Experimental Psychology: General*, 104, 192–233.

Rosch, E., & Mervis, C. B. (1975). Family resemblances: studies in the internal structure of categories. *Cognitive Psychology*, 7, 573–605.

Rosch, E., Mervis, C. B., Gray, W., Johnson, D., & Boyes-Braem, P. (1976). Basic objects in natural categories. *Cognitive Psychology*, 8, 382–439.

Ross, N., Medin, D. L., Coley, J. D., & Atran, S. (2003). Cultural and experiential differences in the development of folkbiological induction. *Cognitive Development*, 18, 25–47.

Shepard, R. N., Hovland, C. I., & Jenkins, H. M. (1961). Learning and memorization of classifications. *Psychological Monographs*, 75 (13).

Smith, E. E., & Medin, D. L. (1981). *Categories and Concepts*. Cambridge, MA: Harvard University Press.

Smith, E. E., Shoben, E. J., & Rips, L. J., (1974). Structure and process in semantic memory: a featural model for semantic decisions. *Psychological Review*, 1, 214–241.

Storms, G., De Boeck, P., & Rits, W. (2000). Prototype and exemplar-based information on natural language categories. *Journal of Memory and Language*, 42, 51–73.

Waxman, S. R. (1989). Linking language and conceptual development: linguistic cues and the construction of conceptual hierarchies. *Genetic Epistemologist*, 17 (2), 13–20.

—— (2002). Links between object categorization and naming: origins and emergence in human infants. In D. H. Rakison & L. M. Oakes (eds.), *Early Category and Concept Development: Making Sense of the Blooming, Buzzing Confusion*. New York: Oxford University Press.

Waxman, S. R., & Lidz, J. (2006). Early word learning. In D. Kuhn & R. Siegler (eds.), *Handbook of Child Psychology* (6th edition, Vol. 2, pp. 299–335). Hoboken, NJ: Wiley.

Wisniewski, E. J. (1997). When concepts combine. *Psychonomic Bulletin & Review*, 4, 167–183.

Wisniewski, E. J., & Medin, D. L. (1994). The fiction and nonfiction of features. In R. S. Michalski & G. D. Tecuci (eds.), *Machine Learning: A Multistrategy Approach* (Vol. 4, pp. 63–84). San Mateo, CA: Morgan Kaufmann.

Index

adaptive clustering, 235
adaptive resonance theory (ART), 221,
    242
ADIT, 135
    comparison, 135–136, 145
aging, 222
ALCOVE, 129–132, 275, 278
    comparison, 34, 78, 112, 136,
    143–145, 229, 231, 241,
    244, 275
Anderson, J. R., 5, 173, 176, 180, 182,
    242, 301
angle categorization, 33
anterior cingulate, 8, 68, 70, 215
anterior striatum, 8
ARACHNE, 269
artificial concepts, 325, 327
Asch, S., 329
Ashby, F. G., 71, 77, 81
associability, 168–169, see also attention,
    selective
ATRIUM, 136–138
    comparison, 145
attention, 14
    executive, 66, 70
    learning, 233
    selective, 5, 7, 9, 19, 29, 33, 42, 168,
    213, 223, 229, 293
    shifting, 134
    shifts, 126–128, 143
attentional learning model, 147
    comparison, 316
attentional weighting, 326
automaticity, 81

backpropagation, 193,
    see also connectionism
backward blocking, see retrospective
    revaluation
Bailey, T., 36, 214
basal ganglia, 70, 215
basic categorization level, 205

basic level categories, 105–108, 270
Bayesian framework, 9, 11
Bayesian inference, 173
Bayesian model, 5, 10
    comparison, 34, 136
Bayesian probabilistic framework, 213
Bayesian reasoning, 260
Baywatch model, 279
Beal, M., 198
Bennett, C. H., 171
Billman, J. D., 267
Blair, M., 46
Blei, D., 198
blocking, 124, 134, see also retrospective
    revaluation
Brooks, L., 66
Brown, G. D. A., 36

Caramazza, A., 315
category coherence, 90, 102–103
category exceptions, 234–236
category learning, 327
category representation, 14, 88,
    89, 274
    multiple, 100–102
category taxonomies, 195
category utility, 12, 258, 269
category utility model, 215
category-based induction, 326
category-specific deficits, 314–315, 317
category-specific proposal, 316
category-specific semantic deficits,
    see category-specific deficits
caudate nucleus, 70
Chater, N., 6, 143, 199, 200, 202, 213,
    216
Chinese restaurant process, 178–179
city-block distance metric, 22, 26,
    42, 228
CLASSIT, 253
Close, J., 213
CLUSTER, 221

clustering, 175, 180, 221, 222,
    223–225
COBWEB models, 253
    assumptions, 254–255
    comparison, 267–270
    details, 255–259
    example, 263–267
    implementation, 261–263
    motivation, 259–261
codelength, 202, 203
Cohen, L., 236
Colreavy, E., 213
complexity, 200
computational level, 173
concept function, 325, 326
concept representation, 256–257
concepts
    splitting, 263
conceptual hierarchies, 11
concurrent presentation, 14
condensation structure, 122
condensation-filtration effect, 193
confidence, 76
configural model, 144, 162
configural representation, 275
connectionism, 9, 241, see parallel
    distributed processing (PDP)
constraint-satisfaction process, 274
contrastive Hebbian learning, 276
correlated structure principle, 318
Corter, J., 258
COVIS, 4, 8–9, 65–67
    comparison, 13, 81–83, 145, 193, 215,
        247, 269
    example, 77–80
    implementation, 67–77
criss-cross categorization, 30
CrossCat, 182–183
cross-cultural differences, 223
CYRUS, 268

DÆDALUS, 253
De Schryver, M., 36
delayed testing, 309
delta learning rule, 232, see also prediction
    error
delta rule, 154–155
    modification, 155–158
    modified, 153
density estimation, 174–176
Denton, S. E., 142, 146
developmental approach, 90–91, 103–105,
    223, 236–238
Devlin, J., 318
diagonal categorization, 31

dimensional shifts, 124–125
dimensional weighting, 213
Dirichlet process mixture model,
    see DPMM
distributed memory model, 92
DIVA, 213
domain-general categorization, 313,
    317
domain-specific hypothesis, 319
dopamine, 9, 70, 75, 80
dot-pattern research, 43
DPMM
    comparison, 316
    implementation, 177–180
    motivation, 175–176
dual systems, 66, 169
dual task, 77–80, 238–241

elemental model, 9, 153, 158–160
    comparison, 166–167, 316
    example, 160–161
Ennis, J. M., 71
EPAM system, 268
episodic memory, 94
Euclidean distance metric, 22, 42, 208
evolutionarily relevant, 319
exemplar, 144
    memory, 129
exemplar model, 174, see also GCM
    comparison, 100, 191, 193, 234,
        244–245, 269
    definition, 35
exemplar representation, 278
exemplar theories, 4
    comparison, 112–113
exemplar-based random walk
    (EBRW), 35
EXIT, 135
    comparison, 145
expertise, 327
explicit system, 68–71
extended generalized context model for
    response times (EGCM-RT), 35

family resemblance, 45
fan effects, 270
Farah, M., 315
feature inference, 329
feature listing tasks, 318
feature-based model, see elemental model
features, 320
filtration structure, 121, 130
Fisher, D. H., 258
flexible prediction, 255
FPC model, 306, 307

GCM, 7–8, *see also* exemplar model
  comparison, 13, 34–36, 41, 42, 46, 58,
  112, 143, 166–167, 212, 214, 269,
  316
  computation assumptions, 21–23
  conceptual overview, 18–20
  example, 29–34
  implementation recommendations,
  27–29
  motivation, 23–27
general knowledge, 7, 12, 216,
  see also prior knowledge
generalization gradient, 162
generalized context model, *see* GCM
Gibbs sampling, 187–189
Gluck, M., 258
Goldstone, R. L., 238–241
Griffiths, T. L., 268, 329
Gureckis, T., 236–241
Guttman-Nahir, T., 170

Haxby, J., 316
HDPMM, 180–182
  comparison, 192–194
  example, 190–192
Hebbian learning, 193
hierarchical Dirichlet process mixed
  model, *see* HDPMM
hierarchical learning, 193
hierarchical representation, 261–262, 268,
  271
hierarchical structure, 255, 257–258
hierarchical updating, 262–263
highlighting, 123, 134–135, 142
hill-climbing algorithm, 53–56
hippocampus, 8, 68, 223
Hoffman, A. B., 281, 286
Homa, D., 43, 46
Hovland, C. L., 24

Iba, W., 267
imaging studies, 315–316
implicit learning system, *see* procedural
  learning system
individual differences approach, 124
induction model, 303–304, 307
inductive projection, 91, 108–110
inference learning, 222, 294
inferotemporal cortex, 8
infinite relational model, 183–184
innate knowledge, 320
integral-dimension stimuli, 23
inter-dimensional multiplicative rule, 27

Jenkins, H. M., 24
Jordan, M., 137
just noticeable difference, 263

Kalman filters, 146
Kanwisher, N., 315
Keele, S. W., 43
Kim, K., 293, 317
knowledge effects, 329
knowledge processes, 294
knowledge resonance, *see* KRES
Kohonen learning rule, 232
Kolmogorov complexity, 200
KOVE, 274–280
  comparison, 286–287, 293
  example, 286, 291–293
  implementation, 281
KRES, 12, 274–280
  comparison, 58, 60, 147, 286–287, 293,
  317, 328
  example, 281–285, 288–291
  implementation, 280–281
Kruschke, J. K., 34, 142, 146, 231, 329

LABYRINTH, 253, 256, 267
Lamberts, K., 35, 166
Langley, P., 267
language concepts, 325, 327
lateral occipital cortex, 215, 315
learned predictiveness effect, 168
learned selective attention, 120–128, 145,
  193, *see also* attention, selective
Lewandowsky, S., 213
linear associator, 133
linear separability constraint, 47,
  54, 61
linearly separable category, 122, 287
linearly separable concepts, 278
Livesey, E. J., 329
local Bayesian learning, 139–142
  comparison, 146
local feature coding, 160
local MAP algorithm, 184–187, 190
López, A., 312
Love, B., 235, 236–238
Luce choice rule, 231

machine learning, 6, 175, 253, 329
  comparison, 34, 192
Mackintosh, N. J., 138, 153
Mackintosh's (1975) model, 138, 145
MÆANDER, 271
Mahon, B., 316
mapping hypothesis, 24–26
Markman, A. B., 326
Markov chain Monte Carlo (MCMC)
  method, 187, 188
Marr, D., 173
Martin, J. D., 260, 267
McClelland, J. L., 5, 92, 99
McLaren, I. P. L., 166, 329

McLaren and Mackintosh model, 145, 153, 157, 165, *see also* elemental model
McLaren, Kaye and Mackintosh model, 153, 157, *see also* elemental model
medial-temporal lobe (MTL) amnesics, 236
Medin, D. L., 7, 18, 23, 26, 46, 48, 52, 328
Medin–Schaffer context model, 23
memory strength, 19, 28
merging concepts, 262
Mervis, C. B., 199, 204
Minda, J. P., 35, 41, 43, 47, 54, 190, 191
minimum description length (MDL), 200
    see also simplicity model
Minkowski power model, 22
mixture models, 175
model limitations, 304–306
model testing, 307–310
Monte Carlo technique, 189
more rational model, 221, 246
Moss, H., 318
motor skills, 271
multidimensional scaling (MDS), 18, 26
Murphy, G. L., 7, 328

narrative comprehension, 300
nearest-neighbour classifier, 22
non-linear similarity rule, 27
non-linearly separable categories, 30, 47, 122
nonparametric Bayesian models, *see* Bayesian model
motivation, 173–176
Nosofsky, R. M., 23, 24, 26, 29, 35, 41, 42, 153, 166, 167, 235

Oakeshott, S. M., 162–165
object recognition, 316
Ockham's razor, 10, 194, 199
ontologies, 253
optimal inference model, *see* Bayesian model
order effects, 226
Osherson, D. N., 303, 326
Osherson *et al.* model, *see* induction model
Oxbow, 253, 256, 267

Palmeri, T. J., 35, 166, 167, 235
parallel distributed processing (PDP), 4
    assumptions, 92–95
    comparison, 110–115, 317
    examples, 100–110
    implementation, 95–100
Parkinson's disease, 71
particle filter, 189–190
patient studies, 314–315

peak shift, 10, 160–165
Pearce, J. M., 144, 153, 162
perceptual discrimination, 222
perceptual representation, 35, 306, 308
perirhinal cortex, 223
POLE, 136–138
Posner, M. I., 43
Pothos, E. M., 6, 36, 143, 199, 200, 202, 213, 214, 216, 329
power-law of learning, 270
prediction error, 36, 75–76, 84, 131, 245
predictions, 301, 311
prefrontal cortex, 8, 68, 70, 215, 223
prior knowledge, 195, 287, 293, *see also* general knowledge
probabilistic categorization, 222
probabilistic concept, 257–258
probabilistic representation, 255, 261–262, 268
probability matching, 21
procedural learning system, 8, 65, 66, 77
prototype, 27, 40, 274
prototype effect, 44, 47, 51
prototype model, 40–41, 174
    comparison, 35, 58, 190, 193, 234, 269, 316
    definition, 35, 40, 41–43
    implementation, 48–57
    motivation, 43–47
prototype representation, 278
prototype theory, 4, 8, 89, 221
    comparison, 113, 212
psychological space, 7, 18, 22–23, 52
Puce, A., 315

quantum probability, 215

Rabinowitz, C., 315
RASHNL, 129–132
    comparison, 132–134, 135–136, 144
rational model, 10, 129, 176, 180, 221, 242, *see also* more rational model
    comparison, 213, 215
recognition memory, 222, 234–236
Rescorla–Wagner model, 75, 145, *see also* prediction error
retrospective revaluation, 136, 139–140
Rex Leopold I model, 36
Rips, L. J., 326
Rogers, T. T., 99
Root mean square deviation (RMSD), 53–56
Rosch, E., 45, 88, 199, 204, 330
Ross, N., 326
Rosseel, Y., 36

rule-based system, 8, 65
rule learning, 66, 169, 194
RULEX, 235, 243
Rumelhart, D. E., 5, 92, 95, 99, 106

Sakamoto, Y., 235
salience, 125–126
Schaffer, M. M., 18, 23, 26, 48, 52
semantic dementia (SD), 90,
    103–105
semantic knowledge, 275
semantic memory, 88–89
semantic system implementation, 93–94
sensory-functional theory, 318
separable-dimension stimuli, 23
Shafir, E., 303
Shallice, T., 318
Shelton, J., 315
Shepard, A. N., 24, 26, 42
sigmoidal activation function, 95
sigmoid-belief network, 147
similarity, 7, 12, 13, 18–19, 21, 22–23, 30,
    41, 42, 200–203, 225, 269, 274, 300,
    304, 306, 307, 309, 328
similarity-choice model (SCM), 24–26
similarity-dissimilarity exemplar model, 36
simplicity, see also Ockham's razor
simplicity model, 6, 10, 199–203, 221
    comparison, 60, 194, 215, 243, 268, 270
    example, 209–212
    implementation, 209
    motivation, 203–207
simplicity principle, 199, 205–207, 225
singleton, 257–258
single-unit recording, 81
Smith, E. E., 46, 326, 330
Smith, J. D., 35, 41, 43, 46, 54, 190, 191
spatial variability, 162–165
Spiering, B. J., 71
spontaneous categorization, 204
spreading activation theory, 89
Stewart, N., 36
Stirling numbers, 203
Storms, G., 35, 327
striatal pattern classifier (SPC), 71
striatum, 8, 68, 72
structured probabilistic approaches
    comparison, 113–115
supervised categorization, 2–3, 13, 226,
    326, 327

SUSTAIN, 3, 11, 13, 150, 220–222,
    223–225
    comparison, 13, 58, 60, 144, 193, 212,
    241–245, 268, 269, 279, 316
    examples, 234–241
    implementation, 227–234
    motivation, 222–223
    principles, 225–227
    symmetry assumption, 201

Teh, Y., 176
Thompson, K., 267
transfer performance, 326, 327
tree structure, 260
trial order, 271
trust, 77
Tversky, A., 201
TWILIX, 253, 267
Tyler, L., 318
Type II categorization, 122, 125
Type IV categorization, 122
typicality effects, 270

unidimensional category structure, 29
unidirectional flow, 274
UNIMEM, 268
unsupervised categorization, 2–3, 6, 10,
    11, 13, 204, 206, 222, 225, 253, 259,
    327, 329
unsupervised clustering, 294

Vandist, K., 36
Vanpaemel, W., 35
varying abstraction model (VAM), 35, 221,
    243
verbalization, 247
verbal models, 300
veridical representation, 279

Waldron, E. M., 71, 77
Waldschmidt, J. G., 81
Warrington, E., 318
Wattenmaker, W. D., 287, 288
Widrow–Hoff error correcting, 155
Wilkie, O., 312
Wisniewski, E. J., 328
Wittgenstein, L., 45
working memory, 66

Younger, B., 236